Annual Editions: Drugs, Society, and Behavior, 32/e

Kim Schnurbush and Mark Pullin

http://create.mheducation.com

ISBN-10: 1260541460   ISBN-13: 9781260541465

1 2 3 4 5 6 QVS 23 22 21 20 19

Contents

Detailed Table of Contents

Understanding Drug Use and Addiction, National Institute on Drug Abuse, *National Institute on Drug Abuse Research Report*, 2016
This article enables readers to better understand drug addiction, prevention, and treatment methods that include a life-long commitment from those affected to ensure their success. The writing includes risk factors as well as positive treatment methods to help reduce drug use and addiction.

What's The Buzz? Treating Prescription Drug Abuse in Youth, Shelley Steenrod, *The New Social Worker*, 2016
Adolescents have been attracted to prescription drugs at an alarming rate. This article discusses how popular prescription drugs vary, their effects on users, the psychological and physiological aspects of use, along with consequences faced by adolescents who consume these popular drugs.

Sex and Gender Differences in Substance Abuse, *National Institute on Drug Abuse*, 2018
In this article, special issues related to hormones, menstrual cycle, fertility, pregnancy, breastfeeding, and menopause that can impact women's struggles with drug use and abuse. Sex and gender differences with both drug use/abuse and other reasons, to include controlling weight, fighting exhaustion, coping with pain and mental health treatment are explored.

Unit 3: The Major Drugs of Use and Abuse

Krokodil: A Monstrous Drug with Deadly Consequences, Danielle M. Matiuk, *Journal of Addictive Disorders*, 2014
Drug use and abuse is not new in the United States, but a deadly drug has recently emerged from Russia called Krokodil, a deadly mixture of codeine tablets crushed up with readily available toxic ingredients such as vehicle gasoline, paint thinner, hydrochloric acid, red phosphorus, and even lighter fluid. Using Krokodil can leave a person mentally and physically incapacitated, and as the name indicates, some users are left with skin that appears crocodile-like when gangrene results. This article discusses this new deadly drug making its way around the globe, the physical effects on users and the efforts being made to discourage use of Krokodil.

Marijuana as Medicine, *National Institute on Drug Abuse*, 2018
Despite both medical and recreational marijuana use being made legal by multiple states across the nation, Federal law and the Drug Enforcement Administration (DEA) still hold marijuana is illegal federally and is a Schedule I drug, which are substances or chemicals with no currently accepted medical use and with a high potential for abuse. Examples of Schedule I drugs are heroin, LSD, ecstasy, and marijuana. This brief report explores the use of marijuana as medicine, explains what cannabinoids are and how they can be used as medicine, and some basic facts surrounding the use of marijuana as a medicine.

Prescription Opioids, *National Institute on Drug Abuse*, 2018
This National Institute on Drug Abuse report explains prescription opioids, common types of opioids, misuse of prescription opioids, how they affect the brain, side effects, overdose information, and opioid addiction.

Hallucinogens and Dissociative Drugs, *National Institute on Drug Abuse*, 2015
Hallucinogens and dissociative drugs such as acid, angel dust, and vitamin K, distort the way a user perceives time, motion, colors, sound, and self (Volkow, 2015). This reading examines some of the popular club drugs and their effects on behavior and the human body.

Drugs, Brains, and Behavior: The Science of Addiction, *National Institute on Drug Abuse*, 2018
Scientist have studied the effects of drugs and it's use for many decades. Issues such as morality, mental health, and environment have all led the research effort at different times, but this article relays some revolutionary discoveries about the human brain that may lead to more effective methods of understanding and responding to drug addiction.

Unit 4: Other Trends in Drug Use

Fentanyl: The Powerful Opioid that Killed Prince, Sara Sidner, *CNN*, 2016
Although the powerful painkiller fentanyl has been around since the 1960's and is potent enough to soothe extreme pain from cancer and similar illnesses, the emergence of fentanyl on the streets across the nation is causing a new health crisis as it only takes a small amount of the drug to kill. This article explores how and why fentanyl is flooding the streets, to include a discussion of how an accidental overdose of this drug killed the popular 1980's music icon Prince.

Unit 6: Creating and Sustaining Effective Drug Control Policy

Unit 7: Prevention, Treatment, and Education

Preface

Humanity has developed an ambiguous relationship with substances we have come to define as drugs, particularly those drugs that alter human consciousness and behavior, psychoactive drugs. The use of such substances has resulted in a social circumstance whereby societies struggle to control human behaviors motivated and altered by their use. Although we consider modern society to function based upon logic, science, and reason, closer to scrutiny of policy, regulation, and control belies this belief. In effect, such attempts at regulation face an enormous biological and psychological challenge: we humans are designed to alter our consciousness, or to use another term familiar to drug use, to "get high." As a result, to significant degree, our societies face a seemingly insurmountable challenge: to control and/or manipulate human behavior with regard to drug using or consciousness-altering behaviors. To this end, societies have, presumably in an attempt to protect their members, developed what they perceive to be rational control mechanisms to protect people from themselves.

Unfortunately, the historical foundations upon which drug regulation and control are based, especially in the United States, have their roots in racism and discrimination. This further complicates society's attempts to address, in a logical and coherent sense, what type of role or relationship humans should have with these substances. The reality of our modern world concerning drugs is unequivocal. Despite repeated resolutions by the U.S. government in an attempt to achieve a "Drug Free America," and the staggering amount of money spent in the attempt to achieve that end, drugs are ubiquitous in American society; they are here to stay. What has come to be defined as deviant and antisocial behaviors in our attempts to "denormalize" drug use has, in fact, resulted in these activities becoming testimony to people's inherent creativity in their never-ending pursuit of states of altered consciousness. When this penchant to "get high" is combined with the precociousness inherent in our species, one ends up with the current circumstance: new substances are discovered regularly, either by scientific research or common curiosity, and the ritual of consciousness alteration begins anew. We currently find ourselves in a conundrum concerning drugs. For whatever reasons, none of which are based upon science or rationality, some drugs are considered to be acceptable and appropriate, while others are seen to be highly dangers and a threat.

One does not need to be a psychopharmacologist or toxicologist to realize that there is very little difference, for instance, between ethyl alcohol and heroin. As a result, we readily accept and condone the use of one (alcohol) while declaring "war" against the other drugs, such as heroin, cocaine, etc. The same situation exists with regard to tobacco, a compound that is among the most toxic and highly addictive known. For these reasons, oftentimes it is in fact impossible to make sense of how modern societies have come to view and address drug using behavior. We hope that the materials presented in this book offer the reader some insight and perspective with regard to understanding the role that drugs play in today's world and how we have come to our current situation concerning drugs and drug use.

The articles contained in *Annual Editions: Drugs, Society, and Behavior* 32/e are a collection of issues and perspectives designed to provide the reader with a framework for examining current drug-related issues and facts. The book is designed to offer students something to think about and *something with which to think*. It is a unique collection of materials of interest to the casual as well as the serious student of drug-related social phenomena. The first section addresses the significance that drugs have in affecting diverse aspect of American life. It emphasizes the often-overlooked reality that drugs—legal and illegal—have remained a pervasive dimension of pas as well as present American history. The unit begins with examples of the multiple ways in which Americans have been and continue to be affected by both legal and illegal drugs. We go on to examine the way drugs affect the mind and body that result in dependence and addiction and the major drugs of use and abuse, along with issues relative to understanding the individual impacts of these drugs on society. Selections address the impacts produced by the legal and illegal drugs and emphasize the alarming nature of widespread prescription drug abuse. We review the dynamic nature of drugs as it relates to changing patterns and trends of use. We give special attention this year to drug trends, particularly those related to prescription drug abuse. Additionally, a section of the book focuses on the social costs of drug abuse and why the costs overwhelm many American institutions. Specific articles have been selected to illustrate the complexity in creating and implementing drug policy, such as that associated with medical marijuana and that associated with foreign drug control policy. The final section concludes the book with discussions of current strategies for preventing and treating drug abuse. Can we deter people from harming themselves with drugs, and can we cure people addicted to drugs? What works and what does not work? Special attention is given to programs that address those at-risk, and programs that reduce criminal offender rehabilitation and recidivism.

Annual Editions: Drugs, Society, and Behavior 32/e contains a number of features that are designed to make the volume user-friendly. These include Learning Outcomes, Critical Thinking Questions, and Internet References for each article that can be used to further explore the topics, and help students better understand what they have read.

Editors of this Volume

Dr. Kim Schnurbush is an Assistant Professor of Criminal Justice at California State University—Sacramento. She received her Bachelor of Arts degree from the University of New Hampshire, her Master's degree from Fitchburg State University, and her PhD in Criminal Justice from Sam Houston State University. She worked for 14 years in the criminal justice system, in a combination of law enforcement and corrections. Dr. Schnurbush also has 15 years of teaching experience at the university level and specializes in teaching drug abuse, law enforcement, and corrections classes. Her research currently centers on wrongful convictions, death penalty, and correctional issues. She is a member of Alpha Phi Sigma, American Correctional Association, Western Association of Criminal Justice, American Society of Criminology, and the Academy of Criminal Justice Sciences.

Dr. Mark Pullin is an Associate Professor at the Center for Security Studies at Angelo State University. He teaches courses in border and homeland security and criminal justice both locally and online to distance-based students.

Professor Pullin has a Bachelor's degree in Criminal Justice from the University of Houston-Victoria, a Master's degree in Criminal Justice Administration from Sam Houston State University, and a doctorate from Sam Houston State University with a dual concentration in Criminal Justice Administration and Legal Aspects of Criminal Justice.

Dr. Pullin spent many years in the private sector managing construction contracts with government environmental agencies at the federal, state, and local level. This work included extensive preparation of contractual and governmental documentation for hearings with jurisdictions concerning the legality and feasibility of large projects.

His work has spanned over much of the southern United States with a concentration in the Midwest and Texas.

Professor Pullin is on the Executive Advisory Board over training and curriculum for The Victoria College Police Training Academy that manages all aspects of training and included preparation for TCOLE examinations. He also is an executive board member for the Criminal Justice Advisory Committee that oversees grant submissions and awards for 15 West Texas counties. Dr. Pullin has authored law enforcement training manuals, police research on citizen perception of law enforcement, as well as authored articles on Emergency Management Preparation post Hurricane Katrina and Rita. This research included the effects of evacuees and human movement on the Criminal Justice System in target cities before, during, and after the effects of natural disasters.

His current research agenda includes human and narcotic trafficking on the southern U.S. border, law enforcement forensic investigative techniques, human and drug trafficking, and issues in Homeland Security.

Academic Advisory Board Members

Members of the Academic Advisory Board are instrumental in the final selection of articles for each edition of Annual Editions. Their review of the articles for content, level, and appropriateness provides critical direction to the editors and staff. We think that you will find their careful consideration well reflected in this volume.

John Janowiak
Appalachian State University

William E. Kelly
Auburn University

Jay Kolick
Rosemont College

Michelle Lomonaco
The Citadel

Patricia Lott
Saint Martin's University

Michael Olivero
Central Washington University Ellensburg

Emmanuel Onyeozili
University of Maryland Eastern Shore

Dennis Schultz
University of Wisconsin, Parkside

Diane Sevening
University of South Dakota

Bruce Sewick
College of DuPage

Brian Starks
Lynchburg College

Caren Steinmiller
University of Toledo

Lea Stewart
Rutgers University

John Stogner
Georgia Southern University

David Tam
University of North Texas

Jennifer Vickery
Winthrop University

Julie Yingling
South Dakota State University

Jodi Zieverink
Central Piedmont Community College

Unit 1

UNIT

Prepared by: Kim Schnurbush, *California State University, Sacramento*
Mark Pullin, *Angelo State University*

Living with Drugs

When attempting to define the U.S. drug experience, one must examine the past as well as the present. Very often, drug use and its associated phenomena are viewed through a contemporary looking glass relative to our personal views, biases, and perspectives. Although today's drug scene is definitely a product of recent historical trends such as the crack trade of the 1980s, the methamphetamine problem, and the turn toward the expanded nonmedical use of prescription drugs, it is also a product of the distant past. This past and the lessons it has generated, although largely unknown, forgotten, or ignored, provide one important perspective from which to assess our current status and to guide our future in terms of optimizing our efforts to manage the benefits and control the harm from legal and illegal drugs.

The U.S. drug experience is often defined in terms of a million individual realities, all meaningful and all different. In fact, these realities often originated as pieces of our historical, cultural, political, and personal past that combine to influence present-day drug-related phenomena significantly. The contemporary U.S. drug experience is the product of centuries of human attempts to alter or sustain consciousness through the use of mind-altering drugs. Early American history is replete with accounts of exorbitant use of alcohol, opium, morphine, and cocaine. Further review of this history clearly suggests the precedents for Americans' continuing pursuit of a vast variety of stimulant, depressant, and hallucinogenic drugs. Drug wars, drug epidemics, drug prohibitions, and escalating trends of alarming drug use patterns were present throughout the early history of the United States. During this period, the addictive properties of most drugs were largely unknown. Today, however, the addictive properties of almost all drugs are known, and research is ongoing into the impact these drugs have on society. So why is it that so many drug-related lessons of the past repeat themselves in the face of such powerful new knowledge? How is it that the abuse of drugs continues to defy the lessons of history? How big is the U.S. drug problem and how is it measured? In addition, prescription drug abuse has become an epidemic in the United States. What is being done to combat this abuse?

One important way of answering questions about drug abuse is by conducting research and analyzing data recovered through numerous reporting instruments. These data are in turn used to assess historical trends and make policy decisions in response to what has been learned. For example, one leading source of information about drug use in America is the annual federal Substance Abuse and Mental Health Services Administration's National Survey on Drug Use and Health. It currently reports that there continues to be more than 19.1 million Americans over 12 years of age who are current users of illicit drugs. The most widely used illicit drug is marijuana with approximately 14 million users—a figure that has remained constant for the past five years. Approximately 51 percent of Americans over 12 are drinkers of alcohol; over 43 percent of full-time enrolled college students are binge drinkers (defined as consuming five or more drinks during a single drinking occasion). Approximately 29 percent of Americans over 12 use tobacco. Almost 23 million people are believed to be drug-dependent on alcohol or illicit drugs. There are approximately 5 million people using prescription painkillers for nonmedical reasons—an alarming trend. The size of the economy associated with drug use is staggering; Americans continue to spend more than $70 billion a year on illegal drugs alone.

Drugs impact our most powerful public institutions on many fronts. Drugs are the business of our criminal justice system, and drugs compete with terrorism, war, and other major national security concerns as demanding military issues. Over $3 billion per year is committed to the Department of Homeland Security to strengthen drug-related land and maritime border interdictions. The cost of illegal street drugs is up, and the post-9/11 national security infrastructure is impacting historical patterns of trafficking. And the relationship between drug trafficking and terrorism has focused added military emphasis on drug fighting. As the war in Iraq, Afghanistan, and Pakistan continues, U.S. drug agents in those countries are increasing efforts to contain the expanding heroin trade, a major source of funding for the Taliban. As you read through the pages of this book, the pervasive nature of drug-related influences on everyday life will become more apparent.

The lessons of our drug legacy are harsh, whether they are the subjects of public health or public policy. Methamphetamine is now recognized as having produced consequences equal to or surpassing those of crack. The entire dynamic of illicit drug use is changing. Once quiet rural towns, counties, and states have reported epidemics of methamphetamine abuse over the past 10 years, and these suggest comparisons to the inner-urban crack epidemics of the 1980s. The current level of drug-related violence in Mexico is out of control and is firmly in control of the U.S. drug market. This issue is the most dangerous emerging drug problem.

Families, schools, and workplaces continue to be impacted by the many facets of drug abuse. One in three Americans has a close relationship to someone who abuses drugs. It is only because of war, terrorism, and a struggling economy that more public attention toward drug problems has been diverted. The articles and graphics contained in this unit illustrate the evolving nature of issues influenced by the historical evolution of legal and illegal drug use in America. The changing historical evolution of drug-related phenomena is reflected within the character of all issues and controversies addressed by this book. This unit presents examples of the contemporary and diverse nature of current problems, issues, and concerns about drugs and how they continue to impact all aspects of public and private life. The drug-related events of today continue to forecast the drug-related events of tomorrow. The areas of public health, public policy, controlling crime, and education exist as good examples for discussion. As you read this and other literature on drug-related events, the dynamics of past and present drug-related linkages will become apparent.

Article Prepared by: Kim Schnurbush, *California State University, Sacramento*
Mark Pullin, *Angelo State University*

History of Alcohol and Drinking Around the World

DAVID J. HANSON

Learning Outcomes

After reading this article, you will be able to:

- Understand the use of alcohol through history.
- Describe various types of alcohol that people use.
- Identify when different types of alcohol became popular and why.

A lcohol is a product that has provided a variety of functions for people throughout all history. From the earliest times to the present, alcohol has played an important role in religion and worship. Historically, alcoholic beverages have served as sources of needed nutrients and have been widely used for their medicinal, antiseptic, and analgesic properties. The role of such beverages as thirst quenchers is obvious and they play an important role in enhancing the enjoyment and quality of life. They can be a social lubricant, can facilitate relaxation, can provide pharmacological pleasure, and can increase the pleasure of eating. Thus, while alcohol has always been misused by a minority of drinkers, it has proved to be beneficial to most.

Ancient Period

While no one knows when beverage alcohol was first used, it was presumably the result of a fortuitous accident that occurred at least tens of thousands of years ago. However, the discovery of late Stone Age beer jugs has established the fact that intentionally fermented beverages existed at least as early as the Neolithic period (cir. 10,000 B.C.) (Patrick, 1952, pp. 12–13), and it has been suggested that beer may have preceded bread as a staple (Braidwood et al., 1953; Katz

and Voigt, 1987); wine clearly appeared as a finished product in Egyptian pictographs around 4,000 B.C. (Lucia, 1963a, p. 216).

The earliest alcoholic beverages may have been made from berries or honey (Blum et al., 1969, p. 25; Roueché, 1960, p. 8; French, 1890, p. 3) and winemaking may have originated in the wild grape regions of the Middle East. Oral tradition recorded in the Old Testament (Genesis 9:20) asserts that Noah planted a vineyard on Mt. Ararat in what is now eastern Turkey. In Summer, beer and wine were used for medicinal purposes as early as 2,000 B.C. (Babor, 1986, p. 1).

Brewing dates from the beginning of civilization in ancient Egypt (Cherrington, 1925, v. 1, p. 404) and alcoholic beverages were very important in that country. Symbolic of this is the fact that while many gods were local or familial, Osiris, the god of wine, was worshiped throughout the entire country (Lucia, 1963b, p. 152). The Egyptians believed that this important god also invented beer (King, 1947, p. 11), a beverage that was considered a necessity of life; it was brewed in the home "on an everyday basis" (Marciniak, 1992, p. 2).

Both beer and wine were deified and offered to gods. Cellars and winepresses even had a god whose hieroglyph was a winepress (Ghaliounqui, 1979, p. 5). The ancient Egyptians made at least seventeen varieties of beer and at least 24 varieties of wine (Ghaliounqui, 1979, pp. 8 and 11). Alcoholic beverages were used for pleasure, nutrition, medicine, ritual, remuneration (Cherrington, 1925, v. 1, p. 405), and funerary purposes. The latter involved storing the beverages in tombs of the deceased for their use in the after-life (King, 1947, p. 11; Darby, 1977, p. 576).

Numerous accounts of the period stressed the importance of moderation, and these norms were both secular and religious (Darby, 1977, p. 58). While Egyptians did not generally appear to define inebriety as a problem, they warned against taverns (which were often houses of prostitution) and excessive drinking (Lutz, 1922, pp. 97, 105–108). After reviewing extensive evidence regarding the widespread but generally moderate use of alcoholic beverage, the historian Darby makes a most important observation: all these accounts are warped by the fact that moderate users "were overshadowed by their more boisterous counterparts who added 'color' to history" (Darby, 1977, p. 590). Thus, the intemperate use of alcohol throughout history receives a disproportionate amount of attention. Those who abuse alcohol cause problems, draw attention to themselves, are highly visible and cause legislation to be enacted. The vast majority of drinkers, who neither experience nor cause difficulties, are not noteworthy. Consequently, observers and writers largely ignore moderation.

Beer was the major beverage among the Babylonians, and as early as 2,700 B.C. they worshiped a wine goddess and other wine deities (Hyams, 1965, pp. 38–39). Babylonians regularly used both beer and wine as offerings to their gods (Lutz, 1922, pp. 125–126). Around 1,750 B.C., the famous Code of Hammurabi devoted attention to alcohol. However, there were no penalties for drunkenness; in fact, it was not even mentioned. The concern was fair commerce in alcohol (Popham, 1978, pp. 232–233). Nevertheless, although it was not a crime, it would appear that the Babylonians were critical of drunkenness (Lutz, 1922, pp. 115–116).

A variety of alcoholic beverages have been used in China since prehistoric times (Granet, 1957, p. 144). Alcohol was considered a spiritual (mental) food rather than a material (physical) food, and extensive documentary evidence attests to the important role it played in the religious life (Hucker, 1975, p. 28; Fei-Peng, 1982, p. 13). "In ancient times people always drank when holding a memorial ceremony, offering sacrifices to gods or their ancestors, pledging resolution before going into battle, celebrating victory, before feuding and official executions, for taking an oath of allegiance, while attending the ceremonies of birth, marriage, reunions, departures, death, and festival banquets" (Fei-Peng, 1982, p. 13).

A Chinese imperial edict of about 1,116 B.C. makes it clear that the use of alcohol in moderation was believed to be prescribed by heaven. Whether or not it was prescribed by heaven, it was clearly beneficial to the treasury. At the time of Marco Polo (1254–1324) it was drunk daily (Gernet, 1962, p. 139) and was one of the treasury's biggest sources of income (Balazs, 1964, p. 97).

Alcoholic beverages were widely used in all segments of Chinese society, were used as a source of inspiration, were important for hospitality, were an antidote for fatigue, and were sometimes misused (Samuelson, 1878, pp. 19–20, 22, 26–27; Fei-Peng, 1982, p. 137; Simons, 1991, pp. 448–459). Laws against making wine were enacted and repealed forty-one times between 1,100 B.C. and A.D. 1,400. (Alcoholism and Drug Addiction Research Foundation of Ontario, 1961, p. 5). However, a commentator writing around 650 B.C. asserted that people "will not do without beer. To prohibit it and secure total abstinence from it is beyond the power even of sages. Hence, therefore, we have warnings on the abuse of it" (quoted in Rouecbe, 1963, p. 179; similar translation quoted in Samuelson, 1878, p. 20).

While the art of wine making reached the Hellenic peninsula by about 2,000 B.C. (Younger, 1966, p. 79), the first alcoholic beverage to obtain widespread popularity in what is now Greece was mead, a fermented beverage made from honey and water. However, by 1,700 B.C., wine making was commonplace, and during the next thousand years wine drinking assumed the same function so commonly found around the world: It was incorporated into religious rituals, it became important in hospitality, it was used for medicinal purposes and it became an integral part of daily meals (Babor, 1986, pp. 2–3). As a beverage, it was drunk in many ways: warm and chilled, pure and mixed with water, plain, and spiced (Raymond, 1927, p. 53).

Contemporary writers observed that the Greeks were among the most temperate of ancient peoples. This appears to result from their rules stressing moderate drinking, their praise of temperance, their practice of diluting wine with water, and their avoidance of excess in general (Austin, 1985, p. 11). An exception to this ideal of moderation was the cult of Dionysus, in which intoxication was believed to bring people closer to their deity (Sournia, 1990, pp. 5–6; Raymond, 1927, p. 55).

While habitual drunkenness was rare, intoxication at banquets and festivals was not unusual (Austin, 1985, p. 11). In fact, the symposium, a gathering of men for an evening of conversation, entertainment, and drinking typically ended in intoxication (Babor, 1986, p. 4). However, while there are no references in ancient Greek literature to mass drunkenness among the Greeks, there are references to it among foreign peoples (Patrick, 1952, p. 18). By 425 B.C., warnings against intemperance, especially at symposia, appear to become more frequent (Austin, 1985, pp. 21–22).

Xenophon (431–351 B.C.) and Plato (429–347 B.C.) both praised the moderate use of wine as beneficial to health and happiness, but both were critical of drunkenness, which appears to have become a problem. Hippocrates (cir. 460–370 B.C.) identified numerous medicinal properties of wine, which had long been used for its therapeutic value (Lucia, 1963a, pp. 36–40). Later, both Aristode (384–322 B.C.) and Zeno (cir. 336–264 B.C.) were very critical of drunkenness (Austin, 1985, pp. 23, 25, and 27).

Among Greeks, the Macedonians viewed intemperance as a sign of masculinity and were well known for their drunkenness. Their king, Alexander the Great (336–323 B.C.), whose mother adhered to the Dionysian cult, developed a reputation for inebriety (Souria, 1990, pp. 8–9; Babor, 1986, p. 5).

The Hebrews were reportedly introduced to wine during their captivity in Egypt. When Moses led them to Canaan (Palestine) around 1,200 B.C., they are reported to have regretted leaving behind the wines of Egypt (Numbers 20:5); however, they found vineyards to be plentiful in their new land (Lutz, 1922, p. 25). Around 850 B.C., the use of wine was criticized by the Rechabites and Nazarites, two conservative nomadic groups who practiced abstinence from alcohol (Lutz, 1922, p. 133; Samuelson, 1878, pp. 62–63).

In 586 B.C., the Hebrews were conquered by the Babylonians and deported to Babylon. However, in 539 B.C., the Persians captured the city and released the Hebrews from their Exile (Daniel 5:1–4). Following the Exile, the Hebrews developed Judaism as it is now known, and they can be said to have become Jews. During the next 200 years, sobriety increased and pockets of antagonism to wine disappeared. It became a common beverage for all classes and ages, including the very young; an important source of nourishment; a prominent part in the festivities of the people; a widely appreciated medicine; an essential provision for any fortress; and an important commodity. In short, it came to be seen as a necessary element in the life of the Hebrews (Raymond, 1927, p. 23).

While there was still opposition to excessive drinking, it was no longer assumed that drinking inevitably led to drunkenness. Wine came to be seen as a blessing from God and a symbol of joy (Psalms 104; Zachariah 10:7). These changes in beliefs and behaviors appear to be related to a rejection of belief in pagan gods, a new emphasis on individual morality, and the integration of secular drinking behaviors into religious ceremonies and their subsequent modification (Austin, 1985, pp. 18–19; Patai, 1980, pp. 61–73; Keller, 1970, pp. 290–294). Around 525 B.C., it was ruled that the Kiddush (pronouncement of the Sabbath) should be recited over a blessed cup of wine. This established the regular drinking of wine in Jewish ceremonies outside the Temple (Austin, 1985, p. 19).

King Cyrus of Persia frequently praised the virtue of the moderate consumption of alcohol (cir. 525 B.C.). However, ritual intoxication appears to have been used as an adjunct to decision making and, at least after his death, drunkenness was not uncommon (Austin, 1985, p. 19).

Between the founding of Rome in 753 B.C. until the third century B.C., there is consensus among historians that the Romans practiced great moderation in drinking (Austin, 1985, p. 17). After the Roman conquest of the Italian peninsula and the rest of the Mediterranean basin (509 to 133 B.C.), the traditional Roman values of temperance, frugality and simplicity were gradually replaced by heavy drinking, ambition, degeneracy and corruption (Babor, 1986, p. 7; Wallbank & Taylor, 1954, p. 163). The Dionysian rites (Bacchanalia, in Latin) spread to Italy during this period and were subsequently outlawed by the Senate (Lausanne, 1969, p. 4; Cherrington, 1925, v. 1, pp. 251–252).

Practices that encouraged excessive drinking included drinking before meals on an empty stomach, inducing vomiting to permit the consumption of more food and wine, and drinking games. The latter included, for example, rapidly consuming as many cups as indicated by a throw of the dice (Babor, 1986, p. 10).

By the second and first centuries B.C., intoxication was no longer a rarity, and most prominent men of affairs (for example, Cato the Elder and Julius Caesar) were praised for their moderation in drinking. This would appear to be in response to growing misuse of alcohol in society, because before that time temperance was not singled out for praise as exemplary behavior. As the republic continued to decay, excessive drinking spread and some, such as Marc Antony (d. 30 B.C.), even took pride in their destructive drinking behavior (Austin, 1985, pp. 28 and 32–33).

Early Christian Period

With the dawn of Christianity and its gradual displacement of the previously dominant religions, the drinking attitudes and behaviors of Europe began to be influenced by the New Testament (Babor, 1986, p. 11). The earliest biblical writings after the death of Jesus (cir. A.D. 30) contain few references to alcohol. This may have reflected the fact that drunkenness was largely an upper-status vice with which Jesus had little contact (Raymond, 1927, pp. 81–82). Austin (1985, p. 35) has pointed out that Jesus used wine (Matthew 15:11; Luke 7:33–35) and approved of its moderate consumption (Matthew 15:11). On the other hand, he severely attacked drunkenness (Luke 21:34, 12:42; Matthew 24:45–51). The later writings of St. Paul (d. 64?) deal with alcohol in detail and are important to Christian doctrine on the subject. He considered wine to be a creation of God and therefore inherently good (1 Timothy 4:4), recommended its use for medicinal purposes (1 Timothy 5:23), but consistently condemned drunkenness (1 Corinthians 3:16–17, 5:11, 6:10; Galatians 5:19–21; Romans 13:3) and recommended abstinence for those who could not control their drinking.

However, late in the second century, several heretical sects rejected alcohol and called for abstinence. By the late fourth and early fifth centuries, the Church responded by asserting that wine was an inherently good gift of God to be used and enjoyed. While individuals may choose not to drink, to despise wine was heresy. The Church advocated its moderate use but rejected excessive or abusive use as a sin. Those individuals who could not drink in moderation were urged to abstain (Austin, 1985, pp. 44 and 47–48).

It is clear that both the Old and New Testaments are clear and consistent in their condemnation of drunkenness. However, some Christians today argue that whenever "wine" was used by Jesus or praised as a gift of God, it was really grape juice; only when it caused drunkenness was it wine. Thus, they interpret the Bible as asserting that grape juice is good and that drinking it is acceptable to God but that wine is bad and that drinking it is unacceptable. This reasoning appears to be incorrect for at least two reasons. First, neither the Hebrew nor Biblical Greek word for wine can be translated or interpreted as referring to grape juice. Secondly, grape juice would quickly ferment into wine in the warm climate of the Mediterranean region without refrigeration or modern methods of preservation (Royce, 1986, pp. 55–56; Raymond, 1927, pp. 18–22; Hewitt, 1980, pp. 11–12).

The spread of Christianity and of viticulture in Western Europe occurred simultaneously (Lausanne, 1969, p. 367; Sournia, 1990, p. 12). Interestingly, St. Martin of Tours (316–397) was actively engaged in both spreading the Gospel and planting vineyards (Patrick, 1952, pp. 26–27).

In an effort to maintain traditional Jewish culture against the rise of Christianity, which was converting numerous Jews (Wallbank & Taylor, 1954, p. 227), detailed rules concerning the use of wine were incorporated into the Talmud. Importantly, wine was integrated into many religious ceremonies in limited quantity (Spiegel, 1979, pp. 20–29; Raymond, 1927, 45–47). In the social and political upheavals that rose as the fall of Rome approached in the fifth century, concern grew among rabbis that Judaism and its culture were in increasing danger. Consequently, more Talmudic rules were laid down concerning the use of wine. These included the amount of wine that could be drunk on the Sabbath, the way in which wine was to be drunk, the legal status of wine in any way connected with idolatry, and the extent of personal responsibility for behavior while intoxicated (Austin, 1985, pp. 36 and 50).

Roman abuse of alcohol appears to have peaked around mid-first century (Jellinek, 1976, pp. 1,736–1,739). Wine had become the most popular beverage, and as Rome attracted a large influx of displaced persons, it was distributed free or at cost (Babor, 1986, pp. 7–8). This led to occasional excesses at festivals, victory triumphs and other celebrations, as described by contemporaries. The four emperors who ruled from A.D. 37 to A.D. 69 were all known for their abusive drinking. However, the emperors who followed were known for their temperance, and literary sources suggest that problem drinking decreased substantially in the Empire. Although there continued to be some criticisms of abusive drinking over the next several hundred years, most evidence indicates a decline of such behavior (Austin, 1985, pp. 37–44, p. 46, pp. 48–50). The fall of Rome

and the Western Roman Empire occurred in 476 (Wallbank & Taylor, 1954, pp. 220–221).

Around A.D. 230, the Greek scholar Athenaeus wrote extensively on drinking and advocated moderation. The extensive attention to drinking, famous drinks, and drinking cups (of which he described 100) reflected the importance of wine to the Greeks (Austin, 1985, pp. 45–46).

The Middle Ages

The Middle Ages, that period of approximately one thousand years between the fall of Rome and the beginning of the High Renaissance (cir. 1500), saw numerous developments in life in general and in drinking in particular. In the early Middle Ages, mead, rustic beers, and wild fruit wines became increasingly popular, especially among Celts, Anglo-Saxons, Germans, and Scandinavians. However, wines remained the beverage of preference in the Romance countries (what is now Italy, Spain, and France) (Babor, 1986, p. 11).

With the collapse of the Roman Empire and decline of urban life, religious institutions, particularly monasteries, became the repositories of the brewing and winemaking techniques that had been earlier developed (Babor, 1986, p. 11). While rustic beers continued to be produced in homes, the art of brewing essentially became the province of monks, who carefully guarded their knowledge (Cherrington, 1925, v. 1, p. 405). Monks brewed virtually all beer of good quality until the twelfth century. Around the thirteenth century, hops (which both flavors and preserves) became a common ingredient in some beers, especially in northern Europe (Wilson, 1991, p. 375). Ale, often a thick and nutritious soupy beverage, soured quickly and was made for local consumption (Austin, 1985, pp. 54, 87–88).

Not surprisingly, the monasteries also maintained viticulture. Importantly, they had the resources, security, and stability in that often-turbulent time to improve the quality of their vines slowly over 1986 (p. 11). While most wine was made and consumed locally, some wine trade did continue in spite of the deteriorating roads (Hyams, 1965, p. 151; Wilson, 1991, p. 371).

By the millennium, the most popular form of festivities in England were known as "ales," and both ale and beer were at the top of lists of products to be given to lords for rent. As towns were established in twelfth-century Germany, they were granted the privilege of brewing and selling beer in their immediate localities. A flourishing artisan brewing industry developed in many towns, about which there was strong civic pride (Cherrington, 1925, v. 1, p. 405; Austin 1985, pp. 68, 74, 82–83).

The most important development regarding alcohol throughout the Middle Ages was probably that of distillation.

Interestingly, considerable disagreement exists concerning who discovered distillation and when the discovery was made. However, it was Albertus Magnus (1193–1280) who first clearly described the process which made possible the manufacture of distilled spirits (Patrick, 1952, p. 29). Knowledge of the process began to spread slowly among monks, physicians and alchemists, who were interested in distilled alcohol as a cure for ailments. At that time it was called aqua vitae, "water of life," but was later known as brandy. The latter term was derived from the Dutch brandewijn, meaning burnt (or distilled) wine (Seward, 1979, p. 151; Roueche, 1963, pp. 172–173).

The Black Death and subsequent plagues, which began in the mid-fourteenth century, dramatically changed people's perception of their lives and place in the cosmos. With no understanding or control of the plagues that reduced the population by as much as 82% in some villages, "processions of flagellants mobbed city and village streets, hoping, by the pains they inflicted on themselves and each other, to take the edge off the plagues they attributed to God's wrath over human folly" (Slavin, 1973, pp. 12–16).

Some dramatically increased their consumption of alcohol in the belief that this might protect them from the mysterious disease, while others thought that through moderation in all things, including alcohol, they could be saved. It would appear that, on balance, consumption of alcohol was high. For example, in Bavaria, beer consumption was probably about 300 liters per capita a year (compared to 150 liters today) and in Florence wine consumption was about ten barrels per capita a year. Understandably, the consumption of distilled spirits, which was exclusively for medicinal purposes, increased in popularity (Austin, 1985, pp. 104–105, 107–108).

As the end of the Middle Ages approached, the popularity of beer spread to England, France, and Scotland (Austin, pp. 118–119). Beer brewers were recognized officially as a guild in England (Monckton, 1966, pp. 69–70), and the adulteration of beer or wine became punishable by death in Scotland (Cherrington, 1929, vol. 5, p. 2,383). Importantly, the consumption of spirits as a beverage began to occur (Braudel, 1974, p. 171).

Early Modern Period

The early modern period was generally characterized by increasing prosperity and wealth. Towns and cities grew in size and number, foreign lands were discovered and colonized, and trade expanded. Perhaps more importantly, there developed a new view of the world. The medieval emphasis on other-worldliness—the belief that life in this world is only a preparation for heaven—slowly gave way, especially among the wealthy

and well educated, to an interest in life in the here and now (Wallbank & Taylor, 1954, p. 513).

The Protestant Reformation and rise of aggressive national states destroyed the ideal of a universal Church overseeing a Holy Roman Empire. Rationality, individualism, and science heavily impacted the prevalent emotional idealism, communalism, and traditional religion (Wallbank & Taylor, 1954, pp. 513–518; Slavin, 1973, ch. 5–7).

However, the Protestant leaders such as Luther, Calvin, the leaders of the Anglican Church, and even the Puritans did not differ substantially from the teachings of the Catholic Church: alcohol was a gift of God and created to be used in moderation for pleasure, enjoyment and health; drunkenness was viewed as a sin (Austin, 1985, p. 194).

From this period through at least the beginning of the eighteenth century, attitudes toward drinking were characterized by a continued recognition of the positive nature of moderate consumption and an increased concern over the negative effects of drunkenness. The latter, which was generally viewed as arising out of the increased self-indulgence of the time, was seen as a threat to spiritual salvation and societal well being. Intoxication was also inconsistent with the emerging emphasis on rational mastery of self and world and on work and efficiency (Austin, 1985, pp. 129–130).

However, consumption of alcohol was often high. In the sixteenth century, alcohol beverage consumption reached 100 liters per person per year in Valladolid, Spain, and Polish peasants consumed up to three liters of beer per day (Braudel, 1974, pp. 236–238). In Coventry, the average amount of beer and ale consumed was about 17 pints per person per week, compared to about three pints today (Monckton, 1966, p. 95); nationwide, consumption was about one pint per day per capita. Swedish beer consumption may have been 40 times higher than in modern Sweden. English sailors received a ration of a gallon of beer per day, while soldiers received two-thirds of a gallon. In Denmark, the usual consumption of beer appears to have been a gallon per day for adult laborers and sailors (Austin, 1985, pp. 170, 186, 192).

However, the production and distribution of spirits spread slowly. Spirit drinking was still largely for medicinal purposes throughout most of the sixteenth century. It has been said of distilled alcohol that "the sixteenth century created it; the seventeenth century consolidated it; the eighteenth popularized it" (Braudel, 1967, p. 170).

A beverage that clearly made its debut during the seventeenth century was sparkling champagne. The credit for that development goes primarily to Dom Perignon, the wine-master in a French abbey. Around 1668, he used strong bottles, invented a more efficient cork (and one that could contain the effervescence in those strong bottles), and began developing the technique of blending the contents. However, another century would pass before problems, especially bursting bottles, would be solved and sparkling champagne would become popular (Younger, 1966, pp. 345–346; Doxat, 1971, p. 54; Seward, 1979, pp. 139–143).

The original grain spirit, whiskey, appears to have first been distilled in Ireland. While its specific origins are unknown (Magee, 1980, p. 7; Wilson, 1973, p. 7) there is evidence that by the sixteenth century it was widely consumed in some parts of Scotland (Roueche, 1963, pp. 175–176). It was also during the seventeenth century that Franciscus Sylvius (or Franz de la Boe), a professor of medicine at the University of Leyden, distilled spirits from grain.

Distilled spirit was generally flavored with juniper berries. The resulting beverage was known as junever, the Dutch word for "juniper." The French changed the name to genievre, which the English changed to "geneva" and then modified to "gin" (Roueche, 1963, pp. 173–174). Originally used for medicinal purposes, the use of gin as a social drink did not grow rapidly at first (Doxat, 1972, p. 98; Watney, 1976, p. 10). However, in 1690, England passed "An Act for the Encouraging of the Distillation of Brandy and Spirits from Corn" and within four years the annual production of distilled spirits, most of which was gin, reached nearly one million gallons (Roueche, 1963, p. 174).

The seventeenth century also saw the Virginia colonists continue the traditional belief that alcoholic beverages are a natural food and are good when used in moderation. In fact, beer arrived with the first colonists, who considered it essential to their well being (Baron, 1962, pp. 3–8). The Puritan minister Increase Mather preached in favor of alcohol but against its abuse: "Drink is in itself a good creature of God, and to be received with thankfulness, but the abuse of drink is from Satan; the wine is from God, but the Drunkard is from the Devil" (quoted in Rorabaugh, 1979, p. 30). During that century the first distillery was established in the colonies on what is now Staten Island (Roueche, 1963, p. 178), cultivation of hops began in Massachusetts, and both brewing and distilling were legislatively encouraged in Maryland (Austin, 1985, pp. 230 and 249).

Rum is produced by distilling fermented molasses, which is the residue left after sugar has been made from sugar-cane. Although it was introduced to the world, and presumably invented, by the first European settlers in the West Indies, no one knows when it was first produced or by what individual. But by 1657, a rum distillery was operating in Boston. It was highly successful and within a generation the manufacture of rum would become colonial New England's largest and most prosperous industry (Roueche, 1963, p. 178).

The dawn of the eighteenth century saw Parliament pass legislation designed to encourage the use of grain for distilling spirits. In 1685, consumption of gin had been slightly over one-half million gallons (Souria, 1990, p. 20). By 1714, gin production stood at two million gallons (Roueche, 1963, p. 174). In 1727, official (declared and taxed) production reached five million gallons; six years later the London area alone produced eleven million gallons of gin (French, 1890, p. 271; Samuelson, 1878, pp. 160–161; Watney, 1976, p. 16).

The English government actively promoted gin production to utilize surplus grain and to raise revenue. Encouraged by public policy, very cheap spirits flooded the market at a time when there was little stigma attached to drunkenness and when the growing urban poor in London sought relief from the new-found insecurities and harsh realities of urban life (Watney, 1976, p. 17; Austin, 1985, pp. xxi–xxii). Thus developed the so-called Gin Epidemic.

While the negative effects of that phenomenon may have been exaggerated (Sournia, 1990, p. 21; Mathias, 1959, p. xxv). Parliament passed legislation in 1736 to discourage consumption by prohibiting the sale of gin in quantities of less than two gallons and raising the tax on it dramatically. However, the peak in consumption was reached seven years later, when the nation of six and one-half million people drank over 18 million gallons of gin. And most was consumed by the small minority of the population then living in London and other cities; people in the countryside largely remained loyal to beer, ale, and cider (Doxat, 1972, pp. 98–100; Watney, 1976, p.17).

After its dramatic peak, gin consumption rapidly declined. From 18 million gallons in 1743, it dropped to just over seven million gallons in 1751 and to less than two million by 1758, and generally declined to the end of the century (Ashton, 1955, p. 243). A number of factors appear to have converged to discourage consumption of gin. These include the production of higher quality beer of lower price, rising corn prices, and taxes which eroded the price advantage of gin, a temporary ban on distilling, a stigmatization of drinking gin, an increasing criticism of drunkenness, a newer standard of behavior that criticized coarseness and excess, increased tea and coffee consumption, an increase in piety and increasing industrialization with a consequent emphasis on sobriety and labor efficiency (Sournia, 1990, p. 22; King, 1947, p. 117; Austin, 1985, pp. xxiii–xxiv, 324–325, 351; Younger, 1966, p. 341).

While drunkenness was still an accepted part of life in the eighteenth century (Austin, 1985, p. xxv), the nineteenth century would bring a change in attitudes as a result of increasing industrialization and the need for a reliable and punctual work force (Porter, 1990, p. xii). Self-discipline was needed in place of self-expression, and task orientation had to replace relaxed conviviality. Drunkenness would come to be defined as a threat to industrial efficiency and growth.

Problems commonly associated with industrialization and rapid urbanization were also attributed to alcohol. Thus, problems such as urban crime, poverty, and high infant mortality rates were blamed on alcohol, although "it is likely that gross overcrowding and unemployment had much to do with these problems" (Soumia, 1990, p. 21). Over time, more and more personal, social, and religious/moral problems would be blamed on alcohol. And not only would it be enough to prevent drunkenness; any consumption of alcohol would come to be seen as unacceptable. Groups that began by promoting temperance—the moderate use of alcohol—would ultimately become abolitionist and press for the complete and total prohibition of the production and distribution of beverage alcohol. Unfortunately, this would not eliminate social problems but would compound the situation by creating additional problems.

Summary and Conclusion

It is clear that alcohol has been highly valued and in continuous use by peoples throughout history. Reflecting its vital role, consumption of alcohol in moderation has rarely been questioned throughout most of recorded time. To the contrary, "Fermented dietary beverage . . . was so common an element in the various cultures that it was taken for granted as one of the basic elements of survival and self-preservation" (Lucia, 1963b, p. 165). Indicative of its value is the fact that it has frequently been acceptable as a medium of exchange. For example, in Medieval England, ale was often used to pay toll, rent, or debts (Watney, 1974, p. 16).

From the earliest times "alcohol has played an important role in religion," typically seen as a gift of deities and closely associated with their worship. Religious rejection of alcohol appears to be a rare phenomenon. When it does occur, such rejection may be unrelated to alcohol per se but reflect other considerations. For example, the nomadic Rechabites rejected wine because they associated it with an unacceptable agricultural life style. Nazarites abstained only during the period of their probation, after which they returned to drinking (Sournia, 1990, p. 5; Samuelson, 1878, pp. 62–63). Among other reasons, Mohammed may have forbidden alcohol in order to further distinguish his followers from those of other religions (Royce, 1986, p. 57).

Alcoholic beverages have also been an important source of nutrients and calories (Braudel, 1974, p. 175). In ancient Egypt, the phrase "bread and beer" stood for all food and was also a common greeting. Many alcoholic beverages, such as Egyptian bouza and Sudanese merissa, contain high levels of protein, fat and carbohydrates, a fact that helps explain the frequent lack of nutritional deficiencies in some populations whose diets are generally poor. Importantly, the levels of amino acids and vitamins increase during fermentation (Ghaliounqui, 1979,

pp. 8–9). While modern food technology uses enrichment or fortification to improve the nutrition of foods, it is possible to achieve nutritional enrichment naturally through fermentation (Steinkraus, 1979, p. 36).

Alcoholic beverages have long served as thirst quenchers. Water pollution is far from new; to the contrary, supplies have generally been either unhealthful or questionable at best. Ancient writers rarely wrote about water, except as a warning (Ghaliounqui, 1979, p. 3). Travelers crossing what is now Zaire in 1648 reported having to drink water that resembled horse's urine. In the late eighteenth century most Parisians drank water from a very muddy and often chemically polluted Seine (Braudel, 1967, pp. 159–161). Coffee and tea were not introduced into Europe until the mid-seventeenth century, and it was another hundred or more years before they were commonly consumed on a daily basis (Austin, 1985, pp. 251, 254, 351, 359, 366).

Another important function of alcohol has been therapeutic or medicinal. Current research suggests that the moderate consumption of alcohol is preferable to abstinence. It appears to reduce the incidence of coronary heart disease (e.g., Razay, 1992; Jackson et al., 1991; Klatsky et al., 1990, p. 745; Rimm *et al.,* 1991; Miller et al., 1990), cancer (e.g., Bofetta & Garfinkel, 1990), and osteoporosis (e.g., Gavaler & Van Thiel, 1992), among many other diseases and conditions, and to increase longevity (e.g., DeLabry et al., 1992). It has clearly been a major analgesic, and one widely available to people in pain. Relatedly, it has provided relief from the fatigue of hard labor.

Not to be underestimated is the important role alcohol has served in enhancing the enjoyment and quality of life. It can serve as a social lubricant, can provide entertainment, can facilitate relaxation, can provide pharmacological pleasure, and can enhance the flavors of food (Gastineau et al., 1979).

While alcohol has always been misused by a minority of drinkers, it has clearly proved to be beneficial to most. In the words of the founding Director of the National Institute on Alcohol Abuse and Alcoholism, ". . . alcohol has existed longer than all human memory. It has outlived generations, nations, epochs, and ages. It is a part of us, and that is fortunate indeed. For although alcohol will always be the master of some, for most of us it will continue to be the servant of man" (Chafetz, 1965, p. 223).

References

Hanson, David J. *Preventing Alcohol Abuse: Alcohol, Culture and Control.* Wesport, CT: Praeger, 1995. www2.potsdam.edu/hansondj/controversies/1114796842.html. Retrieved May 2, 2008.

Marley, David. *Chemical Addiction, Drug Use, and Treatment.* MedScape Today 2001. www.medscape.com/viewarticle/418525. Retrieved May 2, 2008.

Critical Thinking

1. Why have patterns related to alcohol use remained consistent around the world for centuries?
2. Consider the theme(s) of alcohol use throughout history as presented in this article and describe how alcohol use today relates to those themes.

Internet References

National Clearinghouse for Alcohol and Drug Information
www.ncadisamhsa.org

National Institute on Alcoholism and Alcohol Abuse
www.niaaa.nih.gov

Adapted from **DAVID J. HANSON, PHD** *Preventing Alcohol Abuse: Alcohol, Culture, and Control.* Westport, CT: Praeger, 1995.

Article

Prepared by: Kim Schnurbush, *California State University, Sacramento*
Mark Pullin, *Angelo State University*

New Abuse-deterrent Painkiller Approved

STEPHANIE SMITH

Learning Outcomes

After reading this article, you will be able to:

- Understand the impact of Targiniq as an alternative pain medication.

- Be familiar with various pain medications used in the United States, and why Targiniq is a viable alternative for those abusing pain medications.

- Understand various delivery methods for pain killers and why Targiniq may be the answer for many pain medication abusers.

In the painkiller world, oxycodone and naloxone seem like strange bedfellows. Oxycodone is a powerful painkiller, while naloxone is used to reverse painkiller overdose.

On Wednesday, the Food and Drug Administration approved a drug combining the two, called Targiniq ER.

The drug's maker, Purdue Pharma, said the combination is intended to "alleviate pain while also introducing a new method by which to help deter misuse and abuse."

Oxycodone is one in a group of powerful painkillers—called opioid analgesics—that include hydrocodone, morphine, and hydromorphone. It provides pain relief by binding to receptors in the brain that dull the sensation of pain.

So why marry it with naloxone? Simply put, naloxone can unseat oxycodone on those same brain receptors, blocking its ability to provide pain relief.

In the case of Targiniq, it happens only when the pill is crushed. If the pill remains intact, naloxone lies dormant, allowing oxycodone to do its work.

Approval of an abuse-deterrent painkiller such as Targiniq would seem welcome, considering the rampant use of the drugs in the United States. The United States consumes 83% of the world's oxycodone and 99% of its hydrocodone, according to a 2010 International Narcotics Control Board report.

Forty-six people die each day from prescription painkiller overdoses, according to the Centers for Disease Control and Prevention.

Dr. Stephen Anderson, an emergency room physician who sees opioid overdoses on a weekly basis, said Targiniq limits the common abuse delivery routes—such as crushing, dissolving and injecting pills, or crushing and snorting them.

"Well done to the manufacturer for placing some built-in pharmacological protections," said Anderson, past president of the Washington chapter of the American College of Emergency Physicians, in an e-mail. "It won't stop orally ingested overdose deaths, but will limit some of its 'street marketability.'"

And abuse-deterrence seemed to work with another of Purdue Pharma's painkillers, OxyContin: A difficult-to-crush version of the drug was introduced in 2010.

"Before that, OxyContin was the most commonly diverted and abused drug," said Caleb Banta-Green, an opioid overdose researcher and former senior science adviser to the Office of National Drug Control Policy. "After the formulation changed, nobody liked it because they couldn't abuse it."

According to the *New England Journal of Medicine,* before 2010, OxyContin had been considered a primary drug of abuse for about 36% of people surveyed. Twenty-one months after the introduction of the abuse-deterrence version, only 13% abused it.

What impact Targiniq's approval could have on oxycodone abuse remains to be seen.

Targiniq's approval "will better enable the FDA to balance addressing this problem with meeting the needs of the millions of people in this country suffering from pain," said Dr. Sharon Hertz, deputy director of the FDA's Division of Anesthesia, Analgesia and Addiction Products, in a statement.

The FDA said the drug should be prescribed as a last resort, for patients who have exhausted all other attempts to relieve their pain.

Still, experts on addiction said they fear that Targiniq could still be easily abused.

"Naloxone is only active if injected or squirted up the nose," said Andrew Kolodny, chief medical officer of the Phoenix House, an alcohol and drug abuse treatment provider. "That means a patient who chews Targiniq will get the entire dose all at once and the naloxone will have no effect.

When the pills are swallowed, they are as addictive and dangerous as pure oxycodone."

The concern is that people who abuse or misuse opioids (also called opiates) will simply find another route to a high.

"In a sense it's playing a game of whack-a-mole, because if people are addicted to opiates, they will find an opiate," said Banta-Green, who's a senior research scientist at the University of Washington's Alcohol and Drug Abuse Institute.

"This (drug approval) could and will likely help, but it doesn't fix the inherent problem that people addicted to opiates will continue to use them."

Critical Thinking

1. After reviewing the statistics of the consumption of pain medications in the United States, critically analyze why Americans are turning to prescription drugs at such an alarming rate.

2. If prescription pain medications are used to treat pain, why are so many people becoming addicted to them?

3. Will a drug like Targiniq, which changes the delivery route of the medication into the body, ultimately change the way people obtain and/or abuse prescription pain medications?

Internet References

DEA: Drug Enforcement Administration
http://www.justice.gov/dea/index.shtml
Web MD
http://www.webmd.com/drugs/condition-3079-Pain.aspx

Article
         Prepared by: Kim Schnurbush, *California State University, Sacramento*
         Mark Pullin, *Angelo State University*

Heroin Epidemic Increasingly Seeps into Public View

Katharine Q. Seelye

Learning Outcomes

After reading this article, you will be able to:

- Discuss how the current heroin epidemic has affected law enforcement.

- Discuss the effects on the death rates across the country due to heroin.

- Discuss social effects on the community due to heroin addiction.

Cambridge, MA—In Philadelphia last spring, a man riding a city bus at rush hour injected heroin into his hand, in full view of other passengers, including one who captured the scene on video.

In Cincinnati, a woman died in January after she and her husband overdosed in their baby's room at Cincinnati Children's Hospital Medical Center. The husband was found unconscious with a gun in his pocket, a syringe in his arm, and needles strewn around the sink.

Here, in Cambridge a few years ago, after several people overdosed in the bathrooms of a historic church, church officials reluctantly closed the bathrooms to the public.

"We weren't medically equipped or educated to handle overdoses, and we were desperately afraid we were going to have something happen that was way out of our reach," said the Rev. Joseph O. Robinson, rector of the church, Christ Church Cambridge.

With heroin cheap and widely available on city streets throughout the country, users are making their buys and shooting up as soon as they can, often in public places. Police officers are routinely finding drug users—unconscious or dead—in cars, in the bathrooms of fast-food restaurants, on mass transit, and in parks, hospitals, and libraries.

The visibility of drug users may be partly attributed to the nature of the epidemic, which has grown largely out of dependence on legal opioid painkillers and has spread to white, urban, suburban, and rural areas.

Nationally, 125 people a day die from drug overdoses, 78 of them from heroin and painkillers, and many more are revived, brought back from the brink of death—often in full public view. The police in Upper Darby, PA, have even posted a video of another man shooting heroin on a public bus, and then being revived by Narcan, which reverses the effects of a heroin overdose, to demonstrate the drug's effectiveness.

Some addicts even seek out towns where emergency medical workers carry Narcan, "knowing if they do overdose, there's a good likelihood that when police respond, they'll be able to administer Narcan," said Special Agent Timothy Desmond, a spokesman for the New England region of the Drug Enforcement Administration.

In Linthicum, MD, Brian Knighton, a wrestler known as Axl Rotten in Extreme Championship Wrestling, died last month after overdosing in a McDonald's bathroom.

In Cincinnati in 2014, an Indiana couple overdosed on heroin at a McDonald's, collapsing in front of their children in the restaurant's play area.

In Niagara Falls, NY, a man was accused in October of leaving a 5-year-old boy unattended in a Dairy Queen, while he went to the bathroom; he was later found on the floor with a syringe in his arm.

In Johnstown, PA, a man overdosed on heroin on February 19 in a bathroom at the Cambria County Library.

"Users need the fix as quickly as they can get it," said Edward James Walsh, chief of police in Taunton, MA, a city 40 miles south of here that has been plagued with heroin overdoses in recent years. "The physical and psychological need is so great for an addict that they will use it at the earliest opportunity."

That reality has taxed law enforcement and city services across the country and has stretched the tolerance of businesses that allow unfettered access to their bathrooms. Legal liability is an increasing worry.

"Overdosing has become an issue of great societal concern," said Martin W. Healy, chief legal counsel for the Massachusetts Bar Association. "I'm not aware of any seminal cases so far, but this is likely to be a developing area of the law."

After shooting up in public places, people often leave behind dirty needles, posing a health hazard. In response, some groups have called for supervised injection facilities, like those in Canada and Europe, where people can inject themselves under medical supervision. The goal is to keep them from overdosing and to curb infectious diseases. Such facilities are illegal in this country, although the mayor of Ithaca, NY, recently suggested opening one.

In Boston, where pedestrians step over drug users who are nodding off on a stretch of Massachusetts Avenue known as Methadone Mile, an organization for the homeless has planned what it calls a safe space, where users could ride out their high under supervision; it would not allow actual injection on site.

New England has been a cradle of the heroin epidemic. Middlesex County, which encompasses Cambridge, a city of 107,000 just west of Boston, has the highest number of overdose deaths from heroin and prescription pain pills in Massachusetts. From 2000 to 2014, Middlesex, which also includes the city of Lowell, a major heroin hotbed, had 1,634 opioid deaths.

No one keeps track of how many deaths occur in public spaces, but law enforcement officials agree the number is high.

"We quite frequently see folks using public areas," said Robert C. Haas, the Cambridge police commissioner.

It was the fear of someone dying in their bathrooms that led officials at Christ Church Cambridge to close public access to them in 2012. By doing so, the church did not experience the kind of tragic scenes that are occurring around the country, but the decision was difficult.

The church, which opened in 1761 and has a long history of social activism, had kept the bathrooms open to accommodate the homeless people around Harvard Square. But addicts were also using them. Closing them after decades of serving the public represented "a retreat from our ministry," Mr. Robinson said. But in consultation with the Cambridge police, the church reluctantly concluded that leaving the bathrooms open only enabled drug users.

Because there were no freestanding public toilets in Harvard Square, a popular shopping, culture, and dining destination that is visited by eight million tourists a year, the absence of the church bathrooms was felt right away.

"Almost immediately, we began receiving calls saying, basically, 'What the hell just happened?'" said Denise Jillson, executive director of the Harvard Square Business Association. "They were saying, 'Our doorways and alleyways have become public urinals, and people are defecating everywhere.'"

After a campaign by business owners and local activists for a public toilet—which included stickers that read "I Love Toilets" and "Where Would Jesus Go?"—the City of Cambridge spent $400,000 to buy and install Harvard Square's first freestanding public toilet. It was unveiled on February 12. Free to use and open 24 hours a day, it sits in a kiosk on a busy traffic island between the stately brick buildings of Harvard Yard and the weathered headstones in the Old Burying Ground, which dates to 1635.

The kiosk, called the Portland Loo and made in Oregon, was designed specifically to discourage drug use. It has slanted slats at the bottom that allow the police—or anyone—to peer in and see if someone has passed out on the concrete floor. It has no heat, air conditioning or noise insulation, all meant to foil anyone from getting too comfortable inside. The hand washing faucet is outside and an attendant cleans four times a day.

The outcome pleased Mr. Robinson, who said the anguishing decision to close the church bathrooms had "led to a broader response to the needs of the homeless in our neighborhood."

While the new toilet may improve life for some in Harvard Square, many restaurants, parking lots, and other public spaces here and elsewhere remain potential sites for drug activity.

"Until we get a handle on the drug problem," said Capt. Timothy Crowley of the Lowell Police Department, "I think this is an issue we'll be dealing with for a long time."

Critical Thinking

1. Why has heroin become so popular in recent times?
2. How are unsafe using practices creating further health issues?
3. Develop a comprehensive plan to curtain the heroin issues across the country.

Internet References

Addiction Center: Guiding You from Rehab to Recovery—Heroin Treatment and Rehab
   https://www.addictioncenter.com/drugs/heroin/treatment/
Drug Enforcement Administration
   www.dea.gov
National Heroin Threat Assessment Summary—Updated
   https://www.dea.gov/divisions/hq/2016/hq062716_attach.pdf
National Institute on Drug Abuse
   https://www.drugabuse.gov/publications/drugfacts/heroin

Article

Prepared by: Kim Schnurbush, *California State University, Sacramento*
Mark Pullin, *Angelo State University*

Prescription Drug Abuse

Nora D. Volkow

Learning Outcomes

After reading this article, you will be able to:

- Understand how the nonmedical use and abuse of prescription drugs has become a serious health issue in the U.S.
- Discuss the disruption of daily activities as a result of prescription drug abuse.
- Understand the basics of prescription drug addiction and the harmful consequences to social and physical health.

What Is Prescription Drug Abuse?

Prescription drug abuse[1] is the use of a medication without a prescription, in a way other than as prescribed, or for the experience or feelings elicited. According to several national surveys, prescription medications, such as those used to treat pain, attention deficit disorders, and anxiety, are being abused at a rate second only to marijuana among illicit drug users. The consequences of this abuse have been steadily worsening, reflected in increased treatment admissions, emergency room visits, and overdose deaths.

What Are Some of the Commonly Abused Prescription Drugs?

Although many medications can be abused, the following three classes are most commonly abused:

- Opioids—usually prescribed to treat pain;
- Central nervous system (CNS) depressants—used to treat anxiety and sleep disorders;
- Stimulants—most often prescribed to treat attention-deficit hyperactivity disorder (ADHD).

Opioids
What Are Opioids?

Opioids are medications that relieve pain. They reduce the intensity of pain signals reaching the brain and affect those brain areas controlling emotion, which diminishes the effects of a painful stimulus. Medications that fall within this class include hydrocodone (e.g., Vicodin), oxycodone (e.g., OxyContin, Percocet), morphine (e.g., Kadian, Avinza), codeine, and related drugs. Hydrocodone products are the most commonly prescribed for a variety of painful conditions, including dental and injury-related pain. Morphine is often used before and after surgical procedures to alleviate severe pain. Codeine, on the other hand, is often prescribed for mild pain. In addition to their pain-relieving properties, some of these drugs—codeine and diphenoxylate (Lomotil) for example—can be used to relieve coughs and severe diarrhea.

How Do Opioids Affect the Brain and Body?

Opioids act by attaching to specific proteins called opioid receptors, which are found in the brain, spinal cord, gastrointestinal tract, and other organs in the body. When these drugs attach to their receptors, they reduce the perception of pain. Opioids can also produce drowsiness, mental confusion, nausea, constipation, and, depending upon the amount of drug taken, can depress respiration. Some people experience a euphoric response to opioid medications, since these drugs also affect the brain regions involved in reward. Those who abuse opioids may seek to intensify their experience by taking the drug in ways other than those prescribed. For example, OxyContin is an oral medication used to treat moderate to severe pain through a slow, steady release of the opioid. People who abuse OxyContin may snort or inject it,[2] thereby increasing their risk for serious medical complications, including overdose.

What Are the Possible Consequences of Opioid Use and Abuse?

Taken as prescribed, opioids can be used to manage pain safely and effectively. However, when abused, even a single large dose can cause severe respiratory depression and death. Properly managed, short-term medical use of opioid analgesics rarely causes addiction—characterized by compulsive drug seeking and use despite serious adverse consequences. Regular (e.g., several times a day, for several weeks or more) or longer-term use or abuse of opioids can lead to physical dependence and, in some cases, addiction. Physical dependence is a *normal* adaptation to chronic exposure to a drug and is not the same as addiction ("see box 'Dependence versus Addiction'"). In either case, withdrawal symptoms may occur if drug use is suddenly reduced or stopped. These symptoms can include restlessness, muscle and bone pain, insomnia, diarrhea, vomiting, cold flashes with goose bumps ("cold turkey"), and involuntary leg movements.

Dependence versus Addiction

Physical dependence occurs because of *normal* adaptations to chronic exposure to a drug and is not the same as addiction. Addiction, which can include physical dependence, is distinguished by compulsive drug seeking and use despite sometimes devastating consequences.

Someone who is physically dependent on a medication will experience withdrawal symptoms when use of the drug is abruptly reduced or stopped. These symptoms can be mild or severe (depending on the drug) and can usually be managed medically or avoided by using a slow drug taper.

Dependence is often accompanied by tolerance, or the need to take higher doses of a medication to get the same effect. When tolerance occurs, it can be difficult for a physician to evaluate whether a patient is developing a drug problem, or has a real medical need for higher doses to control their symptoms. For this reason, physicians need to be vigilant and attentive to their patients' symptoms and level of functioning to treat them appropriately.

Is It Safe to Use Opioid Drugs with Other Medications?

Only under a physician's supervision can opioids be used safely with other drugs. Typically, they should not be used with other substances that depress the CNS, such as alcohol, antihistamines, barbiturates, benzodiazepines, or general anesthetics, because these combinations increase the risk of life-threatening respiratory depression.

CNS Depressants
What Are CNS Depressants?

CNS depressants, sometimes referred to as sedatives and tranquilizers, are substances that can slow brain activity. This property makes them useful for treating anxiety and sleep disorders. Among the medications commonly prescribed for these purposes are the following:

- **Benzodiazepines,** such as diazepam (Valium) and alprazolam (Xanax), are sometimes prescribed to treat anxiety, acute stress reactions, and panic attacks. The more sedating benzodiazepines, such as triazolam (Halcion) and estazolam (ProSom) are prescribed for short-term treatment of sleep disorders. Usually, benzodiazepines are not prescribed for long-term use because of the risk for developing tolerance, dependence, or addiction.
- **Nonbenzodiazepine sleep medications**, such as zolpidem (Ambien), eszopiclone (Lunesta), and zalepon (Sonata), have a different chemical structure, but act on some of the same brain receptors as benzodiazepines. They are thought to have fewer side effects and less risk of dependence than benzodiazepines.
- **Barbiturates**, such as mephobarbital (Mebaral), phenobarbital (Luminal Sodium), and pentobarbital sodium (Nembutal), are used less frequently to reduce anxiety or to help with sleep problems because of their higher risk of overdose compared to benzodiazepines.

However, they are still used in surgical procedures and for seizure disorders.

Opioids and Brain Damage

While the relationship between opioid overdose and depressed respiration (slowed breathing) has been confirmed, researchers are also studying the long-term effects on brain function. Depressed respiration can affect the amount of oxygen that reaches the brain, a condition called hypoxia. Hypoxia can have short- and long-term psychological and neurological effects, including coma and permanent brain damage.

Researchers are also investigating the long-term effects of opioid addiction on the brain. Studies have shown some deterioration of the brain's white matter due to heroin use, which may affect decision-making abilities, the ability to regulate behavior, and responses to stressful situations.

How Do CNS Depressants Affect the Brain and Body?

Most CNS depressants act on the brain by affecting the neurotransmitter gamma-aminobutyric acid (GABA). Neurotransmitters are brain chemicals that facilitate communication between brain cells. Although the different classes of CNS depressants work in unique ways, it is through their ability to increase GABA—and thereby inhibit brain activity—that they produce a drowsy or calming effect beneficial to those suffering from anxiety or sleep disorders.

What Are the Possible Consequences of CNS Depressant Use and Abuse?

Despite their many beneficial effects, benzodiazepines and barbiturates have the potential for abuse and should be used only as prescribed. The use of nonbenzodiazepine sleep aids is less well studied, but certain indicators have raised concern about their abuse liability as well. During the first few days of taking a prescribed CNS depressant, a person usually feels sleepy and uncoordinated, but as the body becomes accustomed to the effects of the drug and tolerance develops, these side effects begin to disappear. If one uses these drugs long term, larger doses may be needed to achieve the therapeutic effects. Continued use can also lead to physical dependence and withdrawal when use is abruptly reduced or stopped. Because all CNS depressants work by slowing the brain's activity, when an individual stops taking them, there can be a rebound effect, resulting in seizures or other harmful consequences. Although withdrawal from benzodiazepines can be problematic, it is rarely life-threatening, whereas withdrawal from prolonged use of barbiturates can have life-threatening complications. Therefore, someone who is thinking about discontinuing CNS depressant therapy or who is suffering withdrawal from a CNS depressant should speak with a physician or seek immediate medical treatment.

Is it Safe to Use CNS Depressants with Other Medications?

Only under a physician's supervision is it safe to use CNS depressants with other medications. Typically, they should not be combined with any other medication or substance that causes CNS depression, including prescription pain medicines, some OTC cold and allergy medications, and alcohol. Using CNS depressants with these other substances—particularly alcohol—can affect heart rhythm, slow respiration, and even lead to death.

Stimulants
What Are Stimulants?

As the name suggests, stimulants increase alertness, attention, and energy, as well as elevate blood pressure, heart rate, and respiration. Stimulants historically were used to treat asthma and other respiratory problems, obesity, neurological disorders, and a variety of other ailments. But as their potential for abuse and addiction became apparent, the medical use of stimulants began to wane. Now, stimulants are prescribed to treat only a few health conditions, including ADHD, narcolepsy, and occasionally depression—in those who have not responded to other treatments.

How Do Stimulants Affect the Brain and Body?

Stimulants, such as dextroamphetamine (Dexedrine and Adderall) and methylphenidate (Ritalin and Concerta), act in the brain similarly to a family of key brain neurotransmitters called monoamines, which include norepinephrine and dopamine. Stimulants enhance the effects of these chemicals in the brain. The associated increase in dopamine can induce a feeling of euphoria when stimulants are taken nonmedically. Stimulants also increase blood pressure and heart rate, constrict blood vessels, increase blood glucose, and open up breathing passages.

What Are the Possible Consequences of Stimulant Use and Abuse?

As with other drugs of abuse, it is possible for individuals to become dependent upon or addicted to stimulants. Withdrawal

Over-the-Counter Medicines

Over-the-Counter (OTC) medications, such as certain cough suppressants, sleep aids, and antihistamines, can be abused for their psychoactive effects. This typically means taking doses higher than recommended or combining OTC medications with alcohol, or with illicit or prescription drugs. Either practice can have dangerous results, depending on the medications involved. Some contain aspirin or acetaminophen (e.g., Tylenol), which can be toxic to the liver at high doses. Others, when taken for their "hallucinogenic" properties, can cause confusion, psychosis, coma, and even death.

Cough syrups and cold medications are the most commonly abused OTC medications. In 2010, for example, 6.6 percent of high school seniors took cough syrup "to get high." At high doses, dextromethorphan—a key ingredient found in cough syrup—can act like PCP or ketamine, producing dissociative or out-of-body experiences.

Cognitive Enhancers

The dramatic increases in stimulant prescriptions over the last two decades have led to their greater environmental availability and increased risk for diversion and abuse. For those who take these medications to improve properly diagnosed conditions, they can be transforming, greatly enhancing a person's quality of life. However, because they are perceived by many to be generally safe and effective, prescription stimulants, such as Concerta or Adderall, are increasingly being abused to address nonmedical conditions or situations. Indeed, reports suggest that the practice is occurring among some academic professionals, athletes, performers, older people, and both high school and college students. Such nonmedical cognitive enhancement poses potential health risks, including addiction, cardiovascular events, and psychosis.

symptoms associated with discontinuing stimulant use include fatigue, depression, and disturbance of sleep patterns. Repeated abuse of some stimulants (sometimes within a short period) can lead to feelings of hostility or paranoia, even psychosis. Further, taking high doses of a stimulant may result in dangerously high body temperature and an irregular heartbeat. There is also the potential for cardiovascular failure or seizures.

Is it Safe to Use Stimulants with Other Medications?

Stimulants should not be used with other medications unless authorized by a physician. Patients also should be aware of the dangers associated with mixing stimulants and OTC cold medicines that contain decongestants, as combining these substances may cause blood pressure to become dangerously high or lead to irregular heart rhythms.

Trends in Prescription Drug Abuse

How Many People Abuse Prescription Drugs?

According to results from the 2010 National Survey on Drug Use and Health (NSDUH), an estimated 2.4 million Americans used prescription drugs nonmedically for the first time within the past year, which averages to approximately 6,600 initiates per day. More than ½ were females and about a third were aged 12–17. Although prescription drug abuse affects many Americans, certain populations, such as youth, older adults, and women, may be at particular risk.

Adolescents and Young Adults

Abuse of prescription drugs is highest among young adults aged 18–25, with 5.9 percent reporting nonmedical use in the past month (NSDUH, 2010). Among youth aged 12–17, 3.0 percent reported past-month nonmedical use of prescription medications.

According to the 2010 MTF, prescription and OTC drugs are among the most commonly abused drugs by 12th graders, after alcohol, marijuana, and tobacco. While past-year nonmedical use of sedatives and tranquilizers decreased among 12th graders over the last five years, this is not the case for the nonmedical use of amphetamines or opioid pain relievers.

When asked how prescription opioids were obtained for nonmedical use, more than half of the 12th graders surveyed said they were given the drugs or bought them from a friend or relative. Interestingly, the number of students who purchased opioids over the Internet was negligible.

Youth who abuse prescription medications are also more likely to report use of other drugs. Multiple studies have revealed associations between prescription drug abuse and higher rates of cigarette smoking; heavy episodic drinking; and marijuana, cocaine, and other illicit drug use among adolescents, young adults, and college students in the United States.

Older Adults

Persons aged 65 years and older comprise only 13 percent of the population, yet account for more than 1/3 of total outpatient spending on prescription medications in the United States.

Older patients are more likely to be prescribed long-term and multiple prescriptions, and some experience cognitive decline, which could lead to improper use of medications. Alternatively, those on a fixed income may abuse another person's remaining medication to save money.

The high rates of comorbid illnesses in older populations, age-related changes in drug metabolism, and the potential for drug interactions may make any of these practices more dangerous than in younger populations. Further, a large percentage of older adults also use OTC medicines and dietary supplements, which (in addition to alcohol) could compound any adverse health consequences resulting from prescription drug abuse.

Gender Differences

Overall, more males than females abuse prescription drugs in all age groups except the youngest (aged 12–17 years); that is, females in this age group exceed males in the nonmedical use of *all* psychotherapeutics, including pain relievers, tranquilizers, and stimulants. Among *nonmedical users* of prescription drugs, 12- to 17-year-old females are also more likely to meet abuse or dependence criteria for psychotherapeutics.

How Many People Suffer Adverse Health Consequences from Abusing Prescription Drugs?

The Drug Abuse Warning Network (DAWN), which monitors emergency department (ED) visits in selected areas across the Nation, reported that approximately 1 million ED visits in 2009 could be attributed to prescription drug abuse. Roughly 343,000 involved prescription opioid pain relievers, a rate more than double that of five years prior. ED visits also more than doubled for CNS stimulants, involved in nearly 22,000 visits in 2009, as well as CNS depressants (anxiolytics, sedatives, and hypnotics), involved in 363,000 visits. Of the latter, benzodiazepines (e.g., Xanax) comprised the vast majority. Rates for a popular prescribed nonbenzodiazepine sleep aid, zolpidem (Ambien), rose from roughly 13,000 in 2004 to 29,000 in 2009. More than half of ED visits for prescription drug abuse involved multiple drugs.

Preventing and Recognizing Prescription Drug Abuse

The risks for addiction to prescription drugs increase when they are used in ways other than as prescribed (e.g., at higher doses, by different routes of administration, or combined with alcohol or other drugs). Physicians, their patients, and pharmacists all can play a role in identifying and preventing prescription drug abuse.

Physicians

More than 80 percent of Americans had contact with a healthcare professional in the past year, placing doctors in a unique position, not only to prescribe medications, but also to identify abuse (or nonmedical use) of prescription drugs and prevent the escalation to addiction. By asking about *all* drugs, physicians can help their patients recognize that a problem exists, set recovery goals, and seek appropriate treatment. Screening for prescription drug abuse can be incorporated into routine medical visits. Doctors should also take note of rapid increases in the amount of medication needed or frequent, unscheduled refill requests. Doctors should be alert to the fact that those addicted to prescription drugs may engage in "doctor shopping"—moving from provider to provider—in an effort to obtain multiple prescriptions for the drug(s) they abuse.

Preventing or stopping prescription drug abuse is an important part of patient care. However, healthcare providers should not avoid prescribing stimulants, CNS depressants, or opioid pain relievers if needed.

Patients.

For their part, patients can take steps to ensure that they use prescription medications appropriately: always follow the prescribed directions, be aware of potential interactions with other drugs, never stop or change a dosing regimen without first discussing it with a healthcare provider, and never use another person's prescription. In addition to describing their medical problem, patients should always inform their healthcare professionals about all the prescriptions, OTC medicines, and dietary and herbal supplements they are taking, before they obtain any other medications. Additionally, unused or expired medications should be properly discarded per U.S. Food and Drug Administration (FDA) guidelines or at U.S. Drug Enforcement Administration collection sites.

Pharmacists.

Pharmacists dispense medications and can help patients understand instructions for taking them. By being watchful for prescription falsifications or alterations, pharmacists can serve as the first line of defense in recognizing prescription drug abuse. Some pharmacies have developed hotlines to alert other pharmacies in the region when a fraudulent prescription is detected. Moreover, prescription drug monitoring programs (PDMPs), which require physicians and pharmacists to log each filled prescription into a state database, can assist medical professionals in identifying patients who are getting prescriptions from multiple sources. As of May 2011, 48 states and 1 territory have enacted legislation authorizing PDMPs, 34 of which are operational.

Treating Prescription Drug Addiction

Years of research have shown that addiction to any drug (illicit or prescribed) is a brain disease that can be treated effectively. Treatment must take into account the type of drug used and the needs of the individual. Successful treatment may need to incorporate several components, including detoxification, counseling, and sometimes the use of addiction medications. Multiple courses of treatment may be needed for the patient to make a full recovery.

The two main categories of drug addiction treatment are behavioral and pharmacological. Behavioral treatments help patients stop drug use by teaching them strategies to function without drugs, deal with cravings, avoid drugs and situations that could lead to drug use, and handle a relapse should it occur. When delivered effectively, behavioral treatments, such as individual counseling, group or family counseling, contingency management, and cognitive-behavioral therapies, also can help patients improve their personal relationships and their ability to function at work and in the community.

Some addictions, such as opioid addiction, can be treated with medications. These pharmacological treatments counter the effects of the drug on the brain and behavior, and can be used to relieve withdrawal symptoms, help overcome drug cravings, or treat an overdose. Although a behavioral or pharmacological approach alone may be sufficient for treating some patients, research shows that a combined approach may be best.

Treating Addiction to Prescription Opioids

Several options are available for effectively treating prescription opioid addiction. These options are drawn from research on the treatment of heroin addiction and include medications (e.g., naltrexone, methadone, and buprenorphine) as well as behavioral counseling approaches.

Naltrexone is an *antagonist* medication that prevents opioids from activating their receptors. It is used to treat overdose and addiction, although its use for addiction has been limited due to poor adherence and tolerability by patients. Recently, an injectable, long-acting form of naltrexone (Vivitrol), originally approved for treating alcoholism, has also received FDA approval to treat opioid addiction (i.e., heroin or other opioids). Because its effects last for weeks, Vivitrol is ideal for patients who do not have ready access to healthcare or who struggle with taking their medications regularly.

Methadone is a synthetic opioid *agonist* that eliminates withdrawal symptoms and relieves drug cravings by acting on the same brain targets as other opioids like heroin, morphine, and opioid pain medications. It has been used successfully for more than 40 years to treat heroin addiction, but must be dispensed through opioid treatment programs. Buprenorphine is a partial opioid agonist (i.e., it has agonist and antagonist properties), which can be prescribed by certified physicians in an office setting. Like methadone, it can reduce cravings and is well tolerated by patients. NIDA is supporting research needed to determine the effectiveness of these medications in treating addiction to opioid pain relievers.

Treating Addiction to CNS Depressants

Patients addicted to barbiturates and benzodiazepines should not attempt to stop taking them on their own. Withdrawal symptoms from these drugs can be problematic, and—in the case of certain CNS depressants—potentially life-threatening. Research on treating barbiturate and benzodiazepine addiction is sparse; however, addicted patients should undergo medically supervised detoxification, because the dosage they take should be gradually tapered. Inpatient or outpatient counseling

can help individuals through this process. Cognitive-behavioral therapy, which focuses on modifying the patient's thinking, expectations, and behaviors while increasing skills for coping with various life stressors, also has been used successfully to help individuals adapt to discontinuing benzodiazepines.

Often barbiturate and benzodiazepine abuse occurs in conjunction with the abuse of other drugs, such as alcohol or cocaine. In such cases of polydrug abuse, the treatment approach should address the multiple addictions.

Treating Addiction to Prescription Stimulants

Treatment of addiction to prescription stimulants, such as Adderall and Concerta, is based on behavioral therapies used in treating cocaine and methamphetamine addiction. At this time, there are no medications that are FDA-approved for treating stimulant addiction. Thus, NIDA is supporting research in this area.

Depending on the patient's situation, the first steps in treating prescription stimulant addiction may be to taper the drug dosage and attempt to ease withdrawal symptoms. The detoxification process could then be followed by behavioral therapy. Contingency management, for example, uses a system that enables patients to earn vouchers for drug-free urine tests. (These vouchers can be exchanged for items that promote healthy living.) Cognitive-behavioral therapy also may be an effective treatment for addressing stimulant addiction. Finally, recovery support groups may be helpful in conjunction with behavioral therapy.

Chronic Pain Treatment and Addiction

Healthcare providers have long wrestled with how best to treat patients who suffer from chronic pain, roughly 116 million in this country. Their dilemma stems from the potential risks involved with long-term treatment, such as the development of drug tolerance (and the need for escalating doses), hyperalgesia (increased pain sensitivity), and addiction. Patients themselves may even be reluctant to take an opioid medication prescribed to them for fear of becoming addicted. Estimates of addiction among chronic pain patients vary widely—from about 3 percent to 40 percent. This variability is the result of differences in treatment duration, insufficient research on long-term outcomes, and disparate study populations and measures used to assess abuse or addiction.

To mitigate addiction risk, physicians should screen patients for potential risk factors, including personal or family history of drug abuse or mental illness. Monitoring patients for signs of abuse is also crucial, and yet some indicators can signify multiple conditions, making accurate assessment challenging. Early or frequent requests for prescription pain medication refills, for example, could represent illness progression, the development of drug tolerance, or the emergence of a drug problem.

The development of effective, nonaddicting pain medications is a public health priority. A growing elderly population and an increasing number of injured military only add to the urgency of this issue. Researchers are exploring alternative medications that can alleviate pain but have less abuse potential. More research is needed to better understand effective chronic pain management, including identifying factors that predispose some patients to addiction and developing measures to prevent abuse.

Notes

1. Prescription drug abuse, as defined in this report, is equivalent to the term "nonmedical use," used by many of the national surveys or data collection systems. This definition does not correspond to the definition of abuse/dependence listed in the *Diagnostic and Statistical Manual of Mental Disorders,* 4th edition (DSM-IV).

2. Changing the route of administration also contributes to the abuse of other prescription medications, including stimulants, a practice that can lead to serious medical consequences.

Critical Thinking

1. Discuss the high prevalence of prescription drug abuse since the 1990s.

2. What are "doctor shoppers" and how are these people manipulating the prescription system to gain access to drugs?

3. Develop a comprehensive plan to deter prescription drug abuse over the next decade?

Internet References

Centers for Disease Control—Drug Shopping Laws
https://www.cdc.gov/phlp/docs/menu-shoppinglaws.pdf

Foundation for a Drug-Free World
http://www.drugfreeworld.org/drugfacts/painkillers.html

WebMD—Pain Management Health Center
http://www.webmd.com/pain-management/features/painkiller-addiction-warning-signs

Volkow, Nora D., "Prescription Drug Abuse: What Is Prescription Drug Abuse?" *National Institute on Drug Abuse Research Report*, National Institutes of Health, U.S. Department of Health and Human Services, Revised November 2014.

Mental Illness and Homelessness are Connected. But Not How You Might Think by Gale Holland

31

Article

Prepared by: Kim Schnurbush, *California State University, Sacramento*
Mark Pullin, *Angelo State University*

Mental Illness and Homelessness are Connected. But Not How You Might Think

GALE HOLLAND

Learning Outcomes

After reading this article, you will be able to:

- Discuss the controversies surrounding homeless housing projects and community residents.

- Understand the percentage of homeless persons that are mentally ill and how social misconceptions lead to ill-treatment of such persons.

- Discuss the relationship between chronic homelessness and mental health.

Even as Los Angeles starts a $1.2-billion homeless housing construction program, residents from Temple City to Venice are fighting to keep homeless projects out of their neighborhoods.

But since 1995, chronically homeless mentally ill people — a widely shunned subgroup — have been living in Santa Monica's Step Up on Second apartments, a block from the tourist-friendly Third Street Promenade and close enough to the beach to feel the salt air.

"Look around. It's here," Rep. Timothy F. Murphy (R-Pa.) said during a recent visit, describing why he sees Step Up's residential programs as a national model.

Murphy, author of a major 2016 mental health reform bill, was in Santa Monica to tour three of Step Up's permanent supportive housing buildings, which offer apartments and counseling, case management and substance abuse treatment to 267 formerly homeless people with mental health issues.

During the visit, The Times interviewed Step Up Executive Director Tod Lipka, staff members and residents. Dennis Culhane, University of Pennsylvania professor and homelessness researcher, and Andrew Sperling, legislative advocacy director for the National Alliance on Mental Illness, were interviewed later.

Below are their edited responses to common questions about mental illness and homelessness:

Are Most Homeless People Mentally Ill?

A relatively small percentage of all homeless people nation-wide — 13% to 15% — are mentally ill, but their symptoms — paranoia and delusions — draw attention and mislead others into thinking their numbers are greater, Culhane said.

However, Los Angeles' homeless population skews heavily to single adults who have lived in the streets a year or longer — a subgroup with a high incidence of mental health issues. Local authorities estimate that 30% of the county's homeless people have serious mental illness.

Does Chronic Homelessness Cause Mental Illness, or is it the Other Way Around?

Lipka said employees at his agency don't see people developing serious mental illness by virtue of their homelessness. But "I do believe long-term isolation can lead to mental illness," said Steve Elam, Step Up lead life skills coordinator.

Culhane said severely mentally ill people sometimes get treatment and aid that prevents them from becoming homeless.

How Many Homeless People are Physically or Mentally Disabled?

Culhane said half the country's homeless people have a physical or mental disability, or both. But they don't necessarily qualify for federal disability payments, which in any case are too low — about $800 a month — to cover rent, utilities and other needs, even with food stamps tacked on, he added. Welfare reform in 1996 made it difficult for people whose impairment stems largely from substance abuse disorders to receive federal disability aid, Culhane said.

"Instead of looking at individuals and their biographies and conditions, the question is why is the disability system failing?" Culhane said.

Is Mental Illness the Result of Genetics and Brain Chemistry Alone, or Does Trauma Play a Role?

"We're still figuring that one out," Sperling said. A strong case has been made for a genetic role in schizophrenia, but physiological and biological brain development, environmental stressors and childhood trauma are also thought to influence mental health.

"I grew up in Jordan Downs and Watts, I've seen a lot and I've been through two riots," said Step Up resident Marvin Duckworth, 57. "My sense of hope and faith is not that strong."

How Many Mentally Ill Homeless People have Issues with Alcohol and Drug Abuse, and Does Drug Addiction Cause Mental Illness?

About half of the homeless people with severe mental illness also have problems with alcohol or drugs, Culhane said. Lipka put the percentage of his agency's clients even higher — 60% to 70% — but he and the other experts said drug use does not cause severe mental illness. Rather, homeless people with untreated mental illness self-medicate to relieve symptoms, Lipka said.

. . .

What is the Role of Prescribed Medication in Treating Mentally Ill Homeless People? Doesn't it Turn Them All into Zombies?

Medication relieves symptoms, but it "doesn't create purpose or positive meaning in your life, even if you have stabilized with housing," Lipka said.

Paula Boutte, Step Up's Santa Monica program manager, said side effects affect people differently and medications and dosages often have to be adjusted over time. "If you experience drowsiness and can't get up, it's not quality of life," Boutte said.

What About Forced Medication or Other Treatment for the Most Severely Mentally Ill Homeless People?

For the vast majority of homeless people, forcing them to do anything is a mistake, Lipka said.

Sperling said Laura's Law — which authorizes court-ordered mental health treatment for those with serious illness and a recent history of repeated violence, criminal activity or hospitalizations — addresses some cases. But for the 2% to 3% of homeless people so symptomatic that "nothing else works, we may need more options," Lipka said.

Why do People Who Grow up in Foster Care or State Custody End up Homeless?

Children separated from their parents at an early age often suffer anxiety and depression, Sperling said. Lipka said growing up without stable relationships makes it difficult to learn life skills. After years of living in group homes, "the only thing I knew how to do was to shave and take a shower," said Step Up resident Theo Robin, 45.

Most young adults need help from family to go out on their own, and homeless youths are no exception. California's recent law extending the cutoff for aid to foster children from age 18 to 21 has reduced the group's homeless rates, Culhane said.

Do Some Homeless People Prefer to Live that Way?

Lipka said the vast majority of the clients his agency works with — 97% — want housing "if the system we had to get into housing wasn't so complicated." Many have been disappointed by past promises that fell through.

"Housing becomes something not in homeless people's realm of possibility," Lipka said. "The system has failed them, and then we blame it on them."

Can Mentally Ill Homeless People Move on to Jobs and Live Independently or will they Need to be Subsidized Forever?

For the chronically homeless in their 50s and 60s, stabilization in subsidized housing is the most realistic outcome, Lipka said. "We could see less intensive, less costly permanent supportive housing, but that's difficult," he said. "It's either you're in it or you're not."

Homeless young adults with mental health issues do move on to school, jobs, and in some cases, independent living.

"We have a building for transitional-age youth leaving foster care or state custody; they have shorter tenancy, reunite with family, take computer classes and move out and live on their own," Lipka said.

Should the Public Pay for Mentally Ill Homeless People to Live Near the Beach When Most People Can't Afford to?

Lipka said that Santa Monica, which subsidizes Step Up, recognized that its homeless people are residents and that a vibrant city needs diversity.

Housing and support services cost less than we are spending now on police, courts, jails and hospitals to manage homelessness, Lipka said. "Not to mention the nuisance cost of homelessness to a community," he said.

Critical Thinking

1. Why do many people in communities across the nation believe most homeless persons are mentally ill?

2. Is mental illness the result of genetics and brain chemistry or does life trauma play a role?

3. Why is there a correlation between mental illness and being homeless? Is this real or perceived?

4. Should homeless persons with mental illness tendencies be force medicated?

5. Does being homeless become a way of life or a result of life?

Internet References

National Health Care for the Homeless Council
    https://www.nhchc.org/
Substance Abuse and Mental Health Services Administration
    https://www.samhsa.gov

Prepared by: Kim Schnurbush, *California State University, Sacramento*
Mark Pullin, *Angelo State University*

Article

An Inside Look at Homeless Youths' Social Networks: Perceptions of Substance Use Norms[1]

LISA A. MELANDER, KIMBERLY A. TYLER, AND RACHEL M. SCHMITZ

Learning Outcomes

After reading this article, you will be able to:

- Discuss the efforts to understand homeless youth substance abuse issues.

- Gain knowledge of how age of homeless youths affects drug choices and usage.

- Understand how group norms lead to condoning substance abuse and drug safety concerns.

Literature Review
Prevalence of Substance Use

Previous research has found that drug and alcohol use among homeless adolescents is extensive. Alcohol consumption in general is prevalent with over 75% reporting lifetime use (Bailey et al., 1998; Greene, Ennett, & Ringwalt, 1997; Walls & Bell, 2011), and high proportions of both homeless males (83%) and females (79%) have used alcohol in the past (Greene et al., 1997). Other substance use is also common. For example, Hadland and colleagues (2011) found that among their Canadian sample of homeless youth, 24% used marijuana daily, almost 29% reported at least weekly cocaine or crack use, and approximately 23% used heroin at least weekly. Another recent study of homeless adolescents found lifetime methamphetamine use and cocaine use were 34% and 30%, respectively (Rice, Milburn, & Monro, 2011). In addition to high prevalence rates, previous studies with homeless adolescents have found that 40% (Slesnick & Prestopnik, 2005) to 71% (Kipke, Montgomery, Simon, & Iverson, 1997) have met diagnostic criteria for substance use disorders, and many of these young people often meet diagnostic criteria for both drug and alcohol dependence (Bailey et al., 1998; Johnson et al., 2005b; Kipke et al., 1997).

Importance of Homeless Youths' Social Networks

The social networks of homeless youth, which are generally comprised of people with whom a young homeless individual regularly associates and spends the majority of their time (Tyler, 2008), may emerge due to physical propinquity as homeless young people are likely to form ties with those who are in close proximity to themselves (Cairns, Leung, & Cairns, 1995a). Physical propinquity may also explain why the social networks of homeless youth tend to be heterogeneous (Johnson, Whitbeck, & Hoyt, 2005a; Kipke, Unger, O'Connor, Palmer, & LaFrance, 1997; Rice, Milburn, & Rotheram-Bours, 2007), encompassing a wider range of individuals in terms of age, sex, role relationships, and/or housing status (Ennett et al., 1999; Johnson et al., 2005a) compared to those of general adolescent samples (Cairns et al., 1995a; Cotterell, 2007). Another key feature of homeless youths' social networks is that they tend to be smaller on average than those of other adolescents (Cairns, Leung, Buchanan, & Cairns, 1995b). For example, Ennett and colleagues (1999) found that the average size of social networks of homeless youth was 2.6 whereas Cairns et al. (1995b) found the average size to be 4.1 friends and Haynie and Osgood (2005) reported it to be 5.7 friends. As such, the influence of social networks of homeless young people may be different compared to their housed counterparts.

Because of the disturbingly high substance use rates among homeless young people, it is important to understand more about the context in which they become introduced to this lifestyle, the devastating impact of continued use, and the difficulties associated with desistance. The impact of significant others on personal substance use has been documented. For example, Tyler and Johnson (2006) found that a family member initiated 23% of homeless youth into substance use. In addition to family members, social networks may also influence individual behavior.

Homeless youths' social networks perform a variety of functions, some that improve the well-being of the individual members whereas others may engender risk. Social network members may provide sources of companionship, social support, and advice to homeless youth (Johnson, Whitbeck, & Hoyt, 2005b; Molina, 2000; Smith, 2008). They may also protect young members from out-group victimization (Hagan & McCarthy, 1997) and supply information on street survival strategies and safety (Auerswald & Eyre, 2002; Smith, 2008). Conversely, some research finds that certain homeless social network members promote risky activities such as substance use and unsafe sexual behaviors (Ennett et al., 2006; Tyler, 2008).

Importance of Perceived Group Norms on Individual Substance Use Behavior

Because of the salient influence of social network members on homeless youth, it is important to consider how norms regarding prosocial and antisocial behavior are transmitted among members. The behaviors, attitudes, and norms of a social network may be beneficial or detrimental to a homeless young person. If, for example, network norms are consistent with drug and alcohol use and participation in these activities is valued within the group, the young person is afforded more opportunities for substance use and may model the behavior of other members (Bauman & Ennett, 1996; Gomez et al., 2010). Furthermore, homeless adolescents who had more ties to substance using street-based peers were more likely to engage in higher levels of heroin, methamphetamine, alcohol, and marijuana use (Rice et al., 2011; Rice, Milburn, & Rotheram-Borus, 2007).

Individual perceptions of others' behavior may also impact personal decisions regarding their conduct, especially when considering substance use. College and middle school students, for example, have been found to overestimate their peers' drug and alcohol use and these perceptions may influence their own personal substance use (Elek, Miller-Day, & Hecht, 2006; Martens et al., 2006). Arbour-Nicitopoulos and colleagues (2010) found that perceived substance use was a significant predictor of actual individual cigarette, alcohol, and marijuana use. Researchers have also found that general social network drug use shapes individual member behavior: youth who belonged to social groups with drug dependent members were more likely to report personal substance use dependency (Gomez et al., 2010). Consequently, associating with substance abusing peers, who may reinforce and support substance use behaviors, led to increased drug use severity among homeless youth (Gomez et al., 2010). Because of the influence that social network members have on individual substance use behavior, it is imperative that we understand more about the norms that may support or discourage the use of controlled substances as this information may inform intervention efforts to meet the needs of homeless youth.

Theoretical Framework

Two theoretical perspectives informed the current study: coping theory and social norms theory. According to *coping theory*, young people engage in high-risk behaviors such as substance use as a way to cope with negative stimuli. Applied to the current study, homeless youth are often exposed to early abuse in the home as well as other forms of victimization on the street. Moreover, daily survival on the street is also stressful. One way in which youth may cope with these stressful life events or negative stimuli is through alcohol and/or drug use. Some studies examining general population samples have found support for this theory.

Social norms theory holds that people generally do not accurately report the frequency with which their peers engage in risky behaviors such as alcohol use and that these misperceptions influence the person's own behavior. In effect, if the individual thinks the behavior occurs more frequently than it really is, the result is that h/she is more likely to engage in this behavior (Martens et al. 2006). Thus, if homeless youth believe that their network members frequently use alcohol and/or illicit drugs and that their networks are supportive of this behavior, then homeless youth themselves are likely to have higher usage rates.

Research Questions

This project explores homeless youths' perceptions of their social network norms regarding substance use as these informal social rules may influence individual behavior. Although previous research on housed adolescents has found that perceptions of peer substance use influenced personal alcohol and drug use (Andrews, Hampson, Barckley, Gerrad, & Gibbons, 2008; Arbour-Nicitopoulos et al., 2010), little is known about how similar social network norms influence homeless young people. Furthermore, there is a dearth of information regarding the contextual factors surrounding the formation and maintenance of these social rules. As such, this study used a descriptive and exploratory approach instead of a hypothesis testing method to understand these issues. Four predetermined research questions guided this project: (1) What factors are involved in homeless youths' choices to use alcohol and drugs? (2) What safety precautions do homeless youths perceive their network members taking when using substances? (3) What are the ways in which network members influence substance use? and (4) What are the situations in which young homeless ndividuals perceive social network members to use alcohol and drugs? Garnering a fuller understanding of these substance use norms may assist with prevention and intervention efforts that may reduce this health compromising behavior.

Method
Participants
The qualitative data for the present study were from the Social Network and Homeless Youth Project, a larger study designed to examine the effect of social network characteristics on homeless young people's HIV risk behaviors. Over a period of approximately 6 months, 19 homeless youth were interviewed in three Midwestern cities in the United States. Participants for the *qualitative interviews* were selected from the original sample of 249 to represent different gender, racial/ethnic, and sexual orientation groups. There were 13 females (68.4%) and 6 males (31.6%). Females, in general, tend to be slightly over-represented among homeless young people (Rice et al., 2007). Ages ranged from 16 to 21 (M = 19.47 years). The majority was White (n = 11; 57.9%) with the remaining respondents self-identifying as Black (n = 4), Hispanic (n = 2), American Indian (n = 1), and biracial (n = 1). Ten (52.6%) self-identified as gay (n = 2), lesbian (n = 1), bisexual (n = 6), and transgendered (n = 1) (GLBT). Because interviewers were instructed to oversample sexual minorities because of their greater risk for HIV, their numbers in this subsample are higher than what we would typically see in the population of homeless young people. Finally, homeless youth reported having a mean of 5.53 network members whose overall average age was 26.0 years.

Procedure
Three female interviewers conducted the qualitative interviews and were chosen because of their extensive experience working with homeless young people both through shelter service and street outreach. All interviewers completed the Collaborative Institutional Review Board (IRB) Training Initiative course for the protection of human subjects in research. Selection criteria for the larger study required participants to be between the ages of 14 and 21 and meet our definition of runaway or homeless.

Runaway refers to a person under age 18 who has spent the previous night away from home without the permission of parents or guardians. *Homeless* individuals are those who have spent the previous night with a stranger, in a shelter or public place, on the street, in a hotel room, staying with friends (e.g., couch surfing), or other places not intended as their resident domicile (Ennett et al., 1999).

After the completion of the survey instrument, interviewers selected respondents from different demographic groups (discussed above) to participate in an individual in-depth interview approximately one week later. All selected individuals participated in these qualitative interviews, which lasted 1 to 1½ hours and took place in a private room at a shelter. Informed consent was obtained prior to the interview and participants were paid $30 for their participation and offered agency services. Participants were asked a series of open-ended questions, and all interviews were audiotaped and transcribed verbatim. The qualitative themes and subthemes then emerged from the data. Pseudonyms are used to preserve confidentiality, and the IRB at the second author's institution approved this study.

Interviewer Guide
The qualitative interview guide consisted of open-ended questions and probes that expounded upon topics in the quantitative survey where participants could list up to five people that they see or spend most of their time with as well as three people with whom they had sexual relations within the past six months for a total of eight social network members. The sexual partners could be people on their original network list of five or new ones not previously mentioned. In either scenario, sexual partners listed are considered part of the youth's social network. This approach has been used in past research on social networks and high-risk populations of similar age (Montgomery et al., 2002). The qualitative interviews began with the following statement: "Today I would like to talk with you in-depth about the same people that you told me about last time we did your other interview." As a reminder, participants were then given a card with the initials of the people that they discussed in the survey. Interviewers queried respondents about the following topics: (1) alcohol, drug, and/or intravenous (IV) drug use choices among social network members, (2) safety precautions, (3) ways in which network members encourage or discourage substance use, and (4) alcohol and drug use situations.

Data Analysis
The interview transcriptions were imported into ATLAS.ti, a data management software program (Muhr, 2004). The first step in the preliminary data analysis involved rereading each interview transcript in its entirety in order to gain a deeper sense of the data as a whole. Because we were interested in perceived substance use norms within homeless youth's social

networks, we then focused on the transcription sections that related to interview questions on this topic.

We assessed validity by triangulating the data by building evidence for a code or theme (e.g., substance use choices) from several individuals (Creswell & Plano Clark, 2011). For intercoder agreement, we used a predetermined coding scheme and then later identified whether we assigned the same or different codes between text passages (Miles & Huberman, 1994). In cases in which the intercoder agreement between the authors was low or discrepancies existed, we obtained consensus through deliberation and re-evaluating our coding and themes.

Results

Our findings include four main themes regarding the substance use norms of homeless youths and their perceptions of the norms within their social networks. These include: substance use choices, safety concerns, encouraging and discouraging messages, and substance use situations. Each of these four themes and their relevant subthemes are discussed in detail below. Table 1 presents sample quotes for each qualitative theme.

Substance Use Choices

The homeless youth in our sample discussed a wide range of "acceptable" and "unacceptable" drug and alcohol use behaviors. Several reported that when it comes to substance use, "anything goes" and all substances are acceptable whereas others made distinctions between acceptable and unacceptable substances. Alternatively, a few respondents reported that all drug and alcohol use is unacceptable.

Anything goes—Several respondents mentioned that when it comes to social network drug and alcohol use, pretty much anything is regarded as acceptable behavior. For example, when asked about accepted drug use behavior, Megan, a white, 18 year-old said, "Well, even just amongst me, like, I just didn't

Table 1 Individual and Social Network Substance Use Norms Sample Quotes

Qualitative codes and subcodes	Selected qualitative quotes
Substance use choices	
Anything goes	- I just didn't care. I'd do anything. I'd let anybody else do anything.
Undesirable substance use	- I don't condone the use any, any illegal drugs, period. I don't even like drinking or smoking . . . it inhibits you.
Substance use distinctions	- I mean everyone smokes pot sometimes. But it's not like an addiction you know it's smoke here and there and then you know have fun.
Safety concerns	
Knowing your limits	- If I've got a buzz, I got to stop because If I drink more than what I'm supposed to, I get so drunk and I will get myself into trouble.
Drug-related safety	- try a little bit and see how it [the drug] does.
Buddy system	- Stay with the other person [substance user] to make sure they don't . . . end up all fucked up laying somewhere.
Encouraging and discouraging messages	
Offering and visibility	- He'll probably just be like 'come on, just one drink, come on that's it' that kind of pressure.
No encouragement necessary	- I've never needed No encouragement. I just do it on my own.
Words of warning	- All of them say 'Just stay clean.' They, they're always telling me, 'Don't, don't use this, it's just complications.'
Avoidance	- If you are a crack-head, you're gonna have to do it in your tent and nobody else can be around.
Substance use situations	
Managing emotions	- Um back when I was using um, [in] stressful situations, when I was mad, [and] when I was sad. I used emotionally, every emotion.
Managing social situations	- I'll do it because I feel like well if everybody else is getting fucked up that'll give me more of the reason to you know just fit-like go right along with it.

care. I'd do anything. I'd let anybody else do anything . . . I was like, I'm gonna get fucked up, I want everyone else to too." David, a white, 21 year-old male, mentioned that although he does not mind if people in his network use drugs in front of him, there are certain people who should not be around these activities: "If somebody wants to needle push, needle push. So if I say no, you just leave it at that. You can do [substance use] in front of me wherever as long as we're not in front of kids." As such, although general substance use is acceptable among social network members, David believes that children should not witness drug use.

Substance use distinctions—Many homeless young people made distinctions between different types of drugs when considering whether they were acceptable or not within their social networks. Alcohol was a common substance that was viewed as acceptable. Rodrigo and Maria (both 20 year-old Hispanics), for example, mentioned that drinking in moderation is not problematic within their social networks. According to Emily (white, 19 year-old), "Well, like I don't care if someone drinks around me . . . but as far as like any other drugs and stuff like that, I don't really want it around me." Sarah concurred with this statement and mentioned that one of her network members, Dani, "won't have anything to do with anything illegal." As such, it is possible that the legality of alcohol consumption for those 21 years of age and older factors into the acceptability of this particular substance.

In addition to alcohol consumption, several homeless youth believed that marijuana use was viewed as acceptable among their networks. Tyrell (19 year-old, black male), for example, mentioned that he and three of his network members routinely smoke marijuana and it is viewed favorably among their group. As such, these network members distinguish marijuana use from other forms of illicit drugs and view it as a safer or more socially acceptable substance. According to Melissa (white, 20 year-old), marijuana use is very commonplace and thus acceptable among her network, "Um Casey smokes pot but not too much. I mean everyone smokes pot sometimes. But it's not like an addiction you know it's smoke here and there and then you know have fun." It seems that Melissa views marijuana use as universal, although according to the Monitoring the Future Survey, only 6.6% of 12th graders reported using marijuana within the past year (Johnston, O'Malley, Bachman, & Schulenberg, 2011). It is also possible that Melissa believes her peers engage in more marijuana use than they actually do, perhaps influencing her own use. Some homeless young people may not perceive marijuana as having the same addictive properties as other drugs and thus view its use as more acceptable.

Although some respondents such as Darnel (21 year-old, black male) said that their network members tended to perceive experimentation with different substances as acceptable, others such as David mentioned that certain drugs (i.e., meth, heroin, and crack) are unacceptable. Melissa, who lives in a homeless camp community, mentioned that illicit drug use was inconsistent with group norms. When asked what would happen if someone brought heroin or crack into the camp site, Melissa said, "I'd tell them they'd have to leave. Because I'm totally against it and because . . . he's [network member] totally against the whole crack-thing. . . . So if they're gonna do it [use drugs], they gotta go somewhere else, they can't come to camp and do it. That's totally against, kind of a camp code." Consequently, certain social networks appear to have more stringent rules when it comes to acceptable and unacceptable substance use.

Undesirable substance use—Elizabeth (white, 21 year-old) believes that drug and alcohol use is unacceptable within her social network because some members are former users who are trying to stay clean and sober. It is possible that these respondents have learned the deleterious effects of substance abuse the hard way, such as Darnel's previous experiences with incarceration related to drug use, and are perhaps trying to save their friend from a similar fate. For others, such as Stephanie (20 year-old, white female) using alcohol and drugs is not only unacceptable behavior to them but also to their network members: "Oh, well, I know that almost all of them now, um, have a tendency to want to be clean, period, and not abuse anything. . . . I don't condone the use of any, any illegal drugs, period. I don't even like drinking of smoking, because that's just, to me it, it inhibits you." Amanda (white, 20 year-old) adds, "it's [alcohol consumption] not good for your body - neither are drugs or the needle." As such, former alcohol and drug use and health concerns may explain why some view substance use as unacceptable behavior.

Safety Concerns

Safety was a paramount concern for many respondents when discussing substance use norms within their social networks. Specifically, several youth discussed how knowing their limits, drug-related safety, and the buddy system are all important considerations when it comes to substance use. Much of this information, which was transmitted informally among most social networks, may be vital for the young homeless individuals' well-being; however, other advice may actually be detrimental to their health.

Knowing your limits and location—Some respondents discussed how their social networks were supportive of substance use as long as it occurs in moderation. Maria said, "Um, I drink about one or two beers . . . if I've got a buzz, I got to stop because if I drink more than what I'm supposed to, I get so drunk and I will get myself into trouble." Consequently, Maria knows her personal limitations and is aware that consuming too much alcohol will alter her mood such that the larger group will not condone her conduct. Similarly, Lulu (16 year-old American Indian) and Sarah also mentioned that ingesting illicit substances in moderation is crucial and added that location of substance use consumption also matters, such that their social network members are safer when they drink or smoke inside a house. Being inside a dwelling, especially when under the influence of a substance, likely provides a level of protection from stranger and acquaintance victimization that they would not receive if consuming alcohol or drugs on the street.

Drug-related safety—Some network members discussed the importance of checking their drugs prior to consumption as well as using sterile supplies. Jennifer, for example, mentioned that her social network members would "try a little bit and see how it [the drug] does" to ensure that their weed was not laced with a harmful substance. It seems that her network members believe that ingesting a small amount of a tampered substance would not be harmful to them and would actually protect them from an adverse outcome if they were to consume it in a large quantity. Elizabeth and Darnel both say that they have network members who use IV drugs and protect themselves by using sterile needles. It is unclear, however, whether or not these needles were actually thoroughly sterilized. For example, Elizabeth mentions that the safety measures of one of her network members included personally cleaning his needle to sterilize it because he does not trust others doing so. Darnel talked about his own and his network member's IV drug use: "And he'd like - we'd never use the same needles but like I figured if you're shooting up, you don't have to worry about trying to clean the needle if you're using the same needle and nobody else is using the same one, you know?" In general, needles are considered sterile if they have gone through a sterilization process and are properly packaged and stored (Japp, 2008). Although young people may somehow cleanse the needle themselves, it is doubtful that this process would meet precise standards of sterilization. Additionally, homeless youth are unlikely to have a safe place to store used needles or thoroughly cleanse the injection site, thus increasing their risk for infection. It is also possible that like research on condom use (Rose et al., 2009), young people may report that they only inject drugs with a sterile needle but may abandon this general rule when faced with a situation in which clean needles are unavailable.

Buddy system—A few respondents mentioned that their safety measures included having trusted friends around when using controlled substances. Amanda, for example, declared that she and her network members always have a designated driver "who is still sober enough to make sure they don't do anything stupid." Nicole (white, 21 year-old) also reported using the "buddy system" and that her network members will "stay with the other person [substance user] to make sure they don't . . . end up all fucked up laying somewhere." These measures are

enlisted not only to ensure that their network members' physical health is not compromised, but also to prevent other forms of victimization such as robbery or assault from occurring.

Encouraging and Discouraging Messages

There were several ways in which respondents' social networks either implicitly or explicitly encouraged or discouraged substance use. For those who encourage drug or alcohol consumption, they tended to offer or make their own use visible to entice others to engage in similar behavior. In contrast, no encouragement is necessary for some as they believed substance use is a personal choice. Several respondents, however, spoke of the ways in which their network members discouraged substance use through words of warning and avoidance strategies.

Encouraging via offering and visibility—Some homeless youth mentioned that their network members encouraged drug and alcohol use by offering them these substances. Rodrigo talked about how his network member encouraged alcohol use: "He'll probably just be like 'come on, just one drink, come on that's it' that kind of pressure." Tyrell and Sarah echoed these experiences and said that their network members encouraged substance use by explicitly offering the substances and using them in front of the respondent. Another way that social network members may encourage drug use is by "how they act when they're dealing it around others" (Ashley; 18 year-old, white female). Dealing drugs is another method that increases visibility, thereby both condoning and encouraging illicit drug use behavior.

No encouragement necessary—Several respondents talked about how it was unnecessary for network members to encourage substance use as it is a personal choice. Nicole said, "I've never needed no encouragement. I just do it on my own." Within these groups, it seems that personal substance use is not necessarily influenced by the attitudes and behaviors of social network members. Brittany concurred with this sentiment and said that even if their network members drink or use other drugs, they do not encourage or pressure others to do so (18 year-old, bi-racial female). As such, the substance use norms among groups like Brittany's may be more permissive than those of others and thus may result in lower levels of substance use within these particular social networks because there is no direct pressure to use.

Discouraging words of warning—The "Just Say No" campaign from the 1980s seems to have resonated with several of the respondents and their social networks as many youth report that they discourage substance use through words of warning. Stephanie said, "Oh all of them say 'Just stay clean.' . . . they're always telling me, 'Don't, don't use this, it's just complications' . . . Alfred, especially, is always telling me, 'Don't. Do. Drugs.' [laughs]." Others rely on personal stories and tragedies to deter their network members from substance use. Emily, for example, said, "Well just like sometimes they'll tell me some of the experiences that their friends have had when they've . . . done drugs. Or sometimes personal ones too." These network members draw from their personal experiences to detail the negative outcomes associated with substance use in hopes of saving their friends from a similar fate.

Discouraging through avoidance—Others reported that their social network members discourage substance use by simply avoiding it. According to Brittany, some social network members do not allow illicit substances around them or will "throw it out" if it is detected. Melissa spoke of drug use avoidance when discussing the unwritten rules at her homeless camp:

> We-we do have rules down at camp and um thing is: no crack-heads. Um if you are a crack-head, you're gonna have to do it in your tent and nobody else can be around; because we don't want to be around it.

As such, there are severe sanctions for using substances at the homeless camp including isolation, which is difficult for all youth but especially for those who are already disenfranchised.

Substance Use Situations

The final theme centered on different situations in which homeless youth reported that substance use was more likely within their social networks. For example, some respondents mentioned that illicit substances are used to assist them with managing their emotions. Finally, some stated that alcohol and/or drugs were generally consumed within social situations.

Managing emotions—Several homeless youth discussed situations in which they used controlled substances to assist them with managing a range of emotions. For some, drugs and alcohol allowed them to cope with stressful situations such as child abuse (Emily). Megan said, "Um back when I was using um, [in] stressful situations, when I was mad, [and] when I was sad. I used emotionally, every emotion." Others, such as Tyrell and Nicole, also used substances when they were upset or angry. Alcohol and drugs may be used as a method of coping with or relieving negative stimuli such as the stresses associated with street life (Kidd & Kral, 2002; Thompson, Rew, Barczyk, McCoy, & Mi-Sedhi, 2009; Tyler & Johnson, 2006). David and others concur with these statements but also mentioned that they liked how the substances made them feel.

Managing social situations—The respondents also discussed how they are more likely to use substances when they are around certain people and during special occasions. Ashley, for example, was more likely to use substances when around her baby's father as "all he does is drink and smoke." As such, watching someone else consume these substances was too tempting for her and contributed to her personal use. Megan, who was trying to recover from her addiction, also mentioned

that she is more likely to use drugs when she encounters a social situation where drugs are present and she was not mentally prepared beforehand that these substances would be nearby. Brittany and David talked about how they are more likely to use substances on special occasions such as holidays, birthdays, or at other parties. Darnel stated that he is more likely to use substances in social situations:

> I'm not a closet alcoholic anymore, I won't just do it [drink] by myself, it's more so at parties . . . even at parties I'll take it to the extreme but I'll do it because I feel like well if everybody else is getting fucked up that'll give me more of the reason to you know just fit- like go right along with it.

Not only is Darnel more likely to use drugs in a social setting, but he also increases his consumption in these environments. Although usage may be recreational for some, others may continue to use alcohol and drugs as a way to cope with early childhood trauma such as abuse, to manage the stressful circumstances of street life, or to fit in with others around them so that they can feel they are an important part of a group.

Discussion

The narratives of this diverse group of homeless youth reveals important information surrounding substance use and the drug and alcohol consumption norms among members of their social networks. We find that the norms surrounding substance use choices vary considerably among social networks of homeless youth. While some report their networks as being at the extremes of "anything" or "nothing" being acceptable, other networks fell somewhere in between. For those whose network norms support the acceptability of any type of substance, the attitude within these groups tended to be carefree such that everyone should be permitted to do whatever they choose. Those indicating that they did not want to be the only person getting drunk or "high" in the presence of their peers qualified this norm; thus, they were encouraging of everyone using substances. In contrast, others firmly believe that substance use in general is undesirable because some individuals within the group are trying to stay clean and sober and having substance users in close proximity makes this a difficult goal to achieve. Thus, the distinction between these two groups may lie in their earlier exposure to and usage of substances. The final group believes that certain substances such as alcohol and marijuana are socially acceptable within their network as long as they are used in moderation. If over time young people abuse these substances, it is possible that these individuals and their network members may make more refined distinctions between what types of substances are acceptable. Thus it is plausible that the acceptability of alcohol and drugs within networks is a negotiation among its members and that substance use rules ebb and flow over time depending on group composition.

Safety concerns surrounding substance use such as knowing one's limit, drug-related safety, and the buddy system are all important considerations among homeless youth and their social networks. Some respondents describe having "personal limits" when it comes to substance use. Because individual perceptions of others' actions may impact personal decision making regarding their substance use conduct (Arbour-Nicitopoulos et al., 2010; Elek et al., 2006; Martens et al., 2006), it is possible that some network members positively influence homeless youth by limiting their substance use.

The comments of the young people regarding drug related safety indicates their awareness of the potential health hazards of illicit drug use and drug injection; thus, group norms within their networks advocate taking precautions to protect themselves. It is unlikely, however, that all young people belong to networks that have stringent norms and thus many homeless young people are likely at risk for negative health outcomes. Overall, our findings suggest that some are aware of a range of negative outcomes associated with substance use and thus take precautionary measures to reduce their risk. In contrast, others do not have such rigid norms within their networks and thus are likely at greater risk for victimization, physical and mental health problems, and potentially, HIV infection.

Some homeless young people report that their network members encourage drug and alcohol use by making it widely available or by pressuring them to use. This is consistent with the literature which holds that if network norms are consistent with drug and alcohol use and participation in these behaviors is valued within the group, the youth is likely afforded more opportunities to use alcohol and drugs and may model the behavior of other members (Bauman & Ennett, 1996). In contrast several young people stated that it was unnecessary for network members to encourage substance use because they personally make the decision to drink and/or use drugs. It is possible that the young people in this latter group already have high rates of substance use and thus join peer groups where network norms are consonant with their own values, beliefs, and behaviors regarding alcohol and drug use. This finding is consistent with Gomez et al. (2010) who found that those who belonged to social groups with drug dependent members were more likely to report personal substance use dependency. Finally, several describe how their networks discourage substance use through words of warning or through avoidance techniques. It is possible that young people who belong to social networks who do not condone alcohol and drug use are less likely to initially be substance users.

Our final theme, which focuses on situations in which substance use is condoned among homeless young people, is

particularly unique and adds to the existing literature because it reveals circumstances in which alcohol and drug use is more likely to occur within their social networks. Thus, our findings provide insight into why homeless youth view substances as functional and how they are sometimes used to cope with emotions or social situations. Several respondents describe situations in which they use substances to assist with managing feelings of depression, resentment, and sadness associated with experiences of child abuse. Others report using substances to cope with anger and other negative feelings associated with their current circumstances of having to survive on the street. Thus, some drugs may be used as a coping mechanism to relieve numerous stressors, including those associated with street life (Kidd & Kral, 2002; Thompson et al., 2009; Tyler & Johnson, 2006). Finally, some talked about using substances in social situations perhaps because friends were using or because they want to fit in with the group. This may be particularly important for those who are new to the streets and are looking for dependable individuals who will afford them protection and teach them survival techniques. Although not highly desirable, these individuals may join substance using groups because they feel people within these networks are important for their survival on the streets.

There are limitations to this study such as the cross-sectional nature of the data, which do not allow for the changing nature of social networks. Albeit difficult with this population, future research should examine how homeless youth social network norms regarding substance use change over time with a longitudinal sample. Even though our qualitative sample included an overrepresentation of females, GLBT, and young adults, this was purposefully done given that these characteristics are potential sources of variability for our main focus of HIV risk behavior in the full sample. It is possible, however, that the inclusion of more males and heterosexuals may have changed our emergent themes. Furthermore, although our findings are not necessarily representative of all homeless young people, the fact that the majority of them form social networks, often for survival purposes, speaks to the importance of adapting policy changes that address changing substance use norms among these young people within their social networks. Additionally, it is important to recognize that respondents were reporting on their perceptions of their network members' behavior and thus may be over or underreporting certain behaviors. Finally, given the nature of our topic, respondents may have been influenced by social desirability biases that occurred during the interview process.

Overall, the social networks of homeless youth tend to be heterogeneous as some are supportive of substance use whereas other networks are not. Furthermore, some groups advocate substance use in moderation. Although a few respondents have network norms that reflect drug use safety, it is unlikely that these methods are flawless and thus opens up the possibility that at least some of these young people are at risk for negative physical and mental health outcomes. Though some respondents report that their network members routinely make substances readily available or sometimes pressure them to use, others said their networks do not condone substance use and adamantly encourage members to say "No" to drugs. Finally, the narratives of these youth also shed light on particular social situations in which substance use is tolerated because of its comforting ability in light of dealing with stressful circumstances. In conclusion, our study advances the literature on social networks and homeless youth by providing unique insight into the norms associated with alcohol and drug use within these networks and revealing that not everyone in this high-risk population advocates substance use. Even in networks where substance use occurs, there still are explicit norms surrounding safe alcohol and drug use that young people and their network members diligently follow to protect themselves from harmful outcomes.

At the policy level, these findings suggest that intervention could be targeted at two levels. First intervention needs to focus on changing social norms among homeless youth. Previous research with high school samples has focused on pinpointing social situations where substance use occurs and then using interactive video as a way to challenge social norms by teaching young people about social norms, attitudes, and beliefs that are associated with effective refusal skills (Duncan, Duncan, Beauchamp, Wells, & Ary, 2000). These interventions have been effective in changing personal self-efficacy and perceptions about social norms surrounding substance use (Duncan et al., 2000). Second, specific programs that target those with histories of abuse are also needed to assist them with developing healthy coping strategies. Because many of these young people are victims of child abuse and are likely to run away from home to escape these negative circumstances, it is plausible that the majority of youth do not receive appropriate intervention and thus their coping skills may be maladaptive. Intervention programs that teach these individuals alternative coping strategies such as counseling and developing problem-solving skills may result in reducing their likelihood of developing substance abuse problems and future risk for re-victimization. Future research should not only examine the effectiveness of these intervention programs, but also query the youth themselves on other effective ways to prosocially change social network norms regarding unhealthy substance use, especially since some homeless young people may not view alcohol and/or drug use as deviant. Changing homeless youth's social network norms regarding substance use through media sources and street outreach initiatives and providing them with alternative coping mechanisms may significantly improve their quality of life.

Notes

1. This article is based on research supported by a grant from the National Institute on Drug Abuse (DA021079). Dr. Kimberly A. Tyler, PI.

References

Andrews JA, Hampson SE, Barckley M, Gerrad M, Gibbons FX. The effect of early cognitions on cigarette and alcohol use during adolescence. Psychology of Addictive Behaviors. 2008; 22:96–106. [PubMed: 18298235]

Arbour-Nicitopoulos KP, Kwan MY, Lowe D, Taman S, Faulkner GE. Social norms of alcohol, smoking, and marijuana use within a Canadian university setting. Journal of American College Health. 2010; 59:191–196. [PubMed: 21186449]

Auerswald CL, Eyre SL. Youth homelessness in San Francisco: A life cycle approach. Social Science & Medicine. 2002; 54:1497–1512. [PubMed: 12061484]

Bailey SL, Camlin CS, Ennett ST. Substance use and risky sexual behavior among homeless and runaway youth. Journal of Adolescent Health. 1998; 23:378–388. [PubMed: 9870332]

Bauman KE, Ennett ST. On the importance of peer influence for adolescent drug use: Commonly neglected considerations. Addiction. 1996; 91:185–198. [PubMed: 8835276]

Baron SW. Street youths and substance use: The role of background, street lifestyle, and economic factors. Youth & Society. 1999; 31:3–26.

Bousman CA, Blumberg EJ, Shilington AM, Hovell MF, Ji M, Lehman S, Clapp J. Predictors of substance use among homeless youth in San Diego. Addictive Behaviors. 2005; 30:1100–1110. [PubMed: 15925120]

Cairns, RB.; Leung, MC.; Cairns, BD. Social networks over time and space in adolescence. In: Crockett, LJ.; Crouter, AC., editors. Pathways through adolescence: Individual development in relation to social contexts. Mahwah, NJ: Lawrence Erlbaum Associates; 1995a. p. 35-56.

Cairns RB, Leung MC, Buchanan L, Cairns BD. Friendships and social networks in childhood and adolescence: Fluidity, reliability, and interrelations. Child Development. 1995b; 66:1330–1345. [PubMed: 7555219]

Cotterell, J. Social networks in youth and adolescence. 2. New York: Routledge Taylor & Francis Group; 2007.

Creswell, JW.; Plano Clark, VL. Designing and conducting mixed methods research. 2. Thousand Oaks, CA: Sage; 2011.

Duncan TE, Duncan SC, Beauchamp N, Wells J, Ary DV. Development and evaluation of an interactive CD-rom refusal skills program to prevent youth substance use: "Refuse to use. Journal of Behavioral Medicine. 2000; 23:59–72. [PubMed: 10749011]

Elek E, Miller-Day M, Hecht ML. Influences of personal, injunctive, and descriptive norms on early adolescent substance use. Journal of Drug Issues. 2006; 36:147–171.

Ennett ST, Bailey SL, Federman EB. Social network characteristics associated with risky behaviors among homeless and runaway youth. Journal of Health & Social Behavior. 1999; 40:63–78. [PubMed: 10331322]

Ennett ST, Bauman KE, Hussong A, Faris R, Foshee VA, Cai L, DuRant RH. The peer context of adolescent substance use: Findings from social network analysis. Journal of Research on Adolescence. 2006; 16:159–186.

Fisher JD. Possible effects of reference group-based social influence on AIDS-risk behavior and AIDS prevention. American Psychologist. 1988; 43:914–920. [PubMed: 3214003]

Gomez R, Thompson SJ, Barczyk AN. Factors associated with substance use among homeless young adults. Substance Abuse. 2010; 31:24–34. [PubMed: 20391267]

Greene JM, Ennett ST, Ringwalt CL. Substance use among runaway and homeless youth in three national samples. American Journal of Public Health. 1997; 87:229–235. [PubMed: 9103102]

Hadland SE, Marshall BDL, Kerr T, Zhang R, Montaner JS, Wood E. A comparison of drug use and risk behavior profiles among younger and older street youth. Substance Use & Misuse. 2011; 46:1486–1494. [PubMed: 21417557]

Hagan, J.; McCarthy, B. Mean streets: Youth crime and homelessness. New York: Cambridge University Press; 1997.

Haley N, Roy E, Leclerc P, Bourdreau JF, Boivin JF. Characteristics of adolescent street youth with a history of pregnancy. Journal of Pediatric & Adolescent Gynecology. 2004; 17:313–20. [PubMed: 15581776]

Haynie DL, Osgood DW. Reconsidering peers and delinquency: How do peers matter? Social Forces. 2005; 84:1109–1130.

Japp N. Sterilization processes: What every infection control practitioner needs to know. Infection Control Resource. 2008; 5:1–7.

Johnson KD, Whitbeck LB, Hoyt DR. Predictors of social network composition among homeless and runaway adolescents. Journal of Adolescence. 2005a; 28:231–248. [PubMed: 15878045]

Johnson KD, Whitbeck LB, Hoyt DR. Substance abuse disorders among homeless and runaway adolescents. Journal of Drug Issues. 2005b; 35:799–816. [PubMed: 21533015]

Johnston, LD.; O'Malley, PM.; Bachman, JG.; Schulenberg, JE. Monitoring the future: National results on adolescent drug use overview of key findings, 2011. Ann Arbor: Institute for Social Research, The University of Michigan; 2011.

Kidd SA, Kral MJ. Suicide and prostitution among street youth: A qualitative analysis. Adolescence. 2002; 37:411–430. [PubMed: 12144168]

Kipke MD, Montgomery SB, Simon TR, Iverson EF. Substance abuse disorders among runaway and homeless youth. Substance Use & Misuse. 1997; 32:969–986. [PubMed: 9220564]

Kipke MD, Unger JB, O'Connor S, Palmer RF, LaFrance SR. Street youth, their peer group affiliation and differences according to residential status, subsistence patterns, and use of services. Adolescence. 1997; 32:655–669. [PubMed: 9360739]

Lee BA, Tyler KA, Wright JD. The new homelessness revisited. Annual Review of Sociology. 2010; 36:501–521.

Martens MP, Page JC, Mowry ES, Damann KM, Taylor KK, Cimini MD. Differences between actual and perceived student norms: An examination of alcohol use, drug use, and sexual behavior. Journal of American College Health. 2006; 54:295–300. [PubMed: 16539222]

Martino SC, Tucker JS, Ryan G, Wenzel SL, Golinelli D, Munjas B. Increased substance use and risky sexual behavior among migratory homeless youth: Exploring the role of social network composition. Journal of Youth and Adolescence. 2011; 40:1634–1648. [PubMed: 21400037]

Miles, MB.; Huberman, AM. Qualitative data analysis: An expanded sourcebook. 2. Thousand Oaks, CA: Sage; 1994.

Molina E. Informal non-kin networks among homeless Latino and African American men: Form and functions. American Behavioral Scientist. 2000; 43:663–685.

Montgomery SB, Hyde J, De Rosa CJ, Rohrbach LA, Ennett S, Harvey SM, Kipke MD. Gender differences in HIV risk behaviors among young injectors and their social network members. American Journal of Drug & Alcohol Abuse. 2002; 28:453–475. [PubMed: 12211360]

Muhr, T. User's manual for ATLAS.ti 5.0. 2. Berlin, Germany: Scientific Software Development; 2004.

National Institute on Drug Abuse. Medical consequences of drug abuse. Bethesda, MD: National Institutes of Health; 2011. Retrieved from website: http://www.drugabuse.gov/related-topics/medical-consequences-drug-abuse

Rice E, Milburn NG, Monro W. Social networking technology, social network composition, and reductions in substance use among homeless adolescents. Prevention Science. 2011; 12:80–88. [PubMed: 21194011]

Rice E, Milburn NG, Rotheram-Borus MJ. Pro-social and problematic social network influences on HIV/AIDS risk behaviors among newly homeless youth in Los Angeles. AIDS Care. 2007; 19:697–704. [PubMed: 17505933]

Rose E, DiClemente RJ, Wingood GM, McDermott Sales J, Latham TP, Hardin J. The validity of teens' and young adults' self-reported condom use. Archives of Pediatrics & Adolescent Medicine. 2009; 163:61–64. [PubMed: 19124705]

Slesnick N, Prestopnik J. Dual and multiple diagnosis among substance using runaway youth. American Journal of Drug and Alcohol Abuse. 2005; 1:179–201. [PubMed: 15768577]

Smith H. Searching for kinship: The creation of street families among homeless youth. American Behavioral Scientist. 2008; 51:756–771.

Thompson SJ. Risk/protective factors associated with substance use among runaway/homeless youth utilizing emergency shelter services nationwide. Substance Abuse. 2004; 25:13–26. [PubMed: 16150676]

Thompson SJ, Rew L, Barczyk A, McCoy P, Mi-Sedhi A. Social estrangement: Factors associated with alcohol or drug dependency among homeless, street-involved young adults. The Journal of Drug Issues. 2009; 39:905–930.

Tyler KA. Social network characteristics and risky sexual and drug related behaviors among homeless young adults. Social Science Research. 2008; 37:673–685. [PubMed: 19069065]

Tyler KA, Johnson KA. Pathways in and out of substance use among homeless-emerging adults. Journal of Adolescent Research. 2006; 21:133–157.

Walls NE, Bell S. Correlates of engaging in survival sex among homeless youth and young adults. Journal of Sex Research. 2011; 48:423–436. [PubMed: 20799134]

Critical Thinking

1. Why do homeless youth develop drug abuse norms higher than that of non-homeless youth?
2. How does age affect drug use in homeless youth?
3. What factors lead to drug and alcohol choices by homeless youth?
4. How do group norms affect individual drug and alcohol use?

Internet References

Principles of Drug Addiction Treatment: A Research-based Guide
www.drugabuse.gov/PODAT/PODATIndex.html

Substance Abuse and Mental Health Services Administration
https://www.samhsa.gov

U.S. National Institutes of Health's National Library of Medicine (NIH/NLM)
https://www.ncbi.nlm.nih.gov/pmc/

Melander, Lisa A.; Tyler, Kimberly A.; Schmitz, Rachel M., "An Inside Look at Homeless Youths' Social Networks: Perceptions of Substance Abuse Norms," *Journal of Child Adolescent Substance Abuse*, 2016

Descriptive and Injunctive Network Norms Associated with Non Medical Use of Prescription Drugs by Anamika Barman-Adhikari

45

Prepared by: Kim Schnurbush, *California State University, Sacramento*
Mark Pullin, *Angelo State University*

Article

Descriptive and Injunctive Network Norms Associated with Non-medical Use of Prescription Drugs among Homeless Youth

Anamika Barman-Adhikari, et al.

Learning Outcomes

After reading this article, you will be able to:

- Discuss how the use of nonmedical use of prescriptive drugs among homeless youth is resulting in significant public health issues.

- Understand the age, racial, and ethnic disparities with regards to nonmedical prescriptive drug abuse within the homeless youth environment.

- Discuss how social network norms, both street-based and family-based, affect nonmedical prescriptive drug abuse.

1. Introduction
1.1. NMUPD Among Youth and Young Adults

The nonmedical use of prescription drugs (NMUPD) is a serious public health problem in the United States (White House Office of National Drug Control Policy, 2011). NMUPD is defined as using medications that were not prescribed or were taken only for the experience or feeling that they caused, with the most commonly misused drugs being opioid pain relievers, stimulants, tranquilizers, and sedatives. The most recent data from the National Survey on Drug Use and Health indicates that an estimated 655,000, or 2.6% of adolescents'

aged 12 to 17 reported NMUPD in 2014. For those aged 18 to 25, an estimated 1.6 million, or 4.4% of young adults, reported NMUPD in the same year (Center for Behavioral Health Statistics and Quality, 2015). These numbers are concerning, particularly given that NMUPD is associated with a variety of negative health correlates for young adults, such as sexual risk behaviors, mental health concerns, and drug overdose (Drazdowski, 2016; Zullig & Divin, 2012).

1.2. Social Norms of NMUPD

Perception of social norms is an important aspect of drug use. Norms are defined as perceived rules or properties of a group that typify specific beliefs around what behaviors are considered acceptable or common within that group (Kincaid, 2004). Perceived social norms form a crucial component of many common theories of health behaviors (Bandura, 1977; Fishbein, Middlestadt, & Hitchcock, 1994; Fisher & Fisher, 1992), and have been linked to both behavior and behavioral intentions (Barrington et al., 2009). Perceived norms have been generally characterized as descriptive or injunctive norms. Descriptive norms indicate the perceived prevalence of a behavior in a group, whereas injunctive norms refer to perceived approval or disapproval of a behavior (Davey-Rothwell & Latkin, 2007).

Social network analysis provides a fruitful means through which one can assess the prevalence of both descriptive and injunctive norms in naturally occurring social groups

(Latkin et al., 2009). There is an important distinction between "social norms" and "network norms". For example, most studies assessing social norms have used survey data, in which participant respond to a "question regarding the level of drug use their peers engage in" and those responses are used to assess perceived social norms. Researchers have found this to be a little problematic because of the ambiguity regarding who these peers are (i.e., the specificity of the reference group). In a recent meta-analysis, Borsari and Carey (2003) reported that the degree to which youth were able to correctly estimate their peers' drug use depended on the degree of familiarity and proximity of the relationship. Youth generally tend to know better what their close friends are doing compared to a hypothetical or typical peer group (Pape, 2012). The use of network methods partially mitigates this issue because respondents are asked about a very specific network (i.e. people they regularly communicate or interact with) instead of a hypothetical group of people.

Extant research shows that network norms are strongly associated with substance use behavior. However, most of the research describing the association between network norms and drug use behaviors has tended to focus either on college students, especially in relationship to alcohol and marijuana use (Barrett, Darredeau, Bordy, & Pihl, 2005; McCabe, Knight, Teter, & Wechsler, 2006; Rabiner et al., 2009) or regarding adult persons who inject drugs (Knowlton, Hua & Latkin, 2005; Kottiri, Friedman, Neaigus, Curtis, & Des Jarlais, 2002; Latkin, Kuramoto, Davey-Rothwell, & Tobin, 2010).

Additionally, studies have also found that norms are not one-dimensional by nature. More specifically, different kinds of referent groups contribute different kinds of norms surrounding both risk and protective behaviors. For example, while one's family members might promote norms around abstinence, peer groups might promote norms promoting substance use behaviors (Latkin et al., 2009). Conventional wisdom dictated that homeless youth have strained family relationships and their social networks are only comprised of other similarly situated street peers (Whitbeck, 2009). However, evidence from various studies suggests that homeless youth's relationships are not confined to street associations alone (Rice, Milburn & Rotheram-Borus, 2007; Wenzel et al., 2012; Whitbeck & Hoyt, 1999). Homeless youth relationships involve parents, other relatives, home-based peers (peers to whom homeless youths were connected before they became homeless), and social service program staff members (de la Haye et al., 2012; Ennett, Bailey & Federman, 1999; Rice, Milburn, & Monro, 2011). To the best of our knowledge, no study has yet network norms regarding NMUPD vary based on different referent groups in the homeless youth population.

Though less commonly researched, some studies have explored social norms regarding NMUPD. A recent systematic review examined risk and protective factors associated with NMUPD among youth aged 14 to 24 from a social ecological perspective and included 7 longitudinal studies, 36 cross-sectional studies, and 7 reviews (Nargiso et al., 2015). In the interpersonal domain related to peers, the review found that peer approval of substance use (an injunctive norm) and NMUPD were strongly associated, and that a close friend's use of substances (a descriptive norm) was one of the strongest and most consistent risk factors for NMUPD (Nargiso et al., 2015). Several of the studies included in the review analyzed data from the National Survey on Drug Use and Health and the majority of the others used convenience samples from schools and colleges.

1.3. NMUPD Among Homeless Youth: Individual Correlates and the Role of Social Norms

Much less is known about the prevalence of NMUPD among homeless youth and perceived social norms related to nonmedical use of prescription drugs in this population. To the best of our knowledge, this is the first study to investigate associations between social network norms and NMUPD among homeless youth. Extant data from smaller studies of homeless or street-involved youth have reported that 9% to 22% of homeless youth engage in NMUPD (Al-Tayyib, Rice, Rhoades, & Riggs, 2014; Hadland et al. 2014; Rhoades, Winetrobe, & Rice, 2014), which is several times the rate reported in the general population of youth and young adults. One study of 16 to 24 year olds, in which 60% of participants were currently homeless, found that 69% of participants reported lifetime nonmedical use of prescription opioids, tranquilizers, and stimulants (Lankenau et al. 2012).

A vast majority of the literature on NMUPD has been focused on school or college going housed youth (Berenson & Rahman, 2011; Zullig & Divin, 2012). Fewer studies have tried to assess NMUPD specifically among homeless youth (Al-Tayyib, Rice, Rhoades, & Riggs, 2014; Rhoades, Winetrobe, & Rice, 2014). Among youth in the general population, NMUPD has been associated with depression (Zullig & Divin, 2012), post-traumatic stress disorder (PTSD) (Berenson & Rahman, 2011) and use of other substances such as heroin, marijuana and methamphetamine (Lankenau et al., 2012). In samples of homeless youth, NMUPD as been associated with hard drug use, unprotected sex, suicidal ideation and history of foster care (Al-Tayyib, Rice, Rhoades, & Riggs, 2014; Rhoades, Winetrobe, & Rice, 2014). However, beyond these two studies, not much is known about NMUPD among homeless youth.

Notably, interventions attempting to reduce drug use have successfully utilized social networks to disseminate and reinforce behavioral norms that are supportive of protective behaviors related to drug use, especially among hard-to-reach populations (Barrington et al., 2009). Unfortunately, little is known about social norms of NMUPD among homeless youth, leaving researchers and service providers with a dearth of evidence for how to design effective network interventions. Given the paucity of information related to social norms surrounding NMUPD among homeless youth, we sought to understand how social norms regarding NMUPD is associated with self-reported NMUPD in a particularly vulnerable population.

2. Methods
2.1. Procedures
As part of a social network panel study, homeless youth ages 13–24 in Los Angeles (N = 1,046) were surveyed between October 2011 and June 2013. Participants were recruited from three homeless youth drop-in centers in Hollywood and Santa Monica across 4 different waves. Each wave of data collection was approximately 6 months apart. Youth were invited to participate at multiple waves, but only their baseline survey data were used in the current study. Any client receiving services at each respective agency was eligible to participate; this included youth living outdoors or in places not meant for human habitation, youth in shelters or transitional housing programs, and youth living with family, friends, or relatives but spending most of their time on the street. Recruitment was conducted for 19 days at each agency during each wave; during each recruitment period, researchers were present at the agency to approach youth for the duration of service provision hours. Signed voluntary informed consent was obtained from each youth, with caveats that child abuse and suicidal and homicidal intentions would be reported to appropriate authorities. Informed consent was obtained from youth 18 years of age and older and informed assent was obtained from youth 13 to 17 years old. The Institutional Review Board waived parental consent, as homeless youth under 18 years are unaccompanied minors who may not have a parent or adult guardian from whom to obtain consent.

The study consisted of two parts: a computerized self-administered survey and a social network interview. The social network interview was conducted using a free-recall name generator (Rice, Barman-Adhikari, Milburn, & Monro, 2012) to collect names of participants' network members, defined as someone with whom the youth had face-to-face, phone, or Internet contact in the last month. The social network-mapping interview conducted face-to-face by a trained research staff member. (The research team used an iPad application to create the network map.) Respondents are then asked to list as many people as they can. Additionally, 17 follow-up questions were asked about specific types of interactions with each network member, and their perceptions of these youths' behaviors. All

participants received $20 in cash or gift cards as compensation for their time. The Institutional Review Board at the [redacted for review] approved all survey items and procedures. More detailed information about the study's design and data collection procedures may be found elsewhere (blinded for review).

2.2. Measures
NMUPD and Substance Use Behaviors—Recent NMUPD was assessed by asking how many times a participant took a prescription drug without a doctor's prescription, used more of the drug than what was prescribed, or took the drug more often than prescribed within the last 30 days (Eaton et al., 2012; Youth Risk Behavior Survey [YRBS] [CDC, 2012]). Prescription drugs included of sedatives, stimulants and opioids, however youth were not asked to separately specify which type of prescription drug that they had use nonmedically. Similarly, using items adapted from the YRBS (Eaton et al., 2012), we assessed for past 30-day use of binge drinking and marijuana, heroin, and injection drug use. Binge drinking was defined as having 5 or more drinks of alcohol in a row, that is, within a couple of hours.

2.2.2 Sociodemographic Characteristics—Demographics included age, time spent homeless (in years), gender (male vs. female), ethnicity (White, Black, Latino/a, and other and mixed race), and sexual orientation (heterosexual vs. lesbian, gay, bisexual, or queer [LGBQ]). Youth experiencing literal homelessness were defined as those who indicated that they were currently staying in a shelter (emergency or temporary), a stranger's home, hotel, motel, street, beach, tent or campsite, abandoned building, car, or bus (vs. those living with their biological family, foster family, relative, friend, group home, sober living facility, transitional living program, or own apartment but still spent considerable time on the streets).

2.2.3 Health Service Use—The frequency of past month health service utilization was assessed with the question; "I have gone to a place(s) for medical or health care services." Responses ranged from "every day or almost every day" to "not at all this month," and then were dichotomized to indicate health service use versus non-use.

2.2.4 Depression—Depressive symptoms were assessed by the 10-item Center for Epidemiological Studies Depression Scale (CES-D; Kohout, Berkman, Evans, & Cornoni-Huntley, 1993).

2.2.5 Social Norms of NMUPD—We assessed both descriptive as well as injunctive norms. In order to assess descriptive and injunctive norms regarding NMUPD, after youths finished nominating their network members, they were asked: "Out of the people you nominated, how many of them engage in NMUPD, would encourage and object you engaging in NMUPD?" This was calculated as the number of people specified by relationship type (i.e., street peers, home-based peers, family members (which included both biological and foster family, extended relatives and siblings, and finally case-workers/staff members) whom respondents thought engaged in or perceived would object to or encourage them to engage in NMUPD. These network members are all mutually exclusive. However, every youth could have more than one network member type in their total network (i.e. youth who have a family member engaging in NMUPD could also have a street-peer engaging in NMUPD).

To account for varying sized networks, we created network member proportion variables who either engaged in NMUPD, objected to or encourage NMUPD using the total number of network members nominated in the last 90 days as the denominator. However, these proportion variables were skewed as well. Typically, in the social network literature, the way skewness has been handled is to recode proportion into categorical variables (Barrington et al., 2009; Davey-Rothwell & Latkin, 2007; Latkin et al., 2010; Tucker et al., 2011; Tyler, 2013; Valente & Auerswald, 2013). The median is used to create a threshold for measures that are not uniformly distributed (Wang, Fan & Wilson, 1996). Based on the median, the descriptive norm and the injunctive norms (encourage and object NMUPD) were consequently dichotomized as either no network member (coded as 0) or at least one or more network members (coded as 1) who participants believed engaged in NMUPD or would encourage or object to them engaging in NMUPD.

2.3. Analytic Approach

Data analyses were conducted using SAS Version 9.2 (SAS Institute Inc., 2008). Analyses examined bivariate associations between socio-demographic variables and perceived NMUPD social norms and self-reported NMUPD, using chi-square statistics for categorical variables and t-tests for continuous variables. Two-sided significance from Pearson's chi square tests was reported for all categorical variables and t-tests were used for continuous level variables. The degree of freedom for all binary variables was 1. Bivariate tests were not conducted for any of the service-related network variables because of the sparse nature of the cell sizes. Additionally, because these service-related networks could not be independently included in bivariate and multivariate logistic regression models, they were dropped from the subsequent bivariate and multivariate logistic analyses.

To evaluate the significance of the independent associations between perceived NMUPD norms and self-reported NMUPD, logistic regression was conducted. In order to preserve statistical power and degrees of freedom (because of the large number of variables being examined), bivariate analyses were first conducted to examine unadjusted associations between

study variables and outcome measures. Any variable that was significantly associated with the outcome at $p < .10$ was retained in the multivariate model. Multivariate models were then constructed based on these analyses (Hosmer & Lemeshow, 2004). Sociodemographic characteristics (i.e. age, gender, sexual orientation, race/ethnicity) were controlled for regardless of their significance in bivariate analysis. Significance levels were adjusted within each hypothesis using the step-down Bonferroni (Holm) procedure (SAS, 9.2.). The benefit of using step-down methods is that the tests are made more powerful (smaller adjusted p-values) while, in most cases, maintaining strong control of the familywise error rate (Holm, 1979).

Since we were interested in whether or not youth had initiated use and not on dependence or abuse, a dichotomous variable was created to indicate 0 = "no NMUPD use" versus 1 = "recent NMUPD use." It is important to note that dichotomization does not significantly reduce statistical power and yields meaningful effect sizes (i.e. odds ratios) (Farrington & Loeber, 2000). Individual ORs were interpreted in accordance to Chen, Cohen, and Chen's (2010) guidelines for small (OR = 1.46), medium (OR = 2.49), and large (OR = 4.14) effect sizes when predicted outcomes are present in at least or more than 10% of the general population. Tjur R-square (Tjur, 2009) was also used to assess overall strength of association. Tjur R2 was .28, which represents a moderate-to-strong effect size (Ferguson, 2009). Furthermore, multivariate analyses were restricted to participants without missing data for the variables included in the models. Therefore, the sample size for the multivariate model is smaller than the study's total sample size (n = 969).

3. Results
3.1. Descriptive Statistics

Socio demographic characteristics are presented in Table 1. The sample was predominantly male (70.27%) and heterosexual (75.10%). Average age of participants was 21.34 years. In terms of race/ethnicity, Whites represented the largest group (38.24%). A total of 247 youth (23.61%) reported engaging in NMUPD in the past 30 days. Participants differed significantly in their nonmedical use of prescription drugs by variables including race/ethnicity; health care access in the past 30 days; use of heroin, marijuana, or injection drugs in the past 30 days; and depressive symptoms. Participants who reported recent NMUPD compared to those who did not were more likely to be White (44.53% vs. 36.30%, $p < 0.05$) and less likely to be African-American (14.75% vs. 26.03%, $p < .0001$). Youth who accessed health care in the past 30 days were also more likely to report current NMUPD (51.74% vs. 39.41%, $p < .01$). Additionally, use of other substances was significantly associated with self-reported NMUPD, with increased rates of NMUPD

Table 1   Sample Characteristics of Homeless Youth in Los Angeles (*n* = 1,046)

	Full Sample		Recent NMUPD		No NMUPD
	n	%	*n* = 247	% = 23.61	*n* = 799
Gender					
Male	735	70.27	165	66.80	570
Female	311	29.73	82	33.20	229
Sexual Orientation (n = 1,010)					
Heterosexual	759	75.10	159	72.27	600
LGBQ	251	24.90	61	27.73	190
Race/Ethnicity					
African-American	244	23.33	36	14.57	208
Latino	139	13.29	31	12.55	108
Other Race	212	20.26	42	4.02	170
White	400	38.24	110	44.53	290
Traveler					
Yes	377	36.00	99	34.79	278
Accessed Health Care in Past 30 Days (n = 980)					
Yes	411	41.90	104	51.74	307
Alcohol Use (Binge Drinking) in Past 30 Days					
Yes	936	89.50	225	91.09	711
Heroin Use in Past 30 Days					
Yes	157	15.00	113	45.75	134
Marijuana Use in Past 30 Days					
Yes	593	56.70	160	64.78	433
Injection Drug Use in Past 30 Days					
Yes	145	13.90	108	43.72	37
Descriptive Norms					
All Alters Using Prescription Drugs					
Any	360	32.28	131	48.99	229
Street-Based Peer Networks engage in NMUPD					
Any	221	20.99	83	32.68	138
Home-Based Peer Networks engage in NMUPD					
Any	95	9.02	43	16.93	52
Family-Based Networks engage in NMUPD					
Any	41	3.89	16	4.00	25
Service-Related Networks engage in NMUPD					
Any	4	0.38	—	—	—
Injunctive Norms (Encouragement)					
All Alters Encouraging Prescription Drug Use					
Any	156	14.53	70	26.88	86

Street-Based Peer Networks encourage NMUPD					
Any	79	7.50	38	14.96	41
Home-Based Peer Networks encourage NMUPD					
Any	48	4.56	25	9.84	23
Family-Based Networks encourage NMUPD					
Any	28	2.66	8	3.00	20
Proportion of Service Related Networks encourage NMUPD					
Any	2	0.19	—	—	—
Injunctive Norms (Object)					
All Alters Objecting to Prescription Drug Use					
Any	776	73.69	158	70.16	618
Street-Based Peer Networks Object NMUPD					
Any	509	48.34	111	43.70	398
Home-Based Peer Networks Object NMUPD					
Any	502	47.67	108	42.52	394
Family-Based Networks Object NMUPD					
Any	577	54.80	138	45.25	439
Service Related Networks Object NMUPD					
Any	4	0.38	—	—	—
	Mean	**SD**	**Mean**	**SD**	**Mean**
Age	21.34	2.16	21.46	2.12	21.31
Time Homeless (0–7)	3.63	1.35	3.96	1.60	3.52
CESD Score (0–30)	18.37	9.74	18.79	9.00	17.02

Open in a separate window

*p<0.05.

**p<0.01,

***p<0.001,

****p<0.0001

Note: Bivariate tests not conducted for service related networks because of the sparse nature of cell sizes

for participants who reported using heroin (45.75% vs. 5.51%, $p < .0001$), marijuana (64.78% vs. 54.19%, $p < .01$), or injection drug use (43.72% vs. 4.63%, $p < .0001$). On average, participants who reported recent NMUPD had higher depression scores on the CES-D than those who did not report NMUPD ($M = 18.79$ vs. 17.02, $p < .01$).

3.2. Network Norm Characteristics

Social network norm characteristics are also presented in Table 1. A total of 360 participants (32.28%) reported having any network members (aggregated across all network types) that they perceived would engage in NMUPD. There were variations when this was stratified by network type. More youth thought that their street-based peers were more likely to engage in NMUPD (18.99%) compared to home-based peers (9.02%),

family-based network members (3.89%) and service-related network members (0.38%) engaging in NMUPD. In regards to injunctive norms, more youth believed that their network members would object to them engaging in NMUPD relative to perceptions of receiving encouragement from their network members.

Bivariate statistics indicated that participants differed significantly in their self-reported NMUPD based on these social norms especially by network type. Youth were more likely to engage in NMUPD if they had at least one street-based peer (32.68% vs. 17.27%, $p < .0001$) or home-based peer (16.93 vs. 6.51%, $p < .0001$) who engage in NMUPD. Similarly, youth were more likely to endorse recent NMUPD if they had at least one street-based peer (26.88% vs. 10.64%, $p < .0001$) or home-based peer (9.84% vs. 2.88 %, $p < .0001$) who encouraged

Descriptive and Injunctive Network Norms Associated with Non Medical Use of Prescription Drugs by Anamika Barman-Adhikari

51

them to engage in NMUPD. On the contrary, youth who had at least one family member who objected to NMUPD, youth were less likely to engage in NMUPD (45.25% vs. 58.69%, $p< .0001$).

3.3. Bivariate and Multivariate Logistic Regression Analyses

Bivariate and multivariate statistics are presented in Table 2. As noted above, only variables significant in the bivariate model at the $p<.10$ level were included in the bivariate model. In the multivariate model, having accessed health care in the last 30 days, recent heroin, marijuana, injection drug use, and NMUPD. Youth who accessed health care in the past 30 days were 1.91

times more likely to engage in NMUPD ($p < .001$). Youth who reported engaging in recent heroin, marijuana, and injection drug use were 4.50 times ($p < .0001$), 2.64 times ($p < .0001$) and 6.85 times ($p < .0001$) more likely to engage in NMUPD, respectively. Youth who perceived that at least one street-based network member engaged in NMUPD were 1.49 times more likely to report engaging in NMUPD themselves ($p < .001$). Alternatively, youth who perceived that at all family-based people in their network would object to them engaging in NMUPD were 31% less likely to engage in NMUPD ($p < .001$). When the final model was rerun using the more conservative Bonferroni step-down corrected alpha-levels, all variables remained significantly associated with recent NMUPD.

Table 2 Multivariate Logistic Regression of Social Network Norms and Prescription Drug Misuse (PDM)

	Prescription Drug Misuse				
	Unadj OR	95% CI		p	Adj OR
Demographics					
Age	1.03	0.96	1.11		1.04
Male	1.05	0.76	1.46		1.05
LGBQ (Ref = Heterosexual)	1.21	0.87	1.70		1.23
Race (Ref = White)					
African-American	0.47	0.32	0.69	***	0.72
Latino	0.89	0.58	1.36		0.62
Other Race	0.73	0.51	1.06		0.68
Behavioral/Situational Variables					
Traveler	0.61	0.44	0.84	**	—
Accessed Health Care in last 30 days	2.34	1.75	3.12	****	1.91
CESD Score (Depression)	1.02	1.01	1.04	*	1.01
Length of Time Homeless					—
Substance Use (Past 30 Days)					
Alcohol Use (Binge drinking)	1.31	0.80	2.13		—
Heroin Use	15.37	10.39	22.72	****	4.50
Marijuana Use	1.44	1.08	1.92	**	2.64
Injection Drug Use	17.04	11.28	25.73	****	6.85
Perceived Social Norms in Network					
Descriptive Norms					
Street-Based Peer Networks engage in NMUPD	1.62	1.35	1.93	****	1.49
Home-Based Peer Networks engage in NMUPD	1.45	1.15	1.82	***	1.09
Family-Based Networks engage in NMUPD	1.28	0.80	2.03		—

Injunctive Norms (Encouragement)					
Street-Based Peer Networks encourage NMUPD	1.42	1.21	1.68	****	1.12
Home-Based Peer Networks encourage NMUPD	1.62	1.22	2.16	***	1.04
Family-Based Networks encourage NMUPD	1.50	0.88	2.55		—
Injunctive Norms (Object)					
Street-Based Peer Networks Object NMUPD	0.96	0.91	1.00		—
Home-Based Peer Networks Object NMUPD	0.95	0.89	1.01		—
Family-Based Networks Object NMUPD	0.27	0.09	0.80	****	0.69
n					969
AIC					736.50
SC					813.37
−2 log likelihood					704.50
Wald chi-square					147.48****
Tjur R2					0.28

Open in a separate window

Note. LGBQ = lesbian, gay, bisexual, or questioning; OR = odds ratio; CI = confidence interval; AIC = Akaike information criterion; SC = Schwarz criterion; df = degrees of freedom

*$p<0.05$.

**$p<0.01$,

***$p<0.001$,

****$p<0.0001$.

Note: Only variables significant in the bivariate model at $p<.10$ included in the multivariate model.

4. Discussion

The current study advances our understanding of NMUPD among homeless youth, a high-risk and especially hard-to-reach population, in many ways. First, this study, to the best of our knowledge, is the first to demonstrate an association between perceived norms of NMUPD and self-reported NMUPD among homeless youth. Both descriptive and injunctive norms were strongly and significantly associated with NMUPD, a finding consistent with previous research on social norms of NMUPD, although previous studies focused on housed and college attending populations (Meisel & Goodie, 2015).

While less than one-quarter of youth indicated that they had engaged in NMUPD, a greater percentage of youth (32.28%) believed that their network members (aggregating across all network relationships) engaged in NMUPD. This finding indicates that there might be an "overestimation" of the prevalence of NMUPD among homeless youth, perhaps suggesting a "pluralistic ignorance" bias, in which individuals tend to misperceive their peers' drug use, regardless of their own status as users or nonusers (Henry, Kobus, & Schoeny, 2011). Several studies have found evidence consistent with this phenomenon (Bourgeois & Bowen 2001; Henry et al., 2011). The social norms intervention approach, however, is designed to correct the demonstrated inconsistency between actual and perceived behaviors (Ott & Doyle, 2005), and could provide an appropriate approach to address NMUPD with homeless youth. A few interventions have in fact been successful in demonstrating reduced misperceptions of norms of NMUPD (Schinke et al., 2009). The current study was not specifically designed to understand the discrepancy between actual and perceived NMUPD, but given these preliminary findings, it would be prudent to explore this issue further.

Second, our study's focus on injunctive norms furthers our understanding of perceived approval and disapproval as they relate to NMUPD. Injunctive norms continued to be significantly associated with NMUPD even after controlling for (i.e. holding constant) descriptive norms in the multivariate model. Extant research has found that descriptive and injunctive norms have an independent association with behavior across a number of behaviors, including drug use (McMillan & Conner, 2003), engagement in sexual risk (Peterson, Rothenberg, Kraft, Beeker, & Trotter, 2009), physical activity (Rhodes & Courneya, 2003), and violence (Norman, Clark, & Walker, 2005).

Injunctive norms, as noted before, refer to both perceived approval and disapproval of a behavior. What is encouraging about our findings is that while there is significant perceived disapproval of NMUPD use among homeless youths' network members, there is relatively little perceived approval of it. Specifically, in this study, we found that only 7.50% of youth believed that their street-based peers and 4.56% believed that their home-based peers would encourage them to engage in NMUPD. However, a number of preventive interventions have based on the theory that there is active pressure on youth (especially in the form of peer encouragement) to use substances; therefore, interventions have generally sought to provide the young person with social and interpersonal skills that would enable them to resist such proactive pressure (Coggans & McKellar, 1994; Denscombe, 2001). More studies are needed to understand whether the absence of such peer pressure is a matter of perception, or if peer pressure works in other, subtle ways not captured by survey data (Denscombe, 2001). It is possible that observational studies or qualitative studies could better capture the nuances of how such influence is exerted.

Perhaps the most compelling aspects of these data is the finding that the role of descriptive and injunctive norms on NMUPD varies depending on the nature of the referent (Borsari & Carey, 2003; Cho, 2006). Our findings indicate that while the presence of NMUPD engaged street-based and home-based peers increased the likelihood of youth reporting recent NMUPD, objections from family-members decreasing that likelihood. These findings support the "Social Identity Theory" (Turner &Tajfel, 1986), which proposes that norms are linked to specific social groups, and identification with these groups determines what will be regarded as normative. It can be assumed that homeless youth who are connected to family members have more role models to rely on in understanding what can be considered normative behavior. In addition, it is also conceivable that the conversations that youth are having with their family members might act as sources of informational support, which is known, to influence the expression of norms and consequently engagement in behavior. However, it is important to mention that this study did not collect any data on the nature of these interactions, more specifically, what was discussed. A future study that collects detailed network level information on ties and the content of interactions across those ties would do much to increase our understanding of these processes, which could be critical in informing clinical interventions with youth and families.

In addition to network norm characteristics, our study found associations between other sociodemographic and behavioral characteristics and self-reported NMUPD. What is perhaps most compelling is the association between recent health care use and engagement in NMUPD. Nearly half (42%) of participants reported accessing health care in the past 30 days. Emerging research has indicated that one of the principal factors connected to increased NMUPD among youth and young

adults is increased access to these drugs (McCabe, Cranford, Boyd & Teter, 2007). This has been in part attributed to less than conservative prescribing practices of doctors of opioid painkillers and changing medical guidelines (Twombly & Holtz, 2008). However, this also underscores the critical role that physicians can play in screening for and communicating about the negative effects of nonmedical use of prescription drugs with their patients. This may be particularly important for homeless youth, as building trusting relationships with health care providers is one of the key avenues through which substance abusing homeless youth are typically able to access treatment and resources (Hudson, Nyamathi, & Sweat, 2008).

Similar to other studies of NMUPD, we found a significant association between NMUPD and heroin use (Compton, Jones, & Baldwin, 2016). However, much of the existing literature describing the relationship between NMUPD and heroin use is in the adult population. Our findings add to the much smaller body of evidence suggesting that the association between NMUPD and heroin is present at a younger age. Though we did not capture information related to the specific route of administration for heroin, we also found a strong association between NMUPD and injection drug use.

In addition, youth who reported engaging in marijuana use were more likely to engage in NMUPD. This study reinforces previous evidence (Arria et al., 2008; Catalano et al., 2011; Haddox et al., 2014; McCabe et al., 2005), which has found that marijuana and NMUPD are linked especially among college students. This study provides some preliminary evidence that marijuana could prove to be a gateway to NMUPD even among homeless youth. Given that these substance use behaviors are clustered, community-based interventions that address substance misuse more universally could provide a viable means of addressing NMUPD among youth populations.

4.1. Limitations and Conclusions

Certain study limitations must be noted. First, the study includes cross-sectional data, thereby reducing the ability to draw causal conclusions. Thus, it is plausible that substance-using youth are more likely to perceive that their peers also use substances, and/or would approve of their substance use. Future research would benefit from longitudinal investigations of how network dynamics function over time to better discern the causal pathways through which network attributes facilitate the formation of substance use norms among homeless youth. Additionally, all behavioral study variables are self-reported, which could introduce bias. It is perhaps inevitable that some behaviors are under- or over-reported due to social desirability, despite reminders given to participants that data were confidential and that they could skip questions while completing the questionnaire. Further, the study's use of a computer-assisted self-interview modality, which has been shown to diminish threats of social desirability and impression management (Schroder, Carey, & Vanable, 2003), is likely to generate less biased responses. Moreover, norms variables were based on youths' perceptions and, as aforementioned, may not be accurately reflective of reality. Additional research regarding social norms would benefit from further incorporating independent confirmations of norms. Also, we did not assess for perceived availability of prescription drugs in our study. It is possible that perceived norms may have been confounded with availability/access of prescription drugs via network members. However, the social network interview was separate from the individual survey and was interviewer administered. We believe that knowing that these are separate questions assessing their perceptions of their network members' and having an interviewer clarify it for them might have reduced the confusion noted above. Last, but not the least, respondents were not asked to identify the type of prescription drug (i.e., stimulants, sedatives, and/or opioids) that they had use nonmedically. Previous studies (Kelly et al., 2014) have found that young adults who engage in NMUPD have different patterns and clusters of use and therefore are important to assess.

4.2. Conclusion

Our findings help further our understanding of the relationship between perceived norms of NMUPD and self-reported NMUPD among homeless youth. Given that NMUPD may be associated with youths' perceived prevalence of their peers' use (even if an overestimation of that use), and also by their perceived peers' approval or disapproval of NMUPD, such an understanding can help inform development of network interventions that specifically target prevention of NMUPD among homeless youth.

References

Al-Tayyib AA, Rice E, Rhoades H, Riggs P. Association between prescription drug misuse and injection among runaway and homeless youth. Drug and Alcohol Dependence. 2014;134:406–409. [PMC free article] [PubMed]

Arria AM, O'Grady KE, Caldeira KM, Vincent KB, Wish ED. Nonmedical use of prescription stimulants and analgesics: Associations with social and academic behaviors among college students. Pharmacotherapy. 2008;38:1045–1060. [PMC free article] [PubMed]

Bandura A. Self-efficacy: toward a unifying theory of behavioral change. Psychological Review. 1977;84(2):191–215. [PubMed]

Barrett SP, Darredeau C, Bordy LE, Pihl RO. Characteristics of methylphenidate misuse in a university student sample. Canadian Journal of Psychiatry. 2005;50(8):457–461. [PubMed]

Barrington C, Latkin C, Sweat MD, Moreno L, Ellen J, Kerrigan D. Talking the talk, walking the walk: Social network norms, communication patterns, and condom use among the male partners of female sex workers in la Romani, Dominican Republic. Social Science & Medicine. 2009;68(11):2037–2044. [PMC free article] [PubMed]

Berenson AB, Rahman M. Prevalence and correlates of prescription drug misuse among young, low-income women receiving public healthcare. Journal of addictive diseases. 2011;30(3):203–215. [PMC free article] [PubMed]

Borsari B, Carey KB. Descriptive and injunctive norms in college drinking: A meta-analytic integration. Journal of Studies on Alcohol. 2003;64:331–341. [PMC free article] [PubMed]

Bourgeois MJ, Bowen A. Self-organization of alcohol-related attitudes and beliefs in a campus housing complex: An initial investigation. Health Psychology. 2001;20(6):434–437. [PubMed]

Catalano RF, White HR, Fleming CB, Haggerty KP. Is nonmedical prescription opiate use a unique form of illicit drug use? Addictive Behaviors. 2011;36:79–86. [PMC free article] [PubMed]

Center for Behavioral Health Statistics and Quality. (HHS Publication No. SMA 15-4927, NSDUH Series H-50).Behavioral health trends in the United States: Results from the 2014 National Survey on Drug Use and Health. 2015. Retrieved from: http://www.samhsa.gov/data/

Chen H, Cohen P, Chen S. How big is a big odds ratio? Interpreting the magnitudes of odds ratios in epidemiological studies. Communications in Statistics—Simulation and Computation® 2010;39(4):860–864.

Cho H. Influences of norm proximity and norm types on binge and non-binge drinkers: Examining the under-examined aspects of social norms interventions on college campuses. Journal of Substance Use. 2006;11:417–429.

Coggans N, McKellar S. Drug use amongst peers: Peer pressure or peer preference? Drugs: Education, Prevention and Policy. 1994;1(1):15–26.

Compton WM, Jones CM, Baldwin GT. Relationship between Nonmedical Prescription-Opioid Use and Heroin Use. New England Journal of Medicine. 2016;374(2):154–163. [PubMed]

Davey-Rothwell MA, Latkin CA. Gender differences in social network influence among injection drug users: Perceived norms and needle sharing. Journal of Urban Health. 2007;84(5):691–703. [PMC free article] [PubMed]

de la Haye K, Green HD, Jr, Kennedy DP, Zhou A, Golinelli D, Wenzel SL, Tucker JS. Who is supporting homeless youth? Predictors of support in personal networks. Journal of Research on Adolescence. 2012;22:604–616. [PMC free article] [PubMed]

Denscombe M. Peer group pressure, young people and smoking: New developments and policy implications. Drugs: Education, Prevention and Policy. 2001;8(1):7–32.

Drazdowski TK. A systematic review of the motivations for the nonmedical use of prescription drugs in young adults. Drug and Alcohol Dependence. 2016. doi: 10.1016/j.

drugalcdep.2016.01.011. Advance online publication. [PubMed] [CrossRef]

Eaton DK, Kann L, Kinchen S, Shanklin S, Flint KH, Hawkins J, Centers for Disease Control and Prevention (CDC) Youth risk behavior surveillance – United States, 2011. Morbidity and Mortality Weekly Report. 2012;61(4):1–162. [PubMed]

Ennett ST, Bailey SL, Federman EB. Social network characteristics associated with risky behaviors among runaway and homeless youth. Journal of Health and Social Behavior. 1999;40:63–78. [PubMed]

Farrington DP, Loeber R. Some benefits of dichotomization in psychiatric and criminological research. Criminal Behaviour and Mental Health. 2000;10(2):100–122.

Ferguson CJ. An effect size primer: A guide for clinicians and researchers. Professional Psychology: Research and Practice. 2009;40(5):532–538.

Fiellin LE, Tetrault JM, Becker WC, Fiellin DA, Hoff RA. Previous use of alcohol, cigarettes, and marijuana and subsequent abuse of prescription opioids in young adults. Journal of Adolescent Health. 2013;52(2):158–163. [PMC free article] [PubMed]

Fishbein M, Middlestadt SE, Hitchcock PJ. Preventing AIDS. Springer; 1994. Using information to change sexually transmitted disease-related behaviors; pp. 61–78.

Fisher JD, Fisher WA. Changing AIDS-risk behavior. Psychological Bulletin. 1992;111(3):455–474. [PubMed]

Haddox JD, Weiler RM, Pealer LN, Barnett TE. Early initiation of alcohol or marijuana use and nonmedical use of prescription drugs. Drug & Alcohol Dependence. 2014;140:e77.

Hadland SE, DeBeck K, Kerr T, Feng C, Montaner JS, Wood E. Prescription opioid injection and risk of hepatitis C in relation to traditional drugs of misuse in a prospective cohort of street youth. BMJ Open. 2014;4(7) doi: 10.1136/bmjopen-2014-005419. e005419-2014-005419. [PMC free article] [PubMed] [CrossRef]

Henry DB, Kobus K, Schoeny ME. Accuracy and bias in adolescents' perceptions of friends' substance use. Psychology of Addictive Behaviors. 2011;25(1):80–89. [PMC free article] [PubMed]

Holm S. A simple sequentially rejective multiple test procedure. Scandinavian journal of statistics. 1979:65–70.

Hosmer DW, Jr, Lemeshow S. Applied logistic regression. John Wiley & Sons; 2004.

Hudson AL, Nyamathi A, Sweat J. Homeless youths' interpersonal perspectives of health care providers. Issues in Mental Health Nursing. 2008;29(12):1277–1289. [PubMed]

Kelly BC, Wells BE, Pawson M, LeClair A, Parsons JT. Combinations of prescription drug misuse and illicit drugs among young adults. Addictive Behaviors. 2014;39(5):941–944. [PMC free article] [PubMed]

Kincaid DL. From innovation to social norm: Bounded normative influence. Journal of Health Communication. 2004;9(S1):37–57. [PubMed]

Knowlton A, Hua W, Latkin C. Social support networks and medical service use among HIV-positive injection drug users: Implications to intervention. AIDS Care. 2005;17(4):479–492. [PubMed]

Kohout FJ, Berkman LF, Evans DA, Cornoni-Huntley J. Two shorter forms of the CES-D (Center for Epidemiological Studies Depression) depression symptoms index. Journal of Aging and Health. 1993;5(2):179–193. [PubMed]

Kottiri BJ, Friedman SR, Neaigus A, Curtis R, Des Jarlais DC. Risk networks and racial/ethnic differences in the prevalence of HIV infection among injection drug users. Journal of Acquired Immune Deficiency Syndromes (1999). 2002;30(1):95–104. [PubMed]

Lankenau SE, Schrager SM, Silva K, Kecojevic A, Bloom JJ, Wong C, Iverson E. Misuse of prescription and illicit drugs among high-risk young adults in Los Angeles and New York. Journal of Public Health Research. 2012;1(1):22–30. [PMC free article] [PubMed]

Latkin CA, Donnell D, Metzger D, Sherman S, Aramrattna A, Davis-Vogel A, Celentano DD. The efficacy of a network intervention to reduce HIV risk behaviors among drug users and risk partners in Chiang Mai, Thailand and Philadelphia, USA. Social Science & Medicine. 2009;68:740–748. [PMC free article] [PubMed]

Latkin C, Kuramoto S, Davey-Rothwell M, Tobin K. Social norms, social networks, and HIV risk behavior among injection drug users. AIDS and Behavior. 2010;14(5):1159–1168. [PMC free article] [PubMed]

McCabe SE, Knight JR, Teter CJ, Wechsler H. Non-medical use of prescription stimulants among US college students: Prevalence and correlates from a national survey. Addiction. 2005;100(1):96–106. [PubMed]

McCabe SE, Teter CJ, Boyd CJ, Knight JR, Wechsler H. Nonmedical use of prescription opioids among US college students: Prevalence and correlates from a national survey. Addictive behaviors. 2005;30(4):789–805. [PubMed]

McCabe SE, Cranford JA, Boyd CJ, Teter CJ. Motives, diversion and routes of administration associated with nonmedical use of prescription opioids. Addictive behaviors. 2007;32(3):562–575. [PMC free article] [PubMed]

McMillan B, Conner M. Applying an extended version of the theory of planned behavior to illicit drug use among Students1. Journal of Applied Social Psychology. 2003;33(8):1662–1683.

Meisel MK, Goodie AS. Predicting prescription drug misuse in college students' social networks. Addictive Behaviors. 2015;45:110–112. [PubMed]

Nargiso JE, Ballard EL, Skeer MR. A systematic review of risk and protective factors associated with nonmedical use of prescription drugs among youth in the United States: A social ecological perspective. Journal of Studies on Alcohol and Drugs. 2015;76(1):5–20. [PubMed]

Norman P, Clark T, Walker G. The theory of planned behavior, descriptive norms, and the moderating role of group identification. Journal of Applied Social Psychology. 2005;35(5):1008–1029.

Ott CH, Doyle LH. An evaluation of the small group norms challenging model: Changing substance use misperceptions in five urban high schools. The High School Journal. 2005;88(3):45–55.

Pape H. Young people's overestimation of peer substance use: an exaggerated phenomenon? Addiction. 2012;107(5):878–884. [PMC free article] [PubMed]

Peterson JL, Rothenberg R, Kraft JM, Beeker C, Trotter R. Perceived condom norms and HIV risks among social and sexual networks of young African American men who have sex with men. Health Education Research. 2009;24(1):119–127. doi: 10.1093/her/cyn003. [PubMed] [CrossRef]

Rabiner DL, Anastopoulos AD, Costello EJ, Hoyle RH, McCabe SE, Swartzwelder HS. The misuse and diversion of prescribed ADHD medications by college students. Journal of Attention Disorders. 2009;13(2):144–153. doi: 10.1177/1087054708320414. [PubMed] [CrossRef]

Rhoades H, Winetrobe H, Rice E. Prescription drug misuse among homeless youth. Drug and Alcohol Dependence. 2014;138:229–233. [PMC free article] [PubMed]

Rhodes RE, Courneya KS. Investigating multiple components of attitude, subjective norm, and perceived control: An examination of the theory of planned behaviour in the exercise domain. British Journal of Social Psychology. 2003;42(1):129–146. [PubMed]

Rice E, Milburn NG, Rotheram-Borus MJ. Pro-social and problematic social network influences on HIV/AIDS risk behaviours among newly homeless youth in Los Angeles. AIDS Care. 2007;19:697–704. [PMC free article] [PubMed]

Rice E, Milburn NG, Monro W. Social networking technology, social network composition, and reductions in substance use among homeless adolescents. Prevention Science. 2011;12:80–88. [PMC free article] [PubMed]

Rice E, Barman-Adhikari A, Milburn NG, Monro W. Position-specific HIV risk in a large network of homeless youths. American Journal of Public Health. 2012;102(1):141–147. [PMC free article] [PubMed]

Schinke SP, Fang L, Cole KC. Substance use among early adolescent girls: Risk and protective factors. Journal of Adolescent Health. 2008;43(2):191–194. [PMC free article] [PubMed]

Schroder KE, Carey MP, Vanable PA. Methodological challenges in research on sexual risk behavior: I. Item content, scaling, and data analytical options. Annals of Behavioral Medicine. 2003;26(2):76–103. [PMC free article] [PubMed]

Tjur T. Coefficients of determination in logistic regression models—A new proposal: The coefficient of discrimination. The American Statistician. 2009;63(4):366–372.

Tucker JS, Hu J, Golinelli D, Kennedy DP, Green HD, Wenzel SL. Social network and individual correlates of sexual risk behavior among homeless young men who have sex with men. Journal of Adolescent Health. 2012;51(4):386–392. [PMC free article] [PubMed]

Turner JC, Tajfel H. The social identity theory of intergroup behavior. Psychology of intergroup relations. 1986;7:24.

Tyler KA. Homeless youths' HIV risk behaviors with strangers: Investigating the importance of social networks. Archives of sexual behavior. 2013;42(8):1583–1591. [PMC free article] [PubMed]

Twombly EC, Holtz KD. Teens and the misuse of prescription drugs: Evidence-based recommendations to curb a growing societal problem. The journal of primary prevention. 2008;29(6):503–516. [PubMed]

Valente AM, Auerswald CL. Gender differences in sexual risk and sexually transmitted infections correlate with gender differences in social networks among San Francisco homeless youth. Journal of Adolescent Health. 2013;53(4):486–491. [PubMed]

Wang L, Fan X, Willson VL. Effects of nonnormal data on parameter estimates and fit indices for a model with latent and manifest variables: An empirical study. Structural Equation Modeling: A Multidisciplinary Journal. 1996;3(3):228–247.

Wenzel S, Holloway I, Golinelli D, Ewing B, Bowman R, Tucker J. Social networks of homeless youth in emerging adulthood. Journal of Youth and Adolescence. 2012;41(5):561–571. [PMC free article] [PubMed]

White House Office of National Drug Control Policy. Epidemic: Responding to America's prescription drug abuse crisis. 2011 Retrieved from: https://www.whitehouse.gov/sites/default/files/ondcp/policy-and-research/rx_abuse_plan.pdf.

Whitbeck LB, Hoyt DR. Nowhere to grow: Homeless and runaway adolescents and their families. Transaction Publishers; 1999.

Zullig KJ, Divin AL. The association between nonmedical prescription drug use, depressive symptoms, and suicidality among college students. Addictive Behaviors. 2012;37(8):890–899. [PubMed]

Critical Thinking

1. How do homeless youth obtain nonmedical use prescriptive drugs?

2. What are the factors that contribute to homeless youth taking nonmedical use prescriptive drugs in contrast to typical illegal street drugs?

3. Are nonmedical use prescriptive drugs more acceptable within social groups than illegal street drugs?

4. The author suggests that network norms are strongly associated with drug abuse behaviors. Why?

Internet References

Drug and Alcohol Dependence
https://www.drugandalcoholdependence.com/

National Institute on Drug Abuse
https://www.drugabuse.gov/

Principles of Drug Addiction Treatment: A Research-Based Guide
www.drugabuse.gov/PODAT/PODATIndex.html

Barman-Adhikari, Anamika, "Descriptive and Injunctive Network Norms Associated with Non Medical Use of Prescription Drugs among Homeless Youth," HHS Public Access, Addict Behavior, 2017.

Unit 2

UNIT

Prepared by: Kim Schnurbush, *California State University, Sacramento*
Mark Pullin, *Angelo State University*

Understanding How Drugs Work—Use, Dependency, and Addiction

Understanding how drugs act upon the human mind and body is a critical component to the resolution of issues concerning drug use and abuse. An understanding of basic pharmacology is requisite for informed discussion on practically every drug-related issue and controversy. One does not have to look far to find misinformed debate, much of which surrounds the basic lack of knowledge about how drugs work.

Different drugs produce different bodily effects and consequences. All psychoactive drugs influence the central nervous system, which, in turn, sits at the center of how we physiologically and psychologically interpret and react to the world around us. Some drugs, such as methamphetamine and LSD, have great, immediate influence on the nervous system, while others, such as tobacco and marijuana, illicit less-pronounced reactions. Almost all psychoactive drug effects on the body are mitigated by the dosage level of the drug taken, the manner in which it is ingested, and the physiological and emotional state of the user. For example, cocaine smoked in the form of crack versus snorted as powder produces profoundly different physical and emotional effects on the user.

Even though illegal drugs often provide the most sensational perspective from which to view drug effects, the abuse of prescription drugs is being reported as an exploding new component of the addiction problem. Currently, the nonmedical use of pain relievers such as oxycodone and hydrocodone continues at an alarming rate. This trend has been increasing steadily since 1994, and it currently competes with methamphetamine abuse as the most alarming national trend of drug abuse. The National Institute on Drug Abuse reports that, although most Americans take pain medications responsibly, approximately 54 million people (which equates to about 20 percent over the age of 12) have used pain medications for nonmedical reasons at least once.

The continued use of certain drugs and their repeated alteration of the body's biochemical structure provides one explanation for the physiological consequences of drug use. The human brain is the quintessential master pharmacist and repeatedly altering its chemical functions by drug use is risky. Doing such things may produce profound implications for becoming addicted. For example, heroin use replicates the natural brain chemical endorphin, which supports the body's biochemical defense to pain and stress. The continued use of heroin is believed to deplete natural endorphins, causing the nervous system to produce a painful physical and emotional reaction when heroin is withdrawn. Subsequently, one significant motivation for continued use is realized.

A word of caution is in order, however, when preceding through the various explanations for what drugs do and why they do it. Many people, because of an emotional and/or political relationship to the world of drugs, assert a subjective predisposition when interpreting certain drugs' effects and consequences. One person is an alcoholic while another is a social drinker. People often argue, rationalize, and explain the perceived nature of drugs' effects based upon an extremely superficial understanding of diverse pharmacological properties of different drugs. A detached and scientifically sophisticated awareness of drug pharmacology may help strengthen the platform from which to interpret the various consequences of drug use. Drug addiction results as a continuum comprised of experimentation, recreational use, regular use, and abuse. The process is influenced by a plethora of physiological, psychological, and environmental factors. Although some still argue that drug dependence is largely a matter of individual behavior—something to be chosen or rejected—most experts agree that new scientific discoveries clearly define the roots of addiction to live within molecular levels of the brain. Powerful drugs, upon repeated administration, easily compromise the brain's ability to make decisions about its best interest.

One theory used to describe specific drugs as more addictive or less addictive explains a process referred to as "reinforcement." Simply explained, reinforcement is a form of psychological conditioning that results from a drug's influence on a person's brain. Reinforcement is the term use to describe a person's behavior that expresses the uncontrollable need to repeatedly introduce the drug to the body. Powerful drugs such as the stimulant cocaine and the depressant oxycodone influence the brain's reward pathway and promote behavior in which drug seeking is recognized by the brain as actions necessary for survival. Persons addicted to drugs known to be strongly reinforcing typically report that they care more about getting the drug than about anything else—even in the face of self-destruction. Drug addiction and the rate at which it occurs must compete with certain physiological and psychological, as well as environmental, variables that are unique to individuals. A drug user with a greater number of biological markers known to be associated with drug addiction, such as mental illness, alcoholism, and poor physical health, may encourage drug dependency sooner than a person with fewer biological markers. Similarly, a person's positive environmental associations, or "natural reinforcers," such as a strong family structure and healthy personal and professional relationships may not only make experimentation unappealing, it may delay a user's developing drug addiction. Subsequently, one's liability for drug addiction is closely associated with genetics, environment, and the use of psychoactive drugs. Understanding the concept of addiction requires an awareness of these factors. For many people, drug addiction and the reasons that contribute to it are murky concepts.

The articles in this unit illustrate some of the current research and viewpoints on the ways that drugs act upon the human body. New science is suggesting that the new era has begun relative to understanding drugs and their pharmacological influence on the human body. This new science is critical to understanding the assorted consequences of drug use and abuse. Science has taken us closer to understanding that acute drug use changes brain function profoundly and that these changes may remain with the user long after the drug has left the system. New research investigating the liabilities produced by adolescents smoking tobacco suggests that even small amounts produce a remarkable susceptibility for addiction. Subsequently, many new issues have emerged for drug and health-related public policy. Increasingly, drug abuse competes with other social maladies as public enemy number one. Further, the need for a combined biological, behavioral, and social response to this problem becomes more evident. Many health-care professionals and health-care educators, in addition to those from other diverse backgrounds, argue that research dollars spent on drug abuse and addiction should approach that spent on heart disease, cancer, and AIDS. The articles in this unit provide examples of how some new discoveries have influenced our thinking about addiction. They also provide examples of how, even in light of new knowledge, breaking addictions is so very hard to do.

Article   Prepared by: Kim Schnurbush, *California State University, Sacramento*
Mark Pullin, *Angelo State University*

Case Report: The Wide and Unpredictable Scope of Synthetic Cannabinoids Toxicity

JOSE ORSINI, ET AL.

Learning Outcomes

After reading this article, you will be able to:

- Discuss the dangers of synthetic cannabinoids.

- Understand the process as to how synthetic cannabinoids are developed and why they are becoming addictive.

- Discuss the medically issues associated with using synthetic cannabinoids.

Drug use and abuse continue to be a large public health concern worldwide. Over the past decade, novel or atypical drugs have emerged and become increasingly popular. In the recent past, compounds similar to tetrahydrocannabinoid (THC), the active ingredient of marijuana, have been synthetically produced and offered commercially as legal substances. Since the initial communications of their abuse in 2008, few case reports have been published illustrating the misuse of these substances with signs and symptoms of intoxication. Even though synthetic cannabinoids have been restricted, they are still readily available across USA and their use has been dramatically increasing, with a concomitant increment in reports to poison control centers and emergency department (E.D) visits. We describe a case of acute hypoxemic/hypercapmc respiratory failure as a consequence of acute congestive heart failure (CHF) developed from myocardial stunning resulting from a non-ST-segment elevation myocardial infarction (MI) following the consumption of synthetic cannabinoids.

I. Introduction

Synthetic cannabinoids are a heterogeneous group of compounds developed to investigate possible therapeutic effects and to study endocannabinoid receptor systems. Clandestine laboratories subsequently utilized published data to developed synthetic cannabinoids variations marketed as designer drugs, which have been emerging as popular recreational drugs due to their easy accessibility and undetectability on standard toxicology screens. First sold under the name "Spice," the drug has evolved into many different names (e.g., Black Diamond, Mojo, Spice Gold, Aroma, Dream, Genie, and Silver). K2 or "Spice" is made of a C8 homolog of the non-classical cannabinoid CP-47, 497, 497-C8 (cannabicyclohexanol) and a cannabimimetic aminoalkylindole called JWH-018 [1]. They were distributed and sold legally in local smoke shops and gas stations in the USA until November 2010, when they were classified by the USA Drug Enforcement Agency (DEA) as Schedule-I controlled substances. Unlike partial agonist THC molecules, synthetic cannabinoids act as full nonselective agonists of the CB-1 and CB-2 receptors, making the substance 2–100 times more potent and longer lasting than THC [2]. They achieve euphoric effects by inhibiting glutamate synthesis and neurotransmission in the hippocampus [3].

Case reports of synthetic cannabinoids abuse have described patients presenting with alterations in mood and perception [4], xerostomia [5], and tachycardia [6]. Less common signs of intoxication included hypertension, agitation, paranoia, and hypokalemia [6]. There have been few cases describing more drastic features of intoxication such as ST-segment elevation MI [7], recurrent seizures [8], acute kidney injury [9], self-mutilation [10], serotonin syndrome [11], and cardiac arrest [12]. It has been estimated that more than 11,000 patients per year consult ED services in USA because of the side effects of synthetic cannabinoids [13]. As of May 2015, more than 40 deaths related to the use and abuse of synthetic cannabinoids have been reported in the United States [14].

We describe a patient with acute hypoxemic/hypercapnic respiratory failure resulting from acute CHF developed from myocardial stunning as a consequence of a non-ST-segment elevation MI after consumption of synthetic cannabinoids.

2. Case Report

A 41-year-old Hispanic male was brought to our hospital ED after having a witnessed tonic–clonic seizure on the street. His past medical history was significant for polysubstance abuse (heroin, cocaine, benzodiazepines, and methadone) and chronic liver disease (hepatitis C). He had history of multiple admissions to our institution for opiates detoxification. On arrival to ED, his vital signs were as follows: blood pressure of 98/63 mmHg, heart rate of 118 beats/minute, respiratory rate of 48 breaths/minute, temperature of 37.5°C, and an oxygen saturation of 90 percent while receiving oxygen by a non-rebreather mask. Emergency medical services (EMS) staffing reported finding a bag of K2 at the scene. Physical examination was remarkable for bilateral rales on lung auscultation. Old needle puncture areas were found over his arms and legs, without erythema. Pupils were equal with positive light reflex. While in ED, he was combative and developed another tonic–clonic seizure episode. Endotracheal intubation was performed and he was placed on mechanical ventilation. Remarkable laboratory findings included a white blood cell (WBC) count of 29.5 k/mm^3 (4.8–10.8), a bicarbonate level of 15 mmol/L (24–31), a lactic acid level of 4.4 mmol/L (0.5–2.2), and a urine toxicology screen positive for opiates, benzodiazepines, and methadone. Creatine kinase (CK) level was 5,590 U/L (25–215), and troponins were mildly elevated at 1.45 ng/mL (<0.1). Creatinine, coagulation, and liver function profiles were within normal limits. Arterial blood gas (ABG) while on mechanical ventilation and receiving FIO$_2$ of 100 percent showed a pH of 7.14 (7.35–7.45), a pCO$_2$ level of 79 mmHg (34–45), and a paO$_2$ level of 77 mmHg (80–100). Initial chest X-ray (CXR) showed bilateral infiltrates. Electrocardiogram (ECG) showed sinus tachycardia without ST-segment or T-wave abnormalities.

He was admitted to the intensive care unit (ICU) with the diagnosis of acute hypoxemic/hypercapnic respiratory failure presumptively secondary to drug overdose. He required propofol, fentanyl, and midazolam to achieve adequate sedation and ventilatory synchrony. Empiric intravenous antimicrobial therapy consisting of piperacillin/tazobactam (3.375 g every sixhours) was initiated for the possibility of aspiration

pneumonitis. While in ICU, CK and troponin levels continued to increase to 18,589 U/L and 8.76 ng/mL, respectively. A new transthoracic echocardiogram (TTE) showed markedly decreased left ventricular ejection fraction of 30 percent (55–65), with severe global and segmental hypokinesis and no vegetations or valvular dysfunction. Given the echocardiographic and CXR findings as well as the elevated troponin levels, therapy for acute congestive heart failure probably secondary to a non-ST-segment elevation MI was initiated with low-molecular weight heparin, β-blockers, aspirin, clopidogrel, diuretics, statins, and angiotensin-converting enzyme (ACE) inhibitors. Repeated CXR after 24 hours showed near resolution of bilateral infiltrates. Blood, urine, and respiratory cultures were negative, and antimicrobials were discontinued. He was extubated on day 4 of ICU admission but required reintubation because of severe agitation and hypoxemia, which were thought to be a clinical component of a possible withdrawal syndrome. His ICU course was further complicated by fevers, new bilateral infiltrates on CXR, and persistently elevated FIO$_2$ requirements. TTE was repeated, showing a remarkable improvement of left ventricular ejection fraction (63 percent), with a complete resolution of wall motion abnormalities. He was successfully extubated on day 11 of ICU admission, after being treated for acute respiratory distress syndrome (ARDS) secondary to ventilator-associated pneumonia.

3. Discussion

It is known that marijuana has pathophysiological effects on the cardiovascular system, which are mediated by stimulation of the sympathetic nervous system through release of norepinephrine and by parasympathetic blockade [15]. Marijuana consumption increases oxygen demands on the myocardium and also leads to an increase in carboxyhemoglobin levels, which results in decreased oxygen-carrying capacity [16, 17]. Interference with the integrity of peripheral vascular response has been postulated to be one of the mechanisms for cardiac events during cannabis smoking [14]. THC may also be associated with vascular inflammation and increased platelet activation, which is a potential mechanism of plaque rupture [18]. A few cases of MI associated with marijuana use have been reported in the literature [19–22]. Myocardial ischemia has also been reported with the use of synthetic cannabinoids [7, 23, 24]. In a large epidemiological study, THC and derivatives were reported to increase the risk of MI by 4.8 times in the first hour after use [25]. Given the presence of other substances in the urine toxicology screen which have been linked to acute coronary events, it was challenging to categorize the etiology of our patient's cardiovascular findings. Information about heroin-related MI is limited and its mechanisms are not well established. It has been postulated that heroin might have a direct toxic effect on the coronary arteries leading to coronary occlusion, either by provoking a local coronary spasm or inflammation [26]. The hypothesis of heroin-related myocardial injury might include rhabdomyolysis with cardiac involvement, hypoxia, acidosis, and vasoconstrictive substances released by muscle necrosis [27]. This hypothesis may explain the findings of rhabdomyolysis, hypoxia, and acidosis on the patient described in this report. However, the fact that our patient's pupils were not constricted and a bag of K2 was found at the scene makes heroin a less likely etiology for this patient's cardiac abnormalities. Although cases of myocardial ischemia possibly related to methadone use have been reported [28, 29], it has been proposed that methadone possesses cardioprotective properties that include reduction in infarct size in patients with myocardial infarction [30]. Cocaine was not found in the urine toxicology screen in our patient, which makes that substance an extremely unlikely cause for this patient's cardiovascular derangements.

To the best of our knowledge, this is the first report of synthetic cannabinoid-induced non-ST-segment elevation MI resulting in myocardial stunning and acute CHF in a patient without proven history of coronary artery disease. We hypothesized that our patient likely had transient myocardial ischemia resulting in ventricular stunning that might had led to acute CHF. This hypothesis is supported by the fact that subsequent troponin levels normalized within 48 hours and repeated TTE showed complete resolution of wall motion abnormalities with normal left ventricular ejection fraction. Patients with non-ST-segment elevation MI may present with heterogeneous conditions and, therefore, they may have varying degrees of reduction of coronary blood flow but without complete coronary occlusion in combination with distal embolization of thrombotic material and accompanying coronary spasm. In addition, myocardial necrosis (expressed by troponin elevation) may occur in the absence of coronary thrombosis but in the presence of stable but diffuse coronary artery disease and clinical conditions that increase myocardial demands (type-2 MI). Although the most common ECG findings in patients with non-ST-segment elevation MI are ST-segment depression and T-wave inversion, the presence of a normal ECG does not exclude the diagnosis of non-ST-segment elevation MI. Some studies have shown that approximately 1 percent to 6 percent of patients with normal ECGs are found to have either an acute MI or unstable angina [31, 32].

Even though the main limitation of this report is the lack of biological testing of the patient's blood specimen, our subject's toxidrome fits perfectly with K2 overdose. Agitation and tachycardia are known side effects of synthetic cannabinoids [6]. Seizures have been reported in patients with synthetic cannabinoids intoxication [8, 33]. Rhabdomyolysis has been described in individuals abusing synthetic cannabinoids [9, 34]. Surely, the tonic–clonic seizures our patient developed contributed to

the elevated CK levels. It is possible that myositis secondary to an autoimmune reaction to some of the inhaled antigens contained in synthetic cannabinoids may have played a role in the etiology of our patient's rhabdomyolysis. Another potential limitation of this paper is the lack of further follow-up studies, such as coronary angiography and cardiac magnetic resonance imaging.

Our patient displayed other interesting clinical findings not commonly described in the literature. Based on a MEDLINE search and using the words "hypoxemia," "hypercapnea," "respiratory failure," and "synthetic cannabinoids," hypoxemic and/or hypercapnic respiratory failure has been infrequently reported in association with the consumption of synthetic cannabinoids. Berkowitz et al. reported a case series of patients with hypoxemic respiratory failure following the inhalation of synthetic cannabinoids [35]. Similarly, Alhadi et al. described another case of hypoxemia after the use of cannabinoids [36]. Hypoxemia related to synthetic cannabinoids use has also been outlined by Aksel et al. [37]. Diffuse military micronodular infiltrates and centrilobular nodules with tree-in-bud pattern are the most common radiologic findings in patients with respiratory failure resulting from the use of synthetic cannabinoids [35]. The effects of synthetic cannabinoids on respiratory function have not been extensively detailed in humans and likely involve multiple mechanisms. Studies in rats demonstrated a marked respiratory depression, characterized by a decrease in respiratory rate, hypoxia, hypercapnea, and acidosis. Synthetic cannabinoids effect on peripheral receptors, such as chemo- and baroreceptors, increased airway resistance in bronchi, making CB-1 receptors stimulation a possible hypothesis for synthetic cannabinoid-induced respiratory depression [38]. Chemical gases released after inhalation of these substances may also cause damage to the bronchiolar epithelium, leading to acute respiratory distress that may progress to respiratory failure. We hypothesized that the etiology of respiratory failure in our patient was most likely acute congestive heart failure triggered by synthetic cannabinoids overdose.

4. Conclusion

This case illustrates to health care workers the possible life-threatening adverse effects of synthetic cannabinoids abuse. Although there is no specific toxidrome associated with synthetic cannabinoids intoxication, clinicians should suspect their involvement in patients presenting with signs and symptoms of drug overdose. Health-care providers, especially those working in ED and critical care settings, should be on alert for drug-induced toxicities. Further research is needed to identify which contaminants are usually found in synthetic cannabinoids and to understand the interaction between different types of these substances to better predict adverse outcomes.

Conflict of Interests

The authors declare no conflict of interests regarding the publication of this article.

References

1. S. Dresen, N. Ferreirós, M. Pütz, F. Westphal, R. Zimmermann, and V. Auwärter, "Monitoring of herbal mixtures potentially containing synthetic cannabinoids as psychoactive compounds," *Journal of Mass Spectrometry*, vol. 45, no. 10, pp. 1186–1194, 2010.

2. M. S. Castaneto, D. A. Gorelick, N. A. Desrosiers, R. L. Hartman, S. Pirard, and M. A. Huestis, "Synthetic cannabinoids: epidemiology, pharmacodynamics, and clinical implications," *Drug and Alcohol Dependence*, vol. 144, pp. 12–41, 2014.

3. A. F. Hoffman, A. C. Riegel, and C. R. Lupica, "Functional localization of cannabinoid receptors and endogenous cannabinoid production in distinct neuron populations of the hippocampus," *The European Journal of Neuroscience*, vol. 18, no. 3, pp. 524–534, 2003.

4. D. Koethe, C. W. Gerth, M. A. Neatby et al., "Disturbances of visual information processing in early states of psychosis and experimental delta-9-tetrahydrocannabinol altered states of consciousness," *Schizophrenia Research*, vol. 88, no. 1–3, pp. 142–150, 2006.

5. D. M. Berlach, Y. Shir, and M. A. Ware, "Experience with the synthetic cannabinoid nabilone in chronic noncancer pain," *Pain Medicine*, vol. 7, no. 1, pp. 25–29, 2006.

6. M. Hermanns-Clausen, S. Kneisel, B. Szabo, and V. Auwärter, "Acute toxicity due to the confirmed consumption of synthetic cannabinoids: clinical and laboratory findings," *Addiction*, vol. 108, no. 3, pp. 534–544, 2013.

7. A. Mir, A. Obafemi, A. Young, and C. Kane, "Myocardial infarction associated with use of the synthetic cannabinoid K2," *Pediatrics*, vol. 128, no. 6, pp. e1622–e1627, 2011.

8. M. E. Bernson-Leung, L. Y. Leung, and S. Kumar, "Synthetic cannabis and acute ischemic stroke," *Journal of Stroke and Cerebrovascular Diseases*, vol. 23, no. 5, pp. 1239–1241, 2014.

9. G. K. Bhanushali, G. Jain, H. Fatima, L. J. Leisch, and D. Thornley-Brown, "AKI associated with synthetic cannabinoids: a case series," *Clinical Journal of the American Society of Nephrology*, vol. 8, no. 4, pp. 523–526, 2013.

10. K. A. Meijer, R. R. Russo, and D. V. Adhvaryu, "Smoking synthetic marijuana leads to self-mutilation requiring bilateral amputations," *Orthopedics*, vol. 37, no. 4, pp. e391–e394, 2014.

11. C. D. Rosenbaum, S. P. Carreiro, and K. M. Babu, "Here today, gone tomorrow...and back again? A review of herbal marijuana alternatives (K2, Spice), synthetic cathinones (bath salts), kratom, Salvia divinorum, methoxetamine, and piperazines," *Journal of Medical Toxicology*, vol. 8, no. 1, pp. 15–32, 2012.

12. S. Ibrahim, F. Al-Saffar, and T. Wannenburg, "A unique case of cardiac arrest following K2 abuse," *Case Reports in Cardiology*, vol. 2014, Article ID 120607, 3 pages, 2014.

13. L. Fattore and W. Fratta, "Beyond THC: the new generation of cannabinoid designer drugs," *Frontiers in Behavioral Neuroscience*, vol. 5, article 60, 2011.

14. J. Trecki, R. R. Gerona, and M. D. Schwartz, "Synthetic cannabinoid-related illnesses and deaths," *The New England Journal of Medicine*, vol. 373, no. 2, pp. 103–107, 2015.

15. A. Gash, J. S. Karliner, D. Janowsky, and C. R. Lake, "Effects of smoking marihuana on left ventricular performance and plasma norepinephrine: studies in normal men," *Annals of Internal Medicine*, vol. 89, no. 4, pp. 448–452, 1978.

16. J. L. Weiss, A. M. Watanabe, L. Lemberger, N. R. Tamarkin, and P. V. Cardon, "Cardiovascular effects of delta-9-tetrahydrocannabinol in man," *Clinical Pharmacology & Therapeutics*, vol. 13, no. 5, pp. 671–684, 1972.

17. P. F. Renault, C. R. Schuster, R. Heinrich, and D. X. Freeman, "Marihuana: standardized smoke administration and dose effect curves on heart rate in humans," *Science*, vol. 174, no. 4009, pp. 589–591, 1971.

18. M. A. Mittleman, M. Maclure, J. B. Sherwood et al., "Triggering of acute myocardial infarction onset by episodes of anger. Determinants of myocardial infarction onset study investigators," *Circulation*, vol. 92, no. 7, pp. 1720–1725, 1995.

19. G. Kocabay, M. Yildiz, N. E. Duran, and M. Ozkan, "Acute inferior myocardial infarction due to cannabis smoking in a young man," *Journal of Cardiovascular Medicine*, vol. 10, no. 9, pp. 669–670, 2009.

20. L. Bachs and H. Morland, "Acute cardiovascular fatalities following cannabis use," *Forensic Science International*, vol. 124, no. 2–3, pp. 200–203, 2001.

21. Y. Velibey, S. Sahin, O. Tanik, M. Keskin, O. Bolca, and M. Eren, "Acute myocardial infarction due to marijuana smoking in a young man: guilty should not be underestimated," *American Journal of Emergency Medicine*, vol. 33, no. 8, pp. 1114.e1–1114.e3, 2015.

22. C. J. Hodcroft, M. C. Rossiter, and A. N. Buch, "Cannabis-associated myocardial infarction in a young man with normal coronary arteries," *Journal of Emergency Medicine*, vol. 47, no. 3, pp. 277–281, 2014.

23. R. G. McKeever, D. Vearrier, D. Jacobs, G. LaSala, J. Okaneku, and M. I. Greenberg, "K2-not the spice of life; synthetic cannabinoids and ST elevation myocardial infarction: a case report," *Journal of Medical Toxicology*, vol. 11, no. 1, pp. 129–131, 2015.

24. B. C. Clark, J. Georgekutty, and C. I. Berul, "Myocardial ischemia secondary to synthetic cannabinoid (K2) use in pediatric patients," *The Journal of Pediatrics*, vol. 167, no. 3, pp. 757.e1–761.e1, 2015.

25. M. A. Mittleman, R. A. Lewis, M. Maclure, J. B. Sherwood, and J. E. Muller, "Triggering myocardial infarction by marijuana," *Circulation*, vol. 103, no. 23, pp. 2805–2809, 2001.

26. J. Sztajzel, H. Karpuz, and W. Rutishauser, "Heroin abuse and myocardial infarction," *International Journal of Cardiology*, vol. 47, no. 2, pp. 180–182, 1994.

27. R. Melandri, I. De Tommaso, I. Zele et al., "Myocardial involvement in rhabdomyolysis caused by acute heroin intoxication," *Recenti Progressi in Medicina*, vol. 82, no. 6, pp. 324–327, 1991.

28. D. G. Ioseliani, S. P. Semitko, D. G. Gromov et al., "Development of transmural myocardial infarction in young persons with intact coronary arteries during methadone use for the treatment of heroine addiction," *Kardiologiia*, vol. 44, no. 10, pp. 107–112, 2004.

29. M. Backmund, K. Meyer, W. Zwehl, O. Nagengast, and
D. Eichenlaub, "Myocardial infarction associated with
methadone and/or dihydrocodeine," *European Addiction
Research*, vol. 7, no. 1, pp. 37–39, 2001.

30. E. R. Gross, A. K. Hsu, and G. J. Gross, "Acute methadone
treatment reduces myocardial infarct size via the δ-opioid
receptor in rats during reperfusion," *Anesthesia and Analgesia*,
vol. 109, no. 5, pp. 1395–1402, 2009.

31. G. W. Rouan, T. H. Lee, E. F. Cook, D. A. Brand, M. C.
Weisberg, and L. Goldman, "Clinical characteristics and
outcome of acute myocardial infarction in patients with initially
normal or nonspecific electrocardiograms (a report from the
Multicenter Chest Pain Study)," *The American Journal of
Cardiology*, vol. 64, no. 18, pp. 1087–1092, 1989.

32. B. D. McCarthy, J. B. Wong, and H. P. Selker, "Detecting acute
cardiac ischemia in the emergency department: a review of the
literature," *Journal of General Internal Medicine*, vol. 5, no. 4,
pp. 365–373, 1990.

33. C. R. Harris and A. Brown, "Synthetic cannabinoid
intoxication: a case series and review," *Journal of Emergency
Medicine*, vol. 44, no. 2, pp. 360–366, 2013.

34. B. Sweeney, S. Talebi, D. Toro, et al., "Hyperthermia and
severe rhabdomyolysis from synthetic cannabinoids," *American
Journal of Emergency Medicine*, 2015.

35. E. A. Berkowitz, T. S. Henry, S. Veeraraghavan, G. W. Staton,
and A. A. Gal, "Pulmonary effects of synthetic marijuana:
chest radiography and CT findings," *American Journal of
Roentgenology*, vol. 204, no. 4, pp. 750–757, 2015.

36. S. Alhadi, A. Tiwari, R. Vohra, R. Gerona, J. Acharya,
and K. Bilello, "High times, low sats: diffuse pulmonary
infiltrates associated with chronic synthetic cannabinoid use,"
Journal of Medical Toxicology, vol. 9, no. 2, pp. 199–206,
2013.

37. G. Aksel, Ö. Güneysel, T. Tasyürek, E. Kozan, and S. E. Çevik,
"Intravenous lipid emulsion therapy for acute synthetic
cannabinoid intoxication: clinical experience in four cases,"
Case Reports in Emergency Medicine, vol. 2015, Article ID
180921, 5 pages, 2015.

38. K. Schmid, N. Niederhoffer, and B. Szabo, "Analysis
of the respiratory effects of cannabinoids in rats,"
Naunyn-Schmiedeberg's Archives of Pharmacology, vol. 368,
no. 4, pp. 301–308, 2003.

Critical Thinking

1. Discuss the challenges facing drug enforcement professionals to control synthetic cannabinoids.

2. What are some of the attractive attributes of synthetic drugs that make them appealing?

3. Should synthetic cannabinoids be illegal or are they simply a recreational drug?

Internet References

American Association of Poison Control Centers
http://www.aapcc.org/alerts/synthetic-cannabinoids/

American Association of Poison Control Centers Press Release
http://www.aapcc.org/press/43/

Spice Addiction Support
http://spiceaddictionsupport.org/what-is-spice/

Jose Orsini, Christa Blaak, Eric Tam, et al., "The Wide and Unpredictable Scope of Synthetic Cannabinoids Toxicity," *Case Reports in Critical Care*, vol. 2015, Article ID 542490,
5 pages, 2015. doi:10.1155/2015/542490. Reprinted under Creative Commons Attribution License (CC-BY 4.0). https://creativecommons.org/licenses/by/4.0/legalcode

Article

Prepared by: Kim Schnurbush, *California State University, Sacramento*
Mark Pullin, *Angelo State University*

Understanding Drug Use and Addiction

NATIONAL INSTITUTE ON DRUG ABUSE

Learning Outcomes

After reading this article, you will be able to:

- Understand how and why people become addicted to drugs.
- Discuss the addiction process and the complexity of the disease.
- Understand the brain processes from drug addiction and positive recovery efforts.

Many people don't understand why or how other people become addicted to drugs. They may mistakenly think that those who use drugs lack moral principles or willpower and that they could stop their drug use simply by choosing to. In reality, drug addiction is a complex disease, and quitting usually takes more than good intentions or a strong will. Drugs change the brain in ways that make quitting hard, even for those who want to. Fortunately, researchers know more than ever about how drugs affect the brain and have found treatments that can help people recover from drug addiction and lead productive lives.

What Is Drug Addiction?

Addiction is a chronic disease characterized by drug seeking and use that is compulsive, or difficult to control, despite harmful consequences. The initial decision to take drugs is voluntary for most people, but repeated drug use can lead to brain changes that challenge an addicted person's self-control and interfere with their ability to resist intense urges to take drugs. These brain changes can be persistent, which is why drug addiction is considered a "relapsing" disease—people in recovery from drug use disorders are at increased risk for returning to drug use even after years of not taking the drug.

It's common for a person to relapse, but relapse doesn't mean that treatment doesn't work. As with other chronic health conditions, treatment should be ongoing and should be adjusted based on how the patient responds. Treatment plans need to be reviewed often and modified to fit the patient's changing needs.

What Happens to the Brain when a Person Takes Drugs?

Most drugs affect the brain's "reward circuit" by flooding it with the chemical messenger dopamine. This reward system controls the body's ability to feel pleasure and motivates a person to repeat behaviors needed to thrive, such as eating and spending time with loved ones. This overstimulation of the reward circuit causes the intensely pleasurable "high" that can lead people to take a drug again and again.

As a person continues to use drugs, the brain adjusts to the excess dopamine by making less of it and/or reducing the ability of cells in the reward circuit to respond to it. This reduces the high that the person feels compared to the high they felt when first taking the drug—an effect known as tolerance. They might take more of the drug, trying to achieve the same dopamine high. It can also cause them to get less pleasure from other things they once enjoyed, like food or social activities.

Long-term use also causes changes in other brain chemical systems and circuits as well, affecting functions that include:

- learning
- judgment
- decision-making
- stress
- memory
- behavior

Despite being aware of these harmful outcomes, many people who use drugs continue to take them, which is the nature of addiction.

Why Do Some People Become Addicted to Drugs While Others Don't?

No one factor can predict if a person will become addicted to drugs. A combination of factors influences risk for addiction. The more risk factors a person has, the greater the chance that taking drugs can lead to addiction. For example:

- **Biology.** The genes that people are born with account for about half of a person's risk for addiction. Gender, ethnicity, and the presence of other mental disorders may also influence risk for drug use and addiction.

- **Environment.** A person's environment includes many different influences, from family and friends to economic status and general quality of life. Factors, such as peer pressure, physical and sexual abuse, early exposure to drugs, stress, and parental guidance, can greatly affect a person's likelihood of drug use and addiction.

- **Development.** Genetic and environmental factors interact with critical developmental stages in a person's life to affect addiction risk. Although taking drugs at any age can lead to addiction, the earlier that drug use begins, the more likely it will progress to addiction. This is particularly problematic for teens. Because areas in their brains that control decision-making, judgment, and self-control are still developing, teens may be especially prone to risky behaviors, including trying drugs.

Can Drug Addiction be Cured or Prevented?

As with most other chronic diseases, such as diabetes, asthma, or heart disease, treatment for drug addiction generally isn't a cure. However, addiction is treatable and can be successfully managed. People who are recovering from an addiction will be at risk for relapse for years and possibly for their whole lives. Research shows that combining addiction treatment medicines with behavioral therapy ensures the best chance of success for most patients. Treatment approaches tailored to each patient's drug use patterns and any co-occurring medical, mental, and social problems can lead to continued recovery.

More good news is that drug use and addiction are preventable. Results from NIDA-funded research have shown that prevention programs involving families, schools, communities, and the media are effective for preventing or reducing drug use and addiction. Although personal events and cultural factors affect drug use trends, when young people view drug use as harmful, they tend to decrease their drug taking. Therefore,

education and outreach are key in helping people understand the possible risks of drug use. Teachers, parents, and health-care providers have crucial roles in educating young people and preventing drug use and addiction.

Points to Remember

- Drug addiction is a chronic disease characterized by drug seeking and use that is compulsive, or difficult to control, despite harmful consequences.
- Brain changes that occur over time with drug use challenge an addicted person's self-control and interfere with their ability to resist intense urges to take drugs. This is why drug addiction is also a relapsing disease.
- Relapse is the return to drug use after an attempt to stop. Relapse indicates the need for more or different treatment.
- Most drugs affect the brain's reward circuit by flooding it with the chemical messenger dopamine. This overstimulation of the reward circuit causes the intensely pleasurable "high" that leads people to take a drug again and again.
- Over time, the brain adjusts to the excess dopamine, which reduces the high that the person feels compared to the high they felt when first taking the drug—an effect known as tolerance. They might take more of the drug, trying to achieve the same dopamine high.
- No single factor can predict whether a person will become addicted to drugs. A combination of genetic, environmental, and developmental factors influences risk for addiction. The more risk factors a person has, the greater the chance that taking drugs can lead to addiction.
- Drug addiction is treatable and can be successfully managed.
- More good news is that drug use and addiction are preventable. Teachers, parents, and health-care providers have crucial roles in educating young people and preventing drug use and addiction.

Critical Thinking

1. Discuss why some become addicted to drugs and some do not.

2. Can drug addiction be cured or simply maintained?

3. Discuss some prevention methods that are effective in deterring drug addiction.

Internet References

HelpGuide—Overcoming Drug Addiction
http://www.helpguide.org/articles/addiction/overcoming-drug-addiction.htm

National Institute on Drug Abuse
www.nida.nih.gov

Substance Abuse and Mental Health Services Administration
www.samhsa.gov

"Understanding Drug Use and Addiction" National Institute on Drug Abuse Research Report, National Institutes on Drug Abuse, U.S. Department of Health and Human Services, August 2016.

Article

Prepared by: Kim Schnurbush, *California State University, Sacramento*
Mark Pullin, *Angelo State University*

What's The Buzz? Treating Prescription Drug Abuse in Youth

Shelley Steenrod

Learning Outcomes

After reading this article, you will be able to:

- Discuss the attraction of youth to prescription drugs.
- Discuss the variations of popular prescription drugs and their effects on users.
- Understand physiological and psychological aspects that lead to youth consuming prescription drugs and the consequences of such actions.

Mariela is a 16-year-old Caucasian high school student. Prior to her prescription drug abuse, she had above average grades, positive family relationships, and a promising gymnastics career. A year ago, she found a prescription bottle of OxyContin in her family's medicine cabinet and began to experiment with it, loving its relaxing and euphoric effect. Mariela's mother, who uses the medication for chronic lower back pain, failed to notice missing pills for several months, at which point she began to lock the medication up.

Unfortunately, it did not take long for Mariela to figure out how to buy the pills at school, although it was very costly at $30 to $50 per Oxy. As Mariela's dependence grew, her supplier suggested she crush it, to remove the time release coating, and snort it for a more powerful effect. Shortly thereafter, a more addicted Mariela became unable to afford the hefty street price of OxyContin and began to explore alternatives. Heroin, a comparable opiate, sells for only $5 a bag, and Mariela began to snort and then inject this more affordable drug.

Mariela is now in desperate straits. She uses heroin two to three times per day, alone, both for pleasure and to stave off withdrawal symptoms. She stopped attending gymnastic events several months ago, is failing all of her classes, lacks interest in school, and is forgetful. Her friend group has also shifted to other drug users. Mariela has tried to stop using on her own, but quickly returns to heroin or OxyContin as cravings arise or when "triggered" by stressful life events, school pressure, or friends. Mariela's parents, unaware of the seriousness of the situation, realize that something is not right and turn to you, a social worker, for help.

Mariela's story is far from unique. Prescription drug abuse, described by the National Institute on Drug Abuse (NIDA) as "the intentional use of a medication without a prescription; in a way other than as prescribed; or for the experience or feeling it causes" (National Institute on Drug Abuse, 2011), is a serious and growing problem in the United States. The National Survey on Drug Use and Health (NSDUH) reported that nearly 3 percent (or seven million) used prescription medications for non-medical purposes (Substance Abuse and Mental Health Services Administration, 2011).

Myths abound regarding the safety of prescription drugs. Many people believe they are safer than illicit drugs because they were originally prescribed by a doctor. In addition, pharmaceutical treatments of ADHD and chronic pain have flooded the United States, making prescription drugs widely available and increasing the perception that they are inherently safe.

People take prescription drugs for a wide range of reasons. Some take more of a drug than originally prescribed, desiring a more potent impact. Others take medicines, originally prescribed to family or friends, because their own medical symptoms are untreated (a scenario particularly true for individuals without insurance). The unique effect of each drug can also be a big motivator. For example, opioid prescription drugs offer powerful pain relief, in addition to feelings of euphoria and pleasure. Stimulant drugs, such as those prescribed for attention deficit disorder, are often shared between college students for increased focus and energy.

However, prescription drug abuse is accompanied by significant health risks. Many prescription drugs are highly addictive and need to be managed by the prescribing physician to avoid the development of a tolerance or dependence. Alone, or in combination with other drugs and alcohol, illegal use of prescription drugs can also lead to overdose or death. Prescription drug abuse can also be a gateway to illegal street drugs. For example, Mariela switched from OxyContin to heroin, which is cheaper and more potent, but carries an increased risk for blood borne infections, such as HIV, Hepatitis C, and other communicable diseases.

Mariela is also taking risks with her brain. Magnetic resonance imaging (MRI) has firmly established that drug use can permanently change how the brain functions. Mood altering drugs activate the reward, or limbic, system, a crucial area responsible for motivation, reward, and behavior. Also called the pleasure center, this part of the brain makes us feel good when we engage in behaviors that are necessary for survival, such as eating, drinking, and sex. The reward pathway is also responsible for making sure we repeat the same behavior whenever possible by connecting to other areas in the brain that control memory and behavior.

When the limbic system is activated by mood altering drugs, the brain also interprets these chemicals as necessary for survival, thereby sending out increasingly dire cravings for more (and more) of the same. When a user finally succumbs to these intense cravings, the pathway is further reinforced for repeated drug use. Fortunately, research indicates that, over time, some brain function can be repaired, highlighting the importance of appropriate treatment for those with substance use disorders.

There are many important roles for social workers to fill in the identification and treatment of prescription drug addiction and other substance-related disorders. Social workers who work with youth can expect to see an increasing number of adolescents with prescription drug addictions. Because the Patient Protection and Affordable Care Act of 2010 encourages integration between behavioral health care (mental health and substance abuse services) and primary health care, social workers will be called upon to screen and assess adolescents for substance abuse and to provide generalist social work services, including education, brokering, advocacy, and case management.

Screening

The CRAFFT (Knight, Serritt, Harris, & Chang, 2002; Center for Adolescent Substance Abuse Research, n.d.) is a standard screening instrument that quickly assesses for adolescent drug use. It is a face-to-face screen in which a clinician asks three "opening" questions: During the past 12 months, did you:

1. Drink any alcohol?
2. Smoke any marijuana or hashish?
3. Use anything else to get high?

An adolescent who answers "yes" to any of these questions is then asked the following six questions:

C: Have you ever ridden in a CAR driven by someone (including yourself) who was "high" or had been using alcohol or drugs?

R: Do you ever use alcohol or drugs to RELAX, feel better about yourself, or fit in?

A: Do you ever use alcohol or drugs while you are by yourself, or ALONE?

F: Do you ever FORGET things you did while using alcohol or drugs?

F: Do your family or FRIENDS ever tell you that you should cut down on your drinking or drug use?

T: Have you ever gotten into TROUBLE while you were using alcohol or drugs?

The CRAFFT is scored by awarding each affirmative answer one point. A score of zero indicates no risk for a substance related disorder. A score of one point indicates that the client could benefit from education about the risks of drug use and advice on cutting down, or eliminating use. A score of two or greater indicates the need for a more thorough assessment for substance abuse.

Mariela answered five out of six questions affirmatively, strongly indicating the need for further assessment. For example, she reported that she had driven a car while high, used drugs to relax, used drugs alone, forgotten things she had done while high, and been told by family and friends to cut down on her drug use.

Assessment

Substance abuse assessments are appropriate for youth with a "positive" screening result. Assessments allow for deeper examinations of the type, amount, method, and frequency of drug use along with a thorough analysis of the biopsychosocial consequences of such use.

Social workers use the information gleaned from an assessment to formulate a diagnosis and treatment plan. The recently released DSM-5 characterizes substance use disorders as "a cluster of cognitive, behavioral and psychological symptoms indicating that the individual continues using the substance despite significant substance-related problems" (American Psychological Association, 2013, p. 483). Each disorder is specified according to the substance used and may include: alcohol, cannabis, hallucinogens, inhalants, opioids, sedatives, hypnotics, stimulants, anxiolytics (anti-anxiety medications), and other substances.

It is important to note that the DSM-5 does not offer a specific category for prescription drug abuse. Instead, social workers should look to the category of drug that a client is using.

For example, Mariela's drug(s) of choice, first OxyContin and then heroin, are both opioids, so we examine her symptoms according to the 11 diagnostic criteria for Opioid Use Disorder (see DSM-5, Opioid Use Disorder). In Mariela's case, she admits to (1) taking larger amounts of opioids over time; (2) making several unsuccessful efforts to cut down; (3) spending a significant amount of time getting, using, and recovering from opioid use; (4) very strong cravings; (5) failure to meet her academic obligations; (6) regular use despite problems with friends and family; (7) giving up important activities (gymnastics); (8) using in dangerous situations; (9) a growing tolerance; and (10) the experience of withdrawal symptoms between episodes of use.

Mariela's OxyContin and heroin use clearly indicate an opioid use disorder. Further, because she has nine of 11 symptoms, the DSM-5 specifies her disorder as severe.

Next, we look to the biopsychosocial consequences of Mariela's drug use and other elements that are relevant to treatment planning. The American Society of Addiction Medicine (ASAM) recommends consideration of the following dimensions:

1. Acute intoxication and/or withdrawal potential
2. Biomedical conditions and complications
3. Emotional, behavioral or cognitive conditions and complications (dangerousness/lethality, interference with addiction recovery efforts, social functioning, ability for self-care, course of illness)
4. Readiness to change
5. Relapse, continued use, or continued problem potential
6. Recovery environment

The assessment reveals that Mariela is at moderate to severe risk of withdrawal as evidenced by intense cravings and increased tolerance. She is also sharing needles, putting her at risk of communicable, blood borne diseases, including HIV and Hepatitis C. Mariela does not have a history of mental health, behavioral, or cognitive problems. However, she is missing important developmental milestones of adolescence that will ultimately have an impact on her social functioning. The assessment further indicates that Mariela is highly unlikely to stop using drugs in her current environment. She is easily triggered for use, and her parents have been naïvely unaware of the extent of her drug use. She requires intensive motivating strategies and supervision to promote recovery.

Treatment Planning and Levels of Care

The ASAM criteria (Mee-Lee, 2013) also assist clinicians in matching client needs with the best level of care and appropriate treatment resources. To this end, the ASAM criteria describe and delineate the following eight levels of care:

1. Early intervention
2. Outpatient treatment
3. Intensive outpatient treatment
4. Partial hospitalization
5. Clinically managed low-intensity residential treatment
6. Clinically managed medium-intensity residential treatment
7. Medically monitored high-intensity residential/inpatient treatment
8. Medically managed intensive inpatient treatment (see Table 1.)

Descriptions of each level of care are beyond the scope of this article, but it is helpful to imagine the levels of care along a continuum, with early intervention as the least intensive and medically managed intensive inpatient treatment (hospital-based care) as the most intensive. Mariela's status on each biopsychosocial dimension suggests that she initially needs Medically Monitored High-Intensity Residential/Inpatient Treatment to manage her withdrawal symptoms and biomedical needs, but can then likely "step-down" into a lower level of residential treatment to address her ambivalence toward change, likelihood of relapse, and need for a structured and motivational recovery environment.

In addition to screening, assessment and treatment planning, there are several additional social work roles that must be fulfilled to help Mariela and her family. These include educator, broker, advocate, and case manager.

Educator

Mariela and her parents require basic information on addiction and recovery. The entire family will need to understand that addiction is a disease—not a personal failing—which requires life-long management. The first phase of treatment will address Mariela's acute needs, and the second phase of treatment will address the chronicity of addiction.

Both Mariela and her parents will need help understanding that ongoing disease management will require significant lifestyle changes and treatment. An overview of 12-step and other support groups is also important.

Mariela and her family also need education on the treatment options that are available to them. Although the ASAM criteria, an industry standard for treatment and insurance providers, recommend residential care for Mariela, it is always important that clients and social workers collaborate in treatment planning. To this end, Mariela and her family may want to consider medically-assisted therapies in conjunction with other

Table 1 Summary of ASAM Placement Criteria for Adolescents

	Early Intervention	Outpatient	Intensive Outpatient	Partial Hospitalization	Low Intensity Residential	Medium Intensity Residential	High Intensity Residential Inpatient	Hospital Based Treatment
Withdrawal Potential	None	None	Minimal	Mild	Mild-Moderate	Moderate	Severe but manageable	Severe, requires medical management
Biomedical Conditions	None or stable	None or stable	None or stable	None or stable	None or stable	Monitored as needed	Needs medical monitoring	Needs 24-hr medical care
Mental Health Conditions	None or very stable	Minimal	Low to mild	Mild to moderate	Moderate	Moderate to severe	Severe	Very Severe
Readiness to Change	Willing to explore Impact of use	Contemplating change	Needs regular support to promote change	Needs daily monitoring to support change, escalating use, poor treatment engagement	Limited 24-hr supervision to support change	Needs 24-hr supervision to support change	Actively opposed to treatment or needs intensive case management	N/A
Relapse Potential	Needs education and skills	Needs limited support to pursue recovery goals	Needs close monitoring, poor relapse prevention skills	Needs daily monitoring, high risk of relapse	Unable to control use without structured program	Unable to interrupt use and avoid dangerous consequences	N/A	N/A
Recovery Environment	Risk of use is increased by family and peers	Family and environment can support recovery	Living environment impedes recovery	Emerging recovery skills, needs supervision to reinforce recovery skills	Living environment renders recovery unlikely without near-daily monitoring	Environment is dangerous to recovery	Cannot return to environment and will need lower level of care	N/A

treatments. One such medication is Suboxone, a prescription drug that effectively eliminates cravings for opiates. Another medication, recently approved by the FDA, is Vivitrol. It is administered as a monthly injection to block the pleasurable effects of opiates, rendering their use meaningless.

Broker

Mariela may need help accessing appropriate treatment services, because adolescent substance abuse treatment is in short supply across the country. Identifying adolescent-centered services can be a difficult task, but it can be made easier by having a solid understanding of the public and private treatment resources in your particular region. Many states now have toll-free numbers and websites to point clinicians, clients, and families in the right direction. In addition, insurance companies generally contract with specific treatment providers for members of their specific plans.

Advocate

Social workers give voice to client needs when clients are unable to do so themselves. It may be essential to advocate for Mariela on several levels. For example, it may be essential to advocate with her insurance company to pay for the most appropriate treatment. It may also be important to advocate with treatment programs to make Mariela a priority, as they may be inundated with other clients with similar needs.

Case Manager

Mariela also has significant case management needs. Coordinated efforts between her primary care and substance use treatment providers are required, so she is tested for HIV and Hepatitis C and receives treatment specific to those results. Mariela also needs help reengaging in high school. Recovery high schools have become more common over the last few years, and this may be a good choice to meet her academic needs in a drug-free environment, with regular support for sobriety.

Adolescent prescription drug abuse is a serious problem in the United States. Prescription drugs have become readily available to youth and appear safer than illegal drugs. As Mariela's case illustrates, prescription drugs carry substantial risks and can lead to illicit drug use, especially in the transition from OxyContin to heroin. However, with appropriate services, prescription drug abuse is a treatable disease.

Mariela spent four days in a residential treatment program for medical withdrawal from heroin. She then spent six weeks in a second residential program that provided structure and supervision, one-on-one counseling, and motivational groups. At the same time, Mariela's parents attended family psychoeducational meetings, support groups, and family therapy. When Mariela returned home, she enrolled in the recovery high school in her town, where she is back on track academically and attends 12-step groups. Mariela continues to see her original social worker, and they now work on recovery skills.

Visit the following websites for more information:

- http://www.asam.org/research-treatment/treatment
- http://www.ceasar-boston.org/CRAFFT/index.php
- http://www.drugabuse.gov/publications/topics-in-brief/prescription-drug-abuse
- http://www.ncbi.nlm.nih.gov/books/NBK64364/
- http://www.ncbi.nlm.nih.gov/books/NBK64350/

References

American Psychological Association. (2013). *Diagnostic and statistical manual of mental disorders, fifth edition.* Arlington, VA: American Psychological Association.

Center for Adolescent Substance Abuse Research. (n.d.). *The CRAFFT screening tool.* Retrieved May 15, 2014 from http://www.ceasar-boston.org/CRAFFT/index.php.

Knight, J. R., Sherritt, L., Harris, S. K., & Chang, G. (2002, June). Validity of the CRAFFT substance abuse screening test among adolescent clinic patients. *Archives of Pediatrics & Adolescent Medicine, 156:* 607–614.

Mee-Lee, D. (ed.). (2013). *The ASAM criteria: Treatment criteria for addictive, substance-related, and co-occurring condition.* Chevy Chase, MD: American Society of Addiction Medicine.

National Institute on Drug Abuse. (2011). *Topics in brief: Prescription drug abuse.* Retrieved June 06, 2014 from http://www.drugabuse.gov/publications/topics-in-brief/prescription-drug-abuse.

Substance Abuse and Mental Health Services Administration. (2011). *Results from the 2010 national survey on drug use and health: Summary of national findings, NSDUH Series H-41, HHS Publication No. (SMA) 11-4658.* Rockville, MD: Substance Abuse and Mental Health Services Administration.

Critical Thinking

1. Describe some of the pressures that might lead youth to consume prescription drugs.

2. Discuss the risk factors for youth who become addicted to prescription drugs.

3. What does the future look like insofar as drug use by youth is concerned?

Internet References

Inspirations for Youth and Families—Teen Prescriptions & Pills Addiction Rehab

http://www.inspirationsyouth.com/treatments/prescriptions-pills/

National Institute on Drug Abuse—Adolescents and Young Adults

https://www.drugabuse.gov/publications/research-reports/prescription-drugs/trends-in-prescription-drug-abuse/adolescents-young-adults

National Institute on Drug Abuse—Treating Prescription Drug Addiction

https://www.drugabuse.gov/publications/research-reports/prescription-drugs/treating-prescription-drug-addiction

Dr. Shelley Steenrod is an associate professor of social work at Salem State University in Salem, Massachusetts, where she teaches substance abuse and other social work courses. She received her Master of Social Work from Boston University and her PhD. from the Heller School at Brandeis University. Dr. Steenrod's research has focused on the use of standardized screening and assessment tools, patient placement criteria, and practice guidelines by substance abuse treatment professionals and organizations.

Prepared by: Kim Schnurbush, *California State University, Sacramento*
Mark Pullin, *Angelo State University*

Article

Sex and Gender Differences in Substance Abuse

NATIONAL INSTITUTE ON DRUG ABUSE

Learning Outcomes

After reading this article, you will be able to:

- Understand various differences of how drugs impact women versus women.

- Develop a more broad understanding of social issues that result when women abuse substances.

- Understand the broad spectrum of biological issues facing women who abuse illegal drug.

Men are more likely than women to use almost all types of illicit drugs, and illicit drug use is more likely to result in emergency department visits or overdose deaths for men than for women. "Illicit" refers to use of illegal drugs, including marijuana (according to federal law) and misuse of prescription drugs. For most age groups, men have higher rates of use or dependence on illicit drugs and alcohol than do women. However, women are just as likely as men to develop a substance use disorder. In addition, women may be more susceptible to craving and relapse, which are key phases of the addiction cycle.

> Research has shown that women often use drugs differently, respond to drugs differently, and can have unique obstacles to effective treatment as simple as not being able to find child care or being prescribed treatment that has not been adequately tested on women.

Illegal Drugs
Marijuana (Cannabis)

Similar to other addictive drugs, fewer females than males use marijuana. For females who do use marijuana, however, the effects can be different than for male users. Research indicates that marijuana impairs spatial memory in women more than it does in men, while males show a greater marijuanainduced high.

In one study specific to teenagers, male high school students who smoke marijuana reported poor family relationships and problems at school more often than female students who smoke marijuana.However, a few studies have suggested that teenage girls who use marijuana may have a higher risk of brain structural abnormalities associated with regular marijuana exposure than teenage boys.

Animal studies show that female rats are more sensitive to the rewarding, painrelieving, and activityaltering effects of marijuana's main active ingredient, delta9tetrahydrocannabinol (THC). Many of these differences have been attributed to the effects of sex hormones, although rodent research also points to the possibility that there are sex differences in the functioning of the endocannabinoid system, the system of brain signaling where THC and other cannabinoids exert their actions.

Marijuana Use Disorder

Men	Women
Similarities	
- At least one other mental health disorder	
- Low rate of seeking treatment	
Differences	
- Other substance use disorders	- Panic attacks
- Antisocial personality disorder	- Anxiety disorders
- Severity of disorder	- Disorder develops more quickly

For both sexes, marijuana use disorder is associated with an increased risk of at least one other mental health condition, such as depression or anxiety. However, men who are addicted to marijuana have higher rates of other substance use problems as well as antisocial personality disorders. By contrast, women who are addicted to marijuana have more panic attacks and anxiety disorders. Although the severity of marijuana use disorders is generally higher for men, women tend to develop these disorders more quickly after their first marijuana use. Rates of seeking treatment for marijuana use disorder are low for both sexes.

Stimulants (Cocaine and Methamphetamine)

Research in both humans and animals suggests that women may be more vulnerable to the reinforcing (rewarding) effects of stimulants, with estrogen possibly being one factor for this increased sensitivity. In animal studies, females are quicker to start taking cocaine—and take it in larger amounts—than males. Women may also be more sensitive than men to cocaine's effects on the heart and blood vessels. In contrast, female and male cocaine users show similar deficits in learning, concentration, and academic achievement, even if women had been using it longer. Female cocaine users are also less likely than male users to exhibit abnormalities of blood flow in the brain's frontal regions. These findings suggest a sexrelated mechanism that may protect women from some of the detrimental effects of cocaine on the brain.

As for methamphetamine, women report using the drug because they believe it will increase energy and decrease exhaustion associated with work, home care, child care, and family responsibilities. Weight loss is another incentive women cite for methamphetamine use—and one reported significantly more by women than by men. Women also report using methamphetamine because they believe it will increase energy and

decrease exhaustion associated with work, home care, child care, and family responsibilities. Women who use methamphetamine also have high rates of cooccurring depression.

Women tend to begin using methamphetamine at an earlier age than do men, with female users typically more dependent on methamphetamine compared to male users. Women are also less likely to switch to another drug when they lack access to methamphetamine. In addition, as with other substances, women tend to be more receptive than men to methamphetamine treatment.

MDMA (Ecstasy, Molly)

Research suggests that MDMA produces stronger hallucinatory effects in women compared to men, although men show higher MDMA-induced blood pressure increases. There is some evidence that, in occasional users, women are more prone than men to feeling depressed a few days after they last used MDMA. Both men and women show similar increases in aggression a few days after they stop using MDMA.

MDMA can interfere with the body's ability to eliminate water and decrease sodium levels in the blood, causing a person to drink large amounts of fluid. In rare cases, this can lead to increased water in the spaces between cells, which may eventually produce swelling of the brain and even death. Young women are more likely than men to die from this reaction, with almost all reported cases of death occurring in young females between the ages of 15 and 30. MDMA can also interfere with temperature regulation and cause acute hyperthermia, leading to neurotoxic effects and even death.

Heroin

Research suggests that women tend to use smaller amounts of heroin and for less time, and are less likely than men to inject it. Most women who inject heroin point to social pressure and sexual partner encouragement as factors. One study indicates that women are more at risk than men for overdose death during the first few years of injecting heroin, but it is unclear why this might be the case. One possibility is that women who inject heroin are more likely than their male counterparts to also use prescription drugs—a dangerous combination. Women who do not overdose within these first few years are more likely than men to survive in the long term. This could be due to differences in treatment and other environmental factors that impact heroin use.

Compared with men, women who use heroin are:

- younger
- likely to use smaller amounts and for a shorter time
- less likely to inject the drug
- more influenced by drug-using sexual partners

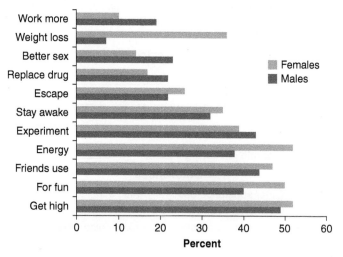

Source: Brecht et al., 2014

Prescription Drugs

Prescription drug misuse is the use of a medication without a prescription, in a way other than as prescribed, or for the experience or feelings elicited. Prescription drug misuse can be dangerous if mixed together without a physician's guidance, or mixed with other drugs or alcohol.

Prescription Opioids

Some research indicates that women are more sensitive to pain than men and more likely to have chronic pain, which could contribute to the high rates of opioid prescriptions among women of reproductive age. In addition, women may be more likely to take prescription opioids without a prescription to cope with pain, even when men and women report similar pain levels. Research also suggests that women are more likely to misuse prescription opioids to self-treat for other problems such as anxiety or tension.

A possible consequence of prescription opioid misuse is fatal overdose, which can occur because opioids suppress breathing. In 2016, 7,109 women and 9,978 men died from prescription opioid overdose (a total of 17,087)* which is about 19 women per day compared to about 27 men dying from overdosing on prescription opioids. However, from 1999 to 2016, deaths from prescription opioid overdoses increased more rapidly for women (596 percent or sevenfold) than for men (312 percent or fourfold). Women between the ages of 45 and 54 are more likely than women of other age groups to die from a prescription opioid overdose.

Alcohol

In general, men have higher rates of alcohol use, including binge drinking. However, young adults are an exception: girls ages 12 to 20 have slightly higher rates of alcohol misuse and binge drinking than their male counterparts.

Drinking over the long term is more likely to damage a woman's health than a man's, even if the woman has been drinking less alcohol or for a shorter length of time. Comparing people with alcohol use disorders, women have death rates 50 to 100 percent higher than do men, including deaths from suicides, alcohol-related accidents, heart disease, stroke, and liver disease. In addition, there are some health risks that are unique to female drinkers. For example, heavy drinking is associated with increased risk of having unprotected sex, resulting in pregnancy or disease, and an increased risk of becoming a victim of violence and sexual assault. In addition, drinking as little as one drink per day is associated with a higher risk of breast cancer in some women, especially those who are postmenopausal or have a family history of breast cancer.

*Note that in this instance, "prescription opioids" includes other opioids and methadone (ICD10 codes T40.2T40.3).

In addition, men and women metabolize alcohol differently due to differences in gastric tissue activity. In fact, after drinking comparable amounts of alcohol, women have higher blood ethanol concentrations. As a result, women become intoxicated from smaller quantities of alcohol than men.

More information on sex and gender differences in alcohol use is available from the National Institute of Alcohol Abuse and Alcoholism (NIAAA).

AntiAnxiety Medications and Sleeping Aids

Women are more likely to seek treatment for misuse of central nervous system depressants, which include sedatives sometimes prescribed to treat seizures, sleep disorders, and anxiety, and to help people fall asleep prior to surgery. Women are also more likely than men to die from overdoses involving medications for mental health conditions, like antidepressants. Antidepressants and benzodiazepines (antianxiety or sleep drugs) send more women than men to emergency departments. Because women are also more at risk than men for anxiety and insomnia, it is possible that women are being prescribed more of these types of medications; greater access can increase the risk of misuse and lead to substance use disorder or overdose.

Nicotine (Tobacco)

Research indicates that men and women differ in their smoking behaviors. For instance, women smoke fewer cigarettes per day, tend to use cigarettes with lower nicotine content, and do not inhale as deeply as men. Women also may smoke for different reasons than men, including regulation of mood and stress. It is unclear whether these differences in smoking behaviors are because women are more sensitive to nicotine, because they find the sensations associated with smoking less rewarding, or because of social factors contributing to the difference; some research also suggests women may experience more stress and anxiety as a result of nicotine withdrawal than men.

Risk of death from smokingassociated lung cancer, chronic obstructive pulmonary disease, heart disease, and stroke continues to increase among women—approaching rates for men. According to data collected from 2005 to 2009, approximately 201,000 women die each year due to factors related to smoking—compared to about 278,000 men. Some dangers associated with smoking—such as blood clots, heart attack, or stroke—increase in women using oral contraceptives.

The number of smokers in the United States declined in the 1970s and 1980s, remained relatively stable throughout the 1990s, and declined further through the early 2000s. Because this decline in smoking was greater among men than women, the prevalence of smoking is only slightly higher for men today than it is for women. Several factors appear to be contributing to this narrowing gender gap, including women being less likely than men to quit and more likely to relapse if they do quit.

Other Substances
Alcohol

In general, men have higher rates of alcohol use, including binge drinking. However, young adults are an exception: girls ages 12 to 20 have slightly higher rates of alcohol misuse and binge drinking than their male counterparts.

Drinking over the long term is more likely to damage a woman's health than a man's, even if the woman has been drinking less alcohol or for a shorter length of time. Comparing people with alcohol use disorders, women have death rates 50 to 100 percent higher than do men, including deaths from suicides, alcohol-related accidents, heart disease, stroke, and liver disease. In addition, there are some health risks that are unique to female drinkers. For example, heavy drinking is associated with increased risk of having unprotected sex, resulting in pregnancy or disease, and an increased risk of becoming a victim of violence and sexual assault. In addition, drinking as little as one drink per day is associated with a higher risk of breast cancer in some women, especially those who are postmenopausal or have a family history of breast cancer.

In addition, men and women metabolize alcohol differently due to differences in gastric tissue activity. In fact, after drinking comparable amounts of alcohol, women have higher blood ethanol concentrations. As a result, women become intoxicated from smaller quantities of alcohol than men.

More information on sex and gender differences in alcohol use is available from the National Institute of Alcohol Abuse and Alcoholism (NIAAA).

Nicotine (Tobacco)

Research indicates that men and women differ in their smoking behaviors. For instance, women smoke fewer cigarettes per day, tend to use cigarettes with lower nicotine content, and do not inhale as deeply as men. Women also may smoke for different reasons than men, including regulation of mood and stress. It is unclear whether these differences in smoking behaviors are because women are more sensitive to nicotine, because they find the sensations associated with smoking less rewarding, or

because of social factors contributing to the difference; some research also suggests women may experience more stress and anxiety as a result of nicotine withdrawal than men.

Risk of death from smoking-associated lung cancer, chronic obstructive pulmonary disease, heart disease, and stroke continues to increase among women—approaching rates for men. According to data collected from 2005 to 2009, approximately 201,000 women die each year due to factors related to smoking—compared to about 278,000 men. Some dangers associated with smoking—such as blood clots, heart attack, or stroke—increase in women using oral contraceptives.

The number of smokers in the United States declined in the 1970s and 1980s, remained relatively stable throughout the 1990s, and declined further through the early 2000s. Because this decline in smoking was greater among men than women, the prevalence of smoking is only slightly higher for men today than it is for women. Several factors appear to be contributing to this narrowing gender gap, including women being less likely than men to quit and more likely to relapse if they do quit.

Critical Thinking

1. How do women use drugs, legal and illegal, differently than men?
2. How do women respond to drug use/abuse compared to men?
3. What are a few of the biological differences of how drugs interact with women's bodies compared to men's bodies?
4. What social issues occur as a result of women's substance abuse? How about biological?
5. What kinds of long-term and even fatal effects are possible when a pregnant mother abuses substances?

Internet References

Centers for Disease Control and Prevention
https://www.cdc.gov/
National Center for Chronic Disease Prevention and Health Promotion
https://www.cdc.gov/chronicdisease/index.htm
National Institute of Child Health and Human Development
https://www.nichd.nih.gov/

National Institute on Drug Abuse, *Sex and Gender Differences in Substance Use.* U.S. Department of Health and Human Services, 2018.

Unit 3

UNIT

Prepared by: Kim Schnurbush, *California State University, Sacramento*
Mark Pullin, *Angelo State University*

The Major Drugs of Use and Abuse

The following articles discuss those drugs that have evolved historically to become the most popular drugs of choice. Although pharmacological modifications emerge periodically to enhance or alter the effects produced by certain drugs or the manner in which various drugs are used, basic pharmacological properties of the drugs remain unchanged. Crack is still cocaine, ice is still methamphetamine, and black tar is still heroin. In addition, all tobacco products supply the drug nicotine, coffee and a plethora of energy drinks provide caffeine, and alcoholic beverages provide the drug ethyl alcohol. All these drugs influence the way we act, think, and feel about ourselves and the world around us. They also produce markedly different effects within the body and within the mind.

To understand why certain drugs remain popular over time, and why new drugs become popular, one must be knowledgeable about the effects produced by individual drugs. Why people use drugs is a bigger question than why people use tobacco. However, understanding why people use tobacco, or cocaine, or marijuana, or alcohol is one way to construct a framework from which to tackle the larger question of why people use drugs in general. One of the most complex relationships is the one between Americans and their use of alcohol. More than 76 million Americans have experienced alcoholism in their families and approximately 28 million children have alcoholic parents.

The most recent surveys of alcohol use estimate that 127 million Americans currently use alcohol. The use of alcohol is a powerful influence that serves to shape our national consciousness about drugs. The relationship between the use of alcohol and tobacco and illicit drugs provides long-standing statistical relationships. The majority of Americans, however, believe that alcohol is used responsibly by most people who use it, despite the fact that approximately 10 percent of users are believed to be suffering from various stages of alcoholism.

Understanding why people initially turn to the nonmedical use of drugs is a huge question that is debated and discussed in a voluminous body of literature. One important reason why the majority of drugs of use and abuse, such as alcohol, nicotine, cocaine, heroin, marijuana, amphetamines, and a variety of prescription, designer, over-the-counter, and herbal drugs,

retain their popularity is because they produce certain physical and psychological effects that humans crave. They temporarily restrain our inhibitions; reduce our fears; alleviate mental and physical suffering; produce energy, confidence, and exhilaration; and allow us to relax. Tired, take a pill; have a headache, take a pill; need to lose weight, take a pill; need to increase athletic performance, take a pill. The options seem almost limitless. There is a drug for everything. Some drugs even, albeit artificially, suggest a greater capacity to transcend, redefine, and seek out new levels of consciousness. Some do that upon demand.

Heroin- and opiate-related drugs such as OxyContin and Vicodin produce, in most people, a euphoric, dreamy state of well-being. The abuse of these prescription painkillers is one of the fastest growing (and alarming) drug trends. Methamphetamine and related stimulant drugs produce euphoria, energy, confidence, and exhilaration. Alcohol produces a loss of inhibitions and a state of well-being. Nicotine and marijuana typically serve as relaxants. Ecstasy and other "club drugs" produce stimulant as well as relaxant effects. Various over-the-counter and herbal drugs attempt to replicate the effects of more potent and often prohibited or prescribed drugs. Although effects and side effects may vary from user to user, a general pattern of effects is predictable from most major drugs of the use and their analogs. Varying the dosage and altering the manner of ingestion is one way to alter the drug's effects. Some drugs, such as LSD and certain types of designer drugs, produce effects on the user that are less predictable and more sensitive to variations in dosage level and the user's physical and psychological makeup.

Although all major drugs of use and abuse have specific reinforcing properties perpetuating their continued use, they also produce undesirable side effects that regular drug users attempt to mitigate. Most often, users attempt to mitigate these effects with the use of other drugs. Cocaine, methamphetamine, heroin, and alcohol have long been used to mitigate each other's side effects. A good example is the classic "speedball" of heroin and cocaine. When they are combined, cocaine accelerates and intensifies the euphoric state of the heroin, while the heroin softens the comedown from cocaine. Add this to the almost limitless combinations of prescription drugs, mixed and traded at "pharming" parties, and an entirely new dimension for altering drugs, physiological effects emerges. Additionally, other powerful influences on drug taking, such as advertising for alcohol, tobacco, and certain prescription drugs, significantly impact the public's drug-related consciousness. The alcohol industry, for example, dissects numerous layers of society to specifically market alcoholic beverages to subpopulations of Americans, including youth. The same influences exist with tobacco advertising.

What is the message in Phillip Morris's advertisements about its attempts to mitigate smoking by youth? Approximately 480,000 Americans die each year from tobacco-related illness. Add to the mix advertising by prescription-drug companies for innumerable human maladies and one soon realizes the enormity of the association between business and drug taking. Subsequently, any discussion of major drugs could begin and end with alcohol, tobacco, and prescription drugs.

Article

Prepared by: Kim Schnurbush, *California State University, Sacramento*
Mark Pullin, *Angelo State University*

Krokodil: A Monstrous Drug with Deadly Consequences[1]

Danielle M. Matiuk

Learning Outcomes

After reading this article, you will be able to:

- Discuss how krokodil come into existence.
- Understand the mental and physical incapacitation krokodil places on individuals.
- Discuss the global outcry and efforts to discourage the use of krokodil and reasons behind such actions.

Introduction

Various drug trends are continually surfacing in the United States and around the globe which is no surprise considering in 2007, the National Survey on Drug Use and Health showed an estimated 208 million people internationally consume illicit drugs (Foundation for a Drug Free World, 2006). Bath salts, synthetic cannabis, "huffing," nutmeg as a hallucinogen and even anti-energy drinks serve as a few examples of fads that have received some attention. However, krokodil, a deadly and incapacitating development, is now receiving more attention throughout the globe, particularly in Russia, with several alleged recent cases in the United States. For many who suffer from addiction, they often feel drugs are a solution to escaping or numbing social and emotional troubles. However, with time and continued abuse, these drugs themselves become the individual's worst predicament. For those who turn to krokodil, this predicament is swift acting and terminal.

Description of Krokodil (Desomorpine)

Krokodil, a crude production of desomorphine, is an opioid drug concocted much like methamphetamines whereby the user can produce it at home with a combination of ingredients. Similar to the production of methamphetamines, krokodil is derived from iodine and red phosphorus. However, it is the use of codeine along with these ingredients that produces krokodil. Specifically, codeine is mixed with toxic products, such as iodine, gasoline, paint thinner, hydrochloric acid, lighter fluid, and red phosphorus; the latter ingredient derived sometimes from the striking plate of match books, since red phosphorus itself is less easy to obtain and more costly. Codeine pills frequently contain caffeine, paracetamol, or diphenhydramine, which is also an opioid potentiator, enhancing sensitization. Tropicamide, found in over the counter eye drops, constitutes another ingredient; krokodil users have been known to incorporate in order to enhance and/or lengthen the experience (Wikipedia.org, Krokodil, 2013). Judging from the aforementioned ingredients, the resulting byproduct is a highly toxic "homemade desomorphine" with many impurities and resulting physical dangers (National Library of Medicine, 2013). After much boiling and distilling, the resulting "grunge" is a caramel colored, acrid smelling concoction that is injected into areas, such as forearms, legs, and even upper body regions where one can obtain vein access (Walker, 2011).

In fact, the name krokodil is indicative of these physical hazards which include an attack on the soft tissues of the skin at the injection site resulting in open sores, phlebitis (vein injury) and even gangrene. Furthermore, continued use causes the skin to become scaly and rough much like a crocodile (Walker, 2011). In the absence of any medical attention, limbs can rot, and amputation becomes a necessary procedure. Internally, due to the iodine content, the endocrine system and muscles can be compromised. High phosphorus levels result in bone damage. Nervous system impairment, liver and kidney inflammation may result from excess iron, zinc, and lead—all byproducts of this chemically toxic homemade substance. Veins can virtually burn up and limbs decompose as a result of excess caustic chemical infiltration (Narconon.org/drug-abuse/desomorphine, 2013). Because krokodil has an extreme analgesic effect, the user often physically and mentally fails to notice these deleterious consequences. Thus, mental impairment including speech impediments can follow resulting in one's inability to sustain normal cognitive functioning with possible brain damage (Lallanilla, 2013).

As krokodil (desomorphine) is an opioid, it produces effects much like heroin, only more potent. However, these effects last for a shorter period of time, thus causing the user to quickly begin feeling the need for more. Heroin is felt for approximately four to eight hours, while krokodil "highs" begin to diminish after one and a half hours. Moreover, the krokodil user will likely begin to feel withdrawal shortly afterwards (Wikipedia, Desomorphine, 2013). Consequently, production is an ongoing "job." Krokodil takes 30–60 min for production, so one can deduce that the individual is starting to make or "cook" more shortly following their injection of each dose.

From a legal standpoint, both heroin and desomorphine are prohibited, Schedule 1 drugs. FDA/ DEA regulation states that Schedule 1 drugs have ". . . (i) no currently accepted medical use in the United States, (ii) a lack of accepted safety for use under medical supervision, and (iii) a high potential for abuse" (FindtheBest.org, 2013). Clinical data suggests that Heroin is classified as having a high incidence of dependency, while krokodil has a "very high" incidence of dependency. Typical heroin routes include inhalation, intravenous, oral, intranasal, and intramuscular, whereas krokodil is characteristically routed intravenously (Wikipedia.org, Heroin and Krokodil, 2013).

Krokodil Chemistry and Pharmacology

Krokodil or Crocodil is the street name for desomorphine (dihydrodesoxymorphine; dihydrodesoxymorphine-D). Its formula, $C17H21NO2$, has a molecular mass of 271.354 g/mol. Chemically, desomorphine and morphine are similar. However, morphine is a true opiate, whereas desomorphine is a semi-synthetic opioid. Due to their structural likeness, it suggests that desomorphine is a potent mu opioid agonist (Erowid, 2013). According to the Drug Enforcement Administration (DEA), when studied on laboratory animals, desomorphine demonstrates stronger than morphine; three times the toxicity, and 10 times as effective as an analgesic. It also works quickly but does not last very long. A slow tolerance develops in rats receiving daily injection and constant dose. In humans, repeated dosing at short intervals in cancer patients has been shown to result in a high level of addiction liability (www.deadiversion.usdoj.gov, 2013).

Historical Data and Growth: Desomorphine

Patented in the United States in 1932, desomorphine had historical use in Switzerland. Specifically, under the brand name Permonid, it was found to produce a faster onset and shorter duration when compared to other pain relievers such as morphine. Desomorphine also initiated less sedative effects and seemed to have favorable post-operative results, such as reduced need for catheterization, less dizziness, and decreased incidence of vomiting when compared to morphine. Medical studies continued to endorse desomorphine for traumatic cases due to its ability to provide a palliative effect on excitement or fear (National Library of Medicine HSDB Database, 2013). For example, 1 mg of desomorphine was equivalent to 10 mg of morphine for pain relief and sleep was produced by 91.8 percent of desomorphine patients compared to 80.5 percent for morphine patients. However, desomorphine was found to wear off quicker, cause faster withdrawal, and it was concluded to have no real overall advantage over morphine (Eddy NB et al., 1957).

Geographic Growth and Specifics

Despite these developments and the obsoleteness of desomorphine in a clinical or medical setting, it has resurfaced predominantly in Russia, the Ukraine, and Georgia with the onset of use beginning around 2002–2003. Russia, Ukraine, and all other former Soviet countries have a history of developing "homemade" opioid and stimulant drugs which are primarily injected. According to Grund et al., when Afghanistan started to import heroin into Russia, most notably in the late 1990s, this served as a replacement to homemade drugs for a while and predominantly in the neighboring cities to the drug trafficking course. However, knowing that it was less expensive to obtain codeine, many drug users with limited funds and resources turned to krokodil. One particularly staggering statistic, suggesting the potential widespread harm desomorphine can produce, shows an estimated 2 million people in Russia who are injecting drugs of some sort into their bodies. To further illustrate and provide a comparison, in 2008, approximately 0.4 percent people use opioids in the Western world, whereas in Russia, this number escalates to 2.3 percent (Grund et al., 2013).

Before June 2012, codeine was sold in Russia without the requirement of a prescription, so it was relatively easy to purchase, along with the other over the counter ingredients. Moreover, the cost of manufacturing krokodil is much less expensive than heroin. In 2011, according to Erowid, 10 over-the-counter codeine tablets cost 120 Russian Rubles (or $3.71). This is a comparable substitute to 500 Rubles (or $15.46) worth of heroin (Erowid, 2013). In the more deprived and low income or unemployed areas of Russia, this price difference proves to be a large reason why krokodil has become such a widespread problem in this country. In fact, according to the DEA, by 2009, desomorphine abuse was increasing among Russian young adults. By 2011, krokodil use in Russia was estimated at approximately 100,000 and in the Ukraine, roughly 20,000 (Grund, J.P. et al., 2013).

Sociological Aspects of Influence

Sociologically, desomorphine users, particularly in Russia, have chosen this route due to low cost and ease of access. Although most of the krokodil users would prefer heroin, krokodil produces a stronger effect and is highly addictive after repeated use. In small towns such as Tver, the ingredients are attainable and sold without a prescription. Although as of June 1, 2012, over-the-counter sales of drugs containing codeine (pentalgin, nurofen, solpadeine, etc.) have been banned in 21 regions of Russia, one can obtain a prescription (Ivan, 2012). Considering the nature of addiction and the individual's drive to obtain drugs in the midst of their cravings and/or withdrawal, one can surmise that codeine is still available to those who have a way of obtaining it and selling it on the black market or simply from one dealer to another. Just because a drug is illegal or requires a prescription does not preclude one with a drug dependency from finding alternative methods of attainment.

Prior to June 1, 2012, Russian pharmacies were making up to a 25 percent profit from the sale of codeine tablets, many of them knowing exactly what customers were using it for. For economic gain and survival in various downtrodden regions, these pharmacies turned a "blind eye" and knowingly sold more than the allotted amount to the same person. According to Erin, in his article, *Krokodil, Homemade Heroin of the Worst Kind*, one user recalls, " . . . I was trying to buy four packs, and the woman told me they could only sell two to any one person. So I bought two packs, then came back five minutes later and bought another two" (Erin, 2011). Pharmacies supporting this habit have enabled those addicted to krokodil to perpetuate their dependency—one that gets increasingly harder to stop and with continued use is ultimately deadly.

As is characteristic in Russia, drug use often begins in the teenage years, particularly in the poorest and more isolated parts of the country. Both male and female users have been identified with no reported statistics on one gender dominating the other. In small towns, such as Vorkuta, they face exceedingly cold winter weather, lasting an average of eight months each year. This results in boredom as teenagers are confined indoors with little entertainment. Drinking is prevalent; however, without employment, this habit becomes costly in the long run. Consequently, many of them turn to stronger drugs such as krokodil (Shuster, 2011).

Simon Shuster, in his article *"The Curse of the Crocodile: Russia's Deadly Designer Drug,"* one 27-year-old female Russian from Vorkuta describes how this epidemic exists in hundreds of towns and villages across northern Russia. She associated with about 12 other krokodil addicts stating that, "Practically all of them are dead now. For some it led to pneumonia, some got blood poisoning, some had an artery burst in their heart, some got meningitis, others simply rot" (Shuster, 2011). She is one of the more fortunate cases who, after being rushed to the emergency room, was offered detox at a drug rehab center in Chichevo (a village several hours east of Moscow). Such centers, however, exist sparingly in this country and are private, often church affiliated and not subsidized by the government.

Recent U.S. Presence and Reports

In 2011, the Drug Enforcement Agency (DEA) reported it was keeping an eye on krokodil overseas but had not yet confirmed its incidence in the United States. In fact, DEA spokesman Rusty Payne told FoxNews.com back in June 2011, "We're looking at it overseas, but we have not seen it yet in the U.S." (Miller, 2013). However, several cases have since been recounted by health officials in the United States in 2012 and 2013.

At the Banner Good Samaritan Medical Center in Phoenix, Arizona, two such cases were reported in September 2013. Having been examined, it was reported by Dr. Frank LoVecchio, co-medical director at Banner Poison, Drug, and Information Center, that " . . . some of the chemicals they're using are very dangerous . . . they've used things like hydrochloric acid . . . paint thinners, gasoline and other stuff that includes phosphorus" (Mendez, 2013). He also stipulated that a daily krokodil user has a life expectancy of approximately two years, with the potential of death occurring before two years as a result of "overwhelming infection."

Such death served as reality for three Oklahoma cases, identified last year. Two of the victims were transported to the burn unit as a result of extensive skin damage but later died from the irreversible damage. A third male individual reportedly died in an Oklahoma city hospital as a result of what was thought to be krokodil use among other drugs found in his system including methamphetamine, morphine and amphetamine. Technically, he died of a heart attack, but presented all the symptoms of krokodil use, most notably, missing chunks of skin (Jeffries, 2013). Dr. William Banner, Director of the Oklahoma Poison Control

Center, warns, "This is an end game move. This is going to kill you" (Jeffries, 2013). For Oklahoma, this presents itself as an eye-opening trend because according to OKCFox.com, "Oklahoma is number one in the Nation for prescription addiction and opiate-abuse, and 'krokodil' is made from prescription drugs" (Henry K, 2013). Chicago has been the third United States city to report the presence of krokodil use. Three individuals, according to CBS Chicago, have received attention at a suburban Chicago hospital (Join Together Staff at drugfree.org, 2013) .

While some doctors and hospitals, particularly in the states described above, are expressing significant concern, others feel the United States is not at any sizable risk. Compared to the socioeconomic and financial state in Russia and its poor suburbs, it seems unlikely the United States will undergo a krokodil epidemic quite to the extent we see in Russia. Moreover, heroin is still widely used and easily obtained in the United States. According to the National Survey on Drug Use and Health (NSDUH), teenagers have reasonably easy access to heroin. For example, 29.7 percent of 12th graders say it is easy to obtain. Even 8th graders (12.6 percent) say they can acquire heroin (HeroinAbuse.us, 2013). None-the-less, such a deadly, incapacitating trend should be recognized and discussed seriously, especially with those who are addicted and dependent upon opioids and who may do anything to maintain their habit.

Interviews and Responses from Individuals Addicted to Heroin

In the interest of obtaining current opinions and feedback on krokodil from actual heroin users, interviews were conducted at MedMark Treatment Center in Hayward, CA. MedMark Treatment Center provides methadone detox and methadone maintenance treatment and counseling to those who have become dependent upon heroin and/or synthetic opiates such as oxycodone. Four subjects who are patients, ranging in age, ethnicity, socio-economic status and gender, agreed to anonymously share their thoughts and responses to several questions pertaining to krokodil. It should be noted, subjects were also carefully selected based upon their perceived level of stability and commitment to their recovery as to not negatively or adversely affect those in early recovery, fragile states or high risk of relapse.

When asked if they knew what krokodil was, three out of the four had no knowledge of the drug. One male, middle-aged, Hispanic patient (Subject A) stated he saw some footage on the internet about krokodil several months ago. Subject A stated, "I saw some pictures and an article about it. It makes your skin rot and fall off. That's just sick." When asked if it would be an option in a desperate situation back when he was in the peak of his drug use, he replied,

Man, I don't know. I was pretty bad and did just about anything on the street. I guess if someone tried to sell me that or tell me about it, I might say 'what the hell,' especially if I was already strung out or desperate. I wouldn't probably know about it, if I were still on the streets I might just go with it. I didn't really care about much back then so I guess you could say it would've been possible.

Subject A has over four years clean of all illicit drugs and is on the methadone maintenance treatment plan at the clinic. He presents as one who is now in a true maintenance stage of change and has rebuilt his life to where he now works, has independent housing, responsibilities and is a healthy, functioning member of the community. He was able to reflect back, however, and admit how addiction to drugs altered his abilities to make intelligent and safe decisions and avoid negative consequences. In fact, three of the four subjects responded similarly to this question in that they felt the severe nature of their addictions could have resulted in using a drug like krokodil simply to satisfy their cravings, especially under dire circumstances.

When interviewing a female, Caucasian patient in her 20s (Subject B), with six months of abstinence from heroin (her drug of choice), she provided a response to the question, "If someone offered you a hit of heroine when you were still using, did you ever question where it came from or what exactly was going into your body?" Prior to her response, she was given a description of krokodil and how it was a cheaper, more dangerous heroin substitute:

When I was using, it was always a full-time job to make sure I got my next fix and sometimes I would start to withdraw and I'd go to some of the worst parts of town – no matter how far I had to go. A lot of times I was so high that I actually would pass out and not remember, so yeah, I guess I never really wondered or cared about the stuff I was getting. I just knew I needed it. I can tell you a couple times it was really bad cuz I remember another girl pulling me into the shower once after I nodded off. I could have died.

Subject B's response indicates the danger involved with those who use drugs heavily to the point where they simply do not know or care what substances are being used to manufacture the drug. She stated that hearing about krokodil scared her and she is grateful it was not something anyone ever gave her because of its highly addictive nature.

Subject C, an elderly black male with over 10 years clean, was a drug dealer and a heroin user in San Francisco. Having spent many years in prison, he is now on a taper plan to transition off methadone and is living a reformed life. When asked if he thinks heroin users would resort to krokodil if they knew how to make it he shares:

I guess that all depends on the person. Me, I was dealing all kinds of stuff and some of it was cut with a lot of crap. I mean, I've had abscesses that were pretty bad and I used to see people with messed up arms, couldn't find a vein. Some people just get like a 'whatever' attitude, they don't care and all common sense is gone. All that matters is the drug, so it's totally possible they'd use anything. As a dealer, I used only the good stuff and so I probably would never have been that hard up. I made good money too so I didn't have to go there.

This individual addresses the importance of recognizing personal circumstances and the drug user's unique situation, socially, demographically, emotionally, and economically. In addition, Subject C acknowledges how drugs effect one's cognition and ability to "care" or have any "common sense." Thus, using something like krokodil in a dire situation may be a reality for those that have lost all sense of true reality.

The last patient, a bi-racial female in her 50s (Subject D) was asked if she thought she would ever contemplate krokodil when she was actively using heroin. She replied:

Honestly, no way. I never used needles and you said krokodil is injected so no. Maybe it seems weird, but for as bad as I got, I never ever resorted to that. It scared me with all the diseases and actually, I have always been afraid of needles, shots – the pain you know? Isn't that crazy though to say that scared me when the whole drug thing shoulda scared me! I guess that's the addiction for you.

Subject D raises an interesting point around the lengths certain addicts will go, which seems to be dependent upon the individual, their experiences and their personal opinions. All four subjects, addicted to the same drug, have shared varying opinions and responses based upon their circumstances. Yet, the commonality lies in the presence of an addiction. The National Institute on Drug Abuse defines addiction as, " . . . a chronic, often relapsing brain disease that causes compulsive drug seeking and use, despite harmful consequences to the addicted individual and to those around him or her" (DrugAbuse.gov, 2012). Consequently, as for the interviewees, addiction can take someone to the point of using something like krokodil with no regard to the potential magnitude of health dangers it presents.

Community Impact: Treatment, Medications, and Rehabilitation

In Russia, where krokodil poses a larger, more widespread and threatening problem, the Federal Antinarcotics Service estimates roughly 1–1.5 million heroin users in Russia, and it could be more (Ivan, 2013). Efforts to curtail heroin trafficking

into Russia, specifically from Afghanistan, is an existing threat to national security. However, Gennady Onishchenko, a predominant Russian public-health official has provided a forewarning that possible increases in heroin flow into Russia may be activated from a withdrawal of troops from Afghanistan (Ivan, 2013). As krokodil is the homemade, less costly alternative, whether heroin availability increases or not, the substantial population of heroin users constitute a huge number of potential krokodil users.

According to Ivan in the article, *Russia's Heroin Habit,* regardless of the aforementioned, staggering number, Russian government offers little assistance and rehabilitation programs for those facing drug dependency issues. Moreover, the country has no state needle-exchange programs to help control and reduce the spread of HIV, AIDS, and Hepatitis C. There are no medication assisted treatment programs (such as methadone or buprenorphine), and in general, those seeking treatment in hospitals are reportedly given substandard care or no attention at all (Ivan, 2013).

From a medication standpoint, there are no specific "pills" or "procedures" a krokodil user can be prescribed short of the necessary pain killers, hospitalization, tranquilizers, skin treatment, and possible amputation in the worst cases. Withdrawal is at its extreme the first 10 days, with continued symptoms and discomfort lasting up to and beyond a month or more. If feasible, the skin must be attended to due to tissue damage and open sores, yet when gangrene sets in, amputation is a necessity (Duncan at krokodildrug.com, 2013).

Attempts to facilitate more social awareness and justice to those in this vicious cycle in Russia, there are people who set up drug awareness foundations, such as the Andrey Rylkov Foundation for Health and Social Justice. This particular nonprofit entity exists to provide support and a voice to those suffering with addiction and in need of help. Andrey began his mission volunteering at a Moscow street-harm reduction project in 2000. As a drug user, he worked toward an awareness of helping those with drug dependency and the diseases often accompanying it, such as HIV and AIDS. This foundation was temporarily shut down by Russian authorities in 2012 as a result of its promoting methadone to be "the most promising way" of battling heroin and opioid addiction (Ivan, 2013).

Recovery Clinics and Social Awareness

As a result, many people in Russia simply do not receive the help that those who struggle in other European or North American countries are more able to obtain through insurance, hospital support, and availability of rehabilitation facilities including methadone clinics. For example, if one were to conduct an internet search on "Drug Addiction Rehabilitation Facilities in Russia," very little options exist.

One such option is a Narconon center located in the Commonwealth of Independent states called Narconon Moscow. The original facility opened in 1994 with Narconon Dimitrovgrad, Narconon Ekaterinburg, Narconon Standard, Narconon South, Narconon St. Petersburg and Narconon Kiev in Ukraine (Narconon International, 2010). Although a nonprofit organization, these facilities still cost money and this is often not a feasible option for those who have very little resources. Narconon provides a drug-free rehabilitation, using only vitamins and minerals to flush toxins out of the body along with counseling and life skills therapy.

Russia covers over six and a half million miles with a population of nearly 142 million. According to Narconon, only about a third of Russia's regions have treatment centers and those that exist are often very inadequate. Specifically, some of these facilities bear resemblance to jail, with substandard living quarters, bars and cell-like accommodations (Narcanon. org, 2010). With the government doing little to assist with more aggressive development of rehab facilities, the Russian union of Evangelical Christians, Pentecostals in majority, runs more than 500 centers with no state support. These church organization rehabs constitute the largest provider of drug rehabilitation in Russia (Shuster, 2011).

Alcoholics Anonymous (AA), whose premise supports a 12-Step, spiritual approach to recovery, exists in Russia, yet mostly in the major cities, such as Moscow and Saint Petersburg. Akin to Narcotics Anonymous, AA provides support and fellowship to those who suffer from addiction so people with alcohol and/or drug problems would be able to access this recovery support. However, considering the nature of the krokodil trend, AA might be difficult to attend due to the isolated locations and distance of the remote krokodil towns from these major thoroughfares. Moreover, krokodil users would perhaps find it difficult to rely on this recovery source alone, simply due to the immediacy of their need to use and the extent of their addictive urgencies.

Such a grim portrait of recovery options suggests the need for greater social awareness, efforts and intervention toward challenging Russia's current views upon opioid substitution treatment and similar medically supervised, more humane treatment options. Currently, Narconon describes Russian drug treatment technology, "narcology," as an "outgrowth of old Russian psychiatry" (Narcanon.org, 2010). Such limited philosophy does little to assist a community of heroin and krokodil addicts who require more hospital attention and rehabilitation therapy.

Warnings via social media, videos, articles, and news stories have provided the Russian and worldwide public with information about krokodil in attempts to warn societies of the dangers this drug presents. Additionally, in 2011, President Dmitry Medvedev ordered websites explaining how to manufacture krokodil be closed down (Erin, 2011), yet some argue this does little to prevent what already exists and it is difficult to monitor all social media activity. However, it serves as a future preventative measure and sends a message of concern as well as distain for such websites.

In sending such alerts, our social media has done an exceptional job providing articles and documentaries about krokodil. Such awareness hopefully provides strong warning signals to the rest of the world. Graphic pictures and documentaries depicting the destitute, harsh reality of the day in the life of a krokodil addict have expectantly caused many individuals to become more aware. As one of the MedMark Treatment Center patients (Subject A) shared, "The pictures of rotting skin and seeing how sick they looked was an eye opener." With continued efforts, one would hope this deadly substance receives the attention it deserves on a political, public and governmental support level in Russia, most notably.

Projections

Where Russia is concerned, the future appears to be an uncertain one with respect to any significant eradication of krokodil and its usage, simply due to the nature of its homemade production and the general nature of addiction in those who suffer from this disease. Just as with any illicit drug, prescription or alcohol abuse, the individual agonizes with a disease that changes the brain in ways that promote further compulsive drug abuse. Consequently, quitting is challenging, even for those who have the desire to do so. Furthermore, the need to address the addict's medical, psychiatric, social, and emotional problems is a unique process requiring dedication of the individual and proper rehabilitation services, which as discussed previously, are sparse in Russia as they continue to face limited progress in harm reduction strategies (Lyuba, 2013). To illustrate the magnitude of this situation, in 1985, the Russian Federal Services for the Control of Narcotics identified four regions in Russia that had more than 10,000 serious drug users. By the year 2000, more than 30 regions claimed roughly this same number of abusers (Narcanon.org, 2010). Due to a continuation of the old ideology about addiction as a criminal or moral deviance rather than a disease, Russia may have ways to go in achieving adequate results and progress towards addiction treatment and therapy.

In contrast, the United States and other European countries have a more accepting stance on those with the disease of addiction. Health care, for example, offers counseling and rehabilitation therapy for those covered with health insurance.

Moreover, we increasingly see the disease of addiction in the media and this often paves the way to better degrees of acceptance around its legitimate diagnosis rather than it being due to "weakness" or being "deviant." Still, considering the ease of manufacture, the potency of high and the similar production process to methamphetamine, which is quite prevalent in the western world, it behooves the U.S. to have an awareness for this phenomenon (Medtox Journal on Drug Abuse Recognition, 2012). As codeine is available only by prescription in the U.S. and heroin is generally not as difficult for the U.S. population to obtain, the Drug Enforcement Agency (DEA) feels that our country is not likely to experience a krokodil epidemic (Sullum, 2013). Nonetheless, Rusty Payne, spokesman for the DEA reports they are,

> . . . aware of and tracking the nationwide reports of alleged abuse of the controlled substance desomorphine that is found in the drug krokodil. To date, none of our forensic laboratories has analyzed an exhibit to contain desomorphine. A sample sent to our Chicago forensic laboratory that was suspected to be krokodil was actually heroin. (Sullom, 2013).

Conclusion

Drug trends continually prove to be an ongoing source of concern in our own local communities as well as worldwide. Whether they originate as a result of factors, such as socioeconomic conditions, political or governmental actions, demographic factors or simply supply and demand issues, they represent a global phenomenon of drug use and/or abuse which continues to be an issue for millions of people.

Sadly, krokodil is one such trend that not only debilitates one's mind and body, but it has the power to abruptly end lives due to its sheer corrosive nature. Addiction dictates that despite these horrific consequences, those who suffer from this disease without help will likely be numb to and indifferent towards their fate. However, just as with any addiction, the addict or user carries their own unique social, emotional, physical, biological, and environmental sigma, which all serve as areas affecting the ability of the individual to seek help, maintain help or even have access to support in the first place.

As our societies are faced with increased, varying drug trends, much can be done locally in more developed countries such as the United States, to address these risks. Family support and involvement, school programs and drug education, hospital support, Employee Assistance Programs (EAP) at work and social media advertising can all facilitate continued awareness in order to help prevent or at least decrease the growth of new and often dangerous drug fads within our communities.

For countries such as Russia, the quality of social support, educational tools, hospital backing (or even participation), EAPs, and overall rehabilitation involvement may be less prevalent or successful. Fortunately, a multitude of efforts pertaining to social awareness through the media, internet and non-profit organizations have been doing their best to make their country and others aware of this potentially epidemic situation. Hopefully, the Russian foundations, churches and social media will continue to rally for support towards recovery and rehabilitation from krokodil, a literally monstrous drug illustrating addiction at its worst with deadly outcomes.

Acknowledgements and Notices

This article may contain opinions that do not reflect the opinion of Breining Institute, and Breining Institute does not warrant the information and/or opinions contained herein.

Note

1. This copyrighted material may be copied in whole or in part, provided that the material used is properly referenced, and that the following citation is used in full: Matiuk, D.M. (2014). Krokodil: A Monstrous Drug with Deadly Consequences. *Journal of Addictive Disorders*. Retrieved from Breining Institute at http://www.breining.edu.

References

Alcoholics Anonymous. (2001). *Alcoholics Anonymous, 4th Edition*. New York: A.A. World Services.

Alcoholics Anonymous—Russia. Retrieved November 26, 2013 from http://www.aa-europe.net/country_map.php?Where=Russia.

Azbel, Lyuba et al. International Journal of Drug Policy, Volume 24, Issue 4. (2013, July). Krokodil and what a long strange trip it's been. IJDP.org. Retrieved November 23, 2013 from the counter from *http://en.rylkov*-fond.org/blog/drug-policy-and-russia/drug-policy-in russia/codeine-prohibition/.2/fulltext.

Drug Enforcement Administration, Office of Diversion Control. Desomorphine (Dihydrodesoxymorphine; dihydrodesoxymorphine-D; Street Name: Krokodil, Crocodil). (2013, October). Retrieved November 24, 2013 from http://www.deadiversion.usdoj.gov/drug_chem_info/desomorphine.pdf.

Duncan (2013, October 15). Desomorphine krokodil drug rehab success rates. Krokodildrug.com. Retrieved November 10, 2013 from http://www.krokodildrug.com.

Duncan (2013, April 3). Detox therapy for krokodil drug users. Krokodildrug.com. Retrieved November 5, 2013 from http://www.krokodildrug.com/.

Eddy N.B. et al. Synthetic Substances with Morphine-like Effect: Clinical Experiences: Potency, Side-Effects, Addiction Liability

(Monographs on Individual Drugs: Desomorphine); Bull World Health Organization 17: 569-863 (1957).

Erowid (2013, October 1). Desomorphine (Krokodil) Basics. Retrieved October 15, 2013 from http://www.erowid.org/chemicals/desomorphine.

FindtheBest.com (2013). Desomorphine – Schedule 1 – Opioids. Retrieved December 6, 2013 the counter from the counter from http://en.rylkov-fond.org/blog/drug-policy-and-russia/drug-policy-in russia/codeine-prohibition/.

Foundation For a Drug Free World (2006). The Truth About Drugs. Retrieved November 15, 2013 from http://www.drugfreeworld.org/drugfacts/drugs/why-do-people-take-drugs.html.

Grund, J. P.C., et al. Breaking Worse: The emergence of krokodil and excessive injuries among people who inject drugs in Eurasia. International Journal of Drug Policy (2013). Retrieved October 22, 2013 from http://dx.doi.org/10.1016/j.drugpo.2013.04.007.

Henry, K. (2013, September 27). Flesh-Eating Drug Makes Its Way to the U.S. Retrieved November 17, 2013 from http://www.okcfox.com/story/23553080/flesh-eating-drug-oklahoma-concerns.

HeroinAbuse.us (2013, December) Heroin Abuse – Statistics, Signs, Treatment. Retrieved November 17, 2013 from http://www.heroinabuse.us/statistics-facts.html.

Ivan (2013, June 1). Andrey Rylkov Foundation for Health and Social Justice. retrieved October 13, 2013 from http://en.rylkov-fond.org/blog/drug-policy-and-russia/drug-policy-inrussia/codeine-prohibition/.

Jeffries, Adrienne (2013, October 10). Reports of flesh rotting drug krokodil popping up in Oklahoma and NYC clubs. Theverge.com. Retrieved October 13, 2013 from http://www.theverge.com/2013/10/10/4824862/reports-of-flesh-rotting-drug-krokodil-popping-up-in-midwestern-suburbs-nyc-clubs.

Jeffries, Adrienne (2013, September 27). The terrifying, flesh-eating drug krokodil has reportedly hit the US – The Verge. TheVerge.com. Retrieved October 15, 2013 from http://www.theverge.com/2013/9/27/4775564/super-addictive-flesh-eating-drug-krokodil-reported-in-the-us.

Join Together Staff (2013, October 10). Krokodil Flesh-eating drug makes appearance in Chicago suburbs. Drugfree.org. Retrieved October 13, 2013 from http://www.drugfree.org/jointogether/community-related/.

Krokodildrug.org (2013, October 21). Krokodil Drug. Retrieved November 22, 2013 from http://krokodil-drug.org.

Lallanilla, Marc (2013, September 26). Deadly Flesh-Eating Drug Arrives in US. News.Yahoo.com. Retrieved October 13, 2013 from http://news.yahoo.com/deadly-flesh-eating-drug-arrives-us-17624875.html.

MedMark Treatment Centers, Inc., Hayward CA. Interviews with patients conducted on the premises. Interview dates: November 13, 2013, November 27, 2013.

Medtox Laboratories. (2012, January). Emerging European drug problem has the attention of U.S. drug experts. Medtox.com. Retrieved November 23, 2013 from www.medtox.com/Resources/Images/7060.pdf.

Mendez, S. (2013, September 27). Flesh Eating Street Drug from Russia Hits the US. ABCNews.go.com. Retrieved October 15, 2013 from http://abcnews.go.com/blogs/headlines/2013/09/flesh-eating-street-drug-from-russia-hits-the-us/.

Miller, Joshua R. (2013, October 10). DEA still dubious despite fresh report of nightmare drug Krokodil surfacing in Illinois. Foxnews.com. Retrieved November 16, 2013 from http://www.foxnews.com/us/2013/10/10/dea-still-dubious-despite-fresh-report-nightmare-drug-krokodil-surfacing-in/.

Narconon.org (2013). Disastrous Effects of Desomporphine Use. Retrieved December 1, 2013 from http://www.narconon.org/drug-abuse/desomorphine-effects.html.

National Institute on Drug Abuse. (2012, November). DrugFacts: Understanding Drug Abuse and Addiction. Drugabuse.gov. Retrieved November 22, 2013 from http://www.drugabuse.gov/publications/drugfacts/understanding-drug-abuse-addiction.

National Institute on Drug Abuse. (2013, September). Emerging Trends "Krokodil." Retrieved October 26, 2013 from http://www.drugabuse.gov/drugs-abuse/emerging-trends.

National Library of Medicine. (2013, September 4). Desomorphine. Retrieved October 13, 2013 from http://toxnet.nlm.nih.gov.RationalWiki, (2013, September 1). Krokodil. Retrieved November 16, 2013 from http://rationalwiki.org.

Shuster, S. Time. (2011, June 20). The Curse of the Crocodile: Russia's Deadly Designer Drug. Retrieved October 15, 2013 from http://content.time.com.

Sullum, Jacob. (2013, November 22). DEA debunks Krokodil sightings. Forbes.com. Retrieved November 23, 2013 from http://www.forbes.com/sites/jacobsullum/2013/11/22/dea-debunks-krokodil-sightings/.

Walker, S. (2011, June 22). Krokodil: The drug that eats junkies. Independent.co.uk. Retrieved October 15, 2013 from http/www.independent.co.uk/news/world/europe/krokodil-the-drug-that-eats-junkies-2300787.html.

Wikipedia, (2013, October 3). Codeine. Retrieved November 3, 2013 from http://en.wikipedia.org/wiki/Codeine.

Wikipedia, (2013, October 11). Desomorphine. Retrieved October 13, 2013 from http://en.wikipedia.org/wiki/Desomorphine.

Wikipedia, (2013, November 8). Heroin. Retrieved November 16, 2013 from http://en.wikipedia.org/wiki/Heroin.

Critical Thinking

1. What is the mental process that would cause a person to use a knowingly destructive drug such as Krokodil?

2. Discuss the chemistry behind krokodil and how the variations in formulas can affect users.

3. Develop a detailed warning campaign that might be successful on a global level and how might this be effective on all levels?

Internet References

Drugs.com—Krokodil Drug Facts
https://www.drugs.com/illicit/krokodil.html

Drug Enforcement Administration—Desomorphine, Street Name: Krokodil
https://www.deadiversion.usdoj.gov/drug_chem_info/desomorphine.pdf

National Institute on Drug Abuse—Emerging Trends "Krokodil"
https://www.drugabuse.gov/drugs-abuse/emerging-trends-alerts

DANIELLE M. MATIUK is a candidate for the Master of Arts in Addictive Disorders Degree from Breining Institute, who is a substance abuse counselor specializing in women's treatment at MedMark Treatment Centers, Inc., holds a Bachelors Degree in Sociology, and has earned Breining Institute-issued professional certifications as a Registered Addiction Specialist (RAS) and Certified Women's Treatment Specialist (CWTS).

Matiuk, Danielle M. (2014), "Krokodil: A Monstrous Drug with Deadly Consequences," *Journal of Addictive Disorders*, Retrieved September 30, 2016 from Breining Institute at http://www.breining.edu.

Article Prepared by: Kim Schnurbush, *California State University, Sacramento*
Mark Pullin, *Angelo State University*

Marijuana as Medicine

NATIONAL INSTITUTE ON DRUG ABUSE

Learning Outcomes

After reading this article, you will be able to:

- Understand why marijuana is not an FDA-approved medicine.
- Discuss how cannabinoids might be useful as medicine.
- Understand the risks to a woman using medical marijuana both during and after her pregnancy.

What Is Medical Marijuana?

The term *medical marijuana* refers to using the whole, unprocessed marijuana plant or its basic extracts to treat symptoms of illness and other conditions. The U.S. Food and Drug Administration (FDA) has not recognized or approved the marijuana plant as medicine.

However, scientific study of the chemicals in marijuana, called *cannabinoids*, has led to two FDA-approved medications that contain cannabinoid chemicals in pill form. Continued research may lead to more medications.

Because the marijuana plant contains chemicals that may help treat a range of illnesses and symptoms, many people argue that it should be legal for medical purposes. In fact, a growing number of states have legalized marijuana for medical use.

Why isn't the Marijuana Plant an FDA-Approved Medicine?

The FDA requires carefully conducted studies (clinical trials) in hundreds to thousands of human subjects to determine the benefits and risks of a possible medication. So far, researchers haven't conducted enough large-scale clinical trials that show that the benefits of the marijuana plant (as opposed to its cannabinoid ingredients) outweigh its risks in patients it's meant to treat.

Can Medical Marijuana Legalization Decrease Prescription Opioid Problems?

Some studies have suggested that medical marijuana legalization might be associated with decreased prescription opioid use and overdose deaths, but researchers don't have enough evidence yet to confirm this finding. For example, one study found that Medicare Part D prescriptions filled for all opioids decreased in states with medical marijuana laws.[1] Another study examined Medicaid prescription data and found that medical marijuana laws and adult-use marijuana laws were associated with lower opioid prescribing rates (5.88 percent and 6.88 percent lower, respectively).[2]

Additionally, one NIDA-funded study suggested a link between medical marijuana legalization and fewer overdose deaths from prescription opioids.[3] These studies, however, are population-based and can't show that medical marijuana legalization caused the decrease in deaths or that pain patients changed their drug-taking behavior.[4,5] A more detailed NIDA-funded analysis showed that legally protected medical marijuana dispensaries, not just medical marijuana laws, were also associated with a decrease in the following:[6]

- opioid prescribing
- self-reports of opioid misuse
- treatment admissions for opioid addiction

Additionally, some data suggests that medical marijuana treatment may reduce the opioid dose prescribed for pain patients,[7,8] while another recent NIH-funded study suggests that cannabis use appears to increase the risk of developing and opioid use disorder.[9] NIDA is funding additional studies to determine the link between medical marijuana use and the use or misuse of opioids for specific types of pain, and also its possible role for treatment of opioid use disorder.

What are Cannabinoids?

Cannabinoids are chemicals related to *delta-9-tetrahydrocannabinol* (THC), marijuana's main mind-altering ingredient that makes people "high." The marijuana plant contains more than 100 cannabinoids. Scientists as well as illegal manufacturers have produced many cannabinoids in the lab. Some of these cannabinoids are extremely powerful and have led to serious health effects when misused.

The body also produces its own cannabinoid chemicals. They play a role in regulating pleasure, memory, thinking, concentration, body movement, awareness of time, appetite, pain, and the senses (taste, touch, smell, hearing, and sight).

How Might Cannabinoids be Useful as Medicine?

Currently, the two main cannabinoids from the marijuana plant that are of medical interest are THC and CBD.

THC can increase appetite and reduce nausea. THC may also decrease pain, inflammation (swelling and redness), and muscle control problems.Unlike THC, CBD is a cannabinoid that doesn't make people "high." These drugs aren't popular for recreational use because they aren't intoxicating. It may be useful in reducing pain and inflammation, controlling epileptic seizures, and possibly even treating mental illness and addictions. The FDA approved a CBD-based liquid medication called Epidiolex® for the treatment of two forms of severe childhood epilepsy, Dravet syndrome and Lennox-Gastaut syndrome.

Are People with Health- and Age-Related Problems More Vulnerable to Marijuana's Risks?

State-approved medicinal use of marijuana is a fairly new practice. For that reason, marijuana's effects on people who are weakened because of age or illness are still relatively unknown. Older people and those suffering from diseases such as cancer or AIDS could be more vulnerable to the drug's harmful effects, but more research is needed.

Many researchers, including those funded by the National Institutes of Health (NIH), are continuing to explore the possible uses of THC, CBD, and other cannabinoids for medical treatment.

For instance, recent animal studies have shown that marijuana extracts may help kill certain cancer cells and reduce the size of others. Evidence from one cell culture study with rodents suggests that purified extracts from whole-plant marijuana can slow the growth of cancer cells from one of the most serious types of brain tumors. Research in mice showed that treatment with purified extracts of THC and CBD, when used with radiation, increased the cancer-killing effects of the radiation.[10]

Scientists are also conducting preclinical and clinical trials with marijuana and its extracts to treat symptoms of illness and other conditions, such as:

- diseases that affect the immune system, including:
  - HIV/AIDS
  - multiple sclerosis (MS), which causes gradual loss of muscle control
- inflammation
- pain
- seizures
- substance use disorders
- mental disorders

Using Medical Marijuana During and After Pregnancy

Some women report using marijuana to treat severe nausea they have during pregnancy. But there's no research that shows that this practice is safe, and doctors generally don't recommend it.

Pregnant women shouldn't use medical marijuana without first checking with their health care provider. Animal studies have shown that moderate amounts of THC given to pregnant or nursing women could have long-lasting effects on the child, including abnormal patterns of social interactions[11] and learning issues.[12,13]

What Medications Contain Cannabinoids?

Two FDA-approved drugs, dronabinol and nabilone, contain THC. They treat nausea caused by chemotherapy and increase appetite in patients with extreme weight loss caused by AIDS. Continued research might lead to more medications.

The United Kingdom, Canada, and several European countries have approved nabiximols (Sativex®), a mouth spray containing THC and CBD. It treats muscle control problems caused by MS, but it isn't FDA-approved.

Points to Remember

- The term *medical marijuana* refers to treating symptoms of illness and other conditions with the whole, unprocessed marijuana plant or its basic extracts.
- The FDA has not recognized or approved the marijuana plant as medicine.
- However, scientific study of the chemicals in marijuana called *cannabinoids* has led to two FDA-approved medications in pill form, dronabinol and nabilone, used to treat nausea and boost appetite.
- Cannabinoids are chemicals related to *delta-9-tetrahydrocannabinol* (THC), marijuana's main mind-altering ingredient.
- Currently, the two main cannabinoids from the marijuana plant that are of interest for medical treatment are THC and *cannabidiol* (CBD).
- The body also produces its own cannabinoid chemicals.
- Scientists are conducting preclinical and clinical trials with marijuana and its extracts to treat symptoms of illness and other conditions.

References

1. Bradford AC, Bradford D, Abraham AJ. Association Between US State Medical Cannabis Laws and Opioid Prescribing in the Medicare Part D Population. *JAMA Intern Med.* April 2018. doi:10.1001/jamainternmed.2018.0266
2. Wen H, Hockenberry J. Association of Medical and Adult-Use Marijuana Laws With Opioid Prescribing for Medicaid Enrollees. *JAMA Intern Med.* doi:10.1001/jamainternmed.2018.1007
3. Bachhuber MA, Saloner B, Cunningham CO, Barry CL. Medical cannabis laws and opioid analgesic overdose mortality in the United States, 1999–2010. *JAMA Intern Med.* 2014;174(10):1668–1673. doi:10.1001/jamainternmed.2014.4005
4. Finney JW, Humphreys K, Harris AHS. What ecologic analyses cannot tell us about medical marijuana legalization and opioid pain medication mortality. *JAMA Intern Med.* 2015;175(4):655–656. doi:10.1001/jamainternmed.2014.8006
5. Bachhuber MA, Saloner B, Barry CL. What ecologic analyses cannot tell us about medical marijuana legalization and opioid pain medication mortality--reply. *JAMA Intern Med.* 2015;175(4):656–657. doi:10.1001/jamainternmed.2014.8027
6. Powell D, Pacula RL, Jacobson M. *Do Medical Marijuana Laws Reduce Addiction and Deaths Related to Pain Killers?*
7. Abrams DI, Couey P, Shade SB, Kelly ME, Benowitz NL. Cannabinoid-opioid interaction in chronic pain. Clin Pharmacol Ther. 2011;90(6):844–851. doi:10.1038/clpt.2011.188
8. Lynch ME, Clark AJ. Cannabis reduces opioid dose in the treatment of chronic non-cancer pain. *J Pain Symptom Manage.* 2003;25(6):496–498.
9. Olfson M, Wall MM, Liu S-M, Blanco C. Cannabis Use and Risk of Prescription Opioid Use Disorder in the United States. *Am J Psychiatry.* 2017;175(1):47–53. doi:10.1176/appi.ajp.2017.17040413
10. Scott KA, Dalgleish AG, Liu WM. The combination of cannabidiol and Δ9-tetrahydrocannabinol enhances the anticancer effects of radiation in an orthotopic murine glioma model. *Mol Cancer Ther.* 2014;13(12):2955–2967. doi:10.1158/1535-7163.MCT-14-0402
11. Trezza V, Campolongo P, Cassano T, et al. Effects of perinatal exposure to delta-9-tetrahydrocannabinol on the emotional reactivity of the offspring: a longitudinal behavioral study in Wistar rats. *Psychopharmacology (Berl).* 2008;198(4):529–537. doi:10.1007/s00213-008-1162-3
12. Antonelli T, Tomasini MC, Tattoli M, et al. Prenatal exposure to the CB1 receptor agonist WIN 55,212-2 causes learning disruption associated with impaired cortical NMDA receptor function and emotional reactivity changes in rat offspring. *Cereb Cortex N Y N 1991.* 2005;15(12):2013–2020. doi:10.1093/cercor/bhi076
13. Mereu G, Fà M, Ferraro L, et al. Prenatal exposure to a cannabinoid agonist produces memory deficits linked to dysfunction in hippocampal long-term potentiation and glutamate release. *Proc Natl Acad Sci U S A.* 2003;100(8):4915–4920. doi:10.1073/pnas.0537849100

RAND Corporation; 2015. http://www.rand.org/content/dam/rand/pubs/working_papers/WR1100/WR1130/RAND_WR1130.pdf. Accessed April 6, 2017.

Critical Thinking

1. Why isn't marijuana an FDA-approved medicine?
2. What are cannabinoids and how might they be useful as medicine?
3. What risks might a woman be taking if she uses medical marijuana during and after her pregnancy?
4. Do you personally believe marijuana will be made legal in the United States for medical purposes in the future? How about recreational? Explain your answers.

Internet References

Centers for Disease Control and Prevention
https://www.cdc.gov/
National Institute on Drug Abuse
https://www.drugabuse.gov/
Substance Abuse and Mental Health Services Administration
https://www.samhsa.gov

Article   Prepared by: Kim Schnurbush, *California State University, Sacramento*
Mark Pullin, *Angelo State University*

Prescription Opioids

NATIONAL INSTITUTE ON DRUG ABUSE

Learning Outcomes

After reading this article, you will be able to:

- Understand what a prescription opioid is and be familiar with some of the common prescription opioids are in the United States.

- Discuss three ways people can misuse prescription opioids.

- Recognize some of the opioid withdrawal symptoms.

What are Prescription Opioids?

Opioids are a class of drugs naturally found in the opium poppy plant. Some prescription opioids are made from the plant directly, and others are made by scientists in labs using the same chemical structure. Opioids are often used as medicines because they contain chemicals that relax the body and can relieve pain. Prescription opioids are used mostly to treat moderate to severe pain, though some opioids can be used to treat coughing and diarrhea. Opioids can also make people feel very relaxed and "high" – which is why they are sometimes used for non-medical reasons. This can be dangerous because opioids can be highly addictive, and overdoses and death are common. Heroin is one of the world's most dangerous opioids, and is never used as a medicine in the United States.

Popular slang terms for opioids include Oxy, Percs, and Vikes.

What are Common Prescription Opioids?

- hydrocodone (Vicodin®) oxycodone (OxyContin®, Percocet®)
- oxymorphone (Opana®)
- morphine (Kadian®, Avinza®)
- codeine
- fentanyl

How do People Misuse Prescription Opioids?

Prescription opioids used for pain relief are generally safe when taken for a short time and as prescribed by a doctor, but they can be misused. People misuse prescription opioids by:

- taking the medicine in a way or dose other than prescribed
- taking someone else's prescription medicine
- taking the medicine for the effect it causes—to get high

When misusing a prescription opioid, a person can swallow the medicine in its normal form. Sometimes people crush pills or open capsules, dissolve the powder in water, and inject the liquid into a vein. Some also snort the powder.

How Do Prescription Opioids Affect the Brain?

Opioids bind to and activate opioid receptors on cells located in many areas of the brain, spinal cord, and other organs in the body, especially those involved in feelings of pain and pleasure.

When opioids attach to these receptors, they block pain signals sent from the brain to the body and release large amounts of dopamine throughout the body. This release can strongly reinforce the act of taking the drug, making the user want to repeat the experience.

What are Some Possible Effects of Prescription Opioids on the Brain and Body?

In the short term, opioids can relieve pain and make people feel relaxed and happy. However, opioids can also have harmful effects, including:

- drowsiness
- confusion
- nausea
- constipation
- euphoria
- slowed breathing

Opioid misuse can cause slowed breathing, which can cause hypoxia, a condition that results when too little oxygen reaches the brain. Hypoxia can have short- and long-term psychological and neurological effects, including coma, permanent brain damage, or death.

Researchers are also investigating the long-term effects of opioid addiction on the brain, including whether damage can be reversed.

What are the Other Health Effects of Opioid Medications?

Older adults are at higher risk of accidental misuse or abuse because they typically have multiple prescriptions and chronic diseases, increasing the risk of drug-drug and drug-disease interactions, as well as a slowed metabolism that affects the breakdown of drugs.

Sharing drug injection equipment and having impaired judgment from drug use can increase the risk of contracting infectious diseases such as HIV and from unprotected sex.

Prescription Opioids and Heroin

Prescription opioids and heroin are chemically similar and can produce a similar high. In some places, heroin is cheaper and easier to get than prescription opioids, so some people switch to using heroin instead. Nearly 80 percent of Americans using heroin (including those in treatment) reported misusing prescription opioids prior to using heroin.[1,2]

However, while prescription opioid misuse is a risk factor for starting heroin use, only a small fraction of people who misuse pain relievers switch to heroin. This

suggests that prescription opioid misuse is just one factor leading to heroin use. . . .

Can I Take Prescription Opioids if I'm Pregnant?

If a woman uses prescription opioids when she's pregnant, the baby could develop dependence and have withdrawal symptoms after birth. This is called neonatal abstinence syndrome, which can be treated with medicines. Use during pregnancy can also lead to miscarriage and low birth weight.

It can be difficult for a person with an opioid addiction to quit, but pregnant women who seek treatment have better outcomes than those who quit abruptly. Methadone and buprenorphine are the standard of care to treat opioid-dependent pregnant women. Methadone or buprenorphine maintenance combined with prenatal care and a comprehensive drug treatment program can improve many of the adverse outcomes associated with untreated opioid addiction. If a woman is unable to quit before becoming pregnant, treatment with methadone or buprenorphine during pregnancy improves the chances of having a healthier baby at birth.

In general, it is important to closely monitor women who are trying to quit drug use during pregnancy and to provide treatment as needed.

Can a Person Overdose on Prescription Opioids?

Yes, a person can overdose on prescription opioids. An opioid overdose occurs when a person uses enough of the drug to produce life-threatening symptoms or death. When people overdose on an opioid medication, their breathing often slows or stops. This can decrease the amount of oxygen that reaches the brain, which can result in coma, permanent brain damage, or death.

Tolerance vs. Dependence vs. Addiction

Long-term use of prescription opioids, even as prescribed by a doctor, can cause some people to develop **a tolerance**, which means that they need higher and/or more frequent doses of the drug to get the desired effects.

Drug **dependence** occurs with repeated use, causing the neurons to adapt so they only function normally in the presence of the drug. The absence of the drug causes several physiological reactions, ranging from mild in the case of caffeine, to potentially life threatening, such as with heroin. Some chronic pain patients are dependent on opioids and require medical support to stop taking the drug.

Drug **addiction** is a chronic disease characterized by compulsive, or uncontrollable, drug seeking and use despite harmful consequences and long-lasting changes in the brain. The changes can result in harmful behaviors by those who misuse drugs, whether prescription or illicit drugs.

How Can an Opioid Overdose be Treated?

If you suspect someone has overdosed, the most important step to take is to call 911 so he or she can receive immediate medical attention. Once medical personnel arrive, they will administer naloxone. Naloxone is a medicine that can treat an opioid overdose when given right away. It works by rapidly binding to opioid receptors and blocking the effects of opioid drugs. Naloxone is available as an injectable (needle) solution, a hand-held auto-injector (EVZIO®), and a nasal spray (NARCAN® Nasal Spray).

Some states have passed laws that allow pharmacists to dispense naloxone without a personal prescription. This allows friends, family, and others in the community to use the auto-injector and nasal spray versions of naloxone to save someone who is overdosing. . . .

Can Use of Prescription Opioids Lead to Addiction?

Yes, repeated misuse of prescription opioids can lead to a substance use disorder (SUD), a medical illness which ranges from mild to severe and from temporary to chronic. Addiction is the most severe form of an SUD. An SUD develops when continued misuse of the drug changes the brain and causes health problems and failure to meet responsibilities at work, school, or home.

People addicted to an opioid medication who stop using the drug can have severe withdrawal symptoms that begin as early as a few hours after the drug was last taken. These symptoms include:

- muscle and bone pain
- sleep problems
- diarrhea and vomiting
- cold flashes with goose bumps

- uncontrollable leg movements
- severe cravings

These symptoms can be extremely uncomfortable and are the reason many people find it so difficult to stop using opioids. There are medicines being developed to help with the withdrawal process, and the U.S. Food and Drug Administration (FDA) approved sale of a device, NSS-2 Bridge, that can help ease withdrawal symptoms. The NSS-2 Bridge device is a small electrical nerve stimulator placed behind the person's ear, that can be used for up to five days during the acute withdrawal phase. There are also medicines being developed to help with the withdrawal process. The FDA approved lofexidine, a non-opioid medicine designed to reduce opioid withdrawal symptoms.

What Type of Treatment Can People Get for Addiction to Prescription Opioids?

A range of treatments including medicines and behavioral therapies are effective in helping people with opioid addiction.

Two medicines, buprenorphine and methadone, work by binding to the same opioid receptors in the brain as the opioid medicines, reducing cravings and withdrawal symptoms. Another medicine, naltrexone, blocks opioid receptors and prevents opioid drugs from having an effect.

Behavioral therapies for addiction to prescription opioids help people modify their attitudes and behaviors related to drug use, increase healthy life skills, and persist with other forms of treatment, such as medication. Some examples include cognitive behavioral therapy which helps modify the patient's drug use expectations and behaviors, and also effectively manage triggers and stress. Multidimensional family therapy, developed for adolescents with drug use problems, addresses a range of personal and family influences on one's drug use patterns and is designed to improve overall functioning. These behavioral treatment approaches have proven effective, especially when used along with medicines. . . .

Points to Remember

- Prescription opioids are used mostly to treat moderate to severe pain, though some opioids can be used to treat coughing and diarrhea.
- People misuse prescription opioids by taking the medicine in a way other than prescribed, taking someone else's prescription, or taking the medicine

to get high. When misusing a prescription opioid, a person may swallow, inject, or snort the drug.

- Opioids bind to and activate opioid receptors on cells located in the brain, spinal cord, and other organs in the body, especially those involved in feelings of pain and pleasure, and can strongly reinforce the act of taking the drug, making the user want to repeat the experience.
- People who use prescription opioids can feel relaxed and happy, but also experience drowsiness, confusion, nausea, constipation, and slowed breathing.
- Prescription opioids have effects similar to heroin. While prescription opioid misuse is a risk factor for starting heroin use, only a small fraction of people who misuse opioid pain relievers switch to heroin.
- A person can overdose on prescription opioids. Naloxone is a medicine that can treat an opioid overdose when given right away.
- Prescription opioid use, even when used as prescribed by a doctor can lead to a substance use disorder, which takes the form of addiction in severe cases. Withdrawal symptoms include muscle and bone pain, sleep problems, diarrhea and vomiting, and severe cravings.
- A range of treatments including medicines and behavioral therapies are effective in helping people with an opioid use disorder. . . .

References

1. Muhuri PK, Gfroerer JC, Davies MC. *Associations of Nonmedical Pain Reliever Use and Initiation of Heroin Use in the United States*. Rockville, MD: Substance Abuse and Mental Health Services Administration; 2013. http://archive.samhsa.gov/data/2k13/DataReview/DR006/nonmedical-pain-reliever-use-2013.pdf. Accessed May 13, 2016.
2. Jones CM. Heroin use and heroin use risk behaviors among nonmedical users of prescription opioid pain relievers - United States, 2002-2004 and 2008-2010. *Drug Alcohol Depend.* 2013;132(1-2):95-100. doi:10.1016/j.drugalcdep.2013.01.007.

Critical Thinking

1. What is a prescription opioid and what are some common ones prescribed in the United States?
2. What are three ways that people can misuse prescription opioids?
3. What are some of the ways prescription opioids impact the human body?
4. If a woman is taking prescription opioids when she is pregnant, what might happen to the baby?
5. What are some of the withdrawal symptoms people may encounter if they have misused prescription opioids?
6. What types of treatment are available for prescription opioid abuse? Can you think of any other types of treatment that may work for people who are addicted to prescription opioid medications?

Internet References

National Center for Chronic Disease Prevention and Health Promotion
 https://www.cdc.gov/chronicdisease/index.htm
National Institute on Drug Abuse
 https://www.drugabuse.gov/
Principles of Drug Addiction Treatment: A Research-Based Guide
 www.drugabuse.gov/PODAT/PODATIndex.html

National Institute on Drug Abuse, *Prescription Opioids*, U.S. Department of Health and Human Services, July 2018.

Prepared by: Kim Schnurbush, *California State University, Sacramento*
Mark Pullin, *Angelo State University*

Article

Hallucinogens and Dissociative Drugs

Including LSD, Psilocybin, Peyote, DMT, Ayahuasca, PCP, Ketamine, Dextromethorphan, and Salvia

NATIONAL INSTITUTE ON DRUG ABUSE

Learning Outcomes

After reading this article, you will be able to:

- Discuss the effects of hallucinogens and dissociative drugs on the brain and body.

- Understand the common hallucinogen and dissociative drugs being used.

- Discuss the reasons people take these drugs and long-term effects of such.

What Are Hallucinogens and Dissociative Drugs?

Hallucinogens are a class of drugs that cause hallucinations—profound distortions in a person's perceptions of reality. Hallucinogens can be found in some plants and mushrooms (or their extracts) or can be man-made, and they are commonly divided into two broad categories: classic hallucinogens (such as LSD) and dissociative drugs (such as PCP). When under the influence of either type of drug, people often report rapid, intense emotional swings and seeing images, hearing sounds, and feeling sensations that seem real but are not.

While the exact mechanisms by which hallucinogens and dissociative drugs cause their effects are not yet clearly understood, research suggests that they work at least partially by temporarily disrupting communication between neurotransmitter systems throughout the brain and spinal cord that regulate mood, sensory perception, sleep, hunger, body temperature, sexual behavior, and muscle control.

from the director:

Hallucinogens and dissociative drugs — which have street names like acid, angel dust, and vitamin K — distort the way a user perceives time, motion, colors, sounds, and self. These drugs can disrupt a person's ability to think and communicate rationally, or even to recognize reality, sometimes resulting in bizarre or dangerous behavior.

Hallucinogens such as LSD, psilocybin, peyote, DMT, and ayahuasca cause emotions to swing wildly and real-world sensations to appear unreal, sometimes frightening. Dissociative drugs like PCP, ketamine, dextromethorphan, and *Salvia divinorum* may make a user feel out of control and disconnected from their body and environment.

In addition to their short-term effects on perception and mood, hallucinogenic drugs are associated with psychotic-like episodes that can occur long after a person has taken the drug, and dissociative drugs can cause respiratory depression, heart rate abnormalities, and a withdrawal syndrome. The good news is that use of hallucinogenic and dissociative drugs among U.S. high school students, in general, has remained relatively low in recent years. However, the introduction of new hallucinogenic and dissociative drugs is of particular concern.

NIDA research is developing a clearer picture of the dangers of hallucinogenic and dissociative drugs. We have compiled the scientific information in this report to inform readers and hopefully prevent the use of these drugs.

Nora D. Volkow, M.D.
Director
National Institute on Drug Abuse

Classic Hallucinogens*

LSD (d-lysergic acid diethylamide)—also known as acid, blotter, doses, hits, microdots, sugar cubes, trips, tabs, or window panes—is one of the most potent mood- and perception-altering hallucinogenic drugs. It is a clear or white, odorless, water-soluble material synthesized from lysergic acid, a compound derived from a rye fungus. LSD is initially produced in crystalline form, which can then be used to produce tablets known as "microdots" or thin squares of gelatin called "window panes." It can also be diluted with water or alcohol and sold

in liquid form. The most common form, however, is LSD-soaked paper punched into small individual squares, known as "blotters."

Psilocybin (4-phosphoryloxy-N, N-dimethyl- tryptamine)—also known as magic mushrooms, shrooms, boomers, or little smoke—is extracted from certain types of mushrooms found in tropical and subtropical regions of South America, Mexico, and the United States. In the past, psilocybin was ingested during religious ceremonies by indigenous cultures from Mexico and Central America. Psilocybin can either be dried or fresh and eaten raw, mixed with food, or brewed into a tea, and produces similar effects to LSD.

Peyote (Mescaline)—also known as buttons, cactus, and mesc—is a small, spineless cactus with mescaline as its main ingredient. It has been used by natives in northern Mexico and the southwestern United States as a part of religious ceremonies. The top, or "crown," of the peyote cactus has disc-shaped buttons that are cut out, dried, and usually chewed or soaked in water to produce an intoxicating liquid. Because the extract is so bitter, some users prepare a tea by boiling the plant for several hours. Mescaline can also be produced through chemical synthesis.

DMT (Dimethyl-tryptamine)—also known as Dimitri—is a powerful hallucinogenic chemical found naturally occurring in some Amazonian plant species (see "Ayahuasca") and also synthesized in the laboratory. Synthetic DMT usually takes the form of a white crystalline powder and is typically vaporized or smoked in a pipe.

Ayahuasca—also known as hoasca, aya, and yagé—is a hallucinogenic brew made from one of several Amazonian plants containing DMT (the primary psychoactive ingredient) along with a vine containing a natural alkaloid that prevents the normal breakdown of DMT in the digestive tract. Ayahuasca tea has traditionally been used for healing and religious purposes in indigenous South American cultures, mainly in the Amazon region.

Dissociative Drugs

PCP (Phencyclidine)—also known as ozone, rocket fuel, love boat, hog, embalming fluid, or superweed—was originally developed in the 1950s as a general anesthetic for surgery. While it can be found in a variety of forms, including tablets or capsules, it is usually sold as a liquid or powder. PCP can be snorted, smoked, injected, or swallowed. It is sometimes smoked after being sprinkled on marijuana, tobacco, or parsley.

Ketamine—also known as K, Special K, or cat Valium—is a dissociative currently used as an anesthetic for humans as well as animals. Much of the ketamine sold on the street has been diverted from veterinary offices. Although it is manufactured as an injectable liquid, ketamine is generally evaporated to form a powder that is snorted or compressed into pills for illicit use. Because ketamine is odorless and tasteless and has amnesia-inducing properties, it is sometimes added to drinks to facilitate sexual assault.

DXM (Dextromethorphan)—also known as robo—is a cough suppressant and expectorant ingredient in some over-the-counter (OTC) cold and cough medications that are often abused by adolescents and young adults. The most common sources of abused DXM are "extra-strength" cough syrup, which typically contains around 15 milligrams of DXM per teaspoon, and pills and gel capsules, which typically contain 15 milligrams of DXM per pill. OTC medications that contain DXM often also contain antihistamines and decongestants.

Salvia divinorum—also known as diviner's sage, Maria Pastora, Sally-D, or magic mint—is a psychoactive plant common to southern Mexico and Central and South America. Salvia is typically ingested by chewing fresh leaves or by drinking their extracted juices. The dried leaves of salvia can also be smoked or vaporized and inhaled.

How Widespread Is the Abuse of Hallucinogens and Dissociative Drugs?

According to the 2013 National Survey on Drug Use and Health, 229,000 Americans ages 12 and older reported current (past-month) use of LSD and 33,000 reported current use of PCP (Substance Abuse and Mental Health Services Administration, 2013). Among high school seniors, salvia was significantly more popular than LSD or PCP when it was added to the Monitoring the Future survey in 2009. Past-year use was reported to be 5.9 percent for salvia, 2.7 percent for LSD, and 1.3 percent for PCP. Fortunately, rates have dropped significantly for saliva—to 1.8 percent in 2014—with LSD and PCP use dropping slightly (Johnston, 2014).

While regular use of hallucinogenic and dissociative drugs in general has remained relatively low in recent years, one study reported that the United States ranks first among 36 nations in the proportion of high school students ever using LSD or other hallucinogens in their lifetime (6 percent versus 2 percent in Europe) (Hibell, 2012).

Additionally, tourism to the Amazon for the purpose of using ayahuasca has become increasingly popular among Americans and Europeans in recent years, and ayahuasca use has also been reported in major cities in Brazil and abroad (Barbosa, 2012; McKenna, 2004). Although DMT is a schedule I drug, plants containing DMT are not scheduled, and there is ambiguity over ayahuasca's legal status in the United States (McKenna, 2004). Two Brazilian churches have obtained permission to import and use these plants in their ceremonies.

Why Do People Take Hallucinogenic or Dissociative Drugs?

Hallucinogenic and dissociative drugs have been used for a variety of reasons (Bogenschutz, 2012; Bonson, 2001). Historically, hallucinogenic plants have been used for religious rituals to induce states of detachment from reality and precipitate "visions" thought to provide mystical insight or enable contact with a spirit world or "higher power." More recently, people report using hallucinogenic drugs for more social or recreational purposes, including to have fun, help them deal with stress, or enable them to enter into what they perceive as a more enlightened sense of thinking or being. Hallucinogens have also been investigated as therapeutic agents to treat diseases associated with perceptual distortions, such as schizophrenia, obsessive-compulsive disorder, bipolar disorder, and dementia. Anecdotal reports and small studies have suggested that ayahuasca may be a potential treatment for substance use disorders and other mental health issues, but no large scale research has verified its efficacy (Barbosa, 2012).

How Do Hallucinogens (LSD, Psilocybin, Peyote, DMT, and Ayahuasca) Affect the Brain and Body?
How Do Hallucinogens Work?

Classic hallucinogens are thought to produce their perception-altering effects by acting on neural circuits in the brain that use the neurotransmitter serotonin (Passie, 2008; Nichols, 2004; Schindler, 2012; Lee, 2012). Specifically, some of their most prominent effects occur in the prefrontal cortex—an area involved in mood, cognition, and perception—as well as other regions important in regulating arousal and physiological responses to stress and panic.

What Are the Short-Term Effects of Hallucinogens?

Ingesting hallucinogenic drugs can cause users to see images, hear sounds, and feel sensations that seem real but do not exist. Their effects typically begin within 20 to 90 minutes of ingestion and can last as long as 12 hours. Experiences are often unpredictable and may vary with the amount ingested and the user's personality, mood, expectations, and surroundings. The effects of hallucinogens like LSD can be described as drug-induced psychosis—distortion or disorganization of a person's capacity to recognize reality, think rationally, or communicate with others. Users refer to LSD and other hallucinogenic experiences as "trips" and to acute adverse or unpleasant experiences as "bad trips." On some trips, users experience sensations that are enjoyable and mentally stimulating and that produce a sense of heightened understanding. Bad trips, however, include terrifying thoughts and nightmarish feelings of anxiety and despair that include fears of losing control, insanity, or death.

Like LSD and psilocybin, DMT produces its effects through action at serotonin (5-HT) receptors in the brain (Strassman, 1996). Some research has suggested that DMT occurs naturally in the human brain in small quantities, leading to the hypothesis that release of endogenous DMT may be involved in reports of alien abductions, spontaneous mystical experiences, and near-death experiences, but this remains controversial (Barker, 2012).

Short-Term General Effects of Hallucinogens
Sensory Effects

- Hallucinations, including seeing, hearing, touching, or smelling things in a distorted way or perceiving things that do not exist
- Intensified feelings and sensory experiences (brighter colors, sharper sounds)
- Mixed senses ("seeing" sounds or "hearing" colors)
- Changes in sense or perception of time (time goes by slowly)

Physical Effects

- Increased energy and heart rate
- Nausea

Specific short-term effects of LSD, psilocybin, peyote, DMT, and ayahuasca include:

LSD

- Increased blood pressure, heart rate, and body temperature
- Dizziness and sleeplessness
- Loss of appetite, dry mouth, and sweating
- Numbness, weakness, and tremors

- Impulsiveness and rapid emotional shifts that can range from fear to euphoria, with transitions so rapid that the user may seem to experience several emotions simultaneously

Psilocybin
- Feelings of relaxation (similar to effects of low doses of marijuana)
- Nervousness, paranoia, and panic reactions
- Introspective/spiritual experiences
- Misidentification of poisonous mushrooms resembling psilocybin could lead to unintentional, potentially fatal poisoning

Peyote
- Increased body temperature and heart rate
- Uncoordinated movements (ataxia)
- Profound sweating
- Flushing

DMT
- Increased heart rate
- Agitation
- Hallucinations frequently involving radically altered environments as well as body and spatial distortions

Ayahuasca
- Increased blood pressure
- Severe vomiting (induced by the tea)
- Profoundly altered state of awareness and perceptions of otherworldly imagery

What Are the Long-Term Effects of Hallucinogens?
LSD users quickly develop a high degree of tolerance to the drug's effects, such that repeated use requires increasingly larger doses to produce similar effects.

Use of hallucinogenic drugs also produces tolerance to other drugs in this class, including psilocybin and peyote. Use of classic hallucinogens does not, however, produce tolerance to drugs that do not act directly on the same brain cell receptors. In other words, there is no cross-tolerance to drugs that act on other neurotransmitter systems, such as marijuana, amphetamines, or PCP, among others. Furthermore, tolerance for hallucinogenic drugs is short-lived—it is lost if the user stops taking the drugs for several days—and physical withdrawal symptoms are not typically experienced when chronic use is stopped.

The long-term residual psychological and cognitive effects of peyote remain poorly understood. Although one study found

no evidence of psychological or cognitive deficits among Native Americans who use peyote regularly in a religious setting, those findings may not generalize to those who repeatedly abuse the drug for recreational purposes (Halpern, 2005). Peyote users may also experience hallucinogen persisting perception disorder (HPPD)— also often referred to as *flashbacks*. The active ingredient mescaline has also been associated, in at least one report, to fetal abnormalities (Gilmore, 2001).

Long-term effects of DMT use and abuse and addiction liability are currently unknown. Unlike most other hallucinogens, DMT does not appear to induce tolerance (Winstock, 2013).

As with some other hallucinogens, there is little information to suggest that ayahuasca use creates lasting physiological or neurological deficits, especially among those using the brew for religious activities.

Overall, two long-term effects— persistent psychosis and HPPD—have been associated with use of classic hallucinogens (see sidebar). Although occurrence of either is rare, it is also unpredictable and may happen more often than previously thought, and sometimes both conditions occur together. While the exact causes are not known, both conditions are more often seen in individuals with a history of psychological problems but can happen to anyone, even after a single exposure. There is no established treatment for HPPD, in which flashbacks may occur spontaneously and repeatedly although less intensely than their initial occurrence. Some antidepressant and antipsychotic drugs can be prescribed to help improve mood and treat psychoses, however. Psychotherapy may also help patients cope with fear or confusion associated with visual disturbances or other consequences of long-term LSD use. More research on the causes, incidence, and long-term effects of both disorders is being conducted.

What Are the Effects of Common Dissociative Drugs on the Brain and Body?
How Do Dissociative Drugs Work?
Laboratory studies suggest that dissociative drugs, including PCP, ketamine, and DXM, cause their effects by disrupting the actions of the brain chemical glutamate at certain types of receptors—called N-methyl-D-aspartate (NMDA) receptors—on nerve cells throughout the brain (Morgan, 2012; Morris, 2005). Glutamate plays a major role in cognition (including learning and memory), emotion, and the perception of pain (the latter via activation of pain- regulating cells outside of the brain). PCP also alters the actions of dopamine, a neurotransmitter responsible for the euphoria and "rush" associated with many abused drugs.

Salvia divinorum works differently. While classified as a dissociative drug, salvia causes its effects by activating the kappa opioid receptor on nerve cells (Cunningham, 2011; MacLean, 2013). These receptors differ from those activated by the more commonly known opioids such as heroin and morphine.

Long-Term Effects of Hallucinogens

Persistent psychosis

- Visual disturbances
- Disorganized thinking
- Paranoia
- Mood disturbances

Hallucinogen Persisting Perception Disorder (HPPD)

- Hallucinations
- Other visual disturbances (such as seeing halos or trails attached to moving objects)
- Symptoms sometimes mistaken for neurological disorders (such as stroke or brain tumor) role

What Are the Short-Term Effects of Dissociative Drugs?

Dissociative drugs can produce visual and auditory distortions and a sense of floating and dissociation (feeling detached from reality) in users. Use of dissociative drugs can also cause anxiety, memory loss, and impaired motor function, including body tremors and numbness. These effects, which depend on the amount of the drug taken, are also unpredictable—typically beginning within minutes of ingestion and lasting for several hours, although some users report feeling the drug's effects for days. See text box for general effects of dissociative drugs.

In addition to these general effects, different dissociative drugs can produce a variety of distinct and dangerous effects. For example, at moderate to high doses, PCP can cause a user to have seizures or severe muscle contractions, become aggressive or violent, or even experience psychotic symptoms similar to schizophrenia. At moderate to high doses, ketamine can cause sedation, immobility, and amnesia. At high doses, ketamine users also report experiencing terrifying feelings of almost complete sensory detachment likened to a near-death experience (called a "K-hole," similar to a bad LSD trip). Salvia users report intense but short-lived effects—up to 30 minutes—including emotional mood swings ranging from sadness to uncontrolled laughter.

DXM, which is safe and effective as a cough suppressant and expectorant when used at recommended doses (typically

General Common Effects of Dissociative Drugs

Low to Moderate Doses	High Doses
Numbness	**Hallucinations**
Disorientation, confusion, and loss of coordination	Memory loss
Dizziness, nausea, vomiting	Physical distress, including dangerous changes in blood pressure, heart rate, respiration, and body temperature
Changes in sensory perceptions (such as sight, sound, shapes, time, and body image)	Marked psychological distress, including feelings of extreme panic, fear, anxiety, paranoia, invulnerability, exaggerated strength, and aggression
Hallucinations	
Feelings of detachment from self and environment	
Increase in blood pressure, heart rate, respiration, and body temperature	Use with high doses of alcohol or other central nervous system depressants can lead to respiratory distress or arrest, resulting in death

15 to 30 milligrams), can lead to serious side effects when abused. For example, use of DXM at doses from 200 to 1,500 milligrams can produce dissociative effects similar to PCP and ketamine and increase the risk of serious central nervous system and cardiovascular effects such as respiratory distress, seizures, and increased heart rate from the antihistamines found in cough medicines.

What Are the Long-Term Effects of Dissociative Drugs?

While the long-term use of most dissociative drugs has not been investigated systematically, research shows that repeated use of PCP can lead to tolerance and the development of a substance use disorder that includes a withdrawal syndrome (including craving for the drug, headaches, and sweating) when drug use is stopped. Other effects of long-term PCP use include persistent speech difficulties, memory loss, depression, suicidal thoughts, anxiety, and social withdrawal that may persist for a year or more after chronic use stops.

References

Barbosa PC, Mizumoto S, Bogenschutz MP, Strassman RJ. Health status of ayahuasca users. *Drug Test Anal.* 2012; 4(7-8):601–609.

Barker SA, McIlhenny EH, Strassman R. A critical review of reportsof endogenous psychedelic N, N-dimethyltryptamines in humans: 1955–2010. *Drug Test Anal.* 2012; Jul-Aug;4(7-8):617–35.

Bogenschutz MP, Pommy JM. Therapeutic mechanisms of classic hallucinogens in the treatment of addictions: from indirect evidence to testable hypotheses. *Drug Test Anal.* 2012;4(7-8):543–555.

Bonson KR. Hallucinogenic drugs. In: *Encyclopedia of Life Sciences.* United Kingdom: Nature Publishing Group; 2001.

Bouso JC, González D, Fondevila S, et al. Personality, psychopathology, life attitudes and neuropsychological performance among ritual users of Ayahuasca: a longitudinal study. *PLoS One.* 2012;7(8).

Cunningham CW, Rothman RB, Prisinzano TE. Neuropharmacology of the naturally occurring kappa-opioid hallucinogen salvinorin A. *Pharmacol Rev.* 2011;63(2):316–347.

Gilmore HT. Peyote use during pregnancy. *S D J Med.* 2001;54(1):27–29.

Halpern JH, Sherwood AR, Hudson JI, Yurgelun-Todd D, Pope HG Jr. Psychological and cognitive effects of long-term peyote use among Native Americans. *Biol Psychiatry.* 2005;58(8):624–631.

Hibell B, Guttormsson U, Ahlström S, et al. *The 2011 ESPAD Report: Substance Use Among Students in 36 European Countries.* Stockholm, Sweden: The Swedish Council for Information on Alcohol and Other Drugs (CAN); 2012.

Johnston LD, O'Malley PM, Bachman JG, Schulenberg JE. *Monitoring the Future national results on drug use: 1975–2014. Overview of key findings on Adolescent Drug Use.* Ann Arbor, MI: Institute for Social Research, The University of Michigan; 2014.

Lee HM, and Roth BL. Hallucinogen actions on human brain revealed. *Proc Natl Acad Sci U S A.* 2012; 109(6):1820–1821.

MacLean KA, Johnson MW, Reissig CJ, Prisinzano TE, Griffiths RR. Dose-related effects of salvinorin A in humans: dissociative, hallucinogenic, and memory effects. *Psychopharmacology (Berl).* 2013;226(2):381–392.

McKenna, DJ. Clinical investigations of the therapeutic potential of ayahuasca: rationale and regulatory challenges. *Pharmacol Ther.* 2004;102(2):111–129.

Morgan CJ, Curran HV, Independent Scientific Committee on Drugs. Ketamine use: a review. *Addiction.* 2012;107(1):27–38.

Morris BJ, Cochran SM, and Pratt JA. PCP: from pharmacology to modelling schizophrenia. *Curr Opin Pharmacol.* 2005;5(1):101–106.

Nichols DE. Hallucinogens. *Pharmacol Ther.* 2004; 101(2):131–181.

Passie T, Halpern JH, Stichtenoth DO, Emrich HM, Hintzen A. The pharmacology of lysergic acid diethylamide: a review. *CNS Neurosci Ther.* 2008;14(4):295–314.

Schindler EA, Dave KD, Smolock EM, Aloyo VJ, Harvey JA. Serotonergic and dopaminergic distinctions in the behavioral pharmacology of (+/-)-1-(2,5-dimethoxy-4-iodophenyl)-2-aminopropane (DOI) and lysergic acid diethylamide (LSD). *Pharmacol Biochem Behav.* 2012;101(1): 69–76.

Strassman RJ. Human psychopharmacology of N,N-dimethyltryptamine. *Behav Brain Res.* 1996;73(1-2):121–124.

Substance Abuse and Mental Health Services Administration. *Results from the 2013 National Survey on Drug Use and Health: Summary of National Findings.* Rockville, MD: Substance Abuse and Mental Health Services Administration; 2014. HHS Publication No. (SMA) 14-4887. NSDUH Series H-49.

Winstock AR, Kaar S, Borschmann R. Dimethyltryptamine (DMT): prevalence, user characteristics and abuse liability in a large global sample. *J Psychopharmacol.* 2014;28(1):49–54.

---

*In this report, the term "hallucinogen" will refer to the classic hallucinogenic drugs LSD and Psilocybin.

Critical Thinking

1. How do hallucinogens affect the brain and body?
2. What are the general common effects of dissociative drugs?
3. List several reasons people take hallucinogenic and dissociative drugs? What is the attractiveness of these drugs?
4. Are these drugs considered more social or recreational drugs than some others?

Internet References

BMC Public Health
https://bmcpublichealth.biomedcentral.com/

National Institute on Drug Abuse
https://www.drugabuse.gov/

Principles of Drug Addiction Treatment: A Research-Based Guide
www.drugabuse.gov/PODAT/PODATIndex.html

National Institute on Drug Abuse, *Hallucinogens and Dissociative Drugs.* U.S. Department of Health and Human Services, 2015.

Article

Prepared by: Kim Schnurbush, *California State University, Sacramento*
Mark Pullin, *Angelo State University*

Drugs, Brains, and Behavior: The Science of Addiction

NATIONAL INSTITUTE ON DRUG ABUSE

Learning Outcomes

After reading this article, you will be able to:

- Understand how people of all ages suffer harmful consequences of drug use and abuse.

- Discuss how science can provide solutions to drug use and addiction.

- Discuss why some become addicted to drugs and other do not.

- Understand risk factors and protective factors to drug use and addiction.

INTRODUCTION
Why study
DRUG USE AND ADDICTION?

Use and misuse of alcohol, nicotine, and illicit drugs, and misuse of prescription drugs cost Americans more than $700 billion a year in increased healthcare costs, crime, and lost productivity.[1,2,3] Every year, illicit and prescription drugs and alcohol contribute to the death of more than 90,000 Americans, while tobacco is linked to an estimated 480,000 deaths per year.[4,5] (Hereafter, unless otherwise specified, *drugs* refers to all of these substances.)

People of All Ages Suffer the Harmful Consequences of Drug Use and Addiction:

- **Teens** who use drugs may act out and may do poorly in school or drop out.[6] Using drugs when the brain is still developing may cause lasting brain changes and put the user at increased risk of dependence.[7]

- **Adults** who use drugs can have problems thinking clearly, remembering, and paying attention. They may develop poor social behaviors as a result of their drug use, and their work performance and personal relationships suffer.

- **Parents'** drug use can mean chaotic, stress-filled homes, as well as child abuse and neglect.[8] Such conditions harm the well-being and development of children in the home and may set the stage for drug use in the next generation.[9]

- **Babies** exposed to drugs in the womb may be born premature and underweight. This exposure can slow the child's ability to learn and affect behavior later in life.[10] They may also become dependent on opioids or other drugs used by the mother during pregnancy, a condition called neonatal abstinence syndrome (NAS).

How Does Science Provide Solutions for Drug Use and Addiction?

Scientists study the effects drugs have on the brain and behavior. They use this information to develop programs for preventing drug use and for helping people recover from addiction. Further research helps transfer these ideas into practice in the community.

The consequences of drug use are vast and varied and affect people of all ages.

Drug Misuse and Addiction

What is DRUG ADDICTION?

Addiction is defined as a chronic, relapsing disorder characterized by compulsive drug seeking and use despite adverse consequences.[†] It is considered a brain disorder, because it involves functional changes to brain circuits involved in reward, stress, and self-control, and those changes may last a long time after a person has stopped taking drugs.[11]

Addiction is a lot like other diseases, such as heart disease. Both disrupt the normal, healthy functioning of an organ in the body, both have serious harmful effects, and both are, in many cases, preventable and treatable. If left untreated, they can last a lifetime and may lead to death.

Why do PEOPLE TAKE DRUGS?

In general, people take drugs for a few reasons:

- **To feel good.** Drugs can produce intense feelings of pleasure. This initial euphoria is followed by other effects, which differ with the type of drug used. For example, with stimulants such as cocaine, the high is followed by feelings of power, self-confidence, and increased energy. In contrast, the euphoria caused by opioids such as heroin is followed by feelings of relaxation and satisfaction.

- **To feel better.** Some people who suffer from social anxiety, stress, and depression start using drugs to try to feel less anxious. Stress can play a major role in starting and continuing drug use as well as relapse (return to drug use) in patients recovering from addiction.

- **To do better.** Some people feel pressure to improve their focus in school or at work or their abilities in sports. This can play a role in trying or continuing to use drugs, such as prescription stimulants or cocaine.

- **Curiosity and social pressure.** In this respect, teens are particularly at risk because peer pressure can be very strong. Teens are more likely than adults to act in risky or daring ways to impress their friends and show their independence from parents and social rules.

If taking drugs makes people feel good or better, WHAT'S THE PROBLEM?

When they first use a drug, people may perceive what seem to be positive effects. They also may believe they can control

their use. But drugs can quickly take over a person's life. Over time, if drug use continues, other pleasurable activities become less pleasurable, and the person has to take the drug just to feel "normal." They have a hard time controlling their need to take drugs even though it causes many problems for themselves and their loved ones. Some people may start to feel the need to take more of a drug or take it more often, even in the early stages of their drug use. These are the telltale signs of an addiction.

Even relatively moderate drug use poses dangers. Consider how a social drinker can become intoxicated, get behind the wheel of a car, and quickly turn a pleasurable activity into a tragedy that affects many lives. Occasional drug use, such as misusing an opioid to get high, can have similarly disastrous effects, including overdose, and dangerously impaired driving.

Do people freely choose to KEEP USING DRUGS?

The initial decision to take drugs is typically voluntary. But with continued use, a person's ability to exert self-control can become seriously impaired; this impairment in self-control is the hallmark of addiction.

Brain imaging studies of people with addiction show physical changes in areas of the brain that are critical to judgment, decision-making, learning and memory, and behavior control.[12] These changes help explain the compulsive nature of addiction.

Why do some people become addicted to drugs, WHILE OTHERS DO NOT?

As with other diseases and disorders, the likelihood of developing an addiction differs from person to person, and no single factor determines whether a person will become addicted to drugs. In general, the more *risk factors* a person has, the greater the chance that taking drugs will lead to drug use and addiction. *Protective factors*, on the other hand, reduce a person's risk. Risk and protective factors may be either environmental or biological.

Risk and Protective Factors for Drug Use, Misuse, and Addiction

RISK FACTORS	PROTECTIVE FACTORS
Aggressive behavior in childhood[13,14]	Good self control[15]
Lack of parental supervision[14,16]	Parental monitoring and support[16–18]
Poor social skills[13,17,18]	Positive relationships[17,19]
Drug experimentation[14,20,21]	Good grades[17,22]
Availability of drugs at school[21,23]	School anti-drug policies[17]
Community poverty[24,25]	Neighborhood resources[26]

[†] *The term addiction as used in this booklet is equivalent to a severe substance use disorder as defined by the Diagnostic and Statistical Manual of Mental Disorders, Fifth Edition (DSM-5, 2013).*

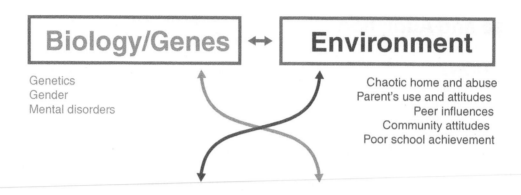

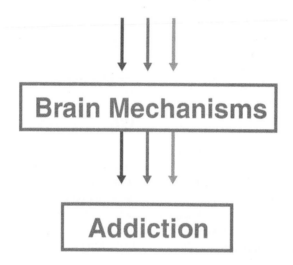

WHAT BIOLOGICAL FACTORS increase the risk of addiction?

Biological factors that can affect a person's risk of addiction include their genes, stage of development, and even gender or ethnicity. Scientists estimate that genes, including the effects environmental factors have on a person's gene expression, called epigenetics, account for between 40 and 60 percent of a person's risk of addiction.[27] Also, teens and people with mental disorders are at greater risk of drug use and addiction than others.[28]

WHAT ENVIRONMENTAL FACTORS increase the risk of addiction?

Environmental factors are those related to the family, school, and neighborhood. Factors that can increase a person's risk include the following:

- **Home and family.** The home environment, especially during childhood, is a very important factor. Parents or older family members who use drugs or misuse alcohol, or who break the law, can increase children's risk of future drug problems.[29]

- **Peers and school.** Friends and other peers can have an increasingly strong influence during the teen years. Teens who use drugs can sway even those without risk factors to try drugs for the first time. Struggling in school or having poor social skills can put a child at further risk for using or becoming addicted to drugs.[30]

What other factors increase the RISK OF ADDICTION?

- **Early use.** Although taking drugs at any age can lead to addiction, research shows that the earlier a person begins to use drugs, the more likely he or she is to develop serious problems.[31] This may be due to the harmful effect that drugs can have on the developing brain.[32] It also may result from a mix of early social and biological risk factors, including lack of a stable home or family, exposure to physical or sexual abuse, genes, or mental illness. Still, the fact remains that early use is a strong indicator of problems ahead, including addiction.
- **How the drug is taken.** Smoking a drug or injecting it into a vein increases its addictive potential.[33,34] Both smoked and injected drugs enter the brain within seconds, producing a powerful rush of pleasure. However, this intense high can fade within a few minutes. Scientists believe this starkly felt contrast drives some people to repeated drug taking in an attempt to recapture the fleeting pleasurable state.

The brain continues to develop into adulthood and undergoes DRAMATIC CHANGES DURING ADOLESCENCE

One of the brain areas still maturing during adolescence is the prefrontal cortex—the part of the brain that allows people to assess situations, make sound decisions, and keep emotions and desires under control. The fact that this critical part of a teen's brain is still a work in progress puts them at increased risk for making poor decisions, such as trying drugs or continuing to take them. Introducing drugs during this period of development may cause brain changes that have profound and long-lasting consequences.

Preventing Drug Misuse and Addiction: The Best Strategy

Why is adolescence a critical time for PREVENTING DRUG ADDICTION?

As noted previously, early use of drugs increases a person's chances of becoming addicted. Remember, drugs change the brain—and this can lead to addiction and other serious problems. So, preventing early use of drugs or alcohol may go a long way in reducing these risks.

Risk of drug use increases greatly during times of transition. For an adult, a divorce or loss of a job may increase the risk of drug use. For a teenager, risky times include moving, family divorce, or changing schools.[35] When children advance from elementary through middle school, they face new and challenging social, family, and academic situations. Often during this period, children are exposed to substances such as cigarettes and alcohol for the first time. When they enter high school, teens may encounter greater availability of drugs, drug use by older teens, and social activities where drugs are used.

A certain amount of risk-taking is a normal part of adolescent development. The desire to try new things and become more independent is healthy, but it may also increase teens' tendencies to experiment with drugs. The parts of the brain that control judgment and decision-making do not fully develop until people are in their early or mid-20s; this limits a teen's ability to accurately assess the risks of drug experimentation and makes young people more vulnerable to peer pressure.[36]

Because the brain is still developing, using drugs at this age has more potential to disrupt brain function in areas critical to motivation, memory, learning, judgment, and behavior control.[12] So, it's not surprising that teens who use alcohol and other drugs often have family and social problems, poor academic performance, health-related problems (including mental health conditions), and involvement with the juvenile justice system.

Can research-based programs prevent DRUG ADDICTION IN YOUTH?

Yes. The term "research-based" or "evidence-based" means that these programs have been designed based on current scientific evidence, thoroughly tested, and shown to produce positive results. Scientists have developed a broad range of programs that positively alter the balance between risk and protective factors for drug use in families, schools, and communities. Studies have shown that research-based programs, such as described in NIDA's *Principles of Substance Abuse Prevention for Early Childhood: A Research-Based Guide* and *Preventing Drug Use among Children and Adolescents: A Research-Based Guide for Parents, Educators, and Community Leaders*, can significantly reduce early use of tobacco, alcohol, and other drugs.[37] Also, while many social and cultural factors affect drug use trends, when young people perceive drug use as harmful, they often reduce their level of use.[38]

How do research-based PREVENTION PROGRAMS WORK?

These prevention programs work to boost protective factors and eliminate or reduce risk factors for drug use. The programs are designed for various ages and can be used in individual or group settings, such as the school and home. There are three types of programs:

- **Universal programs** address risk and protective factors common to all children in a given setting, such as a school or community.
- **Selective programs** are for groups of children and teens who have specific factors that put them at increased risk of drug use.
- **Indicated programs** are designed for youth who have already started using drugs.

Young Brains Under Study

Using cutting-edge imaging technology, scientists from the NIDA's Adolescent Brain Cognitive Development (ABCD) Study will look at how childhood experiences, including use of any drugs, interact with each other and with a child's changing biology to affect brain development and social, behavioral, academic, health, and other outcomes. As the only study of its kind, the ABCD study will yield critical insights into the foundational aspects of adolescence that shape a person's future.

Drugs and the Brain
Introducing the
HUMAN BRAIN

The human brain is the most complex organ in the body. This three-pound mass of gray and white matter sits at the center of all human activity—you need it to drive a car, to enjoy a meal, to breathe, to create an artistic masterpiece, and to enjoy everyday activities. The brain regulates your body's basic functions, enables you to interpret and respond to everything you experience, and shapes your behavior. In short, *your brain is you*—everything you think and feel, and who you are.

How does the
BRAIN WORK?

The brain is often likened to an incredibly complex and intricate computer. Instead of electrical circuits on the silicon chips that control our electronic devices, the brain consists of billions of cells, called *neurons*, which are organized into circuits and networks. Each neuron acts as a switch controlling the flow of information. If a neuron receives enough signals from other neurons connected to it, it "fires," sending its own signal on to other neurons in the circuit.

The brain is made up of many parts with interconnected circuits that all work together as a team. Different brain circuits are responsible for coordinating and performing specific functions. Networks of neurons send signals back and forth to each other and among different parts of the brain, the spinal cord, and nerves in the rest of the body (the peripheral nervous system).

To send a message, a neuron releases a *neurotransmitter* into the gap (or *synapse*) between it and the next cell. The neurotransmitter crosses the synapse and attaches to receptors on the receiving neuron, like a key into a lock. This causes changes in the receiving cell. Other molecules called *transporters* recycle neurotransmitters (that is, bring them back into the neuron that released them), thereby limiting or shutting off the signal between neurons.

How do drugs
WORK IN THE BRAIN?

Drugs interfere with the way neurons send, receive, and process signals via neurotransmitters. Some drugs, such as marijuana and heroin, can activate neurons because their chemical structure mimics that of a natural neurotransmitter in the body. This allows the drugs to attach onto and activate the neurons. Although these drugs mimic the brain's own chemicals, they don't activate neurons in the same way as a natural neurotransmitter, and they lead to abnormal messages being sent through the network.

Other drugs, such as amphetamine or cocaine, can cause the neurons to release abnormally large amounts of natural neurotransmitters or prevent the normal recycling of these brain chemicals by interfering with transporters. This too amplifies or disrupts the normal communication between neurons.

What parts of the brain are
AFFECTED BY DRUG USE?

Drugs can alter important brain areas that are necessary for life-sustaining functions and can drive the compulsive drug use that marks addiction. Brain areas affected by drug use include:

- *The basal ganglia,* which play an important role in positive forms of motivation, including the pleasurable effects of healthy activities like eating, socializing, and sex, and are also involved in the formation of habits and routines. These areas form a key node of what is sometimes called the brain's "reward circuit." Drugs over-activate this circuit, producing the euphoria of the drug high; but with repeated exposure, the circuit adapts to the presence of the drug, diminishing its sensitivity and making it hard to feel pleasure from anything besides the drug.
- *The extended amygdala* plays a role in stressful feelings like anxiety, irritability, and unease, which characterize withdrawal after the drug high fades and thus motivates

the person to seek the drug again. This circuit becomes increasingly sensitive with increased drug use. Over time, a person with substance use disorder uses drugs to get temporary relief from this discomfort rather than to get high.

- *The prefrontal cortex* powers the ability to think, plan, solve problems, make decisions, and exert self-control over impulses. This is also the last part of the brain to mature, making teens most vulnerable. Shifting balance between this circuit and the reward and stress circuits of the basal ganglia and extended amygdala make a person with a substance use disorder seek the drug compulsively with reduced impulse control.

Some drugs like opioids also affect other parts of the brain, such as the brain stem, which controls basic functions critical to life, such as heart rate, breathing, and sleeping explaining why overdoses can cause depressed breathing and death.

How do
DRUGS PRODUCE PLEASURE?

Pleasure or euphoria—the high from drugs—is still poorly understood, but probably involves surges of chemical signaling compounds including the body's natural opioids (endorphins) and other neurotransmitters in parts of the basal ganglia (the reward circuit). When some drugs are taken, they can cause surges of these neurotransmitters much greater than the smaller bursts naturally produced in association with healthy rewards like eating, music, creative pursuits, or social interaction.

It was once thought that surges of the neurotransmitter *dopamine* produced by drugs directly caused the euphoria, but scientists now think dopamine has more to do with getting us to repeat pleasurable activities (reinforcement) than with producing pleasure directly.

How does
DOPAMINE REINFORCE
DRUG USE?

Our brains are wired to increase the odds that we will repeat pleasurable activities. The neurotransmitter dopamine is central to this. Whenever the reward circuit is activated by a healthy, pleasurable experience, a burst of dopamine signals that something important is happening that needs to be remembered. This dopamine signal causes changes in neural connectivity that make it easier to repeat the activity again and again without thinking about it, leading to the formation of habits.

Just as drugs produce intense euphoria, they also produce much larger surges of dopamine, powerfully reinforcing the connection between consumption of the drug, the resulting pleasure, and all the external cues linked to the experience.

Large surges of dopamine "teach" the brain to seek drugs at the expense of other, healthier goals and activities.

Cues in a person's daily routine or environment that have become linked with drug use because of changes to the reward circuit can trigger uncontrollable cravings whenever the person is exposed to these cues, even if the drug itself is not available. This learned "reflex" can last a long time, even in people who haven't used drugs in many years. For example, people who have been drug free for a decade can experience cravings when returning to an old neighborhood or house where they used drugs. Like riding a bike, the brain remembers.

Why are drugs more addictive than
NATURAL REWARDS?

For the brain, the difference between normal rewards and drug rewards can be likened to the difference between someone whispering into your ear and someone shouting into a microphone. Just as we turn down the volume on a radio that is too loud, the brain of someone who misuses drugs adjusts by producing fewer neurotransmitters in the reward circuit, or by reducing the number of receptors that can receive signals. As a result, the person's ability to experience pleasure from naturally rewarding (i.e., reinforcing) activities is also reduced.

This is why a person who misuses drugs eventually feels flat, without motivation, lifeless, and/or depressed, and is unable to enjoy things that were previously pleasurable. Now, the person needs to keep taking drugs to experience even a normal level of reward—which only makes the problem worse, like a vicious cycle. Also, the person will often need to take larger amounts of the drug to produce the familiar high—an effect known as *tolerance.*

Addiction and Health
What are the other health
CONSEQUENCES OF DRUG
ADDICTION?

People with addiction often have one or more associated health issues, which could include lung or heart disease, stroke, cancer, or mental health conditions. Imaging scans, chest X-rays, and blood tests can show the damaging effects of long-term drug use throughout the body.

For example, it is now well-known that tobacco smoke can cause many cancers, methamphetamine can cause severe dental problems, known as "meth mouth," and that opioids can lead to overdose and death. In addition, some drugs, such as inhalants, may damage or destroy nerve cells, either in the brain or the peripheral nervous system (the nervous system outside the brain and spinal cord).

Drug use can also increase the risk of contracting infections. Human immunodeficiency virus (HIV) and hepatitis C (a serious liver disease) infection can occur from sharing injection equipment and from impaired judgment leading to unsafe sexual activity.[40,41] Infection of the heart and its valves (endocarditis) and skin infection (cellulitis) can occur after exposure to bacteria by injection drug use.[42]

Does drug use cause MENTAL DISORDERS OR VICE VERSA?

Drug use and mental illness often co-exist. In some cases, mental disorders such as anxiety, depression, or schizophrenia may come before addiction; in other cases, drug use may trigger or worsen those mental health conditions, particularly in people with specific vulnerabilities.[43,44]

Some people with disorders like anxiety or depression may use drugs in an attempt to alleviate psychiatric symptoms, which may exacerbate their mental disorder in the long run, as well as increase the risk of developing addiction.[43,44] Treatment for all conditions should happen concurrently.

How can addiction HARM OTHER PEOPLE?

Beyond the harmful consequences for the person with the addiction, drug use can cause serious health problems for others. Some of the more severe consequences of addiction are:

- **Negative effects of drug use while pregnant or breastfeeding**
  A mother's substance or medication use during pregnancy can cause her baby to go into withdrawal after it's born, which is called neonatal abstinence syndrome (NAS). Symptoms will differ depending on the substance used, but may include tremors, problems with sleeping and feeding, and even seizures.[45] Some drug-exposed children will have developmental problems with behavior, attention, and thinking. Ongoing research is exploring if these effects on the brain and behavior extend into the teen years, causing continued developmental problems. In addition, some substances can make their way into a mother's breast milk. Scientists are still learning about long-term effects on a child who is exposed to drugs through breastfeeding.
- **Negative effects of secondhand smoke**
  Secondhand tobacco smoke exposes bystanders to at least 250 chemicals that are known to be harmful, particularly to children.[46] Involuntary exposure to secondhand smoke increases the risks of heart disease and lung cancer in people who have never smoked.[5] Additionally, the

known health risks of secondhand exposure to tobacco smoke raise questions about whether secondhand exposure to marijuana smoke poses similar risks. At this point, little research on this question has been conducted. However, a study found that some nonsmoking participants exposed for an hour to high-THC marijuana in an unventilated room reported mild effects of the drug, and another study showed positive urine tests in the hours directly following exposure.[47,48] If you inhale secondhand marijuana smoke, it's unlikely you would fail a drug test, but it is possible.

- **Increased spread of infectious diseases**
  Injection of drugs accounts for 1 in 10 of cases of HIV. Injection drug use is also a major factor in the spread of hepatitis C,[49] and can be the cause of endocarditis and cellulitis. Injection drug use is not the only way that drug use contributes to the spread of infectious diseases. Drugs that are misused can cause intoxication, which hinders judgment and increases the chance of risky sexual behaviors.
- **Increased risk of motor vehicle accidents**
  Use of illicit drugs or misuse of prescription drugs can make driving a car unsafe—just like driving after drinking alcohol. Drugged driving puts the driver, passengers, and others who share the road at risk. In 2016, almost 12 million people ages 16 or older reported driving under the influence of illicit drugs, including marijuana.[50] After alcohol, marijuana is the drug most often linked to impaired driving. Research studies have shown negative effects of marijuana on drivers, including an increase in lane weaving, poor reaction time, and altered attention to the road.

Treatment and Recovery
Can addiction be TREATED SUCCESSFULLY?

Yes, addiction is a treatable disorder. Research on the science of addiction and the treatment of substance use disorders has led to the development of research-based methods that help people to stop using drugs and resume productive lives, also known as being in *recovery*.

Can addiction be CURED?

Like other chronic diseases such as heart disease or asthma, treatment for drug addiction usually isn't a cure. But addiction *can* be managed successfully. Treatment enables people to counteract addiction's disruptive effects on their brain and behavior and regain control of their lives.

Does relapse to drug use mean TREATMENT HAS FAILED?

No. The chronic nature of addiction means that for some people *relapse,* or a return to drug use after an attempt to stop, can be part of the process, but newer treatments are designed to help with relapse prevention. Relapse rates for drug use are similar to rates for other chronic medical illnesses. If people stop following their medical treatment plan, they are likely to relapse.

Treatment of chronic diseases involves changing deeply rooted behaviors, and relapse doesn't mean treatment has failed. When a person recovering from an addiction relapses, it indicates that the person needs to speak with their doctor to resume treatment, modify it, or try another treatment.[52]
Source: JAMA, 284:1689–1695, 2000
Relapse rates for people treated for substance use disorders are compared with those for people treated for high blood pressure and asthma. Relapse is common and similar across these illnesses. Therefore, substance use disorders should be treated like any other chronic illness. Relapse serves as a sign for resumed, modified, or new treatment.

What are the principles of EFFECTIVE TREATMENT?

Research shows that when treating addictions to opioids (prescription pain relievers or drugs like heroin or fentanyl), medication should be the first line of treatment, usually combined with some form of behavioral therapy or counseling. Medications are also available to help treat addiction to alcohol and nicotine.

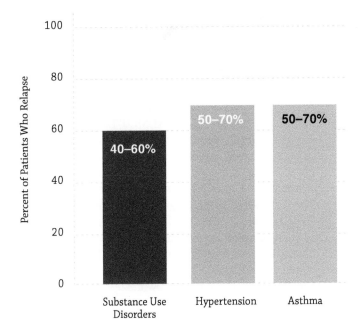

Additionally, medications are used to help people detoxify from drugs, although detoxification is not the same as treatment and is not sufficient to help a person recover. Detoxification alone without subsequent treatment generally leads to resumption of drug use.

For people with addictions to drugs like stimulants or cannabis, no medications are currently available to assist in treatment, so treatment consists of behavioral therapies. Treatment should be tailored to address each patient's drug use patterns and drug-related medical, mental, and social problems.

What medications and devices help TREAT DRUG ADDICTION?

Different types of medications and devices may be useful at different stages of treatment to help a patient stop using drugs, stay in treatment, and avoid relapse.

- **Treating withdrawal.** When patients first stop using drugs, they can experience various physical and emotional symptoms, including restlessness or sleeplessness, as well as depression, anxiety, and other mental health conditions. Certain treatment medications and devices reduce these symptoms, which makes it easier to stop the drug use.
- **Staying in treatment.** Some treatment medications and mobile applications are used to help the brain adapt gradually to the absence of the drug. These treatments act slowly to help prevent drug cravings and have a calming effect on body systems. They can help patients focus on counseling and other psychotherapies related to their drug treatment.
- **Preventing relapse.** Science has taught us that stress cues linked to the drug use (such as people, places, things, and moods), and contact with drugs are the most common triggers for relapse. Scientists have been developing therapies to interfere with these triggers to help patients stay in recovery.

COMMON MEDICATIONS USED TO TREAT DRUG ADDICTION AND WITHDRAWAL
Opioid
  Methadone
  Buprenorphine
  Extended-release naltrexone
  Lofexidine
Nicotine
  Nicotine replacement therapies (available as a patch, inhaler, or gum)
  Bupropion
  Varenicline

Alcohol
 Naltrexone
 Disulfiram
 Acamprosate

How do behavioral therapies TREAT DRUG ADDICTION?

Behavioral therapies help people in drug addiction treatment modify their attitudes and behaviors related to drug use. As a result, patients are able to handle stressful situations and various triggers that might cause another relapse. Behavioral therapies can also enhance the effectiveness of medications and help people remain in treatment longer.

- **Cognitive-behavioral therapy** seeks to help patients recognize, avoid, and cope with the situations in which they're most likely to use drugs.
- **Contingency management** uses positive reinforcement such as providing rewards or privileges for remaining drugfree, for attending and participating in counseling sessions, or for taking treatment medications as prescribed.
- **Motivational enhancement therapy** uses strategies to make the most of people's readiness to change their behavior and enter treatment.
- **Family therapy** helps people (especially young people) with drug use problems, as well as their families, address influences on drug use patterns and improve overall family functioning.
- **Twelve-step facilitation (TSF)** is an individual therapy typically delivered in 12 weekly session to prepare people to become engaged in 12-step mutual support programs. 12-step programs, like Alcoholic Anonymous, are not medical treatments, but provide social and complementary support to those treatments. TSF follows the 12-step themes of acceptance, surrender, and active involvement in recovery.

How do quality treatment programs help patients RECOVER FROM ADDICTION?

Stopping drug use is just one part of a long and complex recovery process. When people enter treatment, addiction has often caused serious consequences in their lives, possibly disrupting their health and how they function in their family lives, at work, and in the community.

Because addiction can affect so many aspects of a person's life, treatment should address the needs of the whole person to

be successful. Counselors may select from a menu of services that meet the specific medical, mental, social, occupational, family, and legal needs of their patients to help in their recovery.

For more information on drug treatment, see *Principles of Drug Addiction Treatment: A Research-Based Guide,* and *Principles of Adolescent Substance Use Disorder Treatment: A Research-Based Guide.*

Advancing Addiction Science and Practical Solutions
Leading the Search for SCIENTIFIC SOLUTIONS

To address all aspects of drug use and its harmful consequences, NIDA's research program ranges from basic studies of the addicted brain and behavior to clinical strategies and health services research. NIDA's research program develops prevention and treatment approaches and ensures they work in real-world settings. As part of this goal, NIDA is committed to research that addresses the vulnerabilities and health differences that exist among ethnic minorities or that stem from gender differences.

Bringing Science to REAL WORLD SETTINGS

- **Clinical Trials Network (CTN):** CTN "road tests" research-based drug use treatments in community treatment programs around the country.
- **Criminal Justice Drug Abuse Treatment Studies (CJDATS):** Led by NIDA, CJ-DATS is a network of research centers, in partnership with criminal justice professionals, drug use treatment providers, and federal agencies, responsible for developing integrated treatment approaches for criminal justice offenders and testing them at multiple sites throughout the Nation.
- **Juvenile Justice Translational Research on Interventions in the Legal System (JJ-TRIALS):** JJ-TRIALS is a seven-site cooperative research program designed to identify and test strategies for improving the delivery of research-based substance use and HIV prevention and treatment services for justice-involved youth.
- **The Adolescent Brain Cognitive Development (ABCD) Study:** ABCD is the largest long-term study of brain development and child health in the United States. The study is following more than 11,000 healthy children ages nine to 10 and follow them into early adulthood to observe brain growth.

Citations

1. National Drug Intelligence Center. *The economic impact of illicit drug use on American society.* Washington, DC: United States Department of Justice, 2011.

2. Rehm J, Mathers C, Popova S, Thavorncharoensap M, Teerawattananon Y, Patra J. Global burden of disease and injury and economic cost attributable to alcohol use and alcohol-use disorders. Lancet 373(9682):2223-2233, 2009.

3. Centers for Disease Control and Prevention. *Best Practices for Comprehensive Tobacco Control Programs* —2014. Atlanta: U.S. Department of Health and Human Services, Centers for Disease Control and Prevention, National Center for Chronic Disease Prevention and Health Promotion, Office on Smoking and Health, 2014.

4. Centers for Disease Control and Prevention (CDC). *Alcohol-Related Disease Impact (ARDI).* Atlanta, GA: CDC.

5. U.S. Department of Health and Human Services. *The Health Consequences of Smoking—50 Years of Progress: A Report of the Surgeon General.* Atlanta, GA: U.S. Department of Health and Human Services, Centers for Disease Control and Prevention, National Center for Chronic Disease Prevention and Health Promotion, Office on Smoking and Health, 2014.

6. Tice P, Lipari R, van Horn S. *Substance Use among 12th Grade Aged Youths, by Dropout Status.* Rockville, MD: Center for Health Statistics and Quality, Substance Abuse and Mental Health Administration; 2017. https://www.samhsa.gov/data/sites/default/files/report_3196/ShortReport-3196.pdf. Accessed June 4, 2018.

7. Chen C-Y, Storr CL, Anthony JC. Early-onset drug use and risk for drug dependence problems. *Addict Behav.* 2009;34(3):319-322. doi:10.1016/j.addbeh.2008.10.021

8. Lander L, Howsare J, Byrne M. The impact of substance use disorders on families and children: from theory to practice. *Soc Work Public Health.* 2013;28(0):194-205. doi:10.1080/19371918.2013.759005

9. Simmons LA, Havens JR, Whiting JB, Holz JL, Bada H. Illicit drug use among women with children in the United States: 2002–2003. *Ann Epidemiol.* 2009;19(3):187-193. doi:10.1016/j.annepidem.2008.12.007

10. Shankaran S, Lester BM, Das A, Bauer CR, Bada HS, Lagasse L, Higgins R. Impact of maternal substance use during pregnancy on childhood outcome. *Semin Fetal Neonatal Med* 12(2): 143-150, 2007.

11. Goldstein RZ, Volkow ND. Dysfunction of the prefrontal cortex in addiction: neuroimaging findings and clinical implications. *Nat Rev Neurosci.* 2011;12(11):652-669. doi:10.1038/nrn3119

12. Fowler JS, Volkow ND, Kassed CA, Chang L. Imaging the addicted human brain. *Sci Pract Perspect* 3(2):4-16, 2007.

13. Grant B, S Stinson F, Harford T. Grant BF, Stinson FS, Harford TC. Age at onset of alcohol use and DSM-IV alcohol abuse and dependence: a 12-year follow-up. *J Subst Abuse.* 2001;13:493-504. doi:10.1016/S0899-3289(01)00096-7

14. Zucker RA, Donovan JE, Masten AS, Mattson ME, Moss HB. Early developmental processes and the continuity of risk for underage drinking and problem drinking. *Pediatrics.* 2008;121 Suppl 4:S252-S272. doi:10.1542/peds.2007-2243B

15. DiClemente CC, Fairhurst SK, Piotrowski NA. Self-efficacy and addictive behaviors. In: *Self-Efficacy, Adaptation, and Adjustment: Theory, Research, and Application.* The Plenum series in social/ clinical psychology. New York, NY, US: Plenum Press; 1995:109-141.

16. Hill KG, Hawkins JD, Catalano RF, Abbott RD, Guo J. Family influences on the risk of daily smoking initiation. *J Adolesc Health Off Publ Soc Adolesc Med.* 2005;37(3):202-210. doi:10.1016/j. jadohealth.2004.08.014

17. Guo J, Hawkins JD, Hill KG, Abbott RD. Childhood and adolescent predictors of alcohol abuse and dependence in young adulthood. *J Stud Alcohol.* 2001;62(6):754-762.

18. Brook JS, Brook DW, Gordon AS, Whiteman M, Cohen P. The psychosocial etiology of adolescent drug use: a family interactional approach. *Genet Soc Gen Psychol Monogr.* 1990;116(2):111-267.

19. Duncan GJ, Wilkerson B, England P. Cleaning up their act: The effects of marriage and cohabitation on licit and illicit drug use. *Demography.* 2006;43(4):691-710. doi:10.1353/dem.2006.0032

20. Chassin L, Pitts SC, Prost J. Binge drinking trajectories from adolescence to emerging adulthood in a high-risk sample: predictors and substance abuse outcomes. *J Consult Clin Psychol.*2002;70(1):67-78.

21. Sher KJ, Rutledge PC. Heavy drinking across the transition to college: predicting first-semester heavy drinking from precollege variables. *Addict Behav.* 2007;32(4):819-835. doi:10.1016/j.addbeh.2006.06.024

22. Bond L, Butler H, Thomas L, et al. Social and school connectedness in early secondary school as predictors of late teenage substance use, mental health, and academic outcomes. *J Adolesc Health Off Publ Soc Adolesc Med.* 2007;40(4):357. e9-e18. doi:10.1016/j.jadohealth.2006.10.013

23. Brook JS, Kessler RC, Cohen P. The onset of marijuana use from preadolescence and early adolescence to young adulthood. *Dev Psychopathol.* 1999;11(4):901-914.

24. Herting JR, Guest AM. Components of satisfaction with local areas in the metropolis. *Sociol Q.* 1985;26(1):99-116. doi:10.1111/j.1533–8525.1985.tb00218.x.

25. Hawkins JD, Arthur MW, Catalano RF. Preventing substance abuse. *Crime Justice.* 1995;19:343-427. doi:10.1086/449234

26. Chalk R, Phillips DA. *Youth Development and Neighborhood Influences: Challenges and Opportunities*. National Academies Press; 1997.

27. Bevilacqua L, Goldman D. Genes and addictions. *Clin Pharmacol Ther*. 2009;85(4):359-361. doi:10.1038/clpt.2009.6

28. Substance Abuse and Mental Health Services Administration. *Mental and Substance Use Disorders*. https://www.samhsa.gov/disorders. Published June 20, 2014. Accessed June 4, 2018.

29. Biederman J, Faraone SV, Monuteaux MC, Feighner JA. Patterns of alcohol and drug use in adolescents can be predicted by parental substance use disorders. *Pediatrics*. 2000;106(4):792-797.

30. Whitesell M, Bachand A, Peel J, Brown M. Familial, social, and individual factors contributing to risk for adolescent substance use. *Journal of Addiction*. https://www.hindawi.com/journals/jad/2013/579310/. Published 2013. Accessed June 4, 2018.

31. Substance Abuse and Mental Health Services Administration. *Mental and Substance Use Disorders*. https://www.samhsa.gov/disorders. Published June 20, 2014. Accessed June 4, 2018.

32. Lynskey MT, Heath AC, Bucholz KK, Slutske WS, Madden PAF, Nelson EC, Statham DJ, Martin NG. Escalation of drug use in earlyonset cannabis users vs co-twin controls. *JAMA* 289: 427-33, 2003.

33. Squeglia LM, Jacobus J, Tapert SF. The influence of substance use on adolescent brain development. *Clin Neurosci Soc ENCS*. 2009;40(1):31-38.

34. Verebey K, Gold MS. From coca leaves to crack: the effects of dose and routes of administration in abuse liability. *Psychiatr Annals* 18:513-520, 1988.

35. Hatsukami DK, Fischman MW. Crack cocaine and cocaine hydrochloride: Are the differences myth or reality. *JAMA* 276:1580-1588, 1996.

36. Krohn MD, Lizotte AJ, Perez CM. The interrelationship between substance use and precocious transitions to adult statuses. *J Health Soc Behav* 38(1):87-103, 1997.

37. Gogtay N, Giedd JN, Lusk L, Hayashi KM, Greenstein D, Vaituzis AC, Nugent TF 3rd, Herman DH, Clasen LS, Toga AW, Rapoport JL, Thompson PM. Dynamic mapping of human cortical development during childhood through early adulthood. *Proc Natl Acad Sci* 101(21):8174-8179, 2004.

38. National Institute on Drug Abuse. *Preventing Drug Abuse among Children and Adolescents: A Research-Based Guide for Parents, Educators, and Community Leaders (Second Edition)* (NIH Publication No. 04-4212[A]). Rockville, MD, 2003.

39. Johnston, LD, O'Malley, PM, Miech, RA, Bachman, JG, & Schulenberg, JE (2014). *Monitoring the Future national survey results on drug use: 1975–2013: Overview, key findings on adolescent drug use*. Ann Arbor: Institute for Social Research, The University of Michigan.

40. Washington State Institute for Public Policy. (2017). Benefitcost results. Retrieved from http://www.wsipp.wa.gov/BenefitCost?topicId=. Accessed on June 14, 2018.

41. El-Bassel N, Shaw SA, Dasgupta A, Strathdee SA. Drug use as a driver of HIV risks: re-emerging and emerging issues. *Curr Opin HIV AIDS*. 2014;9(2):150-155. doi:10.1097/COH.0000000000000035

42. Klevens RM, Hu DJ, Jiles R, Holmberg SD. Evolving epidemiology of hepatitis C virus in the United States. *ClinInfect Dis Off Publ Infect Dis Soc Am*. 2012;55 Suppl 1:S3-S9. doi:10.1093/cid/cis393

43. Moss R, Munt B. Injection drug use and right sided endocarditis. *Heart*. 2003;89(5):577-581.

44. Kelly TM, Daley DC. Integrated treatment of substance use and psychiatric disorders. *Soc Work Public Health*. 2013;28(0):388-406. doi:10.1080/19371918.2013.774673

45. Ross S, Peselow E. Co-occurring psychotic and addictive disorders: neurobiology and diagnosis. *Clin Neuropharmacol*. 2012;35(5):235-243. doi:10.1097/WNF.0b013e318261e193

46. Ko JY, Wolicki S, Barfield WD, et al. CDC Grand Rounds: public health strategies to prevent neonatal abstinence syndrome. *MMWR Morb Mortal Wkly Rep*. 2017;66. doi:10.15585/mmwr.mm6609a2

47. National Cancer Institute. *Secondhand Smoke and Cancer*. National Cancer Institute. https://www.cancer.gov/about-cancer/causesprevention/risk/tobacco/second-hand-smoke-fact-sheet. Published January 12, 2011. Accessed June 4, 2018.

48. Röhrich J, Schimmel I, Zörntlein S, et al. Concentrations of delta9-tetrahydrocannabinol and 11-nor-9-carboxytetra hydrocannabinol in blood and urine after passive exposure to Cannabis smoke in a coffee shop. *J Anal Toxicol*. 2010;34(4): 196-203.

49. Cone EJ, Bigelow GE, Herrmann ES, et al. Non-smoker exposure to secondhand cannabis smoke. I. Urine screening and confirmation results. *J Anal Toxicol*. 2015;39(1):1-12. doi:10.1093/jat/bku116

50. Zibbell JE, Asher AK, Patel RC, et al. Increases in acute hepatitis C virus infection related to a growing opioid epidemic and associated injection drug use, United States, 2004 to 2014. Am J Public Health. 2018;108(2). https://ajph.aphapublications.org/doi/10.2105/AJPH.2017.304132. Accessed June 4, 2018.

51. Center for Behavioral Health Statistics and Quality. *Results from the 2016 National Survey on Drug Use and Health: Detailed Tables*. Rockville, MD: Substance Abuse and Mental Health Services Administration; 2017.

52. Volkow ND, Chang L, Wang GJ, Fowler JS, Franceschi D, Sedler M, Gatley SJ, Miller E, Hitzemann R, Ding YS, Logan J. Loss of dopamine transporters in methamphetamine abusers recovers with protracted abstinence. *J Neurosci* 21(23):9414-9418, 2001.

53. McLellan AT, Lewis DC, O'Brien CP, Kleber HD. Drug dependence, a chronic medical illness: implications for treatment, insurance, and outcomes evaluation. *JAMA* 284(13):1689-1695, 2000.

Critical Thinking

1. What are some factors that increase the risk of becoming addicted to drug use?
2. Are biological factors or environmental factors more of a determination to drug abuse? Or do both coincide?
3. Do drug prevention programs work? Does age make a difference?
4. Why are drugs more addictive than natural rewards?

Internet References

Centers for Disease Control and Prevention
https://www.cdc.gov/
National Drug Intelligence Center
https://www.justice.gov/archive/ndic/
National Institute on Drug Abuse
https://www.drugabuse.gov/

National Institute on Drug Abuse, *Drugs, Brains, and Behavior: The Science of Addiction.* U.S. Department of Health and Human Services, July 20, 2018.

Unit 4

UNIT

Prepared by: Kim Schnurbush, *California State University, Sacramento*
Mark Pullin, *Angelo State University*

Other Trends in Drug Use

Rarely do drug-related patterns and trends lend themselves to precise definition. Identification, measurement, and prediction of the consequence of these trends is an inexact science, to say the least. It is, nevertheless, a very important process. One of the most valuable uses of drug-related trend analysis is the identification of subpopulations whose vulnerability to certain drug phenomena is greater than that of the wider population. These identifications may forewarn of the implications for the general population. Trend analysis may produce specific information that may otherwise be lost or obscured by general statistical indications. For example, tobacco is probably the most prominent of gateway drugs, with repeated findings pointing to the correlation between the initial use of tobacco and the use of other drugs.

The analysis of specific trends related to drug use is very important, as it provides a threshold from which educators, health-care professionals, parents, and policy makers may respond to significant drug-related health threats and issues. Over 24 million Americans report the use of illegal drugs. The current rate of illicit drug use is similar to the rates of the past three years. Marijuana remains as the most commonly used illicit drug with more than 14 million current users. Historically, popular depressant and stimulant drugs—such as alcohol, tobacco, heroin, and cocaine—produce statistics that identify the most visible and sometimes the most constant use patterns. Other drugs such as marijuana, LSD, ecstasy, and other "club drugs" often produce patters widely interpreted to be associated with cultural phenomena such as youth attitudes, popular music trends, and political climate.

Two other continuing trends are those that involve the abuse of prescription drugs and those that involve the use of methamphetamine. Americans are abusing prescription drugs more than ever before with the most frequently mentioned offenders being oxycodone and hydrocodone. Currently, more than 5 million persons use prescription pain relievers for nonmedical reasons. Of those who used pain relievers for nonmedical reasons, 56 percent obtained them for free from a friend or relative. As more and more drugs get prescribed within the population, a steady trend, more and more drugs become easily accessible. The National Institute of Drug Abuse reports that 20 percent of the U.S. population over 12 has used prescription drugs for nonmedical reasons. Currently, prescription drug abuse among youth ranks second behind only marijuana. The good news is that drug use by youth has declined or leveled off in several important categories such as those associated with marijuana, alcohol, and methamphetamine. And although methamphetamine use is down, it is reported by local and state officials in the West and Midwest as the number one illegal drug problem.

Although the federal government has modified its survey methods to more accurately identify the number of meth users, many worry that the meth problem is still understated and greatly outweighs those problems associated with other illegal drugs in the West, Southwest, and Midwest. Information concerning drug-use patterns and trends obtained from a number of different investigative methods is available from a variety of sources. On the national level, the more prominent sources are the Substance Abuse and Mental Health Services Administration, the National Institute on Drug Abuse, the Drug Abuse Warning Network, the national Centers for Disease Control, the Justice Department, the Office of National Drug Control Policy, the surgeon general, and the DEA. On the state level, various departments, including attorney general offices, the courts, state departments of social services, state universities and colleges, and public health offices, maintain data and conduct research. On local levels, criminal justice agencies, social service departments, public hospitals, and health departments provide information. On a private level, various research institutes and universities, professional organizations such as the American Medical Association and the American Cancer Society, hospitals, and treatment centers, as well as private corporations, are tracking drug-related trends. Surveys abound with no apparent lack of available data. As a result, the need for examination of research methods and findings for reliability and accuracy is self-evident. The articles in this unit provide information about some drug-related trends occurring within certain subpopulations of Americans. While reading the articles, it is interesting to consider how the trends and patterns described are dispersed through various subpopulations of Americans and specific geographical areas. Additionally, much information about drugs and drug trends can be located quickly by referring to the list of websites in the front section of the book.

Article
Prepared by: Kim Schnurbush, *California State University, Sacramento*
Mark Pullin, *Angelo State University*

Fentanyl: The Powerful Opioid that Killed Prince

SARA SIDNER

Learning Outcomes

After reading this article, you will be able to:

- Discuss how the illicit drug fentanyl is flooding the streets across the nation

- Understand why fentanyl is so dangerous to users

- Discuss how users, who believe they are buying the popular painkiller Norco illegally on the streets, are dying due to fentanyl overdoses

Sacramento, California (CNN)—America's addiction to opioid-based painkillers and heroin just got exponentially more dangerous. The most potent painkiller on the market, prescribed by doctors for cancer treatment, is being made illicitly and sold on the streets, delivering a super high and, far too often, death.

The drug, fentanyl, has been around since the 1960s. Its potency works miracles, soothing extreme pain in cancer patients who are usually prescribed patches or lozenges. But it can also kill. A medical examination concluded that Prince died of an accidental overdose of fentanyl, ending weeks of speculation on how the singer died.

An illicit version of the drug is flooding into communities across America, and casual users are finding out that their fentanyl pills and powder are delivering a powerful high that is easy to overdose on.

The Drug Enforcement Administration (DEA) and the Centers for Disease Control say we have another national health crisis on our hands. These are just a handful of the people trying to stop it from taking more lives.

The Mother

Natasha Butler stared hard at the pictures laid out in front of her.

But she averted her eyes when they lit on the one that still takes her breath away. It's the one that makes what happened real.

It's the one where the tubes, needles, and respirator are all hooked up to her only son, Jerome, trying to keep him alive. They ultimately didn't.

"I'm dying inside," she said, her voice falling to a whisper and tears streaming down her face. "He was my firstborn. I had him when I was 15. We grew up together."

Addicted? How to Get Help

If you're addicted to prescription drugs, help is available. You can call the Substance Abuse Mental Health Services Administration 24/7 hotline at 1-800-662-HELP(4357) or visit their website.

She had never heard of the substance that killed him. Doctors told her he died from an overdose of fentanyl, which experts say can be 100 times more potent than morphine and 50 times stronger than heroin.

"He came and told me it was an overdose. I'm like, 'An overdose of what?' It wasn't an overdose. This is murder," Butler said. "I taught my kids two things: God, and don't do drugs."

Jerome Butler had not been prescribed the highly controlled narcotic. His mother said she was told that an acquaintance had given Butler what her son thought was a pill of Norco, a less potent opioid-based painkiller, a mix of hydrocodone and acetaminophen.

The sellers knew, Butler alleges, that "the pill had the fentanyl in it, and they killed my son."

Jerome was one of 10 people who died in just 12 days from fentanyl-laced pills in a sudden spike of deaths in Sacramento County, California, in March. More than 50 people overdosed on those pills in the first three months of the year but survived. Investigators are still looking for the source.

Similar clusters of fentanyl-related overdoses and deaths are appearing across the United States.

Like the DEA, the Centers for Disease Control and prevention has issued a health advisory and is stepping in to get health providers and first responders to report fentanyl-related overdoses as well as expand access to naloxone, the drug that counteracts deadly opioid overdoses.

The latest state statistics on fentanyl-related deaths compiled by the CDC tell a sobering story.

Ohio reported 514 fentanyl-related deaths in 2014, up from 93 the year before. Maryland reported 185 fentanyl-related deaths, up from 58 in a year's time. In Florida, the number of deaths jumped to 397 in 2014, from 185. New Hampshire had 151 reported deaths due to fentanyl alone in 2015, five times the number of deaths from heroin, according to the office of the state's chief medical examiner.

No one was more stunned to see those numbers than the mother freshly grieving her son's death from the drug. She didn't know that so many other families had suffered its deadly effects long before it hit hers until she started researching it.

"What are we doing? What are we doing about it?" Butler said, exasperated and weeping. "I'm willing to do everything that I can."

And that is just what Butler intends to do. She's on a mission to warn communities about the opioid-based drugs killing people at alarming rates across America.

She is talking to community groups and has called senators, the California governor, even the White House, looking to tell her story and to build a coalition to help stave off more deaths from opioid use, especially fentanyl.

"I'm mad at the person who sold it. I'm mad at the person who is compressing it. I'm mad at the state for not protecting our people," she said.

Since her son's death, she said, she's heard from so many young people who are addicted to painkillers such as Norco.

"If you feel you don't have that much strength, let's get together," she said. "We can build strength. We can make a difference. We have to."

The Special Agent

Illicit fentanyl is a bestseller on the streets and a prolific killer. It is so potent that when law enforcement goes in to seize it, officers have to wear level A hazmat suits, the highest protection level made, the same kind of suits health care workers use to avoid contamination by the deadly Ebola virus.

"Just micrograms can make a difference between life and death. It's that serious," said DEA Special Agent John Martin, who is based in San Francisco. An amount the size of a few grains of sand of fentanyl can kill you. "All you have to do is touch it. It can be absorbed through the skin and the eyes."

One of the top priorities for Martin and his agency is to stop the flow of fentanyl and other opioids from flooding American communities.

It first showed up in deadly doses on the streets in 2007. The DEA traced the illicit fentanyl to a single lab in Mexico and shut it down. Fentanyl drug seizures subsided for a while, but in 2014, they spiked in 10 states.

It's been an uphill battle. Americans are buying it in record numbers, and highly organized drug cartels are spreading it far and wide.

What is curious is where the drug or elements to make it originate. Its street nickname is "China White" or "China girl," offering a hint at where most of it is coming from.

"DEA investigations reveal that Mexico-based drug cartels are buying fentanyl directly from China," Martin said.

And as far as profits go, the other opioids commonly sold on the streets—heroin, hydrocodone, OxyContin, and Norco—can't even touch fentanyl.

Hydrocodone sells for about $30 a pill on the street. A fentanyl pill may look and cost the same but requires only a fraction of the narcotic to give users an even stronger reaction.

The DEA estimates that drug traffickers can buy a kilogram of fentanyl powder for $3300 and sell it on the streets for more than 300 times that, generating nearly a million dollars.

Fentanyl is often trafficked through the cartels' standard maze of routes through Mexico and into the U.S. But sometimes it's simply ordered on the notorious dark web and shows up straight from China in the buyer's mailbox.

"We're using countless resources to deal with the threat," Martin said.

Seizures of the drug have jumped dramatically, which would seem to be good news for the DEA. But what it indicates is that there is more of it to seize than ever before.

"Everywhere from the Northeast corridor, down to New York, the Midwest and now we're seeing it here out on the West Coast. Fentanyl is everywhere right now," Martin said.

On the East Coast and in the Midwest, it's often sold as powder and mixed with heroin. On the West Coast, it is showing up mostly in pill form.

"It's feeding America's addiction to opioids," Martin said, adding that the cartels have figured out a way to make it more cheaply and easily than heroin.

The Forensic Scientist

"They look like what you're getting from the pharmacy," forensic scientist Terry Baisz said. She was taken aback by just how much the counterfeit pills look like the ones sold by pharmaceutical companies.

After 26 years in the Orange County crime lab, south of Los Angeles, she has never seen anything like what is coming in these days. It worries her.

"I was shocked the first time I tested this stuff and it came back as fentanyl. We hadn't seen it before 2015," Baisz said, "and now we're seeing it a lot."

Fentanyl had entered Orange County, and it was killing people.

Wearing gloves and a lab coat, Baisz looked down at a tiny clear plastic bag under a glass hood with a ventilation system. It was pure fentanyl. A sneeze or deep breath could end in a deadly overdose, so testing it calls for strict protocols. But Baisz said it's the pills that worry her the most as a public threat.

"I wouldn't hold those in a sweaty palm for long. You're bound to get dosed," she said.

In her lab coat and gloves, she pointed to pills spread across a table. They were all labeled as various well-known pharmaceutical drugs. They looked like perfect replicas of the real deal. None was labeled as fentanyl, but that is what most of them actually were.

"Just one could kill you," Baisz said. "We have to test them. We can no longer rely on the database and our naked eye."

The Lawmaker

"It's so dangerous and so lethal, I had to get involved," California state Sen. Patricia Bates said. "Two minutes, and you could be in respiratory arrest and be dead. It's kind of like, get high and die."

Bates knows those details, because the fentanyl overdose deaths started racking up in one of the areas she represents, South Orange County. She is trying to push through a bill that would put harsher penalties on high-volume sellers of fentanyl.

The bill "will enhance the penalties, by weight," Bates said. "We're talking about ... catching the big guys, because when you take them out of the food chain, you really do reduce the incidents of the trafficking and what's available on the streets."

She knows it's a tough sell in a time when California voters have passed laws to lessen prison sentences for nonviolent offenders. And, of course, there is the matter of prison overcrowding in the state. But Bates is pushing it forward, because

she is certain this is the next epidemic, similar to what is happening with heroin but more deadly.

"Addicts are migrating to fentanyl," she said, "They are driven to it because it's a quicker, bigger high. Yet it is something that you don't recover from when you get that super-high."

The Drug Counselor

When fentanyl began showing up in San Francisco in 2015, Eliza Wheeler helped get the word out on the streets about a new, very potent drug in town.

In San Francisco, the drug showed up in the form of white powder and then as pills labeled as Xanax. It turned out to be pure fentanyl. A health advisory warned that more than 75 people had experienced an overdose in July that year.

"People didn't know what it was," Wheeler said. They thought it was heroin, which is far less potent.

Though San Francisco has seen a sudden rise in fentanyl overdoses, the city did not experience the large number of deadly overdoses that other cities have.

Wheeler is a project manager at the DOPE (Drug Overdose Prevention and Education) Project in San Francisco. In cooperation with the city's health department, DOPE and other organizations flooded the streets with fliers warning that "white heroin," promising a super high, was super potent and potentially deadly. The fliers also advised drug users to carry around Narcan, the brand name for naloxone, which blocks or reverses the effects of opioid-based drugs. It is supposed to be used in an emergency such as an overdose.

Since 2003, DOPE has trained about 6000 people on how and when to use Narcan. It can be administered with a needle or as a nasal spray. "We saved countless people by giving easier access to (Narcan) and informing them about the dangers right away," Wheeler said.

Join the conversation

See the latest news and share your comments with CNN Health on Facebook and Twitter.

The San Francisco Department of Public Health sent out a health advisory crediting groups like DOPE with saving lives.

"If you want to do something that will keep people from dying and impact the crisis immediately, then lawmakers should help make more naloxone and training available to the public," Wheeler said.

Natasha Butler, who continues to grieve her only son, would like to see something else, too.

"We have an Amber alert to save children. Why not have a Jerome alert to warn people about this drug?"

Critical Thinking

1. Although legal when prescribed by physicians for a medical condition such as cancer, why are so many people dying after illegally obtaining fentanyl on the streets?

2. What problems face law enforcement when they encounter fentanyl, and how does exposure for law enforcement to fentanyl differ compared to Norco?

3. The popular music icon Prince died of a fentanyl overdose. How can tragedies such as the death of Prince educate the public on the dangers of drugs like fentanyl?

Internet References

Drug Enforcement Administration—Fentanyl
https://www.dea.gov/druginfo/concern_fentanyl.shtml#fentanyl

Narconon-Signs and Symptoms of Fentanyl Abuse
http://www.narconon.org/drug-abuse/fentanyl-signs-symptoms.html

Police One-Fentanyl Exposure: 5 safety tips for cops
https://www.policeone.com/drug-interdiction-narcotics/articles/222385006-Fentanyl-exposure-5-safety-tips-for-cops/

Prepared by: Kim Schnurbush, *California State University, Sacramento*
Mark Pullin, *Angelo State University*

Article

Rash of Hospitalizations in New York State Linked to Synthetic Marijuana

Lorenzo Ferrigno

Learning Outcomes

After reading this article, you will be able to:

- Discuss how synthetic marijuana is marketed and why this marketing appeals to teenagers

- Discuss the dangers of synthetic marijuana, to include the side effects

- Understand how synthetic marijuana is hitting the nation's streets, and why authorities are so concerned about this new "drug"

New York (CNN)—New York state authorities have issued a health alert following a dramatic spike in hospital visits for synthetic marijuana-related emergencies.

Gov. Andrew Cuomo said Friday that more than 160 patients in nine days have been rushed to hospitals across the state for adverse reactions to synthetic cannabinoid, known as "spice" or "K2."

"Spice" and other similar synthetic drugs are often marketed as legal plant material coated with chemicals that are supposed to mimic the effects of marijuana, according to a statement from the governor's office.

"Since the exact compounds contained in synthetic cannabinoid products change so frequently, it's often impossible for users to know exactly what they are putting in their body," acting New York State Health Commissioner Dr. Howard Zucker said.

Symptoms after use have a wide range of severity, from confusion, drowsiness and headaches to increased heart rate, seizures and loss of consciousness, according to the New York State Department of Health.

Synthetic marijuana is popular among teens because it is marketed as incense or natural products to "mask its true purpose," the health department statement said.

"Young people may be fooled into thinking that these substances are safe because they are sold over the counter or are in colorful packaging, but they are not made for human consumption," New York Alcohol and Substance Abuse Services Commissioner Arlene Gonzalez Sanchez said. "They are dangerous and can have significant, long-term effects on the brain."

The recent surge is not isolated in New York; other states across the country have noticed similar trends.

Alabama Department of Public Health issued a statement last week acknowledging a rise of synthetic marijuana usage and said there had been 98 overdoses suspected to be linked with "spice" in the previous month.

Mobile County alone has seen seven cases in 2015 so far, more than the entire previous year, the statement said.

Mississippi health officials are also concerned that synthetic marijuana is on the rise.

Ninety-seven cases over an eight-day span in April were reported to the Mississippi Poison Control Center, a Department of Health press release said.

Critical Thinking

1. Why do you think synthetic marijuana is so appealing to teenagers?

2. What are the various side effects of synthetic marijuana use, and why are medical professionals so concerned about the increase in use of synthetic marijuana across the nation?

3. Why do you believe teenagers are drawn to synthetic marijuana and if you were a parent, what might you tell your teenager about the dangers of synthetic marijuana?

Internet References

National Institute on Drug Abuse—Synthetic Cannabinoid

https://www.drugabuse.gov/publications/drugfacts/synthetic-cannabinoids

Partnership for Drug-Free Kids—Synthetic Marijuana—Nothing Like Real Marijuana, Expert Explains

http://www.drugfree.org/news-service/synthetic-marijuana-nothing-like-real-marijuana-expert-explains/

Spice Addiction Support

http://spiceaddictionsupport.org/side-effects-of-spice-use/

Prepared by: Kim Schnurbush, *California State University, Sacramento*
Mark Pullin, *Angelo State University*

Article

Substance Abuse in the Military

NATIONAL INSTITUTE ON DRUG ABUSE

Learning Outcomes

After reading this article, you will be able to:

- Understand the kinds of issues facing military personnel that can lead to substance use and abuse.

- Discuss ways to address substance abuse in the military.

- Discuss how alcohol, tobacco, and prescription drug abuse may be on the rise in the military, whereas illicit drug use is not when compared to the general public.

Members of the armed forces are not immune to the substance use problems that affect the rest of society. Although illicit drug use is lower among U.S. military personnel than among civilians, heavy alcohol and tobacco use, and especially prescription drug abuse, are much more prevalent and are on the rise.

The stresses of deployment during wartime and the unique culture of the military account for some of these differences. Zero-tolerance policies and stigma pose difficulties in identifying and treating substance use problems in military personnel, as does lack of confidentiality that deters many who need treatment from seeking it.

Those with multiple deployments and combat exposure are at greatest risk of developing substance use problems. They are more apt to engage in new-onset heavy weekly drinking and binge drinking, to suffer alcohol- and other drug-related problems, and to have greater prescribed use of behavioral health medications. They are also more likely to start smoking or relapse to smoking.

Illicit and Prescription Drugs According to the 2008 Department of Defense (DoD) Survey of Health Related Behaviors among Active Duty Military Personnel, just 2.3 percent of military personnel were past-month users of an illicit drug, compared with 12 percent of civilians. Among those age 18–25 (who are most likely to use drugs), the rate among military personnel was 3.9 percent, compared with 17.2 percent among civilians.

A policy of zero tolerance for drug use among DoD personnel is likely one reason why illicit drug use has remained at a low level in the military for 2 decades. The policy was instituted in 1982 and is currently enforced by frequent random drug testing; service members face dishonorable discharge and even criminal prosecution for a positive drug test.

However, in spite of the low level of illicit drug use, abuse of prescription drugs is higher among service members than among civilians and is on the increase. In 2008, 11 percent of service members reported misusing prescription drugs, up from 2 percent in 2002 and 4 percent in 2005. Most of the prescription drugs misused by service members are opioid pain medications.

Mental Health Problems in Returning Veterans

Service members may carry the psychological and physical wounds of their military experience with them into subsequent civilian life. In one study, one in four veterans returning from Iraq and Afghanistan reported symptoms of a mental or cognitive disorder; one in six reported symptoms of post-traumatic stress disorder (PTSD). These disorders are strongly associated with substance abuse and dependence, as are other problems experienced by returning military personnel, including sleep disturbances, traumatic brain injury, and violence in relationships.

Young adult veterans are particularly likely to have substance use or other mental health problems. According to a report of veterans in 2004-2006, a quarter of 18- to 25-year-old veterans met criteria for a past-year substance use disorder, which is more than double the rate of veterans aged 26-54 and five times the rate of veterans 55 or older.

The greater availability of these medications and increases in prescriptions for them may contribute to their growing misuse by service members. Pain reliever prescriptions written by military physicians quadrupled between 2001 and 2009—to almost 3.8 million. Combat-related injuries and the strains from carrying heavy equipment during multiple deployments likely play a role in this trend.

Drinking and Smoking

Alcohol use is also higher among men and women in military service than among civilians. Almost half of active duty service members (47 percent) reported binge drinking in 2008—up from 35 percent in 1998. In 2008, 20 percent of military personnel reported binge drinking every week in the past month; the rate was considerably higher—27 percent—among those with high combat exposure.

In 2008, 30 percent of all service members were current cigarette smokers—comparable to the rate for civilians (29 percent). However, as with alcohol use, smoking rates are significantly higher among personnel who have been exposed to combat.

Suicides and Substance Use

Suicide rates in the military were traditionally lower than among civilians in the same age range, but in 2004 the suicide rate in the U.S. Army began to climb, surpassing the civilian rate in 2008. Substance use is involved in many of these suicides. The 2010 report of the Army Suicide Prevention Task Force found that 29 percent of active duty Army suicides from fiscal year (FY) 2005 to FY 2009 involved alcohol or drug use; and in 2009, prescription drugs were involved in almost one third of them.

Addressing the Problem

A 2012 report prepared for the DoD by the Institute of Medicine (IOM Report) recommended ways of addressing the problem of substance use in the military, including increasing the use of evidence-based prevention and treatment interventions and expanding access to care. The report recommends broadening insurance coverage to include effective outpatient treatments and better equipping healthcare providers to recognize and screen for substance use problems so they can refer patients to appropriate, evidence-based treatment when needed. It also recommends measures like limiting access to alcohol on bases.

The IOM Report also notes that addressing substance use in the military will require increasing confidentiality and shifting a cultural climate in which drug problems are stigmatized and evoke fear in people suffering from them.

Branches of the military have already taken steps to curb prescription drug abuse. The Army, for example, has implemented changes that include limiting the duration of prescriptions for opioid pain relievers to 6 months and having a pharmacist monitor a soldier's medications when multiple prescriptions are being used.

NIDA and other government agencies are currently funding research to better understand the causes of drug abuse and other mental health problems among military personnel, veterans, and their families and how best to prevent and treat them.

Critical Thinking

1. What kinds of issues to military personnel face that may add stress to their lives, which may lead to substance use and abuse?

2. How might the zero tolerance for drug use among military personnel and illicit drug use levels impact military personnel?

3. Why might alcohol, tobacco, and prescription drug use be on the rise, but illicit drug use is not in the military as compared to the general public?

4. What are ways to address substance abuse in the military?

Internet References

Centers for Disease Control and Prevention
https://www.cdc.gov/

National Institute on Drug Abuse
https://www.drugabuse.gov/

U.S. National Institutes of Health's National Library of Medicine (NIH/NLM)
https://www.ncbi.nlm.nih.gov/pmc/

National Institute on Drug Abuse, *Substance Abuse in the Military.* U.S. Department of Health and Human Services, March, 2013.

Article

Prepared by: Kim Schnurbush, *California State University, Sacramento*
Mark Pullin, *Angelo State University*

Alcohol and the Hispanic Community

NATIONAL INSTITUTE ON ALCOHOL ABUSE AND ALCOHOLISM

Learning Outcomes

After reading this article, you will be able to:

- Become familiar with drinking patterns among the Hispanic population.

- Discuss binge drinking and the problems it can cause.

- Understand three factors that predict drinking behavior in the Hispanic community.

Hispanics are the largest and most rapidly growing ethnic group in the United States, making up about 17 percent of the population, or more than 50 million people.

Research shows that drinking patterns among Hispanics are different from those of non-Hispanic Whites and other ethnic or racial groups. Understanding these differences can help prevention, intervention, and treatment programs better serve the Hispanic community.

How Much Do Hispanics Drink?

Overall, Hispanics are less likely to drink at all than are non-Hispanic Whites. In fact, Hispanics have high rates of abstinence from alcohol. But Hispanics who choose to drink are more likely to consume higher volumes of alcohol than non-Hispanic Whites.

Selected Alcohol Consumption Statistics for Women and Men: U.S. Adults 18 Years of Age and Older

	Non-Hispanic White	Hispanic
» % who had at least 1 drink in the past year	70.3	54.5
» % who had at least 1 drink in their lifetime, but not in the past year	13.9	13.2
» % who had at least 1 drink in their lifetime	84.2	67.7
» % total lifetime abstainers (not even 1 drink)	15.5	31.8
» % of past-year drinkers, by usual number of drinks consumed per drinking day:		
1	38.3	31.8
2	30.1	25.8
3+	31.6	42.4
» % of past-year drinkers who drank 4+/5+ drinks:		
At least once in the past year	36.8	41.9
Less than once a month (1 to 11 times in past year, or < monthly)	15.5	15.9
Monthly or more (12+ times in past year)	21.3	26

Sources: Centers for Disease Control and Prevention (CDC). *Summary Health Statistics for U.S. Adults: National Health Interview Survey 2012, Vital Health Statistics.* Series 10, Number 260, February 2014, Table 25; National data collected during 2001–2002.

What Is "Binge Drinking?"

Binge drinking means drinking so much within about 2 hours that blood alcohol concentration (BAC) levels reach 0.08g/dL. For women, this typically occurs after about 4 drinks, and for men, after about 5.

Drinking this way can pose health and safety risks, including car crashes and injuries.

Over the long term, binge drinking damages the liver and other organs.

What Factors Predict Drinking Behavior in the Hispanic Community?

Acculturation

Acculturation is the process of adapting to the beliefs, values, and behaviors of a new culture. A critical factor in predicting drinking patterns in the Hispanic community is level of acculturation.

Living and working in the United States, raising families here, speaking English, and above all, getting an American education all contribute to adapting to American culture. But as acculturation levels increase, so can alcohol consumption. The evidence is clear that as women become acculturated to American life, they tend to drink more alcohol. There is mixed evidence of the same effect for men.

Gender

In traditional Hispanic culture, women typically do not drink alcohol outside of small family gatherings or other private settings. For Hispanics in the United States, though, this cultural norm is changing. Recent evidence shows some young Hispanic women are drinking as much or even more than young Hispanic men.

Attitudes

Research shows that young, U.S.-born Hispanic men who are not Protestant tend to have relaxed attitudes toward drinking. Those who feel this way also are more likely to drink, to drink heavily, and to possibly have alcohol-related problems. Within the Hispanic community, Puerto Ricans and Mexican Americans tend to have more relaxed attitudes about drinking than Cuban Americans.

How Much Is Too Much?

In the United States, a standard drink is one that contains about 14 grams of pure alcohol, which is found in:

- 12 ounces of beer with 5 percent alcohol content
- 5 ounces of wine with 12 percent alcohol content
- 1.5 ounces of distilled spirits with 40 percent alcohol content

Selected Alcohol Consumption Statistics for Women and Men: U.S. Adults 18 Years of Age and Older

	Non-Hispanic White	Hispanic
who had at least 1 drink in the past year	70.3	54.5
» % who had at least 1 drink in their lifetime, but not in the past year	13.9	13.2
» % who had at least 1 drink in their lifetime	84.2	67.7
» % total lifetime abstainers (not even 1 drink)	15.5	31.8
» % of past-year drinkers, by usual number of drinks consumed per drinking day:		
1	38.3	31.8
2	30.1	25.8
3+	31.6	42.4
» % of past-year drinkers who drank 4+/5+ drinks:		
At least once in the past year	36.8	41.9
Less than once a month (1 to 11 times in past year, or < monthly)	15.5	15.9
Monthly or more (12+ times in past year)	21.3	26.0

Sources: Centers for Disease Control and Prevention (CDC). *Summary Health Statistics for U.S. Adults: National Health Interview Survey 2012, Vital Health Statistics.* Series 10, Number 260, February 2014, Table 25; National data collected during 2001–2002.

The USDA defines moderate drinking as:

- Up to 1 drink per day for women
- Up to 2 drinks per day for men

Unfortunately, although the "standard" drink amounts are helpful for following health guidelines, they may not reflect customary serving sizes. A large cup of beer, an overpoured glass of wine, or a single mixed drink could contain much more alcohol than a standard drink. In addition, while the alcohol concentrations listed are "typical," there is considerable variability in alcohol content within each type of beverage (e.g., beer, wine, distilled spirits).

Drinking Trends by Country of National Origin

Trends in drinking among Hispanics vary by country of origin. Among men, Puerto Ricans tend to drink the most and Cubans the least. Among women, Puerto Ricans tend to drink the most and Mexicans the least. Across all Hispanic national groups, beer is the preferred beverage, followed by wine and then liquor.

Consequences of Heavy Drinking
Alcohol Dependence

About 9.5 percent of Hispanics will have alcohol dependence at some point in their lives, as compared with about 13.8 percent

of non-Hispanic Whites. But 33 percent of Hispanics who become alcohol dependent have recurrent or persistent problems compared with 22.8 percent of non-Hispanic Whites.

Drunk Driving

Among Hispanics who drink, Mexican American men and women and South/Central American men are most likely to receive a citation for driving under the influence of alcohol. Research shows that between 1992 and 2002, there was a decrease in the number of Hispanic men (ages 18–29) who received a DUI, but an increase in the number of Hispanic women (ages 18–29) who received this citation.

What Is Alcohol Dependence?

Alcohol dependence is an alcohol use disorder often characterized by:

- Craving or compulsion to drink
- Increased tolerance to alcohol
- Withdrawal symptoms, including shaking, anxiety, or even seizures
- Failed attempts to quit that can result in drinking even greater amounts

Liver Disease

In general, Hispanic men develop liver disease at high rates. In fact, White Hispanic men have the highest rates of alcohol-related cirrhosis, a serious liver disease, of all

Average Number of Drinks Per Week (Beer, Wine, and Liquor) by Country/Nation of Origin

Country/Nation of Origin	Average Number of Drinks/Week for Men (irrespective of beverage)	Average Number of Drinks/ Week for Women (irrespective of beverage)
» Puerto Rico	16.9 (±1.6)	9.5 (±2.3)
» Mexico	15.9 (±1.7)	3.0 (±1.0)
» South/Central America	8.9	3.8 (±0.6)
» Cuba	8.4	3.4 (±1.1)

Percent of Past-year Drinkers Who Binge Drink by Country/Nation of Origin		
Country/Nation of Origin	Who Binge Drink	Who Binge Drink
» Puerto Rico	48.6	51.1
» Mexico	46.2	26.1
» South/Central America	42.9	27.3
» Cuba	27.3	22.4

Source: Ramisetty-Mikler, S.; Caetano, R.; and Rodriguez, L.A. The Hispanic Americans Baseline Alcohol Survey (HABLAS): Alcohol consumption and sociodemographic predictors across Hispanic national groups. *Journal of Substance Use* 15(6): 402–416, 2010.

Within the Hispanic Community, Rates of Alcohol Dependence Vary by Country or Nation of Origin

Country/Nation of Origin	Rate of Alcohol Dependence(Percent)
Puerto Rico	5.5
Mexico	4.7
South/Central America	3.1
Cuba	2.4

Chartier, K., and Caetano, R. Ethnicity and health disparities in alcohol research. *Alcohol Research & Health* 33(1 and 2):154, 2010.

ethnic or racial groups. But Black Hispanic men (e.g., from the Caribbean, the Dominican Republic, or Cuba) have the lowest cirrhosis rates when compared with non-Hispanic Whites.

Do Hispanics Seek Treatment for Alcohol Problems?

About 9.9 percent of Hispanics in the United States needed treatment for alcohol problems in the past year (data collected between 2004 and 2011). Of those in need, about 9.3 percent received treatment in a special facility.1

Limited research shows that treatment can help Hispanics who speak English and who are highly acculturated to American life. Nevertheless, Hispanics with severe alcohol problems are less likely than non-Hispanic Whites to seek the treatment they need. Hispanics also are less likely to join

Within the Hispanic Community, Rates of Alcohol Dependence Vary by Country or Nation of Origin

Country/Nation of Origin	Rate of Alcohol Dependence(Percent)
Mexico	10.4
Puerto rico	10.1
South/Central America	8.2
Other Hispanic	9.1

Source: Substance Abuse and Mental Health Services Administration (SAMHSA).[1]

Alcoholics Anonymous (AA), even though AA groups are available for free and in Spanish.

At Risk

NIAAA defines how much drinking may put people at risk for developing alcohol dependence.

Low-risk drinking limits are:

Women: No more than 7 drinks per week and no more than 3 drinks on any single day.|

Men: No more than 14 drinks per week and no more than 4 drinks on any single day.

To stay low risk, you must keep within both the single-day and weekly limits.

Low risk does not mean no risk. Even within these limits, you can have problems if you drink too quickly or have other health issues. Drinking slowly, and making sure you eat enough while drinking, can help minimize alcohol's effects.

Critical Thinking

1. After examining the chart, "Selected alcohol consumption statistics for women and men: U.S. adults 18 years of age and older," what do the statistics mean to you?

2. Why is it important to understand drinking patterns among the Hispanic population?

3. What is binge drinking and what kinds of problems can binge drinking cause?

4. Explain the three factors that predict drinking behavior in the Hispanic community.

5. We often hear that people consume alcoholic beverages to "relax," however, how much is really too much when it comes to alcohol consumption?

6. How do the average number of alcoholic drinks differ from people from the following countries: Puerto Rico, Mexico, South/Central America, and Cuba?

7. What is alcohol dependence and why is it important to understand the warning signs?

8. What kinds of treatment are available for Hispanics with alcohol problems? Can you suggest any alternatives?

Internet References

Drug and Alcohol Dependence
https://www.drugandalcoholdependence.com/

National Institute of Child Health and Human Development
https://www.nichd.nih.gov/

National Institute on Drug Abuse
https://www.drugabuse.gov/

National Institute on Alcohol Abuse and Alcoholism, *Alcohol and the Hispanic Community.* U.S. Department of Health and Human Services, 2015.

Article

Prepared by: Kim Schnurbush, *California State University, Sacramento*
Mark Pullin, *Angelo State University*

Current Rural Drug Use in the US Midwest

KIRK DOMBROWSKI, ET AL.

Learning Outcomes

After reading this article, you will be able to:

- Discuss how drug use is increasing in the US Midwest and rural areas.
- Understand the types of illicit drugs being used in rural America and the related harms.
- Discuss the complexity of preventing health-related harms from drug use in areas less equipped for medical intervention.

Introduction

The use of illicit drugs affects every region of the United States, but most of our information about drug use comes from large urban areas [1]. This is true despite two decades of increasingly visible rural drug use and its related harms [2, 3]. While once restricted to southern California, methamphetamine has had its largest impacts in rural states such as Oklahoma, Iowa, and Missouri [4]. More recently, Nebraska has joined this list, with increasing evidence of following in its neighbor's footsteps. The most recent Centers for Disease Control and Prevention data for Nebraska reveal that substance abuse treatment rates for prescription opiate use in 2010 was seven times what it was a decade earlier, and opiate-related overdose deaths in Nebraska are rapidly approaching the number of deaths due to automobile accidents [5]. In neighboring Missouri, overdose deaths have exceeded automobile deaths for several years [5].

Understanding and preventing health-related harms arising from drug use is complex [6, 7]. Years of addiction studies point to multifactorial causes for drug abuse, ranging from altered neurological function [8], behavioral factors [9, 10]

and psychosocial determinants [11], all operating in complex feedback loops. Complicating this are the physical, social, and emotional effects of blood born infections such as HIV, hepatitis B and C and tuberculosis, as well as a longer list of sexually transmitted infections frequently contracted in the context of drug use [12]. Although many human-system/virus-system interactions are now understood [13], how these are embedded in specific social contexts often remains unknown [14].

The few studies of rural drug use that exist show marked differences in rural versus urban drug users across demographic variables such as age or gender [15, 16] and large discrepancies in both the contexts of drug use and patterns of drug-related health consequences [17–19]. Other less direct disparities include differing social stressors, lower overall health levels and health care access, a dearth of substance use treatment facilities [20], unstable incomes, sparse social networks, and continuing high levels of social stigma around drug use and its related infections [21]. All of these mark rural drug use as vastly different from use in urban areas. Despite a small number of important exceptions [15, 18, 20], the urgent challenge of understanding drug use in rural settings is significantly under-examined.

The Problem

The United States' relationship with drugs is woven into our national history [22], from tobacco and rum to coffee and stimulant-laced drinks, to the use of performance enhancing drugs in our national pastime. Further, moral, health, economic, and psychological questions around drugs have been continually raised and disputed. This consistency does not reflect stasis, however. The nature and challenge of drug use continues to change rapidly [23], evolving in location and time in reaction to enforcement and education that would curtail use and driven forward by consumer demand and high profits [24]. Because much of this demand (and profit) is rooted in personal addiction, debates about drug use invoke individual and ethical dimensions not associated with other health issues. Recent findings on rising rates of white male mortality, in part due to the increasing numbers of drug-related deaths, has once again raised the question of America's relationship with substance abuse [25] and drugs as they reflect or contribute to national moral decline [26–30].

Beneath the public furor, however, the health sciences have made considerable progress in understanding the etiology of drug use and in uncovering the link between drug use and its myriad associated harms. To name only a few areas of progress, the last three decades have seen remarkable advances in the neurochemistry of drug effects, the virology of pathogens whose spread is often rooted in drug use [13], the understanding of social determinants of drug initiation [31] and clinical approaches to drug cessation. Researchers now speak openly and optimistically about an HIV vaccine and a cure for AIDS. Safer and more reliable forms of opiate inhibitors are emerging every year and as the National Institute on Drug Abuse (NIDA) points out, drug treatment effectiveness is now on par with the success rates of treatments for diabetes and asthma [32].

However, this promising scientific news has not always translated to better health outcomes. An outbreak of HIV infection in southern Indiana in 2015 revealed surprisingly widespread rural drug injection [33]. Current estimates of this outbreak are that 40 percent of the local network of people who inject drugs were infected in less than four months, a scenario not witnessed in urban areas since the early 1980s [33, 34]. The risks go beyond HIV and Clark County, Indiana, where the majority of cases were located. A medical state of emergency was declared in neighboring Madison County based on a high prevalence of hepatitis C virus (HCV) infection discovered in the process of understanding the HIV outbreak [34].

Nationally, overdose-related deaths and rates of opiate addiction in the United States are once again near record highs [35], a situation that Department of Health and Human Services (DHHS) Assistant Secretary Richard Frank recently identified as a top priority for the Administration and DHHS as a whole [36]. Even progress in slowing the use of cocaine cannot mask the immense growth in the use of other stimulants such as methamphetamine [37]. Today, the diversion of prescription and over-the-counter medicines into the illicit drug market is more prominent than at any time since regulation began [38].

These issues are exacerbated by changes in use patterns that have seen a dramatic increase in the use of illicit drugs in rural and sub-urban areas [39]—a change that (perhaps relatedly) locates problems of addiction and drug-related harms in those regions where overall health care infrastructure is struggling to remain viable. As a result, and in ways not seen before, rural drug use has come to urgent national attention. Data on rural drug use and its harms justify this attention. Methamphetamine use in Nebraska, Oklahoma, Iowa, and Missouri now rivals any region in the US [4]. Substance abuse treatment needs in rural states dwarf available services [5], and overdose rates in rural states in the Central Plains exceed 30 deaths per 10,000 residents in some rural counties [40]. Arrest data for cocaine, methamphetamine, or heroin possession in rural counties in the region are similar to urban zones with similar patterns of drug use such as Maricopa County Arizona, and Dallas, Texas [41].

Comparisons of rural to urban drug use within Nebraska show that rural users start using drugs at a younger age, are more likely to use and sell methamphetamine, and use non-marijuana illicit drugs at a higher rate than their urban counterparts [16, 42]. Their methods of use are more risky as well. Between 40 and 50 percent of rural methamphetamine users in Nebraska prefer injection-based use, nearly twice the urban rate and a similar ratio was found for lifetime rates of methamphetamine-related psychosis [16, 43]. Daily count methadone use in Nebraska in 2012 was four times the rate of 2008 and overall estimates suggest that only 8.6 percent of illicit drug-dependent individuals received treatment during 2012 [43]. In all, 3,594 Nebraskans and 8,131 Iowans were admitted for treatment for cocaine, methamphetamine, and opiate abuse in 2013, with methamphetamine by far the most common.

Like rural Indiana prior to the 2015 outbreak, rates of HIV are low in Nebraska, Iowa, and Kansas. However, risk is high. All of these states have highly restrictive syringe access laws [44–46] and high treatment deficits [47, 48]. The current treatment need-to-capacity ratio for opioid addiction in Nebraska is nearly 6:1, ranking third worst in the United States behind Arkansas and South Dakota (each roughly 7:1) and well behind treatment capacity in Connecticut, Massachusetts, and New York, where ratios are roughly 1:1 [49]. Together, these factors foster significant vulnerability to outbreaks like that seen in Indiana and in other rural states [50]. While little surveillance information is available for rural areas in the Central Plains, data from regions with similar use patterns suggest HCV rates of 40 to 50 percent among rural injectors [51–53]. This marks both a hidden precursor to the HIV risk made possible by current drug use patterns and a serious health crisis in the making.

To address this issue, we need to recognize that clear differences exist for rural drug use that make most urban intervention programs ineffective. These differences include: 1) the settings in which drug use takes place (i.e., social, moral, economic, geographical, and environmental contexts); 2) the patterns of use and demographics of rural drug users; and 3) the conditions and capacities for treatment, intervention, and general care.

Current Rural Drug Use in the US Midwest by Kirk Dombrowski et al.

131

Rural Contexts and Drug Use

Elevated levels of behavioral risk for residents of rural areas has been recognized among youth [54] and adults [39, 55], although it is also widely recognized that data on rural risk remain uneven and insufficient [56]. Efforts to understand geographical differences as they influence drug-related risks point to a range of "social ecological" factors underlying these differences [57, 58]. For example, according to Keyes and colleagues [59], the concentration of opiate abuse in rural areas is tied to general structural factors that differentiate rural areas from cities, including: 1) higher rates of opioid prescription, 2) youth outmigration, 3) larger kinship networks that facilitate informal drug trafficking, and 4) more economic stress.

Other approaches note macro-level social structural factors (e.g. marked differences in prisoner re-entry outcomes) for rural areas [60] or differences in rural drug policing [61]. Still others point to radically different racial [62, 63] and economic dynamics [64] related to rural use and risk patterns—factors that require different treatment and intervention strategies. However, not all research takes the urban/rural divide as paramount. Research on rural methamphetamine use points to the importance of local social contexts in creating micro-locational differences within rural areas [65], and research on rural cocaine use finds significant population level differences between users of different stimulants and their respective risk profiles [62]. Some recent evidence even looks at genetic-environment interactions and how these affect substance use susceptibility in rural areas [66, 67]. These approaches could also shed light on rural concentrations of drug use from genetic 'founder effects.' Such findings point to an important consideration—that the causes and implications of rural drug use are highly variegated and may be as different from one region to another, or even one county to another, as they are from generalized urban trends.

Rural Patterns of Drug Use and Demographics of Rural Users

When we shift the focus to rural drug users themselves, there is again evidence of systematic differences between urban and rural areas, including who uses drugs and how [23, 68]. In a wide ranging series of studies in Appalachia, Havens and colleagues found marked differences between rural and urban drug users (mainly users of prescription opiates) in transitions from first use to first injection [17], patterns of initiation of opioids and polysubstance use [15, 69], gender propensities [70], and HCV infection [71], even while patterns of non-fatal overdose were similar [72]. Others have found significant rural/urban differences for methamphetamine users [65]. In Nebraska, Kansas, and Iowa, treatment admissions for methamphetamine

are nearly equal for men and women [73], a startling contrast with other drugs and other regions. According to the Treatment Episodes Data Set (TEDS 2013), in Nebraska, one third of drug treatment admissions were for stimulants, and amphetamines were second only to alcohol in total treatment admissions [47]. Grant and colleagues found that rural methamphetamine users in the state were nearly twice as likely to only inject as their urban counterparts were (37.2 percent versus 20.2 percent) [16]. This risk profile implies radically different potential for HIV and related harms should the virus enter these communities. Other harms have already taken place: in the same report, Grant and colleagues found that lifetime prevalence for meth-related psychosis was much higher for rural (44.9 percent) than urban (28.7 percent) individuals, despite similarities across all other mental health areas [74].

Research on factors influencing user differences within rural areas has focused on many of the same issues that differentiate use among urban populations. Meyers found that adolescent risk and support factors for stimulant users differed along racial lines [75, 76], while Pope found differences for this group were (also) patterned by gender [77]. In both cases, similarities between urban and rural drug users were clear. These results point to an important conclusion—rural users require special consideration for multiple reasons, including decidedly higher rates of methamphetamine use, a higher proportion of users preferring injection, and a user population that is younger and riskier than urban counterparts [51, 78]. This conclusion holds true regardless of whether greater differences exist between urban and rural drug use, or within rural areas themselves,

Rural Capacities for Treatment, Intervention, and Care

Several of the above issues contribute to low treatment success rates in rural areas. In looking at differences within rural areas, Oser and Harp discovered that cultural differences between home and treatment venues played a large role in rural treatment outcomes [79], findings echoed by McMaster for female methamphetamine users [80]. Jackson and Shannon, on the other hand, noted few differences in treatment seeking attitudes in rural versus urban pregnant women [81]. Rather, in their view, and in the view of others, these outcomes for rural treatment seekers may simply reflect a shrinking rural health care infrastructure [21, 64] and decades of general mortality differences across the full continuum of rural settings [82]. There are reasons to suspect this is the case, including a documented lack of available substance use disorder treatment facilities [83] and drug education programs [84] in rural counties. However, these may be only part of the problem, as the treatment needs caused by drug use often go beyond the actual user, affecting family, community, and environment [85]. These findings point to rural conditions that require specific attention to regional issues and differences within rural drug using populations. At the same time, we must keep in mind the clear evidence that larger structural features distinguish rural from urban zones, including differences in care.

In the United States, drug use and its associated health risks have traditionally been considered an urban problem. For example, the Centers for Disease Control and Prevention (CDC)'s National HIV Behavioral Surveillance (NHBS) Program on Injection Drug Use focuses entirely on the nation's 25 largest urban areas, performing extensive surveillance testing among drug using populations in each of these cities every three years. In contrast, drug-related disease surveillance in non-urban zones is largely restricted to local law enforcement programs. In many rural areas, non-prison surveillance is non-existent. In the past, this emphasis on urban drug use has been justified by low rates of drug-related health impacts in non-urban zones. However, the evidence of the last five years shows that this is no longer the case.

Discussion

Rural injection drug use and its related harms have come to national attention at the same time that drug use in the United States has undergone a radical reformulation. New clusters of prescription opiate users (23), significant numbers of whom transition to heroin and the near ubiquity of methamphetamine abuse across rural parts of the country [86] have transformed the national health landscape. Both of these phenomena have significantly impacted the Central Plains, a region one recent author refers to as "Methland" (22) for the sheer scope of use and for its intense impact in a quickly changing rural economic landscape. The harms associated with the use of these drugs goes beyond the more well-known viruses, with implications for sexually transmitted infections contracted in the context of drug use [87], mental health problems [88], and other social and family harms that ripple out from personal centers of addiction [89]. . . .

Despite timely and pressing challenges related to rural drug use, there are crucial limitations in the current state of research surrounding this issue. These challenges must be addressed if we hope to impact rural drug use. In general, the need for reliable physical, contextual and cognitive data related to the onset and desistance of drug use (and behaviors associated with drug use harms) is particularly critical for research on rural illicit drugs users [90]. Indeed, a significant amount of what we know about drug use in urban areas is based on successful, long-term cohort studies [90, 91], some of which continue today such as

ALIVE [92], MIX [93] and VIDUS [94]. However, no rural equivalent currently exists and past rural studies have focused mainly on Appalachia [18].

When we look at the 32 counties in eastern Nebraska, western Iowa, and northern Kansas, we get a sense of the immensity of the challenge. By scaling up [95–97] drug-related (non- marijuana) arrest data from the Department of Justice's Uniform Crime Reporting Program (UCRP; [77]) and hospitalization data from the Substance Abuse and Mental Health Services Administration (SAMHSA; [78]), we can estimate the size of the drug using population in these counties to be ~20,000 individuals (which is ~2.7 percent of the counties' population of ~740,000). This figure is commensurate with national prevalence estimates of drug use as a percentage of total population [79].

While research is needed, immediate solutions to the health risks posed by rural drug use are available. Modern day harm reduction points to three basic means for minimizing the personal and social risks associated with drug use, especially injection drug use preventative strategy. This startlingly contradictory position was underwritten by entrenched (and essentially irrational) opinions about syringe exchange programs—namely, the idea that making clean needles available in exchange for dirty ones somehow encourages drug use among those not already using drugs, or that it increases the level of drug use among those already using. This has been shown repeatedly and uniformly to be false in both cases [98]. To be clear, there is no evidence in three decades of research to suggest either assumption, yet it governs policy in nearly half of the states in the US, and nearly all states in the Central Plains. This is clearly one of area of public health where rational, data-driven outcomes have yet to be adopted in public policy arenas, and thus an area where immediate progress could be made that would save lives and lower treatment costs, even while it protects the wider non-using public from potentially dangerous outbreaks of HIV or hepatitis C. Temporarily closing the barn door long after the horse has left, as was done in Indiana, is unlikely to prevent HIV and hepatitis C outbreaks in places like Nebraska, Missouri, Kansas, Oklahoma or Iowa and much of the Central and Northern Plains [99].

Opiate Substitution Treatment

Treatment of opiate addiction has included opiate substitution for more than five decades. Among the earlier methods was methadone treatment, an opiate that produces less of a "high" that is used in measured and medically supervised program lessen the effects of heroin or opiate withdrawal. Its effectiveness was debated for years, but recent retrospective reviews have found that methadone substitution treatment was highly effective not just in treating addiction, but in lowering on-going risk for infection during the treatment period and beyond [100].

New treatments using substitution drugs such as buprenorphine have proven even more effective than methadone, and have longer lasting success rates. Buprenorphine is a partial opiate agonist, meaning that it bonds to neurological receptors in the brain in a way that is similar to opium (or heroin or a range of opiate-based prescription pain killers), but does not produce the same effects as opiates (i.e., the opiate delirium experienced as a "high") [100]. It is thus highly effective in staving off withdrawal symptoms without fulfilling the psychological need for escape.

By lessening withdrawal effects, buprenorphine allows the user to gradually reduce use and "ease off" of the drug, normally while receiving addiction therapy aimed at understanding and lessening the causes of psychological addiction. By allowing the latter (psychological addiction) to be treated without the experience of withdrawal (physiological addiction), the user stands a greater chance of successfully confronting those issues that inspired drug use/initiation in the past.

Despite these successes, buprenorphine treatment is very rare in the Midwest and Central Plains. Because treatment takes place in a doctor's office and under medical supervision, the availability of treatment is dependent on sufficient numbers of doctors who are willing to participate. Arkansas, North Dakota and Nebraska rank worst in the US in terms of the ratio of opiate addicts to buprenorphine prescribing doctors. This is partly due to the scope of the opiate addiction problem in these states, and partly due to lack of rural medical infrastructure. In some ways, the lack of buprenorphine prescribing doctors reflects the general lack of medical services in rural areas, but in the situation is exaggerated by the stigma attached to drug use and addiction. This is particularly troubling because in these states, opiate addiction is increasingly a rural problem.

This too is a solvable problem, but one that currently lacks political attention. By allowing and promoting buprenorphine services in existing rural facilities, successful treatment for growing opiate addiction in the region could be expanded dramatically in the Central Plains. Given that the treatment is covered by virtually all public and private forms of insurance, the cost to these states, after the initial training and implementation, would be minimal—and the savings in lost productivity time, emergency room visits, and general public risk for drug use related diseases would be substantial.

Naloxone

Where buprenorphine is a partial opiate agonist, naloxone (often known under the commercial name of Narcan) is an opiate antagonist. This means that it operates by blocking the attachments of opium to neurological receptors. In effect, naloxone prevents opium from having an effect on the brain. For this reason, it is often used in emergency situations to reverse an overdose.

As discussed above, drug overdose rates in the Central Plains have grown dramatically over the last decade. Missouri, Oklahoma and Wyoming have rates of overdose nearly double the rates of New York, California, Texas, or Virginia and nearly double the rates of Eastern rural states that have receive considerably more public attention such as Vermont. Notably, some states in the Central Plains still do not make naloxone available to the public, nor have they passed "Good Samaritan" laws protecting bystanders who report overdose incidents to emergency services, or who administer naloxone to someone who has overdosed.

Unlike syringe exchange or buprenorphine availability, considerable progress has been made in this area, however. Central Plains states with high levels of overdose have taken action to make overdose deaths less likely by making naloxone more available and its use in an emergency more protected. Holdouts continue, though, including Missouri, Kansas, South Dakota, Iowa, Minnesota and Wyoming. This is difficult to understand, other than to point out the overall punitive attitude toward addicts in these states. Again, there now exist easy and low cost means to mitigate the relationship between drug use and overdose death, held back only by a seeming desire to punish addicts for their addiction.

Taken together, these three inexpensive and cost effective programs could greatly reduce the disease risk of injection drug use, facilitate addiction recovery, and reverse the rising rate of accidental death associated with overdose. All of these programs have been employed in other regions with considerable success, and with none of the feared side-effects of increased drug use. The lesson that we need to recognize in Nebraska and the Central Plains is that data driven means for dealing with rising rural drug use in our region are available, and acting only after the problem can no longer be ignored ensures that these means will cost more and be more widely needed. In short, the time to act is now.

References

1. Lansky A, Finlayson T, Johnson C, Holtzman D, Wejnert C, Mitsch A, et al. Estimating the number of persons who inject drugs in the United States by meta-analysis to calculate national rates of HIV and hepatitis C Virus infections. PLoS ONE. 2014; 9:1–9.
2. Gfroerer JC, Larson SL, Colliver JD. Drug use patterns and trends in rural communities. J Rural Health. 2007; 23:10–15.

3. Control C for D. Prevention USDH Public Health Service, Services, H. Opioid Overdoses in the United States. J Pain Palliat Care Pharmacother. 2012; 26:44–47. [PubMed: 22448941]

4. Lineberry TW, Bostwick JM. Methamphetamine abuse: A perfect storm of complications. Mayo Clin Proc. 2006; 81:77–84. [PubMed: 16438482]

5. Rudd RA, Paulozzi LJ, Bauer MJ, Burleson RW, Carlson RE, et al. Increases in heroin overdose deaths - 28 States, 2010 to 2012. MMWR Morb Mortal Wkly Rep. 2014; 63:849–854. [PubMed: 25275328]

6. Kalivas PW, Volkow ND. The neural basis of addiction: a pathology of motivation and choice. Am J Psychiatry. 2005; 162:1403–1413. [PubMed: 16055761]

7. Dombrowski K. Topological and historical considerations for infectious disease transmission among injecting drug users in Bushwick, Brooklyn (USA). World J AIDS. 2013; 3:1–9. [PubMed: 24672745]

8. Wise RA, Koob GF. The development and maintenance of drug addiction. Neuropsychopharmacology. 2014; 39:254–262. [PubMed: 24121188]

9. Parvaz MA, Konova AB, Proudfit GH, Dunning JP, Malaker P, et al. Impaired neural response to negative prediction errors in cocaine addiction. J Neurosci. 2015; 35:1872–1879. [PubMed: 25653348]

10. Khan B, Dombrowski K, Saad M. A stochastic agent-based model of pathogen propagation in dynamic multi-relational social networks. Simul Trans Soc Model Simul Int. 2014; 90:460–484.

11. Nestler EJ. Epigenetic mechanisms of drug addiction. Neuropharmacology. 2014; 76(Part B):259– 268. [PubMed: 23643695]

12. Al-Harthi L, Buch S, Geiger JD. Cellular interactions and signaling in neuroAIDS: Emerging issues colloquium. J Neuroimmune Pharmacol. 2014; 9:269–276. [PubMed: 24789373]

13. Khan B, Dombrowski K, Saad M. Network firewall dynamics and the subsaturation stabilization of HIV. Discrete Dyn Nat Soc. 2013; 4:1–16.

14. Friedman SR, Sandoval M, Mateu-Gelabert P. Theory, measurement and hard times: Some issues for HIV/AIDS research. AIDS Behav. 2013; 17:1915–1925. [PubMed: 23564029]

15. Young AM, Havens JR, Leukefeld CG. A comparison of rural and urban nonmedical prescription opioid users' lifetime and recent drug use. Am J Drug Alcohol Abuse. 2012; 38:220–227. [PubMed: 22211586]

16. Grant KM, Kelley SS, Agrawal S. Methamphetamine use in rural Midwesterners. Am J Addict. 2007; 16:79–84. [PubMed: 17453608]

17. Young AM, Havens JR. Transition from first illicit drug use to first injection drug use among rural Appalachian drug users: A cross-sectional comparison and retrospective survival analysis. Addict Abingdon Engl. 2012; 107:587–596.

18. Havens JR, Oser CB, Leukefeld CG. Injection risk behaviors among rural drug users: Implications for HIV prevention. AIDS Care. 2011; 23:638–645. [PubMed: 21293995]

19. Draus PJ, Carlson RG. Needles in the Haystacks: The social context of initiation to heroin injection in rural Ohio. Subst Use Misuse. 2006; 41:1111–1124. [PubMed: 16798679]

20. Young LB, Grant KM, Tyler KA. Community-level barriers to recovery for substance-dependent rural residents. J Soc Work Pract Addict. 2015; 15:307–326.

21. Hartley D. Rural health disparities, population health and rural culture. Am J Public Health. 2004; 94:1675–1678. [PubMed: 15451729]

22. Methland, RN. The death and life of an American small town. Bloomsbury Publishing USA: 2010.

23. Cicero TJ, Ellis MS, Surratt HL. The changing face of heroin use in the United States: A retrospective analysis of the past 50 years. JAMA Psychiatry. 2014; 71:821–826. [PubMed: 24871348]

24. Office of National Drug Control Policy. What America's users spend on illegal drugs: 2000–2010. Office of National Drug Control Policy; 2014.

25. Case A, Deaton A. Rising morbidity and mortality in midlife among white non-Hispanic Americans in the 21st century. Proc Natl Acad Sci. 2015 201518393.

26. Anne Case. Co-author of the White Mortality Paper, Responds to a New Critique of Its Approach to Gender (Updated). Science of US. 2015

27. Kolata G. Death rates rising for middle-aged white Americans, study finds. The New York Times. 2015

28. Cassidy J. Why did the death rate rise among middle-aged white Americans? The New Yorker. 2015

29. Meara E, Skinner J. Losing ground at midlife in America. Proc Natl Acad Sci. 2015 201519763.

30. Angus Deaton's paper on working class white males killing themselves might not be right.

31. Dombrowski K, Khan B, McLean K. A re-examination of connectivity trends via exponential random graph modeling in two IDU risk networks. Subst Use Misuse. 2013; 48:1485–1497. [PubMed: 23819740]

32. How effective is drug addiction treatment?

33. Adams J. HIV outbreak in Indiana. N Engl J Med. 2015; 373:1379–1380.

34. Strathdee SA, Beyrer C. Threading the needle—How to stop the HIV outbreak in rural Indiana. N Engl J Med. 2015; 373:397–399. [PubMed: 26106947]

35. CDC P. et al. Control C for D. CDC grand rounds: prescription drug overdoses-a US epidemic. MMWR Morb Mortal Wkly Rep. 2012; 61:10. [PubMed: 22237030]

36. Rates of drug overdose deaths continue to rise. 2015. HHS.gov

37. Durell TM, Kroutil LA, Crits-Christoph P, et al. Prevalence of nonmedical methamphetamine use in the United States. Subst Abuse Treat Prev Policy. 2008; 3:19. [PubMed: 18655714]

38. Maxwell JC. The prescription drug epidemic in the United States: A perfect storm. Drug Alcohol Rev. 2011; 30:264–270. [PubMed: 21545556]

39. Paulozzi LJ, Xi Y. Recent changes in drug poisoning mortality in the United States by urban–rural status and by drug type. Pharmacoepidemiol Drug Saf. 2008; 17:997–1005. [PubMed: 18512264]

40. Drug overdoses are growing problem in rural Oklahoma. 2015 NewsOK.com.

41. United States Department of Justice. Federal Bureau of Investigation. Uniform Crime Reporting Program Data: County-Level Detailed Arrest and Offense Data, 2012. ICPSR - Interuniversity Consortium for Political and Social Research. 2014

42. Herz, DC. Drugs in the Heartland: Methamphetamine use in rural Nebraska. Vol. 11. Washington, D.C.: National Institute of Justice, U.S. Department of Justice; 2000. Report No.: NCJ 180986

43. Substance Abuse and Mental Health Services Administration. Behavioral health barometer: Nebraska, 2013. Vol. 25. Rockville, MD: 2013. Report No.: HHS Publication No. SMA-13-4796NE

44. Bramson H, Des Jarlais DC, Arasteh K. State laws, syringe exchange, and HIV among persons who inject drugs in the United States: History and effectiveness. J Public Health Policy. 2015; 36:212–230. [PubMed: 25590514]

45. Des Jarlais DC, Nugent A, Solberg A. Syringe service programs for persons who inject drugs in urban, suburban and rural areas-United States. MMWR Morb Mortal Wkly Rep. 2014; 64:1337– 1341.

46. Rich JD, Adashi EY. Ideological anachronism involving needle and syringe exchange programs: Lessons from the Indiana HIV outbreak. JAMA. 2015; 314:23–24. [PubMed: 26000661]

47. Center for Behavioral Health Statistics and Quality S. Treatment Episodes Data Set (TEDS).

48. This family drives 350 miles for what could be a common addiction treatment (2010) The Huffington Post.

49. Jones CM, Campopiano M, Baldwin G. National and State treatment need and capacity for opioid agonist medication-assisted treatment. Am J Public Health. 2015; 105:e55–e63.

50. López LM, de Saxe Zerden L, Bourgois P. HIV/AIDS in Puerto Rican people who inject drugs: Policy considerations. Am J Public Health. 2015; 105:e3–e3.

51. Valdiserri R, Khalsa J, Dan C. Confronting the emerging epidemic of HCV infection among young injection drug users. Am J Public Health. 2014; 104:816–821. [PubMed: 24625174]

52. Cox J, Morissette C, De P. Access to sterile injecting equipment is more important than awareness of HCV status for injection risk behaviors among drug users. Subst Use Misuse. 2009; 44:548– 568. [PubMed: 19242863]

53. Akselrod H, Grau LE, Barbour R. Among injection drug users in Connecticut: Understanding infection and co-infection risks in a non-urban population. Am J Public Health. 2014; 104:1713– 1721. [PubMed: 24134382]

54. Atav S, Spencer GA. Health risk behaviors among adolescents attending rural, suburban and urban schools: A comparative study. Fam Community Health. 2002; 25:53–64. [PubMed: 12010115]

55. Abadie R, Welch-Lazoritz M, Gelpi-Acosta C. Understanding differences in HIV/HCV prevalence according to differentiated risk behaviors in a sample of PWID in rural Puerto Rico. Harm Reduct J. 2016; 13:1. [PubMed: 26743909]

56. Rishel CW, Cottrell L, Kingery T. Preventing adolescent risk behavior in the rural context: An integrative analysis of adolescent, parent, and provider perspectives. J Fam Soc Work. 2012; 15:401–416.

57. Van Gundy KT, Stracuzzi NF, Rebellon CJ. Perceived community cohesion and the stress process in youth. Rural Sociol. 2011; 76:293–318.

58. Burton, LM.; Garrett-Peters, R.; Eason, JM. Morality, identity and mental health in rural ghettos. In: Burton, LM.; Matthews, SA.; Leung, M.; Kemp, SP.; Takeuchi, DT., editors. Communities, Neighbourhoods and Health. New York: Springer; 2011. p. 91–110.

59. Keyes KM, Cerdá M, Brady JE. Understanding the rural–urban differences in nonmedical prescription opioid use and abuse in the United States. Am J Public Health. 2013; 104:e52–e59. [PubMed: 24328642]

60. Wodahl EJ. The challenges of prisoner reentry from a rural perspective. W Criminol Rev. 2006; 7:32–35.

61. Garriott, W. Policing methamphetamine: Narcopolitics in rural America. NYU Press; 2011.

62. Borders TF, Stewart KE, Wright PB. Risky sex in rural America: Longitudinal changes in a community-based cohort of methamphetamine and cocaine users. Am J Addict. 2013; 22:535–542. [PubMed: 24131160]

63. Brown RA. Crystal methamphetamine use among American Indian and White youth in Appalachia: Social context, masculinity and desistance. Addict Res Theory. 2010; 18:250–269. [PubMed: 21637733]

64. Lenardson, JD.; Hartley, D.; Gale, J. Substance use and abuse in rural America. In: Warren, JC.; Smiley, KB., editors. rural public health: Best practices and preventive models. New York: Springer Publishing Company; 2014. p. 95–114.

65. Roussell A, Holmes MD, Anderson-Sprecher R. Community characteristics and methamphetamine use in a rural state an analysis of pre-incarceration usage by prison inmates. Crime Delinquency. 2013; 59:1036–1063.

66. Brody GH, Chen Y-F, Yu T. Life stress, the dopamine receptor gene, and emerging adult drug use trajectories: A longitudinal, multilevel, mediated moderation analysis. Dev Psychopathol. 2012; 24:941–951. [PubMed: 22781864]

67. Brody GH, Yu T, Beach SR. A differential susceptibility analysis reveals the "who and how" about adolescents' responses to preventive interventions: Tests of first-and second-generation Gene$\times$ Intervention hypotheses. Dev Psychopathol. 2015; 27:37–49. [PubMed: 25640829]

68. Novak SP, Kral AH. Comparing injection and non-injection routes of administration for heroin, methamphetamine and cocaine users in the United States. J Addict Dis. 2011; 30:248–257. [PubMed: 21745047]

69. Hall MT, Leukefeld CG, Havens JR. Factors associated with high-frequency illicit methadone use among rural Appalachian drug users. Am J Drug Alcohol Abuse. 2013; 39:241–246. [PubMed: 23841864]

70. Shannon LM, Havens JR, Oser C. Examining gender differences in substance use and age of first use among rural Appalachian drug users in Kentucky. Am J Drug Alcohol Abuse. 2011; 37:98–104. [PubMed: 21142705]

71. Havens JR, Lofwall MR, Frost SDW. Individual and network factors associated with prevalent hepatitis C infection among rural Appalachian injection drug users. Am J Public Health. 2013; 103:e44–e52.

72. Havens JR, Oser CB, Knudsen HK. Individual and network factors associated with non-fatal overdose among rural Appalachian drug users. Drug Alcohol Depend. 2011; 115:107–112. [PubMed: 21126831]

73. National Substance Abuse Index. 2015

74. Grant KM, Kelley SS, Agrawal S. Methamphetamine use in rural midwesterners. Am J Addict. 2007; 16:79–84. [PubMed: 17453608]

75. Myers LL. Substance use among rural African American adolescents: Identifying risk and protective factors. Child Adolesc Soc Work J. 2013; 30:79–93.

76. Myers LL. Health risk behaviors among adolescents in the rural South: A comparison of race, gender and age. J Hum Behav Soc Environ. 2010; 20:1024–1037.

77. Pope SK, Falck RS, Carlson RG. Characteristics of rural crack and powder cocaine use: Gender and other correlates. Am J Drug Alcohol Abuse. 2011; 37:491–496. [PubMed: 21851207]

78. Zibbell JE, Hart-Malloy R, Barry J. Risk factors for HCV infection among young adults in rural New York who inject prescription opioid analgesics. Am J Public Health. 2014; 104:2226–2232. [PubMed: 25211717]

79. Oser CB, Harp KLH. Treatment outcomes for prescription drug misusers: The negative effect of geographic discordance. J Subst Abuse Treat. 2015; 48:77–84. [PubMed: 25200740]

80. MacMaster SA. Perceptions of need, service use and barriers to service access among female methamphetamine users in rural Appalachia. Soc Work Public Health. 2013; 28:109–118. [PubMed: 23461346]

81. Jackson A, Shannon L. Examining barriers to and motivations for substance abuse treatment among pregnant women: does urban-rural residence matter? Women Health. 2012; 52:570–586. [PubMed: 22860704]

82. James WL. All rural places are not created equal: revisiting the rural mortality penalty in the United States. Am J Public Health. 2014; 104:2122–2129. [PubMed: 25211763]

83. Cummings JR, Wen H, Ko M. Race/ethnicity and geographic access to Medicaid substance use disorder treatment facilities in the United States. JAMA Psychiatry. 2014; 71:190–196. [PubMed: 24369387]

84. Williams RD Jr, Barnes JT, Leoni E. Social and epidemiological assessment of drug use: A case study of rural youth in Missouri. Am J Health Stud. 2011; 26:79–86.

85. Sheridan K. A systematic review of the literature regarding family context and mental health of children from rural methamphetamine-involved families: Implications for rural child welfare practice. J Public Child Welf. 2014; 8:514–538.

86. Gruenewald PJ, Johnson FW. Assessing correlates of the growth and extent of methamphetamine abuse and dependence in California. Subst Use Misuse. 2010; 45:1948–1970. [PubMed: 20380553]

87. Wilkerson JM, Noor SW, Breckenridge ED. Substance-use and sexual harm reduction strategies of methamphetamine-using men who have sex with men and inject drugs. AIDS Care. 2015; 27:1047–1054. [PubMed: 25837492]

88. Dew B, Elifson K, Dozier M. Social and environmental factors and their influence on drug use vulnerability and resiliency in rural populations. J Rural Health. 2007; 23(s1):16–21. [PubMed: 18237320]

89. Day C, Conroy E, Lowe J. Patterns of drug use and associated harms among rural injecting drug users: Comparisons with metropolitan injecting drug users. Aust J Rural Health. 2006; 14:120–125. [PubMed: 16706881]

90. Shah NG, Galai N, Celentano DD. Longitudinal predictors of injection cessation and subsequent relapse among a cohort of injection drug users in Baltimore, MD, 1988–2000. Drug Alcohol Depend. 2006; 83:147–156. [PubMed: 16364568]

91. Saxon AJ, Calsyn DA, Jackson TR. Longitudinal changes in injection behaviors in a cohort of injection drug users. Addiction. 1994; 89:191–202. [PubMed: 8173485]

92. Galai N, Safaeian M, Vlahov D. Longitudinal patterns of drug injection behavior in the ALIVE Study cohort, 1988–2000: description and determinants. Am J Epidemiol. 2003; 158:695. [PubMed: 14507606]

93. Horyniak D, Higgs P, Jenkinson R. Establishing the Melbourne injecting drug user cohort study (MIX): Rationale, methods and baseline and twelve-month follow-up results. Harm Reduct J. 2013; 10:11. [PubMed: 23786848]

94. Strathdee SA, Patrick DM, Currie SL. Needle exchange is not enough: Lessons from the Vancouver injecting drug use study. AIDS. 1997; 11:59–65. [PubMed: 9110076]

95. Habecker P, Dombrowski K, Khan B. Improving the network scale-up estimator: Incorporating means of sums, recursive back estimation and sampling weights. PloS One. 2015; 10

96. US Department of Justice. Federal Bureau of Investigation. Uniform Crime Reporting Program Data: County-Level Detailed Arrest and Offense Data (ICPSR 35019). 2012

97. Gibson DR, Flynn NM, Perales D. Effectiveness of syringe exchange programs in reducing HIV risk behavior and HIV seroconversion among injecting drug users. Aids. 2001; 15:1329–1341. [PubMed: 11504954]

98. Laufer FN. Cost-effectiveness of syringe exchange as an HIV prevention strategy. JAIDS J Acquir Immune Defic Syndr. 2001; 28:273–278. [PubMed: 11694836]

99. Indiana's HIV outbreak leads to reversal on needle exchanges. 2016 NPR.org.

100. Fullerton CA, Kim M, Thomas CP. Medication-assisted treatment with methadone: Assessing the evidence. Psychiatr Serv. 2014; 65:146–157. [PubMed: 24248468]

Critical Thinking

1. Why has drug use increased across the country in rural areas?

2. Methamphetamines and opiates have increased greater than seven times in the last decade. Why are these drugs of choice in rural areas?

3. Do enforcement and education issues in rural areas influence increasing drug use?

4. The average age of user is decreasing over time. Why is this? Why are long-term effects of younger drug user numbers increasing?

Internet References

Centers for Disease Control and Prevention
    https://www.cdc.gov/

Drug and Alcohol Dependence
    https://www.drugandalcoholdependence.com/

Drug Policy Alliance
    http://www.drugpolicy.org/

National Center for Chronic Disease Prevention and Health Promotion
    https://www.cdc.gov/chronicdisease/index.htm

© Under License of Creative Commons Attribution 3.0 License **Corresponding author:** Kirk Dombrowski, kdombrowski2@unl.edu, Ph.D., Department of Sociology, Oldfather 708, University of Nebraska-Lincoln, Lincoln, NE 68588, USA. **Tel:** 402-472-3205.

Article

Prepared by: Kim Schnurbush, *California State University, Sacramento*
Mark Pullin, *Angelo State University*

Oil and Drugs: A Toxic Mix

As dollars flow into Permian Basin, dangerous substance abuse increases

COLLIN EATON AND JOHN D. HARDEN

Learning Outcomes

After reading this article, you will be able to:

- Discuss the purpose of the war on drugs in oil and petroleum-based industries.

- Understand the drug trafficking, drug abuse, and drug-related crimes that infuse the oil field industry.

- Discuss how drug abuse in a dangerous industry affect workers as well as cities and communities where oil-related work is conducted.

MIDLAND - Eddy Lozoya never failed a drug test in the three years he hauled water and sand across the West Texas oil patch, even though he used at least $200 a day in cocaine to keep his eyes open on brutally long days behind the wheel of a Kenworth T600 semi-truck.

Lozoya, like his fellow truckers, found ways to beat the tests and keep driving. Earning six-figure salaries, they consumed cocktails of drugs to push themselves to their physical limits on trips between scattered drilling sites that could last 36 to 48 consecutive hours. They would drive their 35-ton vehicles in tight, single-file formations, blowing air horns when the sleepiest among them began drifting off the road.

"We always had cocaine," he said.

Lozoya, a recovering addict at 23, is among the thousands of oil field workers who have succumbed to the mix of money, boredom and drugs that often accompanies energy booms. Drillers of all sizes have poured billions of dollars into the prolific Permian Basin this year, rebuilding operations after a two-year oil bust that devastated the region. But for all the economic benefits of the industry's high-paying jobs, the oil rush again is bankrolling an expanding market for illegal drugs.

Law enforcement officials say drug trafficking, drug abuse and drug-related crimes have spiked in recent years, evidence that energy's boom-and-bust cycles have had enormous social consequences in West Texas. Inside a small Nazarene church in Midland, converted a decade ago into a drug and alcohol addiction treatment center, the number of people seeking help is on track to more than double from last year.

Some 1,200 people have come through the doors of the Palmer Drug Abuse Program in the first six months of the year, one in five of them under 18.

"We're losing a generation of children to drugs and alcohol," said Michele Savage, the longtime director of the program.

Lozoya knows drugs of all kinds are easy to find here. After an injury left him unable to drive commercial trucks, he found another lucrative trucking route, this time transporting narcotic pain medications and other drugs from his home state of California to West Texas. Here, he said, dealers can sell cocaine, marijuana and opioids for two or three times the price in neighboring states because of the remote location and the river of money flowing from the oil patch.

"There's a lot of profit to be made out here because it's in such high demand," he said. "People want it here, and they'll pay for it."

'Meth is Booming'

While the U.S. opioid epidemic has captured national attention, the drug of choice in West Texas is methamphetamine, or crystal meth, a powerful stimulant oil field workers use to cope with long hours in the Texas heat, and one that is increasingly supplied through Mexican drug cartels, according to law enforcement officials. An analysis of data from the Texas Department of Public Safety and the Houston oil field services company Baker Hughes found a strong correlation between the rise of drilling activity and the number of crystal meth seizures in the area surrounding the Permian Basin. Between 2009 and 2016, as oil companies dispatched more rigs into West Texas, the number of meth seizures rose sharply.

The rig count's average of 103 in 2009 increased more than fivefold by 2014, the peak of the oil boom. In the same period, Texas state troopers saw meth seizures jump from 3 to 73, a 4,000 percent increase in the dozens of counties encompassing the Permian Basin.

CRS Diagnostic Service, a drug-testing company in Odessa, found the number of local workers who tested positive for methamphetamine in the first half of this year was more than three times higher than in the first half of 2009, shortly before the so-called shale oil revolution got underway.

"Meth is booming," said Craig Smith, a senior vice president at the company.

For the oil industry, increased drug abuse in West Texas has exacerbated the struggle to find workers as they rebuild labor forces after widespread layoffs during the recent downturn. Patterson-UTI Energy, a Houston drilling and hydraulic fracturing contractor, has hired 4,000 people this year to fill jobs on rigs and fracking fleets, but more job applicants have failed drug tests this year than in 2014, said Diana Dotolo, the company's vice president of human resources.

The Houston firm recruits workers from around the United States, but for local companies without a nationwide reach, the problem is far worse. Dynamic Oilfield Services, an oil-equipment company based in Corpus Christi, has seen roughly half of its job applicants from West Texas fail drug tests this year, and most of its employees in the region are hired from other areas.

Decades ago, biker gangs made meth from phenyl-2- pronopol, which was outlawed in the United States in the 1980s. Now, Mexican drug cartels dominate the commerce of meth, often transporting the substance in liquid form across the U.S.-Mexico border, stored in fake gasoline tanks, iced tea bottles or windshield washer fluid reservoirs, law enforcement officials said.

They take it to stash houses in places like Phoenix and Dallas before it reaches high-demand markets in West Texas, said Will Glaspy, special agent in charge of the Drug Enforcement Agency's El Paso division.

"Oil field workers are big consumers of methamphetamine," Glaspy said. "The Mexican cartels are the biggest sources of supply."

Across the West Texas and New Mexico counties that encompass the Permian Basin, the DEA has seized 2,200 pounds of meth since October 2015, more than triple the amount confiscated in between October 2011 and September 2013. Last year, the agency seized 66 pounds of methamphetamine in the Midland area, compared with 11 pounds in 2012.

"When the oil price is up, there's more methamphetamine in our entire community," said Steve Thomason, executive director at the Springboard Center, an alcohol and drug treatment facility in Midland. It's not uncommon, he said, to see a young oil field worker "roll up to outpatient treatment in a Corvette."

Recovering addicts almost lost their lives to drug use.

Media: Steve Gonzales/chron.com

Failing the Test

In the first six months of this year, more than 1,000 people working or applying for jobs in the oil-producing business failed urine-based drug tests, double the pace of failures last year, according to Houston-based DISA Global Solutions, the largest provider of drug-testing policies to U.S. oil producers. The number of industry workers failing hair follicle tests, which are more effective in detecting long-term drug use, jumped to more than 4,600 over the past 18 months, tripling the number in the two years from 2009 to 2010; the number of people testing positive for methamphetamine jumped five times.

Large oil companies and oil field contractors said they have adopted tougher drug-testing policies in recent years. Houston oil producer Apache Corp., for example, conducts random, pre-employment, post-accident, reasonable-suspicion and random drug tests. If an employee or contractor fails a test, he could face termination.

"We are vigilant about ensuring a drug-free culture," said Castlen Kennedy, a spokeswoman at Apache.

But substance abuse specialists believe drug-test failure figures grossly underestimate the number of oil field workers who abuse drugs. Traces of methamphetamine, for example, linger in a person's system for only few days, making it harder to catch meth abusers. Several recovering drug addicts said managers in the oil patch tip off crews to a random drug test several days before it takes place, some to dodge fines by regulators, others to avoid having to hire new workers.

"There's a million and one ways to beat the drug tests," said Patrice Owens, director of the Greenhouse Outpatient Center, an Arlington addiction treatment facility. "If people want to use drugs, there's always a way."

Even if they get caught using drugs, oil field workers often find their way back to the oil patch. For the seven years Cody Watson worked as an oil field electrician, using meth and cocaine as he worked nonstop for several days at a time when storms knocked out rig powerlines, it wasn't hard to pass drug tests because managers gave him and his crew plenty of advanced warning.

Once, after Watson smashed his finger with a pipe, a drilling company fired him when he came up positive in a post-accident drug test. He drove 18 hours across Texas for a job interview with another company, purging his system with water to erase any trace of drugs. He passed the pre-employment drug test.

"During the boom times, I could leave my job and there'd be plenty of places to work," said Watson, now a 41-year-old recovering addict. "A lot of these guys hop from one rig to another. It's a never-ending cycle."

Breaking the Cycle

Not long ago, drug use on a drilling rig was out in the open, said Kevin Tyson, a 55-year-old recovering addict. He recalled fellow rig workers tying a syringe filled with meth to a machine that pulls pipe out of the earth, then running it up to the derrick hand 90 feet above the rig floor, where the man took a hit.

Meth kept Tyson working and partying for years. They'd go on benders for days and didn't think much of it. Once, he missed a pipe he was supposed to catch. It swung right past him across the rig floor. Another guy smashed a coworker's hand with a sledgehammer. Some would die in oil field accidents, car wrecks or from overdoses. "Oh well," he said, "just keep going."

Doctors told him he weighed 70-something pounds when he arrived at a hospital in Lubbock, where he spent a month in an intensive care unit. He has the paperwork, but he still doesn't know if that is true. One doctor said if he used meth again, he would die. He thought about that for a long time. Four months after his release, he got bored, called his buddy and started shooting meth again.

"I knew I was going to die," said Tyson, who had worked in oil patch for 16 years before he began his recovery in November 2001, at age 39. "But I just figured, let's have a good hard run."

The rules have changed since Tyson began his career, as companies impose stricter testing regimens. But the tough-guy culture still drives roustabouts, mechanics, truckers and rig hands to work long hours under grueling conditions and find ways to beat the tests. And sometimes, it drives them to the breaking point.

In mid-April, around 2 a.m., Robert Orosco Jr. put a gun in his mouth and pulled the trigger. The 34-year-old had lost everything to his relapse with Xanax, a highly addictive medication for anxiety, and cocaine. The drugs were so readily available, he could have them delivered. His wife had left him. He lost his house. He lost his job as an oil-equipment salesman.

In every scenario he played out in his head, his six children were better off without him. The gun didn't fire.

Orosco checked himself in to a treatment facility the next day. Today, a few months sober, Orosco is building a new company that offers drone imaging to oil companies to identify leaks and assemble 3D maps of the earth's surface.

"The boom brings the good and the bad," Orosco said. "There's so much here."

Last month, Lozoya, the former oil field trucker, found a job at a local department store selling women's shoes for $13 an hour, plus commission. He remembers his days as a 19-year old earning paychecks that were five times larger than the average American his age and how he blew it all to feed a habit that eventually cost $500 to $1,000 a day.

He also remembers a downward spiral that cost him his job and led him to steal RVs, dirt bikes and even copper from the oil field. Several times, he nearly overdosed, and ultimately he sought help at a treatment center after his girlfriend and others persuaded him to get clean.

Today, he likes getting dressed up for work, with a suit, tie and well-groomed hair. He hopes to pursue a college degree and, perhaps one day, have his own clothing brand. And, for at least the next few months, he plans to heed the advice his counselors gave him: Don't go back to the oil patch.

"I don't see myself being able to work 100 hours a week sober," he said. "The oil field is tough."

Critical Thinking

1. How can drug abuse be deterred in an industry that demands more than one's physical body can endure?

2. Is social deterrence to reduce drug use an effective measure in the oil industry? Why or why not?

3. Regarding drug testing, are there fail-proof ways to control workers abusing drugs? What are some ways drug tests might improve to decrease "cheating" the test?

Internet References

CATO Institute
   https://www.cato.org/publications

Drug and Alcohol Dependence
   https://www.drugandalcoholdependence.com/

National Drug Intelligence Center
   https://www.justice.gov/archive/ndic/

Article

Prepared by: Kim Schnurbush, *California State University, Sacramento*
Mark Pullin, *Angelo State University*

The Role of Immigration Age on Alcohol and Drug Use Among Border and Non-border Mexican Americans

JENNIFER M. REINGLE, ET AL.

Learning Outcomes

After reading this article, you will be able to:

- Discuss how proximity to the US-Mexico border affects increased risk for alcohol and drug use problems.

- Understand how age of immigration and proximity to the border greatly affect the risk of alcohol and drug use.

- Discuss how different nationalities of Hispanic adults vary in likelihood of drug and alcohol abuse.

The literature is clear that Hispanic immigrants have lower prevalence rates of substance use disorders and other alcohol- and drug-related problems than their U.S.-born counterparts (Grant, Stinson, Hasin, Dawson, Chou, & Anderson, 2004; Maldonado-Molina, Reingle, Jennings, & Prado, 2011). Because Hispanics are a highly heterogeneous group, there are likely to be substantial differences in the prevalence rates in risk behavior between different nationalities of Hispanic adults. For instance, the literature is clear that Mexican Americans and Puerto Ricans have the highest alcohol-related mortality rates among all Hispanic national groups (Caetano, Vaeth, Rodriguez, 2012; Chartier, Vaeth, & Caetano, 2014).

Despite the indisputable evidence in support of the "Immigrant Paradox", in which immigrants have better health outcomes than U.S.-born Hispanics, there is evidence that the corresponding health outcomes of the Hispanic population may depend on the age at which individuals migrate to the U.S (Alegria, 2007; Vega et al., 2004).

Several studies have assessed the impact of age of immigration on health outcomes, including psychiatric disorders and illicit drug use. Alegria et al. (2007) found that adults who immigrated to the United States before age 6 had much higher rates of depressive and anxiety disorders. Rates of substance use disorders in general were also higher among those who immigrated earlier (age 6 or younger) compared to those who immigrated at age 7 or older. Using a sample of Mexican Americans, Vega and colleagues (2004) found qualitative differences in immigrants who migrated at age 13 or younger in mood, anxiety and substance use disorders. Other studies have substantiated this link between immigration age and mental health disorders and alcohol use disorders (Alderete, Vega, Kolody, & Aguilar-Gaxiola, 2000). Further, increased duration of residence in the U.S. has been associated with cigarette, alcohol and illicit drug use among Cuban and Nicaraguan youth (Gfroerer & Tan, 2003). In fact, a study by Cheung et al. (2011) found evidence of a "sensitive period" of acculturation in which those who immigrate as a child become more acculturated than adult immigrants, even when living in the U.S. for the same period of time. Therefore, age of immigration seems to have an effect on risk behavior.

The proposed mechanism for the relationship between these poor alcohol- and drug-related outcomes among early immigrants is rapid acquisition of normative drinking and drug

*Corresponding author: Jennifer M. Reingle, PhD, University of Texas Health Science Center at Houston, 5323 Harry Hines Blvd., V8.112, Dallas, TX 75390, Telephone: 214-648-1519, Fax: 214-648-1081, Jennifer.reingle@utsouthwestern.edu.

using behavior that is often modeled by peers native to the United States. This immigration-assimilation effect has been operationalized by generation and viewed as a linear process, where successive generations experience increasingly negative health outcomes (Maldonado-Molina, Reingle, Jennings, & Prado, 2011). However, in light of the developmental research on immigration, culture, and mental health and substance use outcomes, it is likely that Hispanics who immigrated at a very young age are more amenable to the new culture than those who immigrated during their teenage years or later. Immigration to the US at a young age will increase the time in which a person is exposed to the US culture, potentially in a manner similar to those who are born in the US (Alergria, 2007). The exposure to US culture, assimilation, and adoption of American cultural values, has been consistently identified as having poor effects on several dimensions of health (Maldonado-Molina et al., 2011; Alegria et al., 2007; Caetano et al., 2012). Specifically, Caetano and colleagues (2012) suggested that these alcohol-related problems observed among Mexican Americans may be the result of assimilation and acculturation stress, which in turn, leads to increased levels of alcohol consumption.

Given the theoretical potential for early immigrants to have cultural exposure levels similar to those who were US born, the purpose of this paper is to systematically determine the age of immigration that puts adults who immigrated at a young age at risk for alcohol- and drug use problems in adulthood. To answer this research question, we used two samples of Mexican Americans residing in two distinct contexts: the U.S.-Mexico border, and cities not proximal to the border. In light of the previous research, we hypothesize that adults who immigrated to the United States prior to adolescence have a qualitatively distinct experience in the U.S. compared to adults who immigrate during late adolescence or adulthood. Developmentally, youth are most vulnerable to social pressures during early adolescence, and the combined stresses of adolescence and acculturation may compound the risk of problematic alcohol and drug use. We expect to observe differences between early immigrants and late immigrants in binge drinking, lifetime alcohol status, number of standard drinks consumed each week, DSM-V Alcohol Use Disorder, and illicit drug use. We also hypothesize that those who immigrate before adolescence have alcohol and drug use behavior that mirrors Mexican American adults who were born in the U.S.-born. Finally, we expect to find differences in alcohol (current drinking status, binge drinking, and number of standard drinks per week) and drug use outcomes by age of immigration, across both the U.S.-Mexico border and non-border contexts. We expect that the age of immigration effect may be greater for alcohol and drug use on the border, as earlier immigration implies longer exposure to the border's known risk factors for alcohol use and

risky behavior (Caetano et al., 2012, 2013; Mills et al., 2012; in press; Office of National Drug Control Policy, 1999).

This study is unique in that the population includes a sample of both Mexican Americans living proximal and distal to the U.S.-Mexico border. The U.S.-Mexico border is a unique location, characterized by a high concentration of Mexican Americans, poverty, low education, drug trafficking and related violence (Lusk, Staudt, & Moya, 2012). Alcohol is easily accessible across the border, as the legal drinking age in Mexico is 18; and unlike the U.S., the drinking age is not strictly enforced in Mexico (U.S. Department of State, 2013). Therefore, we are able to compare Mexican Americans living at the border with Mexican Americans living distal to the border, and whether the age of immigration remains a risk factor for alcohol and drug use in both locales.

Methods
Data Collection
These data include two samples of Mexican American adults, one group who resides along the U.S.-Mexico border, and a group of Mexican Americans who reside in large U.S. cities that are not proximal to the border. During March 2009 through July 2010, 1,307 Mexican Americans residing along the border in California (Imperial County, n=365), Arizona (Cochise, Santa Cruz, and Yuma Counties, n=173), New Mexico (Dona Ana County, n=65), and Texas (Cameron, El Paso, Hidalgo and Webb Counties, n=704) were interviewed. Mexican Americans in the non-border group (N=1,288) were interviewed as part of the 2006 Hispanic Americans Baseline Alcohol Survey (HABLAS), a study of more than 5,000 Puerto Rican, Mexican American, Cuban American, and South/Central Americans in five metropolitan areas of the U.S. Most of the 1,288 non-border respondents were interviewed in Los Angeles (n=609) and Houston (n=513); additional interviews were conducted in New York (n=86), Philadelphia (n=59), and Miami (n=21).

The sampling methodology and survey instrument used in both studies were virtually identical, allowing us to pool both samples. Both studies involved a multistage clustered random sample of self-reported Mexican Americans of age 18 or older from areas described above. Trained bilingual interviewers obtained formal informed consent and conducted in-person, at-home Computer Assisted Personal Interviews that lasted approximately one hour. All respondents received a $25 incentive for participating. The only methodological difference between the two samples was that the border study was stratified by county to include primary sampling units from urban areas only. This ensured that the border and metropolitan non-border groups were comparable.

The survey instrument used in both studies was piloted in English, translated into Spanish, and then translated back into English. Weighted response rates for the border and non-border samples were 67% and 76%, respectively. Both surveys were approved by the Committee for the Protection of Human Subjects of the University of Texas Health Science Center at Houston.

Measures

For this study, four alcohol- and drug-related outcomes of immigration age were assessed:

1) lifetime alcohol use status; 2) binge drinking; 3) standard quantity of alcohol consumed each week; and 4) illicit drug use.

Drinking status—Lifetime alcohol use status was categorized as "Abstainers" (never used alcohol during their lifetime), "former drinkers" (drank at some point during their lifetime but not in the past year), and "current drinkers", who reported alcohol use in the past 12 months.

Binge drinking—Binge drinking was defined as drinking 4 (for women) or 5 (for men) standard drinks within a 2-hour period (NIAAA, 2004) at any point within the past 12 months. This variable was dichotomized into "binge drank" or "did not binge drink" in the previous year.

Quantity of alcohol consumed each week—Respondents were provided with explicit examples of what was meant by a standard drink of beer, wine and liquor (such as, "a 12- ounce can of beer", "a 4-ounce glass of wine", or "a mixed drink containing 1 shot of hard liquor"). The average weekly consumption was estimated based upon the graduated frequencies approach to measurement (Greenfield and Kerr, 2008).

Drug use—Due to the low prevalence of specific drug use, participants who reported use of stimulants, crack cocaine, depressants, heroin, methadone or painkillers, hallucinogens, or any other illicit drug were categorized as "users". Those who did not report use of any substances were categorized as "non-users".

Age of immigration to the United States—All respondents were adults (18+) at the time of the interview and retrospectively self-reported the number of years they have been living in the U.S. Immigration age was calculated as the age at the time of the interview minus the number of years living in the U.S. These ages were then categorized as "U.S.- born/ Non-immigrant", or immigrated "less than age 12", "12–14", "15–17", "18–20", or "21+". The initial "<12 years" cut point was determined analytically due to the low prevalence (small n) of alcohol- and drug-related behavior when immigration occurred before age 12. Therefore, a 6-category variable was created for all 'age of immigration' analyses: 1) US-Born

(non-immigrant); 2) immigrated at less than 12 years of age; 3) immigrated at 12–14 years of age; 4) immigrated at 15–17 years of age; 5) immigrated at 18–20 years of age; and 6) immigrated at or after age 21.

Demographic variables—Gender, income (in thousands) and current age were self-reported covariates included in all models. Border or non-border was defined as the location of residence at the time of data collection.

Analytical Plan

To determine the age that qualitatively differentiates "early" versus "late" immigration, we first stratified age of immigration into two-year groups (U.S.-born, <12, 12–14, 15–17, 18–20, and 21+). We used these groupings to examine bivariate differences in each of the four drinking and drug use outcomes by age of immigration. Based upon these analyses, a 12-year cut off point was determined optimal and analyses proceeded using this cutoff age. Bivariate associations between U.S.-born and immigrant status in general and each outcome variable were conducted to determine whether a relationship between immigration and each outcome existed (Model 1 in Tables 2–5). Because all bivariate models resulted in significant age of immigration differences, multivariate analyses were conducted, controlling for age and gender, and stratified by border/non-border location (Model 2 in each outcome table). Depending upon the distribution of the dependent variable, the type of regression differed for each outcome. The relationship between age of immigration and drinking status, binge drinking, and drug use were tested using logistic regression, as these outcomes were binary in nature. The model testing the relationship between age of immigration and the average number of standard drinks per week was evaluated using a zero-inflated Poisson (ZIP) model, as the number of standard drinks per week was highly skewed towards "0". All models were weighted to correct for the unequal probability of selection into the sample. All analyses were conducting using STATA 12 (College Station, TX).

Results
Sample Description

Of the total sample of 2,511 adults, 51% constituted the border sample and 49% constituted the non-border sample. Women comprised 51% of the sample, and the average age of respondents was 39.5 (sd=15.4). Less than 50% of both samples reported having attained a high school diploma (48% in the non-border sample; 49% in the border sample). The mean annual income among non-border adults was $26,000(sd=21.8) and \$28,500 (sd=29.6) among adults residing proximal to the border. Despite the relatively low income in both samples, 61% of the non-border sample and 45% of the border sample was employed full-time. The proportion of respondents who were married or cohabitating did not vary substantial on and off the border (60% and 58%, respectively). A total of 37% of the sample was foreign-born, with 55% of border residents and 71% of non-border residents identifying as being born outside of the U.S. ($x2$=14.6; p<0.001). The average age of arrival among immigrants was 23.2 (sd=11.0), with the average age of arrival on the border at 23.7 years (sd=12.1). Overall, 40% of the respondents were lifelong abstainers, 7% were former drinkers, and 53% were current drinkers. Twenty-one percent of the sample reported binge drinking, and the median number of drinks per week among drinkers was 2.7. Nearly twenty percent (19.1%) reported use of one or more illicit drugs in the past year.

Table 1 depicts the weighted proportions of each alcohol- and drug-related outcome by age of immigration and border/non-border residence. Regardless of location, U.S.-born adults were more likely than those who immigrated at or after age 21 to be current alcohol users, binge drinkers, users of any illicit drugs, and they consumed a greater number of standard drinks per week. On the border only, early immigrants were more likely than late immigrants to be current alcohol users, to be binge drinkers, and to consume a greater number of drinks per week.

Table 2 details the relationship between immigration age and drinking status between U.S.- born participants compared with all immigrants (Model 1), and U.S.-born compared with immigrants broken down by age of immigration (Model 2). Model 1 shows that U.S.-born participants were significantly more likely than immigrants to currently use alcohol among both border and non-border residents. In Model 2, adults who immigrated between the ages of 12 and 14 were nearly three and a half times as likely as late immigrants to be current drinkers among the non-border sample only. As detailed in Table 3, U.S. born adults were more likely to report binge drinking compared to immigrants in the border sample only (Model 1). There were no differences in binge drinking by age of immigration (Model 2).

Being born in the U.S. (compared to being an immigrant) predicted increased weekly drinking volume (Table 4, Model 1) in both samples. However, age of immigration was associated not with higher weekly drinking volume (Table 4, Model 2). Finally, Table 5 shows the relationship between drug use and immigration (Model 1) and drug use and immigration age (Model 2). Model 1 shows that U.S.-born adults are approximately three times more likely to use illicit drugs than those who immigrated at age 21 or older in both samples. Model 2 shows that adults who immigrated at an early age (less than 12) are at least twice as likely as those who immigrated later in life (21+) to use drugs in both samples.

Table 1 Proportions and Means of Alcohol and Drug-Related Risk Behavior by Age of Immigration

	Border	Non-Border	Border	Non-Border	Border	Non-Border	Border	Non-Border	Border	Non-Border	Border	Non-Border
n	614	351	105	84	41	44	72	112	81	164	380	525
Current drinker	.61	.64	.62	.59	.51	.74	.34	.61	.45	.51	.41	.43
Binge Drinker	.29	.24	.29	.26	.18	.28	.12	.28	.13	.21	.14	.15
Any drug use	.29	.30	.24	.21	.10	.12	.07	.16	.17	.12	.15	.08
Standard Drinks/ Week Mean	7.7	6.3	6.1	4.4	2.7	7.3	2.2	5.5	3.2	5.1	2.7	2.7

Note. Binge drinking was defined as consuming 5 (males) or 4 (females) drinks within a two-hour window sometime in the last 12 months. 'Age of immigration' was calculated retrospectively.

Table 2   Multivariate Border/Non-Border Differences in Current Alcohol Use by Immigration Age

	Border N = 1227		Non-Border N = 1284	
	OR	95% CI	OR	95% CI
Model 1: US Born vs. Immigrant				
U.S.-born	1.77**	1.15–2.74	1.79*	1.04–3.06
Immigrant	Ref	--	Ref	--
Covariates				
Gender (Male)	2.71***	1.80–4.08	2.56***	1.66–3.96
Age	0.98*	0.97–0.99	0.99	0.97–1.00
Income	1.01*	1.00–1.02	1.01	0.99–1.02
Employment status				
Full/part time employed	Ref	--	Ref	--
Temporary illness/unemployed	0.73	0.42–1.28	0.40**	0.21–0.70
Retired/disabled/not looking for employment	0.54**	0.34–0.85	0.38***	0.23–0.63
Model 2: Age of Immigration				
U.S.-born	1.76*	1.10–2.80	2.25**	1.25–4.05
Immigrant (age <12)	1.38	0.69–2.74	1.68	0.73–3.90
Immigrant (age 12–14)	0.99	0.44–2.22	4.36*	1.32–14.40
Immigrant (age 15–17)	0.41	0.14–1.19	1.80	0.88–3.66
Immigrant (age 18–20)	1.68	0.71–3.98	1.20	0.65–2.22
Immigrant (ages 21+)	Ref	--	Ref	--
Covariates				
Gender (Male)	2.80***	1.93–4.05	2.59***	1.67–4.00
Age	0.98*	0.97–0.99	0.99	0.98–1.01
Income	1.01	0.99–1.01	1.01	.99–1.02
Employment status				
Full/part time employed	Ref	--	Ref	--
Temporary illness/unemployed	0.68	0.39–1.20	0.39**	0.19–0.78
Retired/disabled/not looking for employment	0.49**	0.31–0.79	0.36***	0.22–0.61

Note. Model 1 uses a binary 'immigrant'/'U.S.-born' variable. Model 2 includes a deconstructed immigration variable broken down by age of immigration, including US Born as a 'non-immigrant' group within the immigration age variable. The reference group for both models is the theoretically least acculturated group ("immigrants" in Model 1' "Immigrant 21+" in Model 2.").

*p<0.05

**p<0.01

***p<0.001

Table 3   Multivariate Logistic Regression Analysis of Border/Non-Border Differences in Binge Drinking by Immigration Age

	Border N = 1269		Non-Border N = 1270	
	OR	95% CI	OR	95% CI
Model 1: US Born vs. Immigrant				
U.S.-born	1.72*	1.08–2.73	1.20	0 0.70–2.05
Immigrant	Ref	--	Ref	--
Covariates				
Gender (Male)	2.84***	1.68–4.81	3.01***	1.71–5.31
Age	0.97***	0.95–0.98	0.97*	0.95–0.99
Income	1.00	0.99–1.01	1.00	0.99–1.01
Employment status				
Full/part time employed	Ref	--	Ref	--
Temporary illness/unemployed	0.78	0.45–0.71	0.71*	0.37-1.38
Retired/disabled/not looking for employment	0.57*	0.33–0.96	0.30**	0.13–0.67
Model 2: Age of Immigration				
U.S.-born	1.55*	0.94–2.54	1.45	0.77–2.75
Immigrant (age <12)	1.33	0.60–2.90	1.48	0.65–3.37
Immigrant (age 12–14)	0.75	0.25–2.29	1.65	0.33–8.21
Immigrant (age 15–17)	0.46	0.12–1.79	1.61	0.68–3.82
Immigrant (age 18–20)	0.70	0.23–2.14	1.18	0.56–2.47
Immigrant (ages 21+)	Ref	--	Ref	--
Covariates				
Gender (Male)	2.87***	1.73–4.77	3.02***	1.70–5.39
Age	0.97***	0.95–0.98	0.98	0.96–1.00
Income	1.00	0.99–1.01	1.00	0.99–1.01
Employment status				
Full/part time employed	Ref	--	Ref	--
Temporary illness/unemployed	0.73	0.41–1.31	0.72	0.36–1.41
Retired/disabled/not looking for employment	0.55*	0.31–0.96	0.29**	0.13–0.66

Note. Model 1 uses a binary 'immigrant'/'U.S.-born' variable. Model 2 includes a deconstructed immigration variable broken down by age of immigration, including US Born as a 'non-immigrant' group within the immigration age variable. The reference group for both models is the theoretically least acculturated group ("immigrants" in Model 1' "Immigrant 21+" in Model 2.").

*p<0.05
**p<0.01
***p<0.001

Table 4 Zero-Inflated Poisson Analysis of Border/Non-Border Differences in Standard Drinking Volume by Immigration Age

	Border N=1287		Non-Border N=1277	
	OR	95% CI	IRR	95% CI
Model 1: US Born vs. Immigrants				
U.S.-born	1.98***	1.48–2.63	1.64*	1.05–2.55
Immigrant	Ref	--	Ref	--
Covariates				
Gender (Male)	3.10***	2.24–4.28	6.21***	2.55–15.11
Age	1.00	0.98–1.01	1.00	0.98–1.01
Income	1.00	0.99–1.00	1.00	0.99–1.01
Employment status				
Full/part time employed	Ref	--	Ref	--
Temporary illness/unemployed	0.98	0.71–1.36	1.40	0.77–2.56
Retired/disabled/not looking for employment	0.53**	0.35–0.81	0.87	0.37–2.04
Model 2: Age of Immigration				
U.S.-born	2.10***	2.52–2.91	2.06**	1.31–3.26
Immigrant (age <12)	1.54	0.92–2.61	1.54	0.59–4.00
Immigrant (age 12–14)	0.63	0.26–1.51	1.56	0.68–3.60
Immigrant (age 15–17)	0.91	0.46–1.80	1.28	0.68–2.42
Immigrant (age 18–20)	1.01	0.38–2.64	1.57	0.91–2.73
Immigrant (ages 21+)	Ref	--	Ref	--
Covariates				
Gender (Male)	3.12***	2.25–4.32	6.22***	2.56–15.12
Age	0.99	0.99–1.01	1.00	0.98–1.02
Income	1.00	0.99–1.00	1.00	0.99–1.01
Employment status				
Full/part time employed	Ref	--	Ref	--
Temporary illness/unemployed	0.98	0.71–1.35	1.43	0.78–2.61
Retired/disabled/not looking for employment	0.51**	0.33–0.77	0.73	0.37–3.98

Note. Model 1 uses a binary 'immigrant'/'U.S.-born' variable. Model 2 includes a deconstructed immigration variable broken down by age of immigration, including US Born as a 'non-immigrant' group within the immigration age variable. The reference group for both models is the theoretically least acculturated group ("immigrants" in Model 1' "Immigrant 21+" in Model 2.").

*p<0.05
**p<0.01
***p<0.001

Table 5 Multivariate Logistic Regression of Border/Non-Border Differences in Drug Use by Immigration Age

	Border N = 1284		Non-Border N = 1277	
	OR	95% CI	OR	95% CI
Model 1: US Born vs. Immigrant				
U.S.-born	2.91***	1.94–4.36	3.20***	1.88–5.45
Immigrant	Ref	--	Ref	--
Covariates				
Gender (Male)	1.56*	1.02–2.37	1.41	0.86–2.31
Age	1.00	0.99–1.02	1.00	0.98–1.02
Income	1.00	0.99–1.00	1.00	0.99–1.02
Employment status				
Full/part time employed	Ref	--	Ref	--
Temporary illness/unemployed	1.07	0.58–1.97	1.04	0.51–2.13
Retired/disabled/not looking for employment	1.31	0.81–2.11	1.38	0.70–2.71
Model 2: Age of Immigration				
U.S.-born	3.27***	1.96–5.43	4.67***	2.43–8.97
Immigrant (age <12)	2.32*	1.08–4.97	3.13*	1.06–9.25
Immigrant (age 12–14)	0.95	0.33–2.72	1.52	0.44–5.29
Immigrant (age 15–17)	0.62	0.16–2.40	2.16	0.90–5.17
Immigrant (age 18–20)	1.25	0.61–2.53	1.52	0.56–4.13
Immigrant (ages 21+)	Ref	--	Ref	--
Covariates				
Gender (Male)	1.58*	1.04–2.39	1.42	0.86–2.34
Age	1.01	0.99–1.02	1.00	0.98–1.02
Income	1.00	0.99–1.00	1.00	0.99–1.02
Employment status				
Full/part time employed	Ref	--	Ref	--
Temporary illness/unemployed	1.03	0.59–1.91	1.08	0.53–2.22
Retired/disabled/not looking for employment	1.27	0.78–2.07	1.39	0.69–2.78

Note. Model 1 uses a binary 'immigrant'/'U.S.-born' variable. Model 2 includes a deconstructed immigration variable broken down by age of immigration, including US Born as a 'non-immigrant' group within the immigration age variable. The reference group for both models is the theoretically least acculturated group ("immigrants" in Model 1' "Immigrant 21+" in Model 2.").

*p<0.05
**p<0.01
***p<0.001

Discussion

The purpose of this study was to examine the age of immigration that most optimally differentiates immigrants and non-immigrants' experience as related to alcohol- and drug use outcomes. We found that adults who immigrated before age 12 have alcohol and drug use patterns similar to U.S.-born adults for many alcohol- and drug-related outcomes (specifically, illicit drug use, and alcohol use status, but not binge drinking or drinking volume per week), while those who immigrate after age 12 have lower rates of alcohol and drug use in adulthood. There were differences in the effects of immigration age across the border and non-border populations. Specifically, early non-border (age 12–14) immigrants were more likely to be current drinkers compared to non-border late immigrants. There were no differences in weekly drinking volume by immigration age. As expected, U.S.-born participants were at risk for nearly all alcohol- and drug-related outcomes, regardless of border/non-border context.

The findings from the current study are in line with the previous research on immigration age and alcohol use (Alderete et al., 2000; Alegia et al., 2008; Grant et al., 2004); however, we were able to expand knowledge on the effect of immigration age beyond alcohol and drug dependence. We assessed specific behavioral outcomes; particularly, binge drinking, lifetime alcohol use status, number of standard drinks consumed per week, and drug use in the past year. In addition, we were able to identify distinct behavioral differences in alcohol- and drug-related risk behavior that qualitatively changes at age 12. This finding is in line with cross-cultural developmental processes, as cultural values from a host country are more strongly solidified when immigration occurs at a young age (Berry, Phinney, Sam, & Vedder, 2006; Cheung et al., 2011). This early immigration may result in higher levels of acculturation stress (Alva & de Los Reyes, 1999) due to school enrollment and peer processes that differentially influence younger immigrants.

One unexpected finding that resulted from this study is that adults who immigrated at young ages who live in non-border regions are more likely to use illicit drugs compared to adults who immigrated later in adolescence or during adulthood. Due to the availability of drugs on the U.S.-Mexico border (Office of National Drug Control Policy, 1999), we expected to find that adults who immigrated at young ages were at risk for drug use if they lived proximal to the border. However, a study by Wallisch & Spence (2006) also found that illicit drug use was lower among U.S.-Mexico border residents compared to the rest of the state of Texas and nationwide. We speculate that, due to the overt drug enforcement that takes place at and near the border, a drug pipeline to other major U.S. cities (El Paso, San Antonio, etc.) has emerged that allows those transporting

drugs to disseminate drugs in a less risky setting (Wallisch & Spence, 2006). This effect could be responsible for the availability and use of drugs in the non-border population.

The current study has several strengths that advance the literature on immigration among Hispanics. First, we were able to examine the effects of immigration age retrospectively among adults across two contexts (the U.S.-Mexico border, and other U.S. cities with a large number of Mexican Americans), one of which is characterized by a great deal of access to alcohol and drug use (Office of Drug Control Policy, 1999). Second, a sample of only Mexican Americans was used, limiting the potential for national origin differences in the effects of immigration age. There are also several limitations that should be noted. First, although we did not detect a significant interaction between border residence and immigration status on any of our outcomes (likely due to insufficient power for several of these outcomes, including illicit drug use), we did plan *a priori* to stratify our analyses by border/non-border regardless of whether border interactions were significant. This was motivated by previous research using these data (which show that border residents are at high risk for alcohol-related problems and other negative health outcomes). Although immigration status as a dummy variable did not vary by border/non-border context in predicting our outcomes, we did observe border differences in the results. Second, there is a potential for recall bias in the immigration age measurement, as well as alcohol and drug use. Also, although the analysis of data from Mexican Americans only is a considerable strength, the national homogeneity of the sample limits the generalizability of the findings to other national groups. Finally, due to the low prevalence of illicit drug use in this population, all types of illicit drugs were grouped together. Although we acknowledge that there may be differential outcomes for different drugs (particularly, marijuana), it remains interesting that we were able to detect an increase in the odds of *any* illicit drug use as a result of immigration patterns.

In conclusion, this study provides evidence that immigration from Mexico to the U.S. before age 12 results in alcohol and drug-related behavior that mirrors the behavior of U.S.-born residents for many alcohol- and drug-related outcomes. Future research on the impact of early immigration on risk behavior should attempt to delineate the social and cognitive processes that produce the increase in alcohol and drug-related risk both on and off the U.S.-Mexico border.

References

Alderete E, Vega W, Kolody B, Aguilar-Gaxiola S. Effects of time in the United States and Indian ethnicity on DSM-III-R psychiatric disorders among Mexican Americans in California. Journal of Nervous and Mental Disorders. 2000; 188:90–100.

Alegría M, Canino G, Shrout PE, Woo M, Duan N, Vila D, Torres M, Chen C, Meng XL. Prevalence of mental illness in immigrant and non-immigrant US Latino groups. The American journal of psychiatry. 2008; 165(3):359. [PubMed: 18245178]

Alva SA, de Los Reyes R. Psychosocial stress, internalized symptoms, and the academic achievement of Hispanic adolescents. Journal of Adolescent Research. 1999; 14(3):343–358.

American Psychiatric Association. Diagnostic and statistical manual of medical disorders. 5. Arlington, VA: American Psychiatric Publishing; 2013.

Berry, JW.; Phinney, JS.; Sam, DL.; Vedder, P., editors. Immigrant youth in cultural transition: Acculturation, identity, and adaptation across national contexts. Psychology Press; 2006.

Caetano, Raul; Vaeth, Patrice AC.; Rodriguez, Lori A. The Hispanic Americans Baseline Alcohol Survey (HABLAS) Acculturation, Birthplace and Alcohol-Related Social Problems Across Hispanic National Groups. Hispanic journal of behavioral sciences. 2012; 34(1):95–117. [PubMed: 22438607]

Chartier, Karen G.; Vaeth, Patrice AC.; Caetano, Raul. Focus on: Ethnicity and the Social and Health Harms From drinking. Alcohol research: current reviews. 2014; 35(2):229. [PubMed: 24881331]

Cheung BY, Chudek M, Heine SJ. Evidence for a sensitive period for acculturation: Younger immigrants report acculturating at a faster rate. Psychological Science. 2011; 22:147–152. [PubMed: 21189354]

Grant BF, Stinson FS, Hasin DS, Dawson DA, Chou SP, Anderson K. Immigration and lifetime prevalence of DSM-IV psychiatric disorders among Mexican Americans and non-Hispanic whites in the United States: results from the National Epidemiologic Survey on Alcohol and Related Conditions. Archives of General Psychiatry. 2004; 61(12):1226. [PubMed: 15583114]

Greenfield TK, Kerr WC. Alcohol measurement methodology in epidemiology: recent advances and opportunities. Addiction. 2008; 103:1082–1099. [PubMed: 18422826]

Gfroerer J, Tan L. Substance Use Among Foreign-Born Youths in the United States: Does the Length of Residence Matter? American Journal of Public Health. 2003; 93(11):1892–1895. [PubMed: 14600061]

Hilbe, JM. Negative binomial regression. University Press; Cambridge: 2011.

Lusk, MW.; Staudt, KA.; Moya, E. Social justice in the US-Mexico Border Region. Springer; 2012.

Maldonado-Molina MM, Reingle JM, Jennings WG, Prado G. Drinking and driving among immigrant and US-born Hispanic young adults: Results from a longitudinal and nationally representative study. Addictive behaviors. 2011; 36(4):381–388. [PubMed: 21216535]

Mills BA, Caetano RC, Vaeth PAC. Elevated alcohol problems among Mexican American youth on the U.S.-Mexico border: A consequence of risky drinking or risky behavior? Alcoholism: Clinical and Experimental Research. (in press).

Mills BA, Caetano RC, Vaeth PAC. What explains higher levels of drinking among Mexican Americans on the U.S-Mexico border? Alcoholism Clinical and Experimental Research. 2012; 36:258.

Office of National Drug Control Policy. Shielding US borders from the drug threat. 1999. Retrieved on November 20, 2013 from https://www.ncjrs.gov/ondcppubs/publications/policy/99ndcs/iv-f.html

U.S. Department of State. Mexico: Country specific information. Feb 15. 2013 Retrieved online on November 21, 2013 from http://travel.state.gov/travel/cis_pa_tw/cis/cis_970.html

Vega WA, Sribney W, Aguilar-Gaxiola S, Kolody B. 12- Month Prevalence of DSM-III-R Psychiatric Disorders Among Mexican Americans: Nativity, Social Assimilation, and Age Determinants. The Journal of Nervous and Mental Disease. 2004; 192(8):532–541. [PubMed: 15387155]

Wallisch LS, Spence RT. Alcohol and drug use, abuse, and dependence in urban areas and colonias of the Texas-Mexico border. Hispanic Journal of Behavioral Sciences. 2006; 28(2):286–307.

Critical Thinking

1. Why should age of immigration and proximity to the border where one lives be an important predictor of alcohol and drug use?

2. The author states that the earlier one immigrates to the US (age 6 or less) the great risk one has of abusing drugs and alcohol? Why is this a risk factor?

3. Why does assimilation and acculturation stress affect drug and alcohol abuse in Hispanic immigrants?

4. Mexican Americans living further from the border have far lower risks of becoming addicted to drugs and alcohol. Why?

Internet References

BMC Public Health
https://bmcpublichealth.biomedcentral.com/

Drug and Alcohol Dependence
https://www.drugandalcoholdependence.com/

National Institute of Alcohol Abuse and Alcoholism
https://www.niaaa.nih.gov/publications

Unit 5

UNIT

Prepared by: Kim Schnurbush, *California State University, Sacramento*
Mark Pullin, *Angelo State University*

Measuring the Social Costs of Drugs

The most devastating effect of drug abuse in America is the magnitude with which it affects the way we live. Much of its influence is not measurable. What is the cost of a son or daughter lost, a parent imprisoned, a life lived in a constant state of fear? The emotional costs alone are incomprehensible. The social legacy of this country's drug crisis could easily be the subject of this entire book. The purpose here, however, can only be a cursory portrayal of drugs' tremendous costs. More than one U.S. president has stated that drug use threatens our national security and well-being. The financial costs of maintaining the federal apparatus devoted to drug interdiction, enforcement, and treatment are staggering. Although yearly expenditures vary due to changes in political influence, strategy, and tactics, examples of the tremendous effects of drugs on government and the economy abound. The federal budget for drug control exceeds $14 billion and includes almost $1.5 billion dedicated to drug fighting in Mexico and Central America under the Merida Initiative. Mexican criminal syndicates and paramilitaries who control trafficking across the U.S. southern border threaten the virtual sovereignty of the Mexican government. Many argue that the situation in Mexico is as dangerous to the United States as the current situation in Afghanistan.

Since 9/11, the restructuring of federal, state, and local law enforcement apparatus in response to terrorism has significantly influenced the nature and extent of drug trafficking in the United States. Huge transnational investigative, intelligence, and enforcement coalitions have formed between the United States and its allies in the war against terrorism. One significant impact of these coalitions has been a tightening of border access and a decreased availability of international trafficking routes. Although drugs are believed to still pour in from Mexico, drug shortages, increased street prices, and a decrease in purity are occurring. Powder heroin is not widely available in the West, and many major U.S. cities are reporting major street declines in the availability of cocaine.

Still, drugs exist, in association with terrorism, as the business of the criminal justice system. Approximately 80 percent of the people behind bars in the country had a problem with drugs or alcohol prior to their incarceration—more of its citizens than almost any other comparable society, and the financial costs are staggering. Doing drugs and serving time produces an inescapable nexus, and it doesn't end with prison. Almost 29 percent of persons on supervised parole or probation abuse drugs. Some argue that these numbers represent the fact that Americans have come to rely on the criminal justice system in an unprecedented way to solve problems of drug abuse. Regardless of the way one chooses to view how various relationships, the resulting picture is numbing.

In addition to the highly visible criminal justice–related costs, numerous other institutions are affected. Housing, welfare, education, and health care provide excellent examples of critical institutions struggling to overcome the strain of drug-related impacts. In addition, annual loss of productivity in the workplace exceeds well over $160 billion per year. Alcoholism alone causes 500 million lost workdays each year. Add to this demographic shifts caused by people fleeting drug-impacted neighborhoods, schools, and businesses, and one soon realizes that there is no victimless public or private institution. Last year, almost 4 million Americans received some kind of treatment related to the abuse of alcohol or other drugs. Almost 23 million Americans need treatment for an illicit drug or alcohol problem. Fetal Alcohol Syndrome is the leading cause of mental retardation in the United States, and still, survey data continue to report that over 11 percent of pregnant women continue to drink alcohol. Add to this injured, drug-related accident and crime victims, along with demands produced by a growing population of intravenous drug users infected with AIDS, a frighteningly overwhelmed health-care system comes to the fore. Health-care costs from drug-related ills are staggering. Drug abuse continues to cost the economy more than $13 billion annually in health-care costs alone. Approximately 71 million Americans over 12 are current users of a tobacco product.

It should be emphasized that the social costs exacted by drug use infiltrate every aspect of public and private life. The implications for thousands of families struggling with the adverse effects of drug-related woes may prove the greatest and most tragic of social costs. Children who lack emotional support, self-esteem, role models, a safe and secure environment, economic opportunity, and an education because of a parent on drugs suggest costs that are difficult to comprehend or measure.

In some jurisdictions in California and Oregon, as many as 50 percent of child welfare placements are precipitated by methamphetamine abuse.

When reading this unit of this book, consider the diversity of costs associated with the abuse of both legal and illegal drugs. As you read the following articles, consider the historical progressions of social costs produced by drug abuse over the past century. How are the problems of the past replicating themselves and how have science, medicine, and social policy changed in an attempt to mitigate these impacts? Ample evidence informs us that there is no single approach to mitigate the diverse nature of drug-related social impacts. Further, some of the most astounding scientific discoveries about how addiction develop remains mysterious when compared to the reality of the lives of millions who find drugs an end in themselves. Some have argued that the roots of drug-related problems today seem even more elusive, complicated, and desperate. Good progress has been made in treating drug addiction, but only moderate progress has been made in preventing it in the first place. What are the disproportionate ways in which some populations of Americans are harmed by drugs? Are there epidemics within epidemics? How is drug abuse expressed within different populations of Americans? How do the implications for Native American families and culture differ from those for other racial and ethnic groups? What are the reasons for these disparities and how should they be addressed?

Article

Prepared by: Kim Schnurbush, *California State University, Sacramento*
Mark Pullin, *Angelo State University*

Dealing with Opioid Abuse Would Pay for Itself

Austin Frakt

Learning Outcomes

After reading this article, you will be able to:

- Understand why opioid painkillers have become such a problem in the United States for both patients and authorities.

- Discuss the social costs of opioid painkillers, to include the effects on the user/abuser to how society will suffer from this spike in addicts as well.

- Understand that although legal, addiction to opioid painkillers can be more devastating than addiction to illegal substances.

Once championed as the answer to chronic pain, opioid medications and painkillers have become a large and costly problem in the United States. Fatal overdoses have quadrupled in the last 15 years, and opioids now cause more deaths than any other drug, over 16,000 in 2010. Prescription opioid abuse is also costly, sapping productivity and increasing health care and criminal justice costs to the tune of $55.7 billion in 2007, for example.

Addressing this problem would cost money, too, but evidence suggests it would pay for itself.

Much of the problematic use of opioids like Vicodin and OxyContin, originates with a prescription to treat pain. Prescriptions can be of tremendous help to certain patients. But doctors write a lot more of them for opioids in the United States than they should, enough for every American adult to have a bottle of opiate painkillers each year, according to the U.S. Centers for Disease Control and Prevention.

One approach to the problem, therefore, is to attempt to reduce the number of prescriptions written by targeting use

to patients for whom the medications are most appropriate. In July 2012, for example, Blue Cross Blue Shield of Massachusetts began requiring prior authorization for more than a 30-day supply of opioid medication within a two-month period. After 18 months, the insurer estimates that it cut prescriptions by 6.6 million pills.

Except for Missouri, all states have or plan to soon have drug databases in place that can be used to track prescribers of opioid painkillers and those that use them. Not all states require doctors to check the database before prescribing the medications, though—a provision that has been demonstrated to reduce overuse. For example, in 2012, the states of New York and Tennessee began requiring doctors to check their states' drug monitoring databases before prescribing opiate painkillers. Both states saw substantial drops in patients who received duplicate prescriptions of drugs from different doctors, one pathway for overuse and overdose.

Prevention and better targeting are sensible, but they do little to assist patients already dependent on opioids. Those patients need help, and more than just a short stint in a detox facility. The modern view of opioid dependency is that it's akin to a chronic disease, like diabetes or hypertension, which requires maintenance therapy: long-term treatment with a craving-relieving substitution agent like methadone or buprenorphine, sometimes combined with other medications.

Such treatment isn't free, of course, but many studies have shown it's worth the cost. Just considering health care costs alone, studies have shown it to be cost-effective with substantial offsets in reduced spending on other types of health care. For example, methadone treatment limits the spread of HIV. by reducing the use and sharing of needles. It also reduces hospitalization and emergency department use, such as treatment of trauma, perhaps from accidents. Considering the broader, social costs of opioid dependence as well—those due to lost productivity and crime—the case that maintenance therapy for opioid dependence is cost saving is even stronger.

Recently, the Comparative Effectiveness Public Advisory Council conducted an economic analysis of expanding opioid treatment in New England states. The council found that as access to treatment increased, total costs of treatment also grew, but savings to society increased even more rapidly. The result is that greater treatment actually saves society money. For instance, New England states could save $1.3 billion by expanding treatment of opioid-dependent persons by 25 percent.

If maintenance therapy is such a good deal, why don't we more readily provide it? One answer is that, though treatment works, its benefits are diffuse. A great deal of the cost of treatment would be borne by insurers and public health programs. But a great deal of the savings would be captured by society at large (through a reduction in crime, for example). As my colleague Keith Humphreys and coauthors wrote, "If, for example, one is held responsible to keep a hospital budget in balance, spending scarce funds on [substance use disorder] treatment does not become more attractive just because it saves money for the prison system."

Another reason maintenance therapy for opioid dependency is underprovided is that it is still misunderstood. Culturally, there's a temptation to view dependency as a result of poor lifestyle choices, not as a chronic disease, and to view maintenance treatment as merely substituting one addiction for another. (This is akin to viewing chronic insulin use as a mere substitute for chronic diabetes.) And, to be fair, there are real issues, such as the potential for misuse and diversion, associated with maintenance drug therapy for opioid dependency. Those deserve some attention, but not out of proportion to the problems they pose.

It's clear that treatment for opioid dependency is underprovided for a variety of reasons, and that this, in turn, helps promote the growth in the problems dependency causes. But it's also clear that those dependent on opioids aren't the only victims. Because of the social costs the problem causes, many others are as well.

Critical Thinking

1. Discuss the recent spike in opioid painkiller deaths, and why this is presenting a problem to both medical personnel and law enforcement.

2. Opioid painkillers are legal, yet, they are responsible for the largest number of addicted patients in the nation over the past 15 years. Why would someone who is addicted to a legal opioid struggle with admitting they're an "addict" compared to someone who abuses heroin, cocaine, or similar?

3. Do you believe all states should provide lowcost or even free treatment for opioid treatment? Why or why not?

Internet References

Centers for Disease Control and Prevention, Opioid Painkiller Prescribing

http://www.cdc.gov/vitalsigns/opioid-prescribing/index.html?s_cid=cdc_homepage_feature_001

National Institute on Drug Abuse, America's Addiction to Opioids: Heroin and Prescription Drug Abuse

https://www.drugabuse.gov/about-nida/legislative-activities/testimony-to-congress/2016/americas-addiction-to-opioids-heroin-prescription-drug-abuse

United States Department of Justice, Drug Enforcement Agency, Diversion Control Division-State Prescription Drug Monitoring Programs

https://www.deadiversion.usdoj.gov/faq/rx_monitor.htm

AUSTIN FRAKT is a health economist with several governmental and academic affiliations. He blogs at *The Incidental Economist*.

Article

Prepared by: Kim Schnurbush, *California State University, Sacramento*
Mark Pullin, *Angelo State University*

Alcohol: A Women's Health Issue

U.S. DEPARTMENT OF HEALTH AND HUMAN SERVICES

Learning Outcomes

After reading this article, you will be able to:

- Understand what categories of people should avoid the consumption of alcohol.

- Explore why lower levels of alcohol are recommended for women compared to men.

- Discuss some consequences of unsafe drinking for women.

Women and Drinking

Alcohol presents yet another health challenge for women. Even in small amounts, alcohol affects women differently than men. In some ways, heavy drinking is much more risky for women than it is for men.

With any health issue, accurate information is key. There are times and ways to drink that are safer than others. Every woman is different. No amount of drinking is 100 percent safe, 100 percent of the time, for every woman. With this in mind, it's important to know how alcohol can affect a woman's health and safety.

How Much Is Too Much?

Sixty percent of U.S. women have at least one drink a year. Among women who drink, 13 percent have more than seven drinks per week.

For women, this level of drinking is above the recommended limits published in the *Dietary Guidelines for Americans*, which are issued jointly by the U.S. Department of Agriculture and the U.S. Department of Health and Human Services. (The *Dietary Guidelines* can be viewed online at www.nutrition.gov.)

The *Dietary Guidelines* define moderate drinking as no more than one drink a day for women and no more than two drinks a day for men.

The *Dietary Guidelines* point out that drinking more than one drink per day for women can increase the risk for motor vehicle crashes, other injuries, high blood pressure, stroke, violence, suicide, and certain types of cancer.

What Is a Drink?

In the United States, a standard drink is one that contains about 14 grams of pure alcohol, which is found in:

- 12 ounces of beer with 5 percent alcohol content
- 5 ounces of wine with 12 percent alcohol content
- 1.5 ounces of distilled spirits with 40 percent alcohol content

Unfortunately, although the "standard" drink amounts are helpful for following health guidelines, they may not reflect customary serving sizes. A large cup of beer, an overpoured glass of wine, or a single mixed drink could contain much more alcohol than a standard drink. In addition, while the alcohol concentrations listed are "typical," there is considerable variability in alcohol content within each type of beverage (e.g., beer, wine, distilled spirits).

Some people should not drink at all, including:

- Anyone under age 21
- People of any age who are unable to restrict their drinking to moderate levels
- Women who may become pregnant or who are pregnant
- People who plan to drive, operate machinery, or take part in other activities that require attention, skill, or coordination
- People taking prescription or overthecounter medications that can interact with alcohol.

Why are lower levels of drinking recommended for women than for men? Because women are at greater risk than men for developing alcoholrelated problems. Alcohol passes through the digestive tract and is dispersed in the water in the body. The more water available, the more diluted the alcohol. As a rule, men weigh more than women, and, pound for pound, women have less water in their bodies than men. Therefore, a woman's brain and other organs are exposed to more alcohol and to more of the toxic byproducts that result when the body breaks down and eliminates alcohol.

Moderate Drinking: Benefits and Risks

Moderate drinking can have short and longterm health effects, both positive and negative:

- **Benefits**

Heart disease: Once thought of as a threat mainly to men, heart disease also is the leading killer of women in the United States. Drinking moderately may lower the risk for coronary heart disease, mainly among women over age 55. However, there are other factors that reduce the risk of heart disease, including a healthy diet, exercise, not smoking, and keeping a healthy weight. Moderate drinking provides little, if any, net health benefit for younger people.

(Heavy drinking can actually damage the heart.)

- **Risks**

Drinking and driving: It doesn't take much alcohol to impair a person's ability to drive. The chances of being killed in a singlevehicle crash are increased at a blood alcohol level that a 140lb. woman would reach after having one drink on an empty stomach.

Medication interactions: Alcohol can interact with a wide variety of medicines, both prescription and overthecounter. Alcohol can reduce the effectiveness of some medications, and it can combine with other medications to cause or increase side effects. Alcohol can interact with medicines used to treat conditions as varied as heart and blood vessel disease, digestive problems, and diabetes. In particular, alcohol can increase the sedative effects of any medication that causes drowsiness, including cough and cold medicines and drugs for anxiety and depression. **When taking any medication, read package labels and warnings carefully.**

Breast cancer: Research suggests that as little as one drink per day can slightly raise the risk of breast cancer in some women, especially those who are postmenopausal or have a family history of breast cancer. It is not possible, however, to predict how alcohol will affect the risk for breast cancer in any one woman.

Fetal Alcohol Syndrome: Drinking by a pregnant woman can harm her unborn baby, and may result in a set of birth defects called fetal alcohol syndrome (FAS).

Fetal Alcohol Syndrome

Fetal alcohol syndrome (FAS) is the most common known preventable cause of mental impairment. Babies with FAS have distinctive changes in their facial features and they may be born small. The brain damage that occurs with FAS can result in lifelong problems with learning, memory, attention, and problem solving. These alcoholrelated changes in the brain may be present even in babies whose appearance and growth are not affected. It is not known if there is any safe drinking level during pregnancy; nor is there any stage of pregnancy in which drinking—at any level—is known to be risk free. **If a woman is pregnant, or wants to become pregnant, she should not drink alcohol.** Even if she is pregnant and already has consumed alcohol, it is important to stop drinking for the rest of her pregnancy. Stopping can reduce the chances that her child might be harmed by alcohol.

Another risk of drinking is that a woman may at some point abuse alcohol or become alcoholic (alcohol dependent). Drinking four or more drinks on any given day OR drinking eight or more drinks in a typical week increases a woman's risk of developing alcohol abuse or dependence.

The ability to drink a man—or anyone—under the table is not a plus: it is a red flag. Research has shown that drinkers who are able to handle a lot of alcohol all at once are at higher—not lower—risk of developing problems, such as dependence on alcohol.

Heavy Drinking

An estimated 5.3 million women in the United States drink in a way that threatens their health, safety, and general wellbeing. A strong case can be made that heavy drinking is more risky for women than men:

- *Heavy drinking increases a woman's risk of becoming a victim of violence and sexual assault.*
- *Drinking over the long term is more likely to damage a woman's health than a man's, even if the woman has been drinking less alcohol or for a shorter length of time than the man.*

The health effects of alcohol abuse and alcoholism are serious. Some specific health problems include:

- *Alcoholic liver disease:* Women are more likely than men to develop alcoholic hepatitis (liver inflammation) and to die from cirrhosis.
- *Brain disease:* Most alcoholics have some loss of mental function, reduced brain size, and changes in the function of brain cells. Research suggests that women are more vulnerable than men to alcoholinduced brain damage.

- *Cancer:* Many studies report that heavy drinking increases the risk of breast cancer. Alcohol also is linked to cancers of the digestive tract and of the head and neck (the risk is especially high in smokers who also drink heavily).
- *Heart disease:* Chronic heavy drinking is a leading cause of cardiovascular disease. Among heavy drinkers, women are more susceptible to alcoholrelated heart disease, even though women drink less alcohol over a lifetime than men.

Finally, many alcoholics smoke; smoking in itself can cause serious longterm health consequences.

Alcohol in Women's Lives
Adolescence

Despite the fact that drinking is illegal for anyone under the age of 21, the reality is that **many** adolescent girls drink. Research shows that about 37 percent of 9th grade girls—usually about 14 years old—report drinking in the past month. (This rate is slightly more than that for 9th grade boys.) Even more alarming is the fact that about 17 percent of these same young girls report having had five or more drinks on a single occasion during the previous month.

Consequences of Unsafe Drinking

- Drinking under age 21 is illegal in every State.
- Drunk driving is one of the leading causes of teen death.
- Drinking makes young women more vulnerable to sexual assault and unsafe and unplanned sex. On college campuses, assaults, unwanted sexual advances, and unplanned and unsafe sex are all more likely among students who drink heavily on occasion—for men, five drinks in a row, for women, four. In general, when a woman drinks to excess she is more likely to be a target of violence or sexual assault.
- Young people who begin drinking before age 15 have a 40 percent higher risk of developing alcohol abuse or alcoholism some time in their lives than those who wait until age 21 to begin drinking. This increased risk is the same for young girls as it is for boys.

Alcohol's Appeal for Teens. Among the reasons teens give most often for drinking are to have a good time, to experiment, and to relax or relieve tension. Peer pressure can encourage drinking. Teens who grow up with parents who support, watch over, and talk with are less likely to drink than their peers.

Staying Away From Alcohol. Young women under age 21 should not drink alcohol. Among the most important things

parents can do is to talk frankly with their daughters about not drinking alcohol.

Women in Young and Middle Adulthood

Young women in their twenties and early thirties are more likely to drink than older women. No one factor predicts whether a woman will have problems with alcohol, or at what age she is most at risk. However, there are some life experiences that seem to make it more likely that women will have drinking problems.

Heavy drinking and drinking problems among White women are most common in younger age groups. Among African American women, however, drinking problems are more common in middle age than youth. A woman's ethnic origins—and the extent to which she adopts the attitudes of mainstream vs. her native culture—influence how and when she will drink. Hispanic women who are more "mainstream" are more likely to drink and to drink heavily (that is, to drink at least once a week and to have five or more drinks at one time).

Research suggests that women who have trouble with their closest relationships tend to drink more than other women. Heavy drinking is more common among women who have never married, are living unmarried with a partner, or are divorced or separated. (The effect of divorce on a woman's later drinking may depend on whether she is already drinking heavily in her marriage.) A woman whose husband drinks heavily is more likely than other women to drink too much.

Many studies have found that women who suffered childhood sexual abuse are more likely to have drinking problems.

Depression is closely linked to heavy drinking in women, and women who drink at home alone are more likely than others to have later drinking problems.

Stress and Drinking

Stress is a common theme in women's lives. Research confirms that one of the reasons people drink is to help them cope with stress. However, it is not clear just how stress may lead to problem drinking. Heavy drinking by itself causes stress in a job and family. Many factors, including family history, shape how much a woman will use alcohol to cope with stress. A woman's past and usual drinking habits are important. Different people have different expectations about the effect of alcohol on stress. How a woman handles stress, and the support she has to manage it, also may affect whether she uses alcohol in response to stress.

Consequences of Unsafe Drinking

- The number of female drivers involved in alcoholrelated fatal traffic crashes is going up, even as the number of male drivers involved in such crashes has decreased.

This trend may reflect the increasing number of women who drive themselves, even after drinking, as opposed to riding as a passenger.

- Longterm health problems from heavy drinking include liver, heart, and brain disease; suppression of the immune system; and cancer.
- Because women are more likely to become pregnant in their twenties and thirties, this age group faces the greatest risk of having babies with the growth and mental impairments of fetal alcohol syndrome, which is caused by drinking during pregnancy.

Older Women

As they grow older, fewer women drink. At the same time, research suggests that people born in recent decades are more likely to drink—throughout life—than people born in the early 1900s. Elderly patients are admitted to hospitals about as often for alcoholrelated causes as for heart attacks.

Older women may be especially sensitive to the stigma of being alcoholic, and therefore hesitate to admit if they have a drinking problem.

Consequences of Unsafe Drinking

- Older women, more than any other group, use medications that can affect mood and thought, such as those for anxiety and depression. These "psychoactive" medications can interact with alcohol in harmful ways.
- Research suggests that women may be more likely to develop or to show alcohol problems later in life, compared with men.

Age and Alcohol. Aging seems to reduce the body's ability to adapt to alcohol. Older adults reach higher blood levels of alcohol even when drinking the same amount as younger people. This is because, with aging, the amount of water in the body is reduced and alcohol becomes more concentrated. But even at the same blood alcohol level, older adults may feel some of the effects of alcohol more strongly than younger people.

Alcohol problems among older people often are mistaken for other aging-related conditions. As a result, alcohol problems may be missed and untreated by health care providers, especially in older women.

Staying Well. Older women need to be aware that alcohol will "go to their head" more quickly than when they were younger. Also, caregivers need to know that alcohol may be the cause of problems assumed to result from age, such as depression, sleeping problems, eating poorly, heart failure, and frequent falls.

The National Institute on Alcohol Abuse and Alcoholism recommends that people ages 65 and older limit their consumption of alcohol to one drink per day.

An important point is that older people with alcohol problems respond to treatment as well as younger people. Those with shorter histories of problem drinking do better in treatment than those with longterm drinking problems.

Women and Problem Drinking
An Individual Decision

A woman's genetic makeup shapes how quickly she feels the effects of alcohol, how pleasant drinking is for her, and how drinking alcohol over the long term will affect her health, even the chances that she could have problems with alcohol. A family history of alcohol problems, a woman's risk of illnesses like heart disease and breast cancer, medications she is taking, and age are among the factors for each woman to weigh in deciding when, how much, and how often to drink.

What Are Alcohol Abuse and Alcoholism?

Alcohol abuse is a pattern of drinking that is harmful to the drinker or others. The following situations, occurring repeatedly in a 12 month period, would be indicators of alcohol abuse:

- Missing work or skipping child care responsibilities because of drinking
- Drinking in situations that are dangerous, such as before or while driving
- Being arrested for driving under the influence of alcohol or for hurting someone while drunk
- Continuing to drink even though there are ongoing alcoholrelated tensions with friends and family.

Alcoholism or alcohol dependence is a disease. It is chronic, or lifelong, and it can be both progressive and life threatening. Alcoholism is based in the brain. Alcohol's shortterm effects on the brain are what cause someone to feel high, relaxed, or sleepy after drinking. In some people, alcohol's longterm effects can change the way the brain reacts to alcohol, so that the urge to drink can be as compelling as the hunger for food. Both a person's genetic makeup and his or her environment contribute to the risk for alcoholism. The following are some of the typical characteristics of alcoholism:

- *Craving:* a strong need, or compulsion, to drink
- *Loss of control:* the inability to stop drinking once a person has begun
- *Physical dependence:* withdrawal symptoms, such as nausea, sweating, shakiness, and anxiety, when alcohol use is stopped after a period of heavy drinking
- *Tolerance:* the need for increasing amounts of alcohol to get "high."

Know the Risks

Research suggests that a woman is more likely to drink excessively if she has any of the following:

- Parents and siblings (or other blood relatives) with alcohol problems
- A partner who drinks heavily
- The ability to "hold her liquor" more than others
- A history of depression
- A history of childhood physical or sexual abuse.

The presence of any of these factors is a good reason to be especially careful with drinking.

How Do You Know if You Have a Problem?

Answering the following four questions can help you find out if you or someone close to you has a drinking problem.

- Have you ever felt you should cut down on your drinking?
- Have people annoyed you by criticizing your drinking?
- Have you ever felt bad or guilty about your drinking?
- Have you ever had a drink first thing in the morning to steady your nerves or to get rid of a hangover?

One "yes" answer suggests a possible alcohol problem. If you responded "yes" to more than one question, it is very likely that you have a problem with alcohol. In either case, it is important that you see your health care provider right away to discuss your responses to these questions.

Even if you answered "no" to all of the above questions, if you are having drinkingrelated problems with your job, relationships, health, or with the law, you should still seek help.

Treatment for Alcohol Problems

Treatment for an alcohol problem depends on its severity. Women who have alcohol problems but who are not yet alcohol dependent may be able to stop or reduce their drinking with minimal help. Routine doctor visits are an ideal time to discuss alcohol use and its potential problems. Health care providers can help a woman take a good hard look at what effect alcohol is having on her life and can give advice on ways to stop drinking or to cut down.

Research Directions

Finding out what makes some women drink too much is the first step to preventing alcohol problems in women. Scientists are studying the role of genetics and family environment in increasing or decreasing the risk of alcohol problems. They also are studying other features of a woman's life, such as the type of job she has; whether she combines family and work; life changes like marriage, divorce, and the birth and departure of children; infertility; relationship and sexual problems; and ethnic background.

Scientists want to know why women in general seem to develop longterm health problems from drinking more quickly than men. Researchers are examining issues like alcohol and breast cancer in women, and the extent to which alcohol may lower the risk of heart disease, and possibly osteoporosis, in some women.

Finally, research is helping determine how to identify women who may be at risk for alcohol problems, and to ensure that treatment will be effective.

Getting Help and More Information

Alcoholics Anonymous (AA) World Services
Internet address: www.aa.org
Phone: 212–870–3400

Makes referrals to local AA groups and provides informational materials on the AA program. Many cities and towns also have a local AA office listed in the telephone book.

AlAnon Family Group Headquarters
Internet address: www.alanon.alateen.org
For locations of AlAnon or Alateen meetings worldwide, call 888–4AL–ANON (888–425–2666), Monday through Friday, 8 a.m.–6 p.m. (EST)
For free informational materials, call 757–563–1600, Monday through Friday, 8 a.m.–6 p.m.

Makes referrals to local AlAnon groups, which are support groups for spouses and other significant adults in an alcoholic person's life. Also makes referrals to Alateen groups, which offer support to children of alcoholics.

National Association for Children of Alcoholics (NACoA)
Internet address: www.nacoa.net Email: nacoa@nacoa.org
Phone: 888–554–COAS or 301–468–0985

Works on behalf of children of alcohol- and drug-dependent parents.

National Clearinghouse for Alcohol and Drug Information (NCADI)
Internet address: www.samhsa.gov
Phone: 800–729–6686

Provides alcohol and drug abuse information produced by the Substance Abuse and Mental Health Services Administration, U.S. Department of Health and Human Services.

National Council on Alcoholism and Drug Dependence (NCADD)
Internet address: www.ncadd.org
Phone: 800–NCA–CALL (800–622–2255)

Provides telephone numbers of local NCADD affiliates (who can provide information on local treatment resources) and educational materials on alcoholism.

National Institute on Alcohol Abuse and Alcoholism (NIAAA)
5635 Fishers Lane, MSC 9304
Bethesda, Maryland 20892–9304
Internet address: www.niaaa.nih.gov
Phone: 301–443–3860

Offers a free 12minute video, Alcohol: A Woman's Health Issue, profiling women recovering from alcohol problems and describing the health consequences of heavy drinking in women. Other publications also are available from NIAAA and feature information on a wide variety of topics, including fetal alcohol syndrome, the dangers of mixing alcohol with medications, family history of alcoholism, and preventing underage drinking. See "Additional Reading," on page 20, for information on ordering NIAAA materials.

Substance Abuse Treatment Facility Locator
Internet address: www.findtreatment.samhsa.gov
Phone: 800–662–HELP(800–662–4357)

Offers alcohol and drug information and treatment referral assistance. (This service is provided by the Substance Abuse and Mental Health Services Administration, U.S. Department of Health and Human Services.)

Additional Reading

A *Family History of Alcoholism: Are You at Risk?*—offers easytoread information for anyone who is concerned about a family history of alcoholism. English version: NIH Publication Number 03–5340; Spanish version: NIH Publication Number 04–5340–S.

Drinking and Your Pregnancy—explains how drinking can hurt a developing baby, the problems that children born with fetal alcohol syndrome have, how to stop drinking, and where to go for help. English version: NIH Publication Number 96–4101; Spanish version: NIH Publication Number 97–4102.

Make a Difference: Talk to Your Child About Alcohol—offers guidance to parents and caregivers of young people ages 10 to 14 on preventing underage drinking. English version: NIH

Publication Number 06–4314; Spanish version: NIH Publication Number 06–4314–S.

Rethinking Drinking: Alcohol and Your Health—offers valuable researchbased information on "lowrisk" versus "highrisk" drinking. Includes tips, tools, and resources for people who choose to cut down or to quit drinking. English version: NIH Publication Number 10–3770; Spanish version: NIH Publication Number 10–3770–S.

To order, write to: National Institute on Alcohol Abuse and Alcoholism, Publications Distribution Center, P.O. Box 10686, Rockville, MD 20849–0686. The full text of all of the above publications is available on NIAAA's Web site (www.niaaa.nih.gov).

Critical Thinking

1. How much is "too much" when it comes to consuming alcoholic beverages?
2. What categories of people should avoid drinking alcohol?
3. Why are lower levels of alcohol recommended for women compared to men?
4. What are some risks of consuming alcohol for women in particular?
5. What are some consequences of unsafe drinking for women?
6. How does someone know they have a problem with alcohol?

Internet References

National Center for Chronic Disease Prevention and Health Promotion
https://www.cdc.gov/chronicdisease/index.htm

National Center for Complementary and Integrative Health
https://nccih.nih.gov/

National Institute of Alcohol Abuse and Alcoholism
https://www.niaaa.nih.gov/publications

The Office of Research on Women's Health (ORWH) serves as the focal point for women's health research at NIH. ORWH works in a variety of ways to encourage and support researchers to find answers to questions about diseases and conditions that affect women and how to keep women healthy, and to establish a research agenda for the future. ORWH encourages women of all racial and ethnic backgrounds to participate in clinical studies to help increase knowledge of the health of women of all cultures, and to understand the health-related similarities and differences between women and men. The office also provides opportunities and support for the advancement of women in biomedical careers.

National Institute of Health, National Institute on Alcohol Abuse and Alcoholism, Alcohol: *A Women's Health Issue.* U.S. Department of Health and Human Services, 2015.

Article

Prepared by: Kim Schnurbush, *California State University, Sacramento*
Mark Pullin, *Angelo State University*

The Effect of Sanctuary City Policies on the Ability to Combat the Opioid Epidemic

U.S. House Judiciary Committee Subcommittee on Immigration and Border Security

JESSICA M. VAUGHAN

Learning Outcomes

After reading this article, you will be able to:

- Explore how we can tackle the "War on Drugs" in the future and how addiction issues impact Sanctuary Cities.

- Discuss the pros and cons of Sanctuary Cities with regard to the opioid crisis.

- Understand "The Chilling Effect" Myth and how it relates to the opioid crisis in the United States.

Thank you, Chairman Labrador and Ranking Minority Member Lofgren, for the opportunity to participate in this important hearing. The epidemic of opioid addiction and overdoses that is ravaging our communities is tragic. I am reminded of it every single day that I drive around near my family's house in Massachusetts, where ubiquitous lawn signs bear the simple message "#2069" in black and white, to memorialize the number of lives lost in the state in 2016 as a direct result of opioid abuse and addition.

This epidemic, according to virtually every law enforcement officer ever asked to comment on it, is like nothing we have ever experienced before, at least in New England. Those individuals who are struggling with addiction and substance abuse need help, no question, and they and their families need and deserve

our support. But we will not make progress on this crisis unless we also take steps to disrupt and dismantle the criminal organizations that bring these illegal and deadly substances to our communities.

Sanctuary policies deliberately limit, block, or prohibit communication and cooperation with federal immigration agencies, and they inevitably result in the release of criminal aliens back to the streets instead of back to their home country. These politically motivated policies are particularly destructive to law enforcement efforts to combat the opioid epidemic. In many parts of the country, most of the drugs that have fueled this epidemic — primarily fentanyl, which is now responsible for more deaths in New England than heroin—are brought in by foreign drug cartels and distributed by rings that are often staffed by illegal aliens.

The sanctuary policies thus prevent local law enforcement agencies from working effectively with immigration agencies, which are among the federal agencies that are best equipped to fight the opioid epidemic. They also exacerbate the problem by enabling some of the criminals who are distributing the opioids to remain in the communities, where, like American citizen criminals, they often re-offend.

The misguided officials who impose sanctuary policies on state and local law enforcement agencies will not reverse these policies on their own. Congress must act to clarify immigration authorities and to impose consequences on sanctuary jurisdictions and the officials who are responsible for these destructive policies. In addition, Congress should act to strengthen laws on identity theft and fraud, which are commonly used by foreign drug traffickers and dealers to conceal their identity and their criminal activity.

Immigration Enforcement Is Necessary to Combat the Opioid Epidemic.

According to the Drug Enforcement Administration (DEA) and other federal and local law enforcement experts, approximately 80 percent of the illegal opioids sold in this country are brought in by foreign criminal organizations, primarily the Mexico-based drug cartels. The dominant organization is the Sinaloa cartel, but there are numerous others, with shifting associations and geographic territory. The drugs often are smuggled in vehicles across the U.S.-Mexico border and taken to distribution hubs in cities around the country. Beginning around 2015, Mexican drug trafficking organizations had taken over heroin markets throughout the country, displacing Asian suppliers.[1]

The cartels have cells within the United States and work with other criminal groups, sometimes street gangs with foreign members, such as MS-13, to distribute the drugs. In New England, opioid distribution is handled primarily by trafficking organizations rather than street gangs. A 2016 Boston fusion center analysis found that the vast majority of Class A drug (including opioids) trafficking arrests were citizens of the Dominican Republic, many of whom were fraudulently using the identity of a citizen of Puerto Rico.[2]

The agencies of the Department of Homeland Security (DHS), especially Customs and Border Protection (CBP) and Immigration and Customs Enforcement (ICE) are among the best equipped agencies to help state and local law enforcement agencies deal with opioid trafficking. They have expertise and intelligence on cross-border drug trafficking and smuggling, attaches in foreign countries and relationships with foreign and international law enforcement agencies, and extensive databases of foreign gang members and other criminals, including biometrics, and including information on the movement of individuals across borders. They are not limited in jurisdiction by state or city boundaries.

For example, this week ICE led an operation in Oklahoma in which 10 people were arrested on state felony charges of heroin trafficking, possession of drug proceeds, and other charges. Six of the 10 suspects arrested were illegal aliens from Mexico. In addition, two others were arrested for immigration violations. In addition to agents from the federal immigration agencies and the DEA, officers from several local police departments and state law enforcement agencies participated as willing partners. According to ICE, the targets of the operation supplied as much as two-thirds of the heroin sold in the Tulsa area.

In addition to information and intelligence, these federal agencies have unique immigration authorities that can be particularly effective in addressing the problem of opioid trafficking. These authorities include the ability to charge criminal aliens with immigration violations such as illegal entry, overstaying a visa, re-entry after deportation, failure to appear for immigration proceedings, illegal possession of a firearm, identity or document fraud, immigration fraud, alien smuggling, immigration charges based on prior commission of serious crimes (aggravated felonies), and other prosecutorial tools.[3]

Immigration authorities can be extremely valuable when dealing with informants. The prospect of removal, while not truly punishment compared to a prison sentence, can be a powerful incentive for criminal aliens to cooperate with authorities. ICE agents can offer certain protections to illegal alien offenders who become assets on investigations, and these protections repeatedly have been used successfully by ICE agents working with local drug and gang investigators. Immigration agents can provide immigration documents for use by investigators in penetrating transnational crime organizations. These transactions often produce evidence and even biometric information that can be used against the criminal enterprises.

In addition, U.S. Citizenship and Immigration Services and the immigration courts (part of the Department of Justice) maintain records related to application and awarding of immigration benefits that may be helpful in a criminal investigations. Information from immigration files can be of great importance in providing evidence at bail hearings as to the defendant's track record of failures to appear for immigration proceedings. This information can help a judge make a more informed decision about granting a defendant the opportunity to post bail (rates of absconding by released criminal aliens are significant, as discussed below).

Equally important, the involvement of immigration special agents can spur cooperation of informants or witnesses that might otherwise be difficult to obtain. More traditional types of incentives used by local law enforcement usually involve monetary rewards or mitigating a criminal charge or punishment. The immigration tools can supplement these methods or even supplant them, because to a foreign national, the ability to stay in the United States might be the most powerful incentive possible.[4] These incentives include:

- **Significant Public Benefit Parole.** Provides victims, witnesses and cooperators with temporary lawful immigration status. This is one of the easiest immigration incentives to obtain on behalf of a partnering law enforcement agency. Another big advantage is that it can be cancelled at any time by the controlling ICE agent with immediate consequences to the alien (such as detention) should the alien cease cooperating. There are currently no statutory numerical limits to grants of parole.

- **Work Permits (Employment Authorization Documents).** Allows informants or witnesses to legally work and support themselves while they are assisting authorities.
- **S Visa.** A temporary visa for aliens assisting with criminal and national security investigations and prosecutions, with a path to permanent residency and citizenship. There is a numerical limit of 250 issuances, plus family members, per year.
- **U Visa.** A temporary visa for alien victims of crime, who have suffered substantial harm, cooperate with prosecution of the perpetrator, and have information of value to the case. This visa has a direct path to permanent residency and citizenship. It has become controversial because of fraudulent applications and inadequate screening of applicants. Congress provided for the issuance of 10,000 per year, but applications are currently in excess of 50,000 per year.

Sanctuary Policies Interfere with Local-Federal Cooperation.

Sanctuary policies are destructive to local and federal efforts to combat the opioid epidemic because they interfere with communication and cooperation that could lead to disruption and dismantling of trafficking and distribution organizations that are led by non-citizens. They deny both federal and local agencies the partnership and collaboration that is essential to succeed in fighting transnational criminal organizations. In addition, sanctuary policies inevitably result in the release of criminal aliens back to the streets where they can and do re-offend. Finally, sanctuary policies can act as a magnet for foreign criminal organizations whose operatives are in the country illegally, because they know that immigration violations will be overlooked and that their use of fraudulent documents and identities is less likely to be detected.

Different people and groups may have different definitions of a sanctuary, and there is a spectrum of such policies across the nation. By my definition, a sanctuary is a jurisdiction that has a law, ordinance, policy, practice, or rule that deliberately

obstructs immigration enforcement, restricts interaction with federal immigration agencies, or shields illegal aliens from detection. In addition, federal law includes two key provisions that forbid certain practices: one that forbids policies restricting communication and information sharing (8 U.S.C. Section 1373)[5] and one that forbids harboring illegal aliens or shielding them from detection (8 U.S.C. Section 1324).[6]

For the purposes of eligibility to receive certain grants from the Department of Justice, the Trump administration has defined sanctuary jurisdictions as those that are in violation of 8 USC 1373 by restricting communication with federal agencies regarding immigration or citizenship status, that deny ICE officers access to jails to interview inmates, and/or that refuse to provide ICE with adequate notification of a criminal alien's release who is the subject of an ICE detainer. An immigration detainer is filed by an ICE officer to signal intent to take custody of aliens for purposes of removal once state or local justice system proceedings are concluded, and to request that the local agency keep the alien in custody for up to 48 hours or notify ICE of the date and time of the alien's release so that they can arrive in time to take the alien into custody.

There are approximately 300 sanctuary jurisdictions in the country, and they include municipalities, counties, and states.[7] Clearly this is a small fraction of all of the law enforcement agencies in the country, but these policies exist in places that have severe problems with drug trafficking in general and opioids in particular.

The most common type of sanctuary policy adopted by municipalities is to prohibit police officers from questioning suspects about their immigration status and to prohibit police officers from contacting ICE to report or inquire about a suspect's immigration status. For example, the code of the city of Chicago states:

> No agent or agency shall request information about or otherwise investigate or assist in the investigation of the citizenship or immigration status of any person unless such inquiry or investigation is required by Illinois State Statute, federal regulation, or court decision.[8]

The result of this policy is that if a Chicago police officer were to arrest or investigate a drug dealer or drug trafficker, the officer would not be able to ask the suspect about citizenship or immigration status, or submit an inquiry to ICE to determine the suspect's immigration status, even if the officer has articulable suspicion or cause to believe that the suspect is a foreign national and/or in the country illegally. For example, the officer would be unable to make a routine, automated query or phone call to the Law Enforcement Support Center, which was established by ICE specifically to respond to such queries.[9] Even if a suspect voluntarily disclosed that he was in the country illegally, or had been deported before, the officer would be prohibited from contacting ICE to enable ICE to question or charge the individual with immigration violations that would lead to his deportation.

The ability to communicate with ICE and other federal immigration agencies is particularly important for law enforcement agencies in areas where foreign drug trafficking organizations operate. As stated above, many of the individuals who are involved in drug trafficking are foreign nationals and/or in the United States illegally. It has been well established that many of them are using aliases and stolen or fraudulent identity documents. This is especially common if the criminal alien has been deported before. Local law enforcement agencies typically are not trained to recognize immigration documents or signs of identity theft by foreign nationals, and need to have the discretion to contact the DHS agencies that can assist in identifying criminal aliens involved in the drug trade.

For example, some law enforcement agencies in New England have adopted protocols to detect these instances of identity theft and foreign drug traffickers using the identities of criminals who are U.S. citizens from Puerto Rico. However, for the protocols to be effective, the local law enforcement agencies must be working in cooperation with ICE, the State Department, and state motor vehicle departments.[10]

Because ICE does not patrol the streets of our communities to search for deportable criminal aliens, it is local police and sheriff's officers who are the most likely to encounter them first. They are the ones who know who the drug dealers and opioid traffickers are and where they operate. When they have reasonable suspicion that one of these criminals is in the country illegally, or is not a citizen, and cannot pass that information along to the federal agency that is responsible for enforcing those laws, they are enabling that criminal alien to remain in the country, and they are deprived of the ability to remove that criminal from the community and deprived of the opportunity to spare its peaceful residents from the destructive and dangerous activity of that criminal.

Another common sanctuary policy is to prohibit state and local law enforcement agencies from honoring ICE detainers. The city of Lawrence, Mass., is a regional fentanyl distribution hub for the Sinaloa cartel, where the fentanyl distribution is handled primarily by illegal aliens from the Dominican Republic. Approximately 70 percent of the opioid related deaths last year were linked to fentanyl, and a study by Dartmouth College's school of medicine found that more than half of opioid users they interviewed said that they got their drugs in Lawrence, which is within an hour's drive of most of the population of New Hampshire, Maine, and Massachusetts.[11] Yet the

city council (over the objections of the mayor) has maintained a sanctuary ordinance that forbids local police from cooperating with ICE in any way. It says:

> [N]o officer of employee of a City of Lawrence law enforcement agency shall arrest or detain an individual solely on the basis of an immigration [detainer]. This includes extending length of custody by any amount of time once an individual is released from local custody. . . . No officer or employee of a City of Lawrence law enforcement agency shall respond to any ICE notification request seeking information about an individual's incarceration status, length of detention, home address, work address, personal information, hearing information, or pending release. . . . no officer or employee of a City of Lawrence law enforcement agency shall allow ICE agents access to or use of facilities, records/databases, booking lists, or individuals in custody either in person or via telephone or video conference."[12]

The practical result of such policies is the release of deportable criminal aliens who are involved in the trafficking of narcotics back to the streets of the communities, where they are likely to resume their criminal activities, instead of back to their home countries. There is ample evidence that criminal aliens who are released by sanctuary policies are as likely to offend as any other convicted criminal. Acting ICE Director Tom Homan has stated that since January 2014, there have been 10,000 criminal aliens who were released by sanctuaries and who were then subsequently arrested for additional crimes. Homan said that the recidivism rate for released criminal aliens could be as high as 70 percent, which is consistent with the recidivism rate for all offenders in the United States.[13]

According to ICE records, the number of criminal aliens that ICE is forced to release pursuant to a Ninth Circuit Court of Appeals decision, who then go on to commit new crimes is significant. Approximately 35 percent of the aliens released under this court-imposed mandate have been subsequently re-arrested for other crimes within three to four years after their release.[14]

Additionally, there is a significant chance that these aliens will abscond from their immigration hearings and become fugitives. According to immigration court records, in 2015 the percentage of detained aliens who were subsequently released by ICE on bond or their own recognizance and then skipped out on their hearings hit a record high of 41 percent in 2015.

One example of a violent criminal alien who was reportedly an operative of the Sinaloa cartel and who may have been shielded by sanctuary policies of local police agencies in Utah is Luis Enrique Monroy Bracamontes. This week Bracamontes was found guilty of killing two California sheriff's deputies, Michael Davis, Jr., and Danny Oliver.[15]

Justifications Given for Sanctuary Policies Are False

Proponents of sanctuary policies commonly invoke two main reasons for imposing restrictions on local law enforcement agencies: they maintain that cooperation with federal immigration authorities will erode immigrants' trust in local law enforcement and cause immigrants to refrain from reporting crimes, and that they lack the authority to honor immigration detainers. Both of these rationales are false.

1. "The Chilling Effect" Myth. Sanctuary proponents often assert that non-cooperation policies are needed to enable immigrants to feel comfortable reporting crimes. This frequently heard claim has never been substantiated and, in fact, has been refuted by a number of reputable studies. No evidence of a "chilling effect" from local police cooperation with ICE exists in federal or local government data or independent academic research.

It is important to remember that crime reporting can be a problem in any place, and is not confined to any one segment of the population. In fact, most crimes are not reported, regardless of the victim's immigration status or ethnicity. According to the Bureau of Justice Statistics (BJS), in 2012 only 44 percent of violent victimizations and about 54 percent of serious violent victimizations were reported to police. In 2012, the percentage of property victimizations reported to police was just 34 percent.[16]

In addition, data from the Bureau of Justice Statistics show no meaningful differences among ethnic groups in crime reporting. Overall, Hispanics are slightly more likely to report crimes. Hispanic females especially are slightly more likely than white females and more likely than Hispanic and non-Hispanic males to report violent crimes.[17] This is consistent with academic surveys finding Hispanic females to be more trusting of police than other groups.[18]

A multitude of other studies refute the notion that local-federal cooperation in immigration enforcement causes immigrants to refrain from reporting crimes:

- A major study completed in 2009 by researchers from the University of Virginia and the Police Executive Research Forum (PERF) found no decline in crime reporting by Hispanics after the implementation of a local police program to screen offenders for immigration status and to refer illegals to ICE for removal. This examination of Prince William County, Virginia's,

287(g) program is the most comprehensive study to refute the "chilling effect" theory. The study also found that the county's tough immigration policies likely resulted in a decline in certain violent crimes.[19]

- The most reputable academic survey of immigrants on crime reporting found that by far the most commonly mentioned reason for not reporting a crime was a language barrier (47 percent), followed by cultural differences (22 percent), and a lack of understanding of the U.S. criminal justice system (15 percent) — not fear of being turned over to immigration authorities.

- The academic literature reveals varying attitudes and degrees of trust toward police within and among immigrant communities. Some studies have found that Central Americans may be less trusting than other groups, while others maintain that the most important factor is socio-economic status and feelings of empowerment within a community, rather than the presence or level of immigration enforcement. (See Davis and Henderson's 2003 study of New York and Menjivar and Bejarano's 2004 study of Phoenix).

- A 2009 study of calls for service in Collier County, Fla., found that the implementation of the 287(g) partnership program with ICE enabling local sheriff's deputies to enforce immigration laws, resulting in significantly more removals of criminal aliens, did not affect patterns of crime reporting in immigrant communities. (Collier County Sheriff's Office).

- Data from the Boston, Mass., Police Department, one of two initial pilot sites for ICE's Secure Communities program, show that in the years after the implementation of this program, which ethnic and civil liberties advocates alleged would suppress crime reporting, showed that calls for service decreased proportionately with crime rates. The precincts with larger immigrant populations had less of a decline in reporting than precincts with fewer immigrants. (Analysis of Boston Police Department data by Jessica Vaughan, 2011).

- Similarly, several years of data from the Los Angeles Police Department covering the time period of the implementation of Secure Communities and other ICE initiatives that increased arrests of aliens show that the precincts with the highest percentage foreign-born populations do not have lower crime reporting rates than precincts that are majority black, or that have a smaller foreign-born population, or that have an immigrant population that is more white than Hispanic. The crime-reporting rate in Los Angeles is most affected by the amount of crime, not by race, ethnicity, or size of the foreign-born population. (Analysis of Los Angeles Police Department data by Jessica Vaughan, 2012).

Recent studies based on polling of immigrants about whether they might or might not report crimes in the future based on hypothetical local policies for police interaction with ICE, such as one recent study entitled "Insecure Communities", by Nik Theodore of the University of Illinois, Chicago, should be considered with great caution, since they measure emotions and predict possible behavior, rather than record and analyze actual behavior of immigrants. Moreover, the Theodore study is particularly flawed because it did not compare crime reporting rates of Latinos with other ethnic groups.

For these reasons, law enforcement agencies across the country have found that the most effective ways to encourage crime reporting by immigrants and all residents are to engage in community outreach, hire personnel who speak the languages of the community, establish anonymous tip lines, and set up community sub-stations with non-uniform personnel to take inquiries and reports — not by suspending cooperation with federal immigration enforcement efforts.

2. Legal Issues on Detainers. Some jurisdictions have adopted sanctuary policies that prohibit agencies from honoring ICE detainers. Sometimes these policies are imposed by elected officials and sometimes they are recommended by county attorneys or adopted by sheriffs who are concerned about liability for lawsuits. While there remains an outstanding legal controversy over policies of honoring all ICE detainers, there should be no controversy whatsoever regarding a local agency's ability to honor a detainer in cases of alien drug offenders. In cases of aliens arrested for controlled substance offenses, federal law explicitly permits local officers to notify federal immigration authorities to request a detainer, and directs federal immigration authorities to decide promptly if a detainer can be issued, and to act to take the alien in custody if appropriate (8 USC 1357(d).[20] There is no valid reason or excuse for local law enforcement agencies not to be contacting ICE and requesting detainers for alien drug offenders — especially for those who traffic in heroin, fentanyl, or other opioids.

According to my colleague Dan Cadman, who is a retired senior ICE official, this provision ironically was enacted by Congress because of widespread frustration among local law enforcement agencies and their congressional representatives, who saw the value of immigration enforcement for public safety, and who recognized the nexus between drug trafficking and immigration security, that the federal immigration agency (INS) was not responding to their requests to remove drug offenders from their community. This was a time when there were significantly

fewer than 1,000 investigative agents available to conduct their work for the entire United States. While detainers routinely were filed by INS agents for serious offenders, among those who fell through the cracks were second-tier drug offenders.

This so angered police and sheriffs offices that they lobbied Congress to require INS agents to respond by filing a detainer if the arresting police agency requested it. Fast forward a few decades, and we now have substantially more agents and officers in ICE, the successor agency to the INS, but now we have police, sheriff's departments, and even some correctional agencies, that decline to honor immigration detainers, meaning many non-citizen drug offenders are able to remain here with impunity, thanks to the sanctuary policies.[21]

Recommendations. There are a number of steps Congress should take to clarify the law to make it easier for local law enforcement agencies to push back on politically-motivated sanctuary policies and to impose consequences on those jurisdictions that refuse to follow federal law and that maintain deliberate sanctuary policies. Many of these provisions are found in the Secure America's Future Act, which is a product of this committee and the House Committee on Homeland Security.

- Update the law to explicitly set out the authorities of immigration agencies and state and local law enforcement agencies to make use of detainers.
- Update the law to prohibit non-cooperation and non-communication policies that are being adopted today.
- Stipulate that eligibility for certain federal law enforcement grants is contingent on cooperating with federal immigration agencies. Establish benchmarks for cooperation, to include unfettered communication between local officials and federal immigration officials, honoring detainers, and providing immigration officials with access to jails, courthouses, and all public spaces.
- Require all state motor vehicle agencies and State Department passport offices to adopt identity verification programs to detect imposters and use of stolen identities, such as programs now in use in New England designed to identify foreign drug traffickers using stolen Puerto Rican identities.
- Revise the grounds of inadmissibility and removability to facilitate the removal of drug traffickers and gang members and to prevent them from obtaining immigration benefits of any kind.
- Update the provisions in 8 USC 1324 to facilitate the prosecution or imposition of penalties on local officials who impose egregious sanctuary policies.
- Provide for a private right of action for citizens or residents who suffer harm from criminal aliens who

were released in defiance of federal efforts to take custody.

End Notes

1. See "United States: Areas of Influence of Major Mexican Transnational Criminal Organizations", DEA-DCT-065-15, Drug Enforcement Administration, July 2015.

2. "2016 Heroin Overdose Report: Exploring Narcotic Related Illness in Boston", Boston Regional Intelligence Center, June 2016.

3. For more information see Claude Arnold, "Immigration Authorities and Gang Enforcement", U.S. Attorney's Bulletin 47, May 2006.

4. Jessica M. Vaughan and Jon D. Feere, "Taking Back the Streets: ICE and Local Law Enforcement Target Immigrant Gangs", Center for Immigration Studies, October 2008.

5. 8 USC 1373 states: "a Federal, State, or local government entity or official may not prohibit, or in any way restrict, any government entity or official from sending to, or receiving from, [federal immigration authorities] information regarding the citizenship or immigration status, lawful or unlawful, of any individual."

6. 8 USC 1324 states: "Any person who…knowing or in reckless disregard of the fact that an alien has come to, entered, or remains in the United States in violation of law, conceals, harbors, or shields from detection, or attempts to conceal, harbor, or shield from detection, such alien in any place, …; encourages or induces an alien to come to, enter, or reside in the United States, knowing or in reckless disregard of the fact that such coming to, entry, or residence is or will be in violation of law; or engages in any conspiracy to commit any of the preceding acts, or aids or abets the commission of any of the preceding acts, shall be….fined under title 18, imprisoned not more than 5 years, or both..."

7. See the Center for Immigration Studies map and lists of sanctuary jurisdictions.

8. Chapter 2-173-020 of the Chicago City Code.

9. See "Law Enforcement Support Center" on the ICE website.

10. Kathy Curran and Kevin Rothstein, "Heroin dealers use assumed IDs to elude police", WCVB5 in Massachusetts, February 25, 2016; and "Benefits for the poor diverted to help fuel heroin trade", May 2, 2016.

11. Brian MacQuarrie, "N.E. fentanyl deaths 'like no other epidemic'", Boston Globe, July 27, 2017.

12. Lawrence, Mass. Trust Ordinance, Chapter 9.20 of the city ordinances, adopted on June 8, 2015.

13. Acting ICE Director Tom Homan in remarks in Miami, Florida, as reported by Fox News, "ICE Director: Sanctuaries 'Pulling their own funding' by disobeying feds", August 16, 2017.

14. Letter from Daniel H. Ragsdale, Deputy Director of ICE, in response to questions from Senator Jeff Flake, May 16, 2016.

15. Jessica Vaughan, "Lax Immigration Policies May Have Shielded Killer of California Deputies", Center for Immigration Studies, October 27, 2014.

16. Jennifer Truman, Lynn Langton, and Michael Planty, "Criminal Victimization, 2012", Bureau of Justice Statistics, October 2013.

17. See additional data from the National Crime Victimization Survey here.

18. Lynn Langton, Marcus Berzofsky, Christopher Krebs, and Hope Smiley-McDonald, "Victimizations Not Reported to the Police, 2006-2010", Bureau of Justice Statistics report, August 2012.

19. "Evaluation Study of Prince William County's Illegal Immigration Enforcement Policy: FINAL REPORT 2010", Prince William Board of County Supervisors, November 2010.

20. 8 USC 1357(d) states:

    Detainer of aliens for violation of controlled substances laws. In the case of an alien who is arrested by a Federal, State, or local law enforcement official for a violation of any law relating to controlled substances, if the official (or another official)—

    (1) has reason to believe that the alien may not have been lawfully admitted to the United States or otherwise is not lawfully present in the United States,

    (2) expeditiously informs an appropriate officer or employee of the Service authorized and designated by the Attorney General of the arrest and of facts concerning the status of the alien, and

    (3) requests the Service to determine promptly whether or not to issue a detainer to detain the alien, the officer or employee of the Service shall promptly determine whether or not to issue such a detainer. If such a detainer is issued and the alien is not otherwise detained by Federal, State, or local officials, the Attorney General shall effectively and expeditiously take custody of the alien.

21. Dan Cadman, "An Anti-Sanctuary Bill Doesn't Quite Get to the Goal Line", Center for Immigration Studies, February 11, 2018.

Topics: Sanctuary Cities
Testimony

Critical Thinking

1. Why is it important for people who work in the field, such as this author, to share their experience and research with policymakers?

2. If about 80% of the illegal opioids being brought into the United States are being trafficked in by foreign criminal organizations, how do you propose we tackle the "War on Drugs" in the future? How do you see this impacting addiction issues in Sanctuary cities?

3. How do Sanctuary Policies interfere with local to Federal law enforcement?

4. Do you see Sanctuary cities as being a positive or negative aspect with regards to the opioid crisis in the Untied States? Explain your answer.

5. What is "The Chilling Effect" Myth, and how does it relate to the opioid crisis in the United States?

6. Review the seven recommendations made by the author that she believes should make alleviate at least part of the opioid crisis in Sanctuary cities. Do you agree or disagree with her recommendations? Which ones do you agree/disagree with and why? Do you have any further recommendations, that if you were addressing Congress, you believe may have a positive impact on this issue?

Internet References

BMC Public Health
https://bmcpublichealth.biomedcentral.com/

Principles of Drug Addiction Treatment: A Research-Based Guide
www.drugabuse.gov/PODAT/PODATIndex.html

Substance Abuse and Mental Health Services Administration
https://www.samhsa.gov

WebMD
https://www.webmd.com/

Vaughan, Jessica M., "The Effect of Sanctuary City Policies on the Ability to Combat the Opioid Epidemic," U.S. House Judiciary Committee Subcommittee on Immigration and Border Security, Subcommittee on Immigration and Border Security, 2018.

Article

Prepared by: Kim Schnurbush, *California State University, Sacramento*
Mark Pullin, *Angelo State University*

As Opioid Overdoses Rise, Police Officers Become Counselors, Doctors, and Social Workers

Katie Zezima

Learning Outcomes

After reading this article, you will be able to:

- Understand how the traditional role of police officer is changing to meet the needs to the opioid crisis.

- Discuss how the opioid crisis is financially impacting police departments across the nation.

- Propose solutions on how to ease the burden placed on law enforcement by the opioid crisis.

The nation's opioid epidemic is changing the way law enforcement does its job, with police officers acting as drug counselors and medical workers and shifting from law-and-order tactics to approaches more akin to social work.

Departments accustomed to arresting drug abusers are spearheading programs to get them into treatment, convinced that their old strategies weren't working. They're administering medication that reverses overdoses, allowing users to turn in drugs in exchange for treatment, and partnering with hospitals to intervene before abuse turns fatal.

"A lot of the officers are resistant to what we call social work. They want to go out and fight crime, put people in jail," said Capt. Ron Meyers of the police department in Chillicothe, Ohio, a 21-year veteran who is convinced that punitive tactics no longer work against drugs. "We need to make sure the officers understand this is what is going to stop the epidemic."

Officers are finding children who were barricaded in rooms while their parents got high, and they are responding to the same homes for the same problems. Feelings of exasperation course through some departments in which officers are interacting with the same drug users over and over again, sometimes saving their lives repeatedly with naloxone, a drug that reverses an opiate overdose.

"You're tired of dealing with this person because it saps your resources and it's frustrating, and sometimes that manifests itself in a poor attitude or police officer becoming cynical or sarcastic," said Officer Jamie Williamson of the police department in Ithaca, N.Y., where he said heroin is on every corner of the city. "But you want to get them the help so you don't have to deal with them and so that person gets to a better place."

According to the Centers for Disease Control and Prevention, more than 33,000 people died from opiate overdoses in 2015, a record. Opioids now kill more people than car accidents, and in 2015 the number of heroin deaths nationwide surpassed the number of deaths from gun homicides. The expansion of the problem has forced officers to fundamentally rethink their work.

"When I came out of the police academy, it was law enforcement enforcing the law," said Kevin Coppinger, the sheriff in Essex County, Mass., and a former police chief in Lynn, Mass. "Now police officers have to be generalists. You have to enforce the law, you have to be social-service workers and almost mental-health workers."

Last Wednesday morning in Chillicothe, Meyers, Ross County Deputy Sheriff J. David Weber and three others sat in a conference room, reviewing police reports about six white men between the ages of 26 and 34 who overdosed the week before. One needed four doses of naloxone to survive.

The officers are part of the Ross County Post Overdose Response Team, known as PORT, which visits the home of each person in the county who overdosed during the prior week. Sometimes family members don't know that their loved one overdosed, but most people are receptive to the intervention, said Teri Minney, the partnership's coordinator.

The group provides information that includes a list of support group meetings, a brochure on how to contact treatment providers and detox centers and a primer on naloxone.

Weber said he and the team are blunt, telling victims that they are playing "Russian roulette." Though the team hopes the person won't use drugs again, it knows they likely will. So it implores them to do so in the presence of others, so someone can call for help.

"This is just one piece of the puzzle," Minney said.

Police must also work as front-line social-service providers in homes where children are present during an overdose.

"We're struggling to get them somewhere safe," Meyers said. "You could send them to grandma's house, but she's also a heroin addict. You have to vet everyone who you send those kids to."

Officials said drugs are taking a particular toll on children. In Martinsburg, W.Va., police have partnered with the Berkeley County Schools and Shepherd University to form the Martinsburg Initiative. It links schools, law enforcement, families and the community to help children who are living in traumatic situations, such as having an incarcerated parent or a history of domestic violence, and connects the families with available resources. Police Chief Maury Richards said it is based on data showing that children who grow up in dysfunctional households are more likely to use drugs.

"Unless we get a handle on this, it could really unravel our entire community and society as a whole," Richards said.

Even run-of-the-mill calls such as shoplifting and car break-ins now have a drug connection, as do more serious ones like robberies. In large cities such as Cincinnati and small towns including Mount Sterling, Ky., calls for overdoses sometimes overwhelm local emergency response systems.

Louisville's emergency medical services are making "overdose run after overdose run," said spokesman Mitchell Burmeister. In February, the system received 52 overdose calls in 32 hours, most of which were believed to be related to heroin or fentanyl.

Authorities say last August provides an example of how a powerful batch of drugs can quickly cause devastation. In Ohio, 174 overdoses were reported in Hamilton County, which

includes Cincinnati, in less than a week. In Charleston, W.Va., 26 people overdosed in a matter of hours, as did 14 in Jennings County, Ind. In Mount Sterling — population 6,900 — at least 18 people overdosed in a matter of hours that month.

Police blame the spikes on a rash of potent synthetic drugs. They include fentanyl and carfentanil, an opiate typically used as a large animal tranquilizer that can kill people when taken in even minuscule amounts.

According to the CDC, the number of drug overdose deaths involving synthetic drugs like fentanyl rose from 8 percent in 2010 to 18 percent in 2015.

Drugs that can kill instantly and massive spikes in overdose calls are the new normal, said Van Ingram, executive director of the Kentucky Office of Drug Control Policy.

"Drugs are being introduced into the illicit drug supply that are more powerful than anything we've ever seen before, and it's taxing our law enforcement resources, our EMS resources, our emergency departments and hospitals, and it's difficult to manage," Ingram said.

These drugs also pose a danger for first responders. Many officers are now carrying extra doses of naloxone to use on officers or K-9s should they accidentally breathe in drugs or handle ones that are particularly potent.

Other departments across the country no longer allow officers to process drugs at crime scenes because of the risk of exposure, instead sending the drugs directly to labs.

In Hartford, Conn., a doctor goes with police on raids so he can treat officers who might encounter drugs; he was on vacation when 11 SWAT officers were exposed to fentanyl and heroin that was atomized by a flash grenade the officers used to burst into a drug stash house, according to Hartford Deputy Chief Brian Foley. Three were sickened and all were sent to the hospital.

In Hamilton County, Ohio, which saw the rash of overdoses blamed on carfentanil last year, 414 people died of a drug overdose, compared with 298 the year before, according to the county coroner's office.

Tom Synan, chief of the Newtown, Ohio, police department and a leader of the Hamilton County Heroin Coalition, said the staggering numbers are difficult because "we are in this job to help people" and often the resources are not there to do it correctly. He said his biggest source of frustration is sitting across from parents of drug addicts knowing there are few resources available that can help their children.

"Law enforcement has been forced to take the lead on this, and we probably are not the best profession to be doing this because our job really is to enforce laws," he said, noting that he has seen family after family torn apart by addiction. He keeps in touch with the children of some who have died. "I never got into police work thinking I'd watch an entire generation die of drugs."

Critical Thinking

1. Police officers are being called out to deal with opioid abusers, which has slightly changed their traditional police officer role to more of a social worker role. Why?

2. How is the opioid crisis, in particular, taking a toll on the nation's children?

3. How is the opioid crisis financially impacting police departments across the nation?

4. What solutions can you propose to ease the burden placed upon law enforcement by the opioid crisis?

Internet References

Centers for Disease Control and Prevention
https://www.cdc.gov/

Drug and Alcohol Dependence
https://www.drugandalcoholdependence.com/

Drug Policy Alliance
http://www.drugpolicy.org/

National Institute on Drug Abuse
https://www.drugabuse.gov/

KATIE ZEZIMA is a national correspondent covering drugs, guns, gambling and vice in America. She covered the 2016 election and the Obama White House for The Washington Post.

Prepared by: Kim Schnurbush, *California State University, Sacramento*
Mark Pullin, *Angelo State University*

Article

Declaring Addiction a Health Crisis Could Change Criminal Justice

The surgeon general's new approach on substance abuse has policy implications for law enforcement.

JULEYKA LANTIGUA-WILLIAMS

Learning Outcomes

After reading this article, you will be able to:

- Discuss the purpose of the criminal-justice system regarding treating addiction.

- Understand the reasons the U.S. Surgeon General has declared substance abuse a public-health crisis in the United States.

- Discuss how treating drug addiction as a health-care issue can be more productive to deter drug use than harsh sentences in the criminal-justice system.

For the first time ever, a sitting U.S. surgeon general has declared substance abuse a public-health crisis. "It's time to change how we view addiction," Vivek Murthy said in a statement last week, which was accompanied by a lengthy report on the issue. "Not as a moral failing, but as a chronic illness that must be treated with skill, urgency and compassion. The way we address this crisis is a test for America."

Murthy's statement is a major victory for those advocates who have long hoped addiction would be viewed through a physical- and mental-health lens. But this new approach—if it were to become widespread—could also profoundly impact the criminal-justice system, where addicts often end up.

Murthy's report provides an update on drug and alcohol users in the country. According to its figures, in the last year alone, about 48 million Americans used or abused illegal or

prescription drugs and 28 million drove under the influence. It also details how 21 million Americans currently suffer from addiction—or as the medical community refers to it, substance-use disorder. Currently, over 300,000 inmates sit in state and federal prisons for convictions related to drugs, according to the Prison Policy

Initiative. A recent study estimates that of the nation's more than 2 million inmates, 65 percent "meet the criteria for substance-abuse addiction."

These numbers have severe ramifications in the criminal-justice system. Scores of those Americans were among the 11 million admissions to local and county jails last year. Tens of thousands lost their driving privileges due to strict state guidelines against driving drunk. Millions served time, were put on probation, entered rehabilitation programs in exchange for reduced sentences, or became further entrenched in the justice system due to repeated violations.

Health professionals and recovery experts, including social psychologist and University of California, Irvine, criminologist Mona Lynch, agree that the criminal-justice system is not the place to treat addiction. According to Lynch, the existing system cannot deliver adequate services and that attempting to integrate health care into the criminal-justice system can lead to negative consequences. "We need to have the investment in public health and treatment programs," said Lynch, who wrote a book on how federal drug laws are used, among other things, to coerce guilty pleas and secure long sentences. "The criminal-justice system is, of course, a really expensive way to deliver health care. The punitive side of it can be counterproductive, particularly for addicts."

According to the surgeon general's report, substance-use disorder costs the country $442 billion annually in health-care and criminal-justice spending, as well as in lost productivity. Lynch told me that relying on criminal law to be "the stick" that keeps addicts in line is not "responsive to the public-health problem or to the person's health problems." And when the criminal-justice system does offer treatment alternatives, they're usually organized so that failures are harshly penalized. If, for example, a treatment participant fails a drug test or misses a court check-in, he or she could face jail time, suspension from the program, or the revocation of other privileges. Lynch said such consequences are antithetical to treatment because they imply a straight line toward recovery. Addressing addiction individually "is not one strike and you're out," she said. "There are going to be failures, there are going to be setbacks. It's a relatively long and arduous process to try and address addiction."

Reformers view unnecessarily punitive federal sentencing guidelines as harmful legal responses to problems that often require medical or therapeutic interventions. Unless those guidelines are altered, a new approach focusing on health would have little practical application. Lynch said that separating the dealer, or "the criminal," from "the user" during sentencing is essentially a distinction without a difference that has resulted in "a system that recycles addicts through jails' revolving doors." That's because designations do nothing to address the underlying issue of addiction: Labels don't get people sober. Lynch said that parsing between dealers and users has been detrimental to getting adequate medical, psychological, and social services to those in need.

Most troubling, the criminal-justice system is often the first institution to "catch" those suffering from substance-use disorders. As a result, many people only receive treatment once the situation is critical—like after getting arrested and involved with the criminal-justice system, or after a medical crisis, such as an overdose. Lynch takes a hard line on the system's capacity to provide care: "I would like to see addiction not go through the criminal-justice system," she said.

"You see that in higher economic strata of our society," she said. "People whose children become addicts and they have resources to mobilize all kinds of private interventions that don't involve the criminal-justice system." People with means can intervene much earlier than others, including by paying for expensive private-treatment facilities or by keeping a loved one safe at home and off the street to limit their potential interactions with law enforcement. It "gets so raced and classed," Lynch said, describing how users in certain ethnic and

economic groups have fewer treatment options and far more legal consequences.

Yet even if state and federal governments take cues from the surgeon general—and begin addressing addiction as a health crisis first—any reforms to the existing criminal-justice system would have immediate, unintended economic effects via institutional competition. "There's now huge, monstrous criminal-justice institutions that have been built over 30 or 40 years in our country at the state and federal level that are going to be resistant to shrinking," Lynch said. If treating addiction as a public-health problem gains more traction—and federal dollars are redirected to health-care programs—then penal "institutions are going to compete to deal with it. They're going to seek money to deal with addiction through the criminal-justice system," she said.

The "starved" mental-health and public-health institutions that would, in advocates' view, be better suited to treat people "are not going to have the same power to say, 'We need resources to be able to do this; we're fit to be able to do this,'" without major federal buy-in, Lynch said. Setting up any statewide or national approach for diverting addicts into treatment and away from jails is a massive undertaking that will probably not happen in the near future. But there are steps that towns and cities can take in that direction.

One of them is to offer crisis-intervention training for officers so they can identify mental-health crises during emergency calls. Several cities, like San Antonio, Texas, have found this approach successful in reducing arrests, identifying repeat users, and reducing housing costs in their facilities. But with over 18,000 police departments in the country, the cumulative effect of local efforts will be limited if the message that addiction is a health issue—and not a criminal one—does not become part of the modus operandi for criminal-justice practitioners. And it will be especially limited if the federal government, more than any other body, does not get fully on board.

Critical Thinking

1. What is the purpose of treating drug addiction through health care rather than the criminal-justice system?

2. Are drug abusers more likely to trick the system in a health-care treatment facility rather than a correctional facility?

3. Are "labels" as a drug or alcohol abuser an effective deterrent? Why or why not?

4. How does the 4th Amendment relate to treating drug offenders medically?

Internet References

BMC Public Health
https://bmcpublichealth.biomedcentral.com/

CATO Institute
https://www.cato.org/publications

Drug Policy Alliance
http://www.drugpolicy.org/

JULEYKA LANTIGUA-WILLIAMS is a former staff writer at The Atlantic, where she covered criminal justice.

Unit 6

UNIT

Prepared by: Kim Schnurbush, *California State University, Sacramento*
Mark Pullin, *Angelo State University*

Creating and Sustaining Effective Drug Control Policy

The drug problem consistently competes with all major public policy issues, including the wars in Iraq and Afghanistan, the economy, education, and foreign policy. Drug abuse is a serious national medical issue with profound social and legal consequences. Formulating and implementing effective drug control policy is a troublesome task. Some would argue that the consequences of policy failures have been worse than the problems that the policies were attempting to address. Others would argue that although the world of shaping drug policy is an imperfect one, the process has worked generally well as could be expected. The majority of Americans believe that failures and breakdowns in the fight against drug abuse have occurred in spite of various drug policies, not because of them. Although the last few years have produced softening attitudes and alternatives for adjudicating cases of simple possession and use, the get-tough stay-tough enforcement policies directed at illegal drug trafficking remain firmly in place and widely supported. Policy formulations are not a process of aimless wandering.

Various levels of government have responsibility for responding to problems of drug abuse. At the center of most policy debate is the premise that the manufacture, possession, use, and distribution of psychoactive drugs without government authorization is illegal. The federal posture of prohibition is an important emphasis on state and local policymaking. Federal drug policy is, however, significantly linked to state-by-state data, which suggests that illicit drug, alcohol, and tobacco use vary substantially among states and regions. The current federal drug strategy began in 2001 and set the goals of reducing drug use by young persons by 25 percent over five years. In 2008, President Bush announced that drug use by the population in this age group was down by 24 percent. President Obama has continued the basic strategic constructs of the Bush policy. Core priorities of the overall plan continue to stop drug use before it starts, heal America's drug users, and disrupt the illegal market. These three core goals are reinforced by objectives outlined in

a policy statement produced by the White House Office of Drug Control Policy. All three goals reflect budget expenditures related to meeting goals of the overall policy. The current drug control policy, in terms of budget allocations, continues to provide for over $1.5 billion to prevent use before it starts, largely through education campaigns, which encourage a cultural shift away from drugs, and more than $3.4 billion to heal America's users. Each year produces modifications to the plan as a result of analysis of trends and strategy impacts. Allocations for interdiction, largely a result of the attempt to secure the borders and frustrate allegiances between drug traffickers and terrorists, remain the most significant component of the budget at $10 billion.

One exception to prevailing views that generally support drug prohibition is the softening of attitudes regarding criminal sanctions that historically applied to cases of simple possession and use of drugs. There is much public consensus that incarcerating persons for these offenses is unjustified unless they are related to other criminal conduct. The federal funding of drug court programs remains a priority with more than $38 million dedicated to state and local operation. Drug courts provide alternatives to incarceration by using the coercive power of the court to force abstinence and alter behavior through a process of escalating sanctions, mandatory drug testing, and outpatient programs. Successful rehabilitation accompanies the reentry to society as a citizen, not a felon. The drug court program exists as one important example of policy directed at treating users and deterring them from further involvement in the criminal justice system. Drug courts are now in place in all 50 states.

The majority of Americans express the view that legalizing, and in some cases even decriminalizing, dangerous drugs is a bad idea. The fear of increased crime, increased drug use, and the potential threat to children are the most often state reasons. Citing the devastating consequences of alcohol and tobacco use, most Americans question society's ability to use any addictive, mind-altering drug responsibly. Currently, the public favors supply reduction, demand reduction, and an increased emphasis on prevention, treatment, and rehabilitation as effective strategies in combating the drug problem. Shaping public policy is a critical function that greatly relies upon public input. The policymaking apparatus is influenced by public opinion, and public opinion is in turn influenced by public policy. When the president refers to drugs as threats to national security, the impact on public opinion is tremendous. Currently, record amounts of opium are being produced in Afghanistan, and the implications for its providing support for the Taliban and terrorism are clear. Opium production in Southwest Asia, an entrenched staple in the region's overall economic product, continues as a priority of U.S. national security. The resulting implications for sustaining enforcement-oriented U.S. drug policy are also clear; and in the minds of most Americans, they are absolutely necessary. The U.S. Department of State alone will receive $336 million for alternative crop production, diplomacy, interdiction, and enforcement.

Although the prevailing characteristic of most current drug policy still reflects a punitive, "get tough" approach to control, an added emphasis on treating and rehabilitating offenders is visible in policy changes occurring over the past 10 years. Correctional systems are reflecting with greater consistency the view that drug treatment made available to inmates is a critical component of rehabilitation. The California Department of Corrections, the largest in the nation, was recently named the California Department of Corrections and Rehabilitation. A prisoner with a history of drug abuse, who receives no drug treatment while in custody, is finally being recognized as a virtual guarantee to reoffend. In 2006, the National Institute of Drug Abuse published the first federal guidelines for administering drug treatment to criminal justice populations.

Another complicated aspect of creating national as well as local drug policy is consideration of the growing body of research on the subject. The past 20 years have produced numerous public and private investigations, surveys, and conclusions relative to the dynamics of drug use in U.S. society. Although a historical assessment of the influence of research on policy produces indirect relationships, policy decisions of the last few years and be directly related to evidence-based research findings and not just political views. One example is the consistently increasing commitment to treatment. This commitment comes as a direct result of research related to progress achieved in treating and rehabilitating users. Treatment, in terms of dollars spent, can compete with all other components of drug control policy.

One important issue affecting and sometimes complicating the research/policymaking relationship is that the policymaking community, at all levels of government, is largely composed of persons of diverse backgrounds, professional capacities, and political interests. Some are elected officials, others are civil servants, and many are private citizens from the medical, educational, and research communities. In some cases, such as with alcohol and tobacco, powerful industry players assert a tremendous influence on policy. As you read on, consider the new research-related applications for drug policy, such as those related to the rehabilitation of incarcerated drug offenders.

Article

Prepared by: Kim Schnurbush, *California State University, Sacramento*
Mark Pullin, *Angelo State University*

Hawaii's Radical Drug Use Experiment

KEVIN SABET

Learning Outcomes

After reading this article, you will be able to:

- Describe the HOPE Program.
- Discuss the theory that explains Hawaii's HOPE Program's success.
- Explain the trends with alternative sentencing.

When I was a kid, my mom would often ask me to clean my room. Most of the time, I did it with little fuss. But on those days when I was playing *The Legend of Zelda* or busy shooting hoops with friends, she would use modest and credible threats to get me to act—and they almost always worked. "Kevin," she would say, "If you don't clean up your room right now, you can't have friends over tonight and you can forget about going to that movie you wanted to see tomorrow. So get to work!" That got me every time. The godfather of public policy, Thomas Schelling, used to say that the best threat is the one which is *never carried out*. And my mom was a pro at making that happen.

In my work with criminal populations, I have learned that criminals are a lot like kids: both groups have poor impulse control, a propensity to attribute their misfortunes in life to either bad luck or actions beyond their own control, and a tendency to value immediate gratification even if delaying gratification would result in a bigger payoff. So for both kids and crooks, psychologists and criminologists have long known that credible threats—usually swift, certain, but modest sanctions that are imposed very soon after the time of offense—are much more effective at changing behavior than, say, severe threats to be carried out in the distant future (or not carried out at all). Therefore it comes as no surprise that the largest segment of our criminal justice system—those in the community on probation or parole—often do not heed severe threats issued by the bench. Instead, they go on reoffending at the cost of billions of dollars to society. They are expected to change their behavior after hearing this from the equivalent of mom: "If you don't clean up your room right now, there is a 45 percent chance that in 19½ you will be grounded for three whole years!" It is these kinds of threats that have resulted in today's broken probation system.

That is why a once obscure program in Hawaii, aptly titled HOPE (Hawaii's Opportunity Probation with Enforcement), has received a lot of notice lately. Tired of seeing the same offenders recidivating in his Hawaiian circuit court, Judge Steve Alm decided that he was going to start getting smart about sanctioning his probationers. Applying what we know about deterrence, he started issuing *swift, certain, and modest* sanctions *every time* one of his probationers reoffended. Beginning with a formal warning hearing, Judge Alm openly explained to his probationers that continued violations would not be tolerated and that each violation would result in an immediate jail stay. To track their behavior, offenders were assigned a color and had to call in every morning to see if their color was mentioned by the automated system. If it was, they had to report at once for a drug test; no shows were treated as positives and a warrant was immediately issued. Reoffenders appeared before Judge Alm within 1–2 days and were offered treatment first. If they refused, they immediately spent the next two days (not years or decades) in jail (weekends for employed probationers). After they served their time, they continued in the program, with sanctions slowly escalating (repeat offenders were refered to a drug court or other treatment option). Skeptics worried that without mandating treatment for all probationers at the start, many would reoffend and take up drugs again. Others were concerned that the jail population would skyrocket—now that, you know, the law was *actually being carried out*.

What resulted was nothing short of revolutionary. Transforming the criminal justice system in a way unseen since drug courts (which also owe their success to applying these principles of deterrence), HOPE shattered myths about sentence length, drug use behavior, and the ability of offenders and public administrators to change their ways. In a randomly controlled trial, HOPE far outperformed traditional probation. Missed appointments and positive drug tests fell by over 80%. Positive findings persisted for those who were in the program longer. Jail stays decreased, and real dollars were saved. The traditional probation group—surprise—found no improvement in drug use, and their percentage of missed appointments actually increased. HOPE probationers viewed their sentences as fair, crime fell (arrests for new crimes was cut in half, to be exact), and, best of all, people's lives turned around. Additionally, scarce treatment slots were reserved for those with the most serious addictions (those who could not stop through HOPE). A 1 year randomized control experiment done by the National Institute of Justice confirmed these results.

HOPE may be Hawaii's best export since pineapples. Faced with overcrowding criminal justice systems and continued drug-related crime, several jurisdictions around the country have implemented similar programs. In Alaska, the Probationer Accountability with Certain Enforcement (PACE) program reduced drug use and helped offenders stay out of court. Results are now in from the Washington Intensive Supervision Program (WISP) program in Washington State: Offenders supervised under the intensive model were two-thirds less likely to test positive in randomly assigned drug tests than offenders in a control group. In Delaware, the White House/Justice Department funded Decide Your Time program looks promising, as does Arizona's Swift, Accountable, Fair Enforcement (SAFE) program. This pioneering approach is also being applied in California, Alabama, Arkansas, Georgia, Kentucky, Louisiana, Montana, and Virginia. The Office of National Drug Control Policy (ONDCP) and National Institute of Justice (NIJ) just announced four new HOPE (renamed nationally as the "Honest Opportunity Probation with Enforcement" program) sites: Clackamas County, Oregon; Essex County, Massachusetts;

Saline County, Arkansas; and Tarrant County, Texas. We owe much to Directors Gil Kerlikowske (ONDCP) and John Laub (NIJ) for making that happen in this funding environment.

While applying HOPE principles to probation programs around the country is new, the underpinnings of the program are well established. The first Director of the National Institute on Drug Abuse, Bob DuPont, a national treasure, utilized similar strategies with resounding success among a population of drug-using physicians through the Physician Health Program. Additionally, as mentioned, thousands of drug courts across the country are predicated on swift and certain sanctions, combined with treatment, and have been extremely successful in reducing drug use and reshaping lives and communities.

HOPE and similar programs like drug courts shatter the myth that the criminal justice system can play no positive role in changing behavior, lowering drug use, and making our communities safer. The only real issue that remains is whether those we entrust with running the criminal justice system—the Steve Alms of the world—will try something new or stick with business as usual. As an evaluation of a HOPE-like program once concluded, "Changing addict behavior is easy. Changing judge behavior is hard." Here's to having HOPE that change comes sooner rather than later.

Critical Thinking

1. Discuss at least two programs similar to the HOPE program.
2. Identify the key elements of success of HOPE and similar programs.
3. Discuss the challenges of HOPE and similar programs.

Internet References

National Criminal Justice Reference Service
https://www.ncjrs.gov/
The Sentencing Project
http://www.sentencingproject.org/template/page.cfm?id5128

Article   Prepared by: Kim Schnurbush, *California State University, Sacramento*
                                         Mark Pullin, *Angelo State University*

Company Denies Drug to Dying Child

Elizabeth Cohen

Learning Outcomes

After reading this article, you will be able to:

- Understand compassionate use as it relates to the use of drugs not approved by the FDA.
- Recognize the "red tape" some patients have to go through in order to receive a treatment that works for their medical condition.

In an intensive care unit in Memphis, a virus ravages the body of a 7-year-old who's in heart and kidney failure. He vomits blood several times an hour as his family gathers in vigil.

In a cabinet in Durham, North Carolina, there's a drug that could likely help Josh Hardy, but the drug company won't give it to him. They're adamant that spending the time to help Josh and others like him will slow down their efforts to get this drug on the market.

Helping Josh, they say, means hurting others.

When asked how he will feel if Josh dies—and he's in critical condition, so sadly that could happen soon—the president of the company that makes the drug doesn't hesitate to answer.

"Horrible," said Kenneth Moch. He would feel horrible and heartbroken.

But still, he said there's no way he's going to change his mind. There's no way he's going to give Josh this drug.

"We're Begging Them"

It's called "compassionate use," but sometimes it feels anything but compassionate.

Here's the way it works: According to the Food and Drug Administration, if someone has a serious or immediately life-threatening disease and has tried and failed other available treatments, they can ask a drug company for an experimental drug, one that they're still studying and has not yet been approved by the FDA.

Companies often say yes: The FDA approved 974 compassionate use arrangements in fiscal year 2013.

In Cancer Drug Battle, Both Sides Appeal to Ethics

But pharmaceutical companies often say no, as they did to Josh Hardy.

"Our son will die without this drug," said Todd Hardy, Josh's father. "We're begging them to give it to us."

So now, like many families, the Hardys have turned to the media, Facebook, and change.org to pressure the drug company to change its mind.

Countless members of "Josh's army" have responded with angry tweets to @chimerix, telling them to "open their hearts," asking the executives how they can sleep at night.

"Everyone is watching," one tweeter warned the company. Others have tweeted out the e-mail addresses of the company's board members. Chimerix executives say they've received physical threats.

Moch, the company president, has read these tweets and said he is heartbroken, but the issue is complex and unsuitable for a 144-long character debate.

At its very simplest, this is it: Chimerix is going full speed ahead to get the drug on the market hopefully by the end of 2016, and if they spend time and money on compassionate use cases, it would greatly hinder their effort to get the drug, brincidofovir, on the market and available to everyone.

The company would have to dish out $50,000 per compassionate-use patient, since insurance doesn't usually pay for experimental drugs, Moch said. And perhaps even more important than the money, it would divert manpower in this 50-person company, since they'd have to handle the requests and then get the patient's records and follow up with them, as required by the FDA.

"If this were just one patient wanting this drug, then this would be a very different question," he said. "But it's yes to all or no to all."

From 2009 to 2012, the company did give out the drug under compassionate use to 451 patients, Moch said, but at least at that time, the information gleaned from those 451 compassionate use patients was helpful to the Chimerix study and helped move the science along. But currently doctors don't really learn very much, if anything, from compassionate use patients, so the patients don't help get the drug to market.

Beat cancer four times

Josh's journey began when he was diagnosed with a rare form of kidney cancer at 9 months old. Over the years, cancer turned up in his thymus, lung, and bone marrow, and each time Josh beat it.

But a bone marrow transplant left Josh without much of an immune system, and in February doctors diagnosed him with an adenovirus that spread through his body.

They gave him an antiviral drug, an intravenous form of brincidofovir, but it ravaged his kidneys.

His doctors at St. Jude's Children's Research Hospital said not to give up hope. Since they'd been part of the brincidofovir studies, they'd seen how in sometimes just a week or two, the the oral form of the drug could get rid of an adenovirus without damaging the kidneys. Now all they had to do was ask the company that makes brincidofovir: Chimerix, Inc.

On February 12, the St. Jude's doctors called a Chimerix executive, Dr. Marion Morrison, and asked for permission to use brincidofovir. She said no.

On March 5, the doctors asked again. Two days later they got an answer by e-mail from another executive, Dr. Herve Mommeja-Marin, who said the company was not "in a position to provide drug for this and other subjects in similar circumstances due to a limited inventory and our limited resources."

He holds our son's life in his hands

Moch wants you to know that he has children of his own, and if his child had an aggressive adenovirus like Josh, he'd be doing the same thing as Todd and Aimee Hardy.

"There are no words to express our compassion for this young boy and his family and what they're going through," he said.

Art Caplan, a bioethicist at NYU Langone Medical Center, said he feels for both the Hardys and for Moch.

"We can't ask the company to turn into a philanthropy or their investors will back out," he said.

It's not just the $50,000 per patient that might make investors squeamish, Caplan said, but compassionate cases can make a drug look bad. By definition, compassionate use patients are extremely sick, and might not do well with the drug. Companies have to report that poor outcome to the FDA in its application to market the drug.

Perhaps there's another way to handle compassionate use requests, Caplan suggests. Perhaps a company like Chimerix could agree to give the drug only to the very most dire cases, and put a cap on the number of patients they help.

"They might want to open the door a little more broadly," he said. "They might want to show a little compassion."

But right now, Chimerix stands firm that their compassionate use program is almost completely over.

"We've had employees who ask for the drug for family members who are close to death, and the answer has been no," said Mommeja-Marin, the Chimerix executive.

But that's not good enough for the Hardys.

"He holds our son's life in his hands," Todd Hardy said. "This is just beyond belief to me."

Critical Thinking

1. If funding doesn't exist to test and manufacture a drug, some patients will die. Should drug companies be able to give experimental drugs to patients, as long as patients are well aware of the risks and sign waivers?

2. Should compassionate use of pharmaceutical drugs even be considered if a drug hasn't been approved by the FDA?

Internet References

United States Food and Drug Administration
http://www.fda.gov/
Mayo Clinic
http://www.mayoclinic.org/healthy-living/consumer-health/expert-answers/compassionate-use/faq-20058036

Prepared by: Kim Schnurbush, *California State University, Sacramento*
Mark Pullin, *Angelo State University*

Article

Judges to Explore Whether 'Habitual Drunkards' Can Appeal Deportation

KIMBERLY LEONARD

Learning Outcomes

After reading this article, you will be able to:

- Understand how the 9th Circuit Court of Appeals in California found regarding classification of people with chronic alcoholism and how it applies to illegal immigrants.

- Explore how alcoholism, as a disease, compares to other diseases such as heart disease, cancer, diabetes, and HIV.

- Discuss the impact alcoholism may have to future illegal immigrants.

A FEDERAL APPEALS COURT is reviewing a case that will determine whether someone who entered the U.S. illegally and is a "habitual drunkard" can be deemed ineligible to fight deportation under a 50-year-old statute that says such people lack "good moral character."

A three-judge panel of the 9th U.S. Circuit Court of Appeals in California ruled 2-1 in March that classifying people with chronic alcoholism as immoral was unconstitutional, arguing that alcoholism is a medical disability. They determined that the law violates equal-protection guarantees under the Constitution that also apply to non-U.S. citizens.

The full court on Wednesday agreed to consider the case, which follows a growing consensus among medical providers that addiction should be treated as a disease rather than a moral or justice issue.

Federal law allows the attorney general to cancel the deportation of someone who entered the country illegally or to permit such a person to depart voluntarily if they have good moral character. Other than habitual drinking, the law specifies other behaviors that would make people ineligible for such

consideration, including if they engage in gambling, serious felonies, genocide or torture.

The case centers on Salomon Ledezma-Cosino, who came to the U.S. illegally from Mexico in 1997. He has eight children, five of whom are U.S. citizens, and supports his family by working in the construction industry.

The court filings show that Ledezma-Cosino drank an average of a liter of tequila per day for a decade and has alcoholism, acute alcoholic hepatitis and decompensated cirrhosis of the liver. He also was convicted of a DUI.

His lawyers submitted a supplemental brief to the panel judges arguing that it was irrational to distinguish between habitual drunkards and people who have heart disease, cancer, diabetes, syphilis and HIV.

"The government is wrong," Judge Stephen Reinhardt, who was appointed by President Jimmy Carter, wrote for the majority in the panel ruling. "Just as a statute targeting people who exhibit manic and depressive behavior would be, in effect, targeting people with bipolar disorder ... a statute targeting people who habitually and excessively drink alcohol is, in effect, targeting individuals with chronic alcoholism."

In his dissent, Judge Richard R. Clifton, who was appointed by George W. Bush, argued that alcoholism was different from being a habitual drunkard and said Ledezma-Cosino must have had some degree of free will because he was eventually able to quit drinking. Unlike other medical conditions, he pointed out, alcoholism is tied to public safety issues, including abuse or motor vehicle accidents.

"The majority assumes that a person found to be a habitual drunkard is in that state only because of factors beyond his control, such that it is irrational to hold him accountable for it," Clifton wrote. "But chronic alcoholics do not have to be habitual drunkards."

Critical Thinking

1. What did the three-panel of the 9th U.S. Circuit Court of Appeals in California find regarding the classification of people with chronic alcoholism? How does it apply to an illegal immigrant?

2. On what grounds did Ledezma-Cosino's lawyers file a supplemental brief?

3. Does alcoholism differ from other diseases, such as heart disease, cancer, diabetes, and HIV? If so, how does it differ? If not, why?

4. What impact might this case have in the future with regard to illegal immigrants who are alcoholics?

Internet References

Drug and Alcohol Dependence
https://www.drugandalcoholdependence.com/

National Institute of Alcohol Abuse and Alcoholism
https://www.niaaa.nih.gov/publications

WebMD
https://www.webmd.com/

KIMBERLY LEONARD is a former health care reporter for the News division at U.S. News. Previously she worked in Health Rankings as a multimedia producer and reporter. You can follow her on Twitter, connect with her on LinkedIn, circle her on Google+ or e-mail her at kleonard@usnews.com.

Article

Prepared by: Kim Schnurbush, *California State University, Sacramento*
Mark Pullin, *Angelo State University*

Some People Still Need Opioids

The crackdown on pain medication prescribing is intended to help the addiction crisis—but it's leaving chronic pain patients in untenable situations.

STEFAN KERTESZ AND SALLY SATEL

Learning Outcomes

After reading this article, you will be able to:

- Discuss how reducing the availability of pain medication is leaving patients with chronic pain.

- Understand the results of limited pain medication prescriptions by doctors leaving them in ethical dilemmas.

- Discuss how over-prescribing pain medication pills in the past has led to overcorrection by state and federal health authorities creating restricting limits on these medications.

On July 26, Todd Graham, 56, a well-respected rehabilitation specialist in Mishawaka, Indiana, lost his life. Earlier that day, a woman complaining of chronic pain had come to Graham's office in hope of receiving an opioid such as Percocet, Vicodin, or long-acting OxyContin. He reportedly told her that opioids were not an appropriate first-line treatment for long-term pain—a view now shared by professionals—and she, reportedly, accepted his opinion. Her husband, however, became irate. Later, he tracked down the doctor and shot him twice in the head.

This horrific story has been showcased to confirm that physicians who specialize in chronic pain confront real threats from patients or their loved ones, particularly regarding opioid prescriptions. But Graham's death also draws attention to another fraught development: In the face of an ever-worsening opioid crisis, physicians concerned about fueling the epidemic are increasingly heeding warnings and feeling pressured to constrain prescribing in the name of public health. As they do

so, abruptly ending treatment regimens on which many chronic pain patients have come to rely, they end up leaving some patients in agonizing pain or worse.

Last month, one of us was contacted by a 66-year old orthopedic surgeon in Northern California, desperate to find a doctor for herself. Since her early 30s, Dr. R suffered from an excruciating condition called Interstitial Cystitis (IC). She described it as a "feeling like I had a lit match in my bladder and urethra." Her doctor placed her on methadone and she continued in her medical practice on a relatively low dose, for 34 years. As Dr. R told one of us, "Methadone has saved my life. Not to sound irrational, but I don't think I would have survived without it." Then a crisis: "Unfortunately for me, the feds are clamping down on docs prescribing opiates. My doctor decided that she did not want to treat me anymore, didn't give me a last prescription, and didn't wait until I found another pain doctor who would help me." For the past 30 years, Dr. R has been an advocate for better treatment of IC and reports "many suicides in the IC patient population due to the severity of the pain."

Thankfully, Dr. R found someone to treat her. Doug Hale, 53, of Vermont was less fortunate. On Oct. 11, 2016, he died by suicide.

"My husband Doug took his own life after being cut off abruptly from his long-term therapy for intractable chronic pain," his wife, Tammi, wrote in a survey collected by a rehabilitation scholar. His pain was caused by interstitial cystitis, severe migraines, and a back condition. A doctor had prescribed methadone and oxycodone since 2001, according to Tammi Hale, but then "said he would not risk his [medical] license." Her husband "lasted six weeks, all the while desperately searching for help" but he made a conscious choice not to pursue alcohol or illegal drugs. He said he wanted to live to see his grandchildren and to grow old with me, his wife wrote, "but the pain drove him to suicide as he could not bear a life of intractable pain."

So, he waited until his wife was out running errands, went to the far end of their backyard, and shot himself. Doug Hale left a suicide note stating that no one but his wife had helped him and that "the doctors were all puppets who basically just wanted to cover their own backs well."

In 2016, a physician wrote a searing personal account of losing his sister, a chronic pain patient, in the *Journal of the American Medical Association*. William Weeks of Dartmouth Geisel School of Medicine, described Hailey's death. A "caring, devoted, and motivated woman," Haley injured her back at 35 when she was thrown from a horse. Her back never got better, and she qualified for federal disability payments. Over 14 years she received opioids and sedatives from a single pain physician, reaching high doses of both. When illness struck her physician, he retired, leaving her with a one-month prescription and a list of doctors.

As Weeks wrote, "My sister made appointments with several of the physicians [but at] every appointment, she was told that the physician would be unwilling to prescribe her current medication regimen. At every appointment, she was told that she would need to dramatically reduce her use of opioids and benzodiazepines. At every appointment, she felt that the medical establishment, which had prescribed these medications for a decade and a half, had abandoned her. Having not found a physician to manage her medications, she tried to wean herself, if only to extend her medication supply." She accelerated her alcohol use, wound up in an emergency room—and then a jail cell where she died, six weeks after her last prescription. Finally, there is the anguished report from Mark Ibsen, a doctor based in Montana. On Aug. 4, he posted a video of himself with a distraught patient. "This patient is suicidal due to sudden severe cuts in her medications," reads the tagline. Ibsen, who is currently entwined in a legal battle over his own practice of prescribing opioids to people with chronic pain, explains the urgency:

> This is Kirsten. She's here for a cannabis card. And we're going to approve her. She has been on chronic pain medication. And the reason I want to show you this is that she can't move her neck. She is operating stiffly. She lost all her muscles in her neck, when she had hardware placed by a doctor and it got infected, and she has had chronic pain since then. She has been on opiates for 11+ years. She is suddenly weaning, due to her doctor's insistence. Just see your scar back here. That's her scar. And this lady is in agony... She is on a third of her morphine and

> a third of her oxycodone. She is suicidal. And she has been abandoned by the medical profession. ... And we just talked about how if she were an animal, we would euthanize her for this kind of suffering... So I am sending out a plea. I don't know what I am pleading for, except this lady is suicidal, and this is a preventable suicide. If she could get her opiates, she wouldn't be trying to kill herself. ...This is a crime scene... as this lady deteriorates and gets more and more suicidal. Senator Tester can you help us?

The ordeals of Dr. R, Doug Hale, Hailey Weeks, and Kristin are being replicated across the country. Every week, one of us receives notice of suicides and overdoses by patients across the country who are distraught in the wake of having their dosages reduced. Eighteen months ago, Kertesz cared for a patient who had shot himself in the hand in the parking lot of a local hospital after his primary care doctor stopped maintaining even stable patients on opioids. That doctor had bought into a fallacy that's been circulating medical practices: that the Centers for Disease Control and Prevention said all prescribing should stop.

It is no secret that one contributing factor to the current opioid crisis is the overreliance on and, at least in retrospect, irresponsible use of opioid-based pain medication. Promiscuous prescribing by physicians gained momentum in the early 1990s and continued for much of the next decade. Aggressive marketing by makers of long-acting painkillers, along with unfounded reassurances that they were safe, played a role in the explosion of prescribing—as did the culture of medical practice which rewarded hospitals based on patient satisfaction ratings, hurried visits, and a dearth of ready insurance-covered alternatives.

It should be noted that the chief risk of liberal prescribing—that is, giving a month's worth of pills when two days were needed; prescribing opioids when extra-strength aspirin and a heating pad would do—was not so much that the patient for whom painkillers would become addicted or overdose. That can happen, particularly when the patient is also depressed, chronically anxious, or has a history of substance abuse, but it is not especially common: "Rates of carefully diagnosed addiction have averaged less than 8 percent [of patients receiving prescriptions] in published studies," a 2016 review in the *New England Journal of Medicine* found. Others offer figures of 0.7 percent to 6 percent, a figure cited by the CDC itself. While those figures are high enough to merit a serious doctor-patient conversation, the bigger danger has always been that excess medication was feeding the rivers of pills coursing through many neighborhoods, and that as more painkillers circulated, more opportunities arose for nonpatients to obtain them, abuse them, and die.

As the pill problem has grown, physicians, medical centers, and state health authorities sought to bring prescribing under better control with education, new norms, and prescription registries that pharmacists and doctors could use to detect patients who "doctor shopped" for painkillers and even forged prescriptions. To a welcome degree, this worked: Since 2010, when opioid prescribing peaked, painkiller-related overdose deaths have begun to decline. (Now, heroin and illicit fentanyl are responsible for most opioid-related deaths.) Seventeen states have passed laws or regulations that limit doses or duration for acute pain, and several federal bills are under consideration. Last year, the American Medical Association recommended that pain be removed as a "fifth vital sign" in professional medical standards, another attempt to limit the overprescribing of opioid pain medication.

The pendulum has swung back in the other direction. We are now experiencing the painful backlash to overzealous prescribing of opioid painkillers (that was itself a backlash to the under-treatment of unremitting noncancer pain). The bad news is that many patients treated with high opioid regimens have been caught in the crossfire. Amid regulations, pharmacy payment restrictions, and intimations that doctors are the major culprits in this epidemic, doctors are increasingly sensing pressure to reduce doses, even among patients who are benefiting from the medication and using it responsibly.

On Oct. 1, for example, Colorado's Medicaid requirement on dose-lowering goes into effect. It requires physicians to reduce the number of painkillers already being prescribed to patients with chronic pain to a one-size-fits-all threshold. Exception clauses do exist but given the notorious inefficiency of state bureaucracy and the priming of physician anxiety lest they not act, more needless suffering may well be an unintended fallout.

What's more, there is no consensus among physicians on the proper role of opioids in the management of chronic pain. There is a "civil war" between clinicians who treat pain, according to Daniel B. Carr, president of the American Academy of Pain Medicine. "One group believes the primary goal of pain treatment is curtailing opioid prescribing," he explained. "The other group looks at the disability, the human suffering, and the expense of chronic pain."

The debate would recede if only there were reliable data to guide physicians. But the wisdom of involuntary reduction is not backed by evidence, according to a recent review in the *Annals of Internal Medicine* titled "Patient Outcome in Dose Reduction or Discontinuation in Long Term Opioid Therapy." Comprehensive longitudinal data regarding opioids' benefits in chronic pain patients is mostly lacking, as is the case for nearly all alternatives.

The 2016 Guideline for Prescribing Opioids for Chronic Pain from the CDC was introduced to provide general principles for how to treat people with chronic pain. It does not endorse mandated reduction. Instead the guideline indicates, correctly, that opioids should rarely be a first option for chronic pain. Indeed, some patients now on chronic treatment might have been successfully directed toward alternative remedies, such as physical therapy, anti-convulsant drugs, localized injections, or electrical stimulation when they first became ill, diverting them from opioids in the first place.

The guideline also recommends that doctors carefully weigh the risks and benefits of maintaining the current doses of opioids in patients already on them. This means, to us, that doctors should discuss reductions with patients on long-term opioids, offer other options, and proceed with very slow tapering if the patient is interested. It turns out, in fact, that some patients welcome the chance to reduce the dose and even feel more alert once this is done. Nonetheless, there exists a contingent for whom only opioids work and who seem to benefit at a stable dose.

We seem to have come, in a tragic way, full circle. Doctors, in particular, have been open in acknowledging their role in the opioid crisis and are trying to balance appropriate prescribing with a duty to treat pain in an effective and compassionate way. Their challenge today is the mirror image of the balancing act they tried to perform back in the 1990s, when efforts to compensate undertreatment of pain gained momentum and led to overcorrection.

Everyone is trying to do the right thing, but the system sometimes fails patients who need opioids to manage chronic pain. As physicians negotiate this uneasy terrain, they need more data, less ideology—no matter how well-intentioned—and a case-by-case mentality. Until then, the clinical anecdotes that are accumulating should serve as powerful cautionary tales.

Critical Thinking

1. Where is the balance between those who need pain medications and the overuse of the same? Can there be an equilibrium reached?

2. Should opioids be unrestricted to medical and scientific research? Where should restrictions rest to control abuse?

3. Is aggressive marketing by the makers of long-acting painkillers, with unfounded reassurances that they are safe, to blame for steep rise in the use of painkillers over the past 20 years?

4. Should pain medications be prescribed in limited numbers to reduce selling of "excess" pills? What is an adequate number of pills at one time?

Internet References

Principles of Drug Addiction Treatment: A Research-Based Guide
www.drugabuse.gov/PODAT/PODATIndex.html

Substance Abuse and Mental Health Services Administration
https://www.samhsa.gov

U.S. National Institutes of Health's National Library of Medicine (NIH/NLM)
https://www.ncbi.nlm.nih.gov/pmc/

WebMD
https://www.webmd.com/

Article

Prepared by: Kim Schnurbush, *California State University, Sacramento*
Mark Pullin, *Angelo State University*

Illegal Drug Laws: Clearing a 50-Year-Old Obstacle to Research

DAVID NUTT

Learning Outcomes

After reading this article, you will be able to:

- Discuss how many drugs are made illegal to reduce their availability and how this hinders scientific and medical research

- Understand the different chemical structures in illegal drugs can be used to create medications to further pharmacology.

- Discuss how simple redefinition of certain drugs by the UN will allow hospitals and medical research institutions to develop and test drugs easier

Introduction

Many drugs are made "illegal" in an attempt to reduce their availability and so their harms. This control occurs at both national and international levels—in the latter case, in the United Nations conventions that make a whole range of drugs from cannabis to heroin "illegal." Many people are aware of the challenges to this system of control in terms of human rights abuses by those who seek to implement a prohibitionist approach to drug control, as well as the failure of, and massive collateral damage from, the "War on Drugs" that is currently being waged to stop drug use (http://www.lse.ac.uk/IDEAS/publications/reports/pdf/LSE-IDEAS-DRUGS-REPORT-FINAL-WEB.pdf). Less well known are the perverse restrictions that these laws have had on pharmacology and therapeutics research. Here I will show how they have led to censoring of life science and medical research, with disastrous consequences that have lasted for more than 50 years and counting.

Recently additional controls have started to be developed, provoked by the fear of so-called "legal highs." These are drugs that mimic the actions of controlled drugs but are of different chemical structures, so they fall outside the UN conventions or local laws. So, for example, the Republic of Ireland has now banned the sale of any chemical that might be used recreationally, a move that if enforced could stop all pharmaceutical research and development in the country. In the United States, city and state governments often move to outlaw novel drugs before the federal government believes it has sufficient evidence to make that determination. Some have been extreme in their lack of understanding of pharmacology. For example, a bill in Maryland would have outlawed any compound with any binding to any cannabinoid receptor, with no mention of thresholds for binding affinity, whether the ligand had agonist or antagonist efficacy, or whether actions at other receptor sites might moderate overall abuse potential (http://mgaleg.maryland.gov/2013RS/bills/sb/sb0109f.pdf). This demonstrates a very extreme version of prohibition, in which molecular entities that have yet to exist are deemed Schedule 1, as if we had absolute ability to perfectly predict the activity of a novel chemical structure.

Drug Control Laws

Most national laws controlling "illegal" drugs are based on the UN Single Convention on Narcotic Drugs (1961) and the Convention on Psychotropic Substances (1971) that define a range of substances that are supposedly sufficiently harmful to be removed from the usual sales regulations (see Table 1). They are made "illegal," which means that punishments are implemented for sale and, in most cases, possession. Some of these can be very severe; e.g., some countries have the death penalty for personal possession of heroin and other opioids [1].

However, many "illegal" drugs have medicinal uses: for example, opioids for pain, amphetamines for narcolepsy and attention deficit hyperactivity disorder (ADHD), and even cocaine for local blood control and anaesthesia in ear nose and throat (ENT) surgery. In most Western countries there is an attempt to make the medical use of these exempt from the legal controls that try to limit recreational use. So, in the United Kingdom and US, drugs such as morphine and amphetamine are exempted from the most severe controls that apply to non-medical drugs, such as crack cocaine and crystal meth (see [1]). In practice this means that they are available from pharmacies and most universities can hold them for research purposes.

The problem for researchers comes from two sources: (1) the banning of certain medicines and (2) current regulations limiting the study of the medical potential of drugs, e.g. LSD, psilocybin, and MDMA, that are subject to the most stringent level of control.

The Banning of Certain Medicines

Many traditional medicines have been defined out of the pharmacopeia by international and national conventions. These include plant sources of DMT such as ayahausca and ibogaine, but the most obvious one is cannabis. Cannabis has been used medically for over 4,000 years [2], yet since the 1961 UN Single Convention on Narcotic Drugs, it has been defined as not having such value. As a result, cannabis is put into Schedule 1. Drugs located in Schedule 1 are subject to the most stringent level of control in most countries in the world (see [1] for a fuller description of these schedules and laws justifying them). This status means that researchers (both preclinical and clinical) require a special licence to hold the drug. In the UK only four (out of many hundred) hospitals have such a licence, though all can hold heroin, a much more harmful and sought-after drug by anyone's estimate, because heroin is in Schedule 2. These restrictions have meant that research on the medical uses of cannabis has hardly occurred in the past 50 years, despite substantial increase in knowledge of the many pharmacologically active components of the cannabis plant, many of which have medical potential [2]. Moreover, what little research has taken place—such as the development of the cannabis oral spray Sativex—has been delayed by the question of what licence it would be given (now in the UK, it is Schedule 4 despite being identical in pharmaceutical content to plant cannabis, which is still held in Schedule 1).

Similar controls apply in the US, where therapeutic studies on cannabis products have been hampered by intense regulations: in the US only three people hold Drug Enforcement Agency licences to research cannabis clinically. As a result, in many US states the population defied Federal laws and voted for the legalization of medical cannabis (with Colorado and Washington State making recreational use legal as well: http://en.wikipedia.org/wiki/Medical_cannabis_in_the_United_States).

In the UK sub-national democracy for health issues does not exist, so it is estimated that over 30,000 people use medical cannabis illegally, and many get arrested for doing so, particularly as, since 2005, self-medication with cannabis has been specifically excluded as a defence in UK law (despite the fact that it can still be pleaded as a defence for the use of any other "illegal" drug for self-medication) [3].

How the Law Stops Innovation of New Medicines

Table 2 shows that many popular "illegal" drugs have plausible medical uses. Some of these come from studies that were conducted when they were legal. For instance, LSD was tested in six clinical trials for alcoholism before it was banned in the 1960s. A recent meta-analysis of these studies found an effect-size equal to that of any current treatment for this addiction [4]. So why has the therapeutic potential of LSD not been developed for the past 50 years? The answer is that, because of its Schedule 1 status, research is almost impossible. Most hospitals are banned from holding it, as are many university research institutions. Getting a Schedule 1 licence in the UK takes about a year and costs around £5,000, with £3,000 for the licence and £2,000 for the other requirements such as extra security for the drug cabinets, police checks, etc.

Additionally, there is often considerable extra bureaucracy with the need and cost of import licences, since most suppliers are overseas. Moreover, sourcing an LSD formulation for human clinical trial use is close to impossible under current UK and European clinical trial guidelines that require Good Manufacturing Practice (GMP) production compliance (http://eur-lex.europa.eu/legal-content/EN/TXT/PDF/?uri=CELEX:32014R0536&from=EN), as no company we know of in the world is currently approved for this. The situation is somewhat easier in the US and Switzerland, where drugs sourced to high purity, though without the full GMP accreditation, can be used in clinical studies (see [1]). Thus, academic chemistry departments and small chemistry producers can act as providers.

Similar considerations apply to all the drugs in Table 2, although the rising interest in psilocybin as a neuroscience tool and as a possible treatment for obsessive compulsive disorder (OCD) [5] and depression has led to one company developing a GMP supply. However, this does not end the regulatory hurdles as the tableting and dispensing still requires a Schedule licenced site, which are scarce, and as mentioned above, only four hospitals in the UK have a Schedule 1 dispensing licence. Our own experience has shown that overcoming these hurdles—if at all possible—takes several years and increases the cost of this research by about 10-fold over that for "legal" drugs.

The regulations can also be applied arbitrarily to new drugs that are under research. For example, based on the clinical case reports of MDMA helping in the dyskinesia of Parkinson's disease [6] we began to develop a series of legal MDMA analogues for this indication. In parallel, "head-shops" began selling similar analogues for recreational use. Following some media hysteria, these drugs became banned in the UK, but the legislation was vey broad and so included the compounds we were working on [7]. As a result, this research has now had to stop because not all the various sites on which the work was conducted can afford Schedule 1 licences.

Another recent example is that of ketamine analogues that were being developed as new treatments for pain and depression [1, 8]. Because one or two became available for recreational use (though without any deaths), these and hundreds of other analogues were banned and put in Schedule 1. This effectively stopped research in this field, leaving only ketamine (as it is Schedule 2) available for research. Ketamine is well known to be dependence inducing and to produce significant bladder damage in a proportion of users, so finding safer alternatives was a priority; the fact that all known analogues, including many that may never be developed—let alone tested—are now Schedule 1 drugs means that finding a safer alternative is now almost certainly never going to happen. The pharmaceutical industry is very reluctant to develop drugs that are controlled because of the significant cost implications of the regulatory hurdles and because investors often consider working in the "illegal" drug space to be condoning drug abuse.

One further absurdity of the current approach is that it takes no notice of amount. This means that a single molecule of an "illegal" drug is illegal. This is already limiting PET research with new 5HT2A receptor tracers, where picogramme quantities required for tracer production (well below quantities having psychological effects) need licences [7]. Similarly, research on the epidemiology of new psychoactive substances is limited because once they are made illegal, transferring tiny (sub-active) amounts between research labs becomes subject to complex licence and import–export regulations. In the UK such licences are required for each and every drug separately which massively increases costs. Moreover each are time-limited to only 8 weeks so they need to be renewed repeatedly.

Our work on cannabis has been delayed because it turned out that cannabis placebo is considered a Schedule 1 drug in the UK. This meant that placebo had to be added to our licence and that import and export licences were then required for obtaining it from overseas suppliers. As these licences only last for 8 weeks, they commonly time-expire before the university or the supplier have dealt with the contractual documents. We are currently on our third licence for placebo cannabis and still awaiting supply.

Most researchers do not have the time, money, or energy to work their way through the regulatory jungle. We are the first group in the UK ever to study psilocybin and the first in the 50 years since the regulations were brought in to study LSD. Already the insights gained have transformed our understanding of the role of these drugs and, by inference, the role of 5HT2A receptors in brain function [9], and these findings have now been back-translated into preclinical studies with considerable value [10].

Maybe one could argue that the impairment of research produced by the regulations on "illegal" drugs is worth it because recreational use is reduced. However, it is highly doubtful that this is the case with any of these drugs since they are all readily available from dealers or even over the Internet. Moreover, we can find no instances of diversion of Schedule 1 or Schedule 2 drugs from research labs. So the law simply censors research rather than protects the public; indeed the limitation to clinical research produced by the regulations almost certainly has done much more harm than good to society by impeding medical progress.

What Is the Solution?

This is remarkably simple; all that needs to happen is for each national government to redefine UN Schedule 1 drugs as Schedule 2 in their country. The governments would still be complying with the UN conventions (i.e., the drugs would still be "illegal"), but the drugs could be held by research establishments and hospitals alongside drugs currently in Schedule 2, e.g., opioids and stimulants. There would be no increased risk of diversion, but a significant easing of the regulatory burden for research. A more rational European approach to GMP production of research compounds for Phase I and II clinical trials would also make clinical research much easier without any significant risk to participants.

As we work towards lifting the ban on pharmacological innovation and research with current Schedule 1 drugs, it will be important to encourage and support the efforts of scientists to oppose harmful new legislation, such as blanket bans on chemical or pharmacological series. In the US, researchers have intervened in these political processes when city-based or state-based proposed legislation has threatened current or upcoming medical research projects (see for example, the testimony to the Maryland Senate provided in the following: http://www.drugpolicy.org/docUploads/Salvia_Packet_02_02_11.pdf).

References

1. Nutt DJ, King LA, Nichols DE (2013) Effects of Schedule I drug laws on neuroscience research and treatment innovation. Nat Rev Neurosci. 14(8):577–85. Epub 2013 Jun 12. doi: 10.1038/nrn3530 PMID: 23756634

2. Pertwee R (2014) Handbook of Cannabis. Oxford: Oxford University Press.

3. Nutt DJ (2010) Necessity or nastiness? The hidden law denying cannabis for medical use. http://profdavidnutt.wordpress.com/2010/12/13/necessity-or-nastiness-the-hidden-law-denying-cannabis-for-medicinal-use/. 13 December 2010.

4. Krebs T, Johansen P-Ø (2012) Lysergic acid diethylamide (LSD) for alcoholism: a meta-analysis of controlled trials. J. Psychopharmacol. 26: 994–1002. doi: 10.1177/0269881112439253 PMID: 22406913

5. Moreno FA, Wiegand CB, Taitano EK, Delgado PL (2006) Safety, tolerability and efficacy of psilocybin in 9 patients with obsessive-compulsive disorder. J. Clin. Psychiatry 67, 1735–1740. doi: 10.4088/JCP.v67n1110 PMID: 17196053

6. Huot PH, Johnston TH, Lewis KD, Koprich JB, Reyes G, Fox SH, Piggott MJ, Brotchie JM (2011) Characterization of 3,4-methylenedioxymethamphetamine (MDMA) enantiomers *in vitro* and in the MPTP-lesioned primate: *R*-MDMA reduces severity of dyskinesia, whereas *S*-MDMA extends duration of ON-time. J. Neurosci. 31, 7190–7198. doi: 10.1523/JNEUROSCI.1171-11.2011 PMID: 21562283

7. Nutt DJ, King LA, Nichols DE (2013). New victims of current drug laws. Nat Rev Neurosci 14: 877. doi: 10.1038/nrn3530-c2 PMID: 24149187

8. Coppola M, Mondola R (2012) Methoxetamine: from drug of abuse to rapid-acting antidepressant. Med. Hypotheses 79, 504–507. doi: 10.1016/j.mehy.2012.07.002 PMID: 22819129

9. Carhart-Harris RL, Erritzoe D, Williams T, Stone JM, Reed LJ, et al. (2012) Neural correlates of the psychedelic state as determined by fMRI studies with psilocybin. Proc. Natl Acad. Sci. USA 109, 2138–2143. doi: 10.1073/pnas.1119598109 PMID: 22308440

10. Riga MS, Soria G, Tudela R, Artigas F, Celada P (2014) The natural hallucinogen 5-MeO-DMT, component of ayahuasca, disrupts cortical function in rats. International Journal of Neuropsychopharmacology, 17, 1269–1282. doi: 10.1017/S1461145714000261 PMID: 24650558

Critical Thinking

1. Has banning opioids and cannabis delayed medicinal breakthroughs in scientific and medical research?

2. When was the "War on Drugs" declared, and what was the original purpose? How has this affected the pharmacology industry?

3. Are drug laws aimed at reducing availability to all persons or are they aimed at controlling social availability?

Internet References

Drug Policy Alliance
   http://www.drugpolicy.org/

National Center for Chronic Disease Prevention and Health Promotion
   https://www.cdc.gov/chronicdisease/index.htm

National Drug Intelligence Center
   https://www.justice.gov/archive/ndic/

Unit 7

UNIT

Prepared by: Kim Schnurbush, *California State University, Sacramento*
Mark Pullin, *Angelo State University*

Prevention, Treatment, and Education

There are no magic bullets for preventing drug abuse and treating drug-dependent persons. Currently, more than 22 million Americans are classified as drug dependent on illicit drugs and/or alcohol. Males continue to be twice as likely to be classified as drug dependent as females. Research continues to establish and strengthen the role of treatment as a critical component in the fight against drug abuse. Some drug treatment programs have been shown to dramatically reduce the costs associated with high-risk populations of users. For example, recidivism associated with drug-related criminal justice populations has shown to decrease by 50 percent after treatment. Treatment is a critical component in the fight against drug abuse but is not a panacea. Society cannot "treat" drug abuse away just as it cannot "arrest" it away.

Drug prevention and treatment philosophies subscribe to a multitude of modalities. Everything seems to work a little and nothing seems to work completely. The articles in this unit illustrate the diversity of methods utilized in prevention and treatment programs. Special emphasis is given to treat the drug problems of those who are under the supervision of the criminal justice system. All education, prevention, and treatment programs compete for local, state, and federal resources. Current treatment efforts at all public and private levels are struggling to meet the demands for service due to the impacts from the U.S. economic crisis of the past few years.

Education: One critical component of drug education is the ability to rapidly translate research findings into practice, and today's drug policy continues to emphasize this in its overall budget allocations. Funding for educational research and grants is generally strong with the trend being toward administering funds to local communities and schools to fund local proposals. For example, in 2011, more than $50 million was again made available to schools for research-based assistance for drug prevention and school safety programs. Another example is the refunding of the $120 million National Youth Media Campaign designed to help coach parents in processes of early recognition and intervention. Encouraging successful parenting is one primary emphasis in current federal drug policy. Other significant research efforts continue to support important

education prevention, and treatment programs such as The National Prevention Research Initiative, Interventions and Treatment for Current Drug Users Who Are Not Yet Addicted, the National Drug Abuse Treatment Clinical Trail Network, and Research Based Treatment Approaches for Drug Abusing Criminal Offenders. In 2011, federal research-related grants totaling almost $100 million were made available to local and state school jurisdictions.

Prevention: A primary strategy of drug prevention programs is to prevent and/or delay initial drug use. A secondary strategy is to discourage use by persons minimally involved with drugs. Both strategies include (1) educating users and potential users; (2) teaching adolescents how to resist peer pressure; (3) addressing problems associated with drug abuse such as teen pregnancy, failure in school, and law breaking; (4) creating community support and involvement for prevention activities; and (5) involving parents in deterring drug use by children. Prevention and education programs are administered through a variety of mechanisms, typically amidst controversy relative to what works best. Schools have been an important delivery apparatus. Funding for school prevention programs is an important emphasis within the efforts to reduce the demand for drugs. Subsequently, an increase in federal money was dedicated to expanding the number of high school programs that implement student drug testing. Drug testing in high schools, authorized by the Supreme Court in a 2002 court decision, has produced a positive and measurable deterrent to drug use. Despite its controversy, school drug testing is expanding as a positive way to reinforce actions of parents to educate and deter their children from use. The testing program provides for subsequent assessment, referral, and intervention process in situations where parents and educators deem it necessary.

In addition, in 2011, approximately $90 million in grant funds were again dedicated to support the federal Drug-Free Communities Program, which provides funds at the community level to anti-drug coalitions working to prevent substance abuse among young people in local neighborhoods. There are currently more than 700 local community coalitions working under this program nationwide. Also, there are community-based drug prevention programs sponsored groups, and private corporations. All programs pursue funding through public grants and private endowments. Federal grants to local, state, and private programs are critical components to program solvency. The multifaceted nature of prevention programs make them difficult to assess categorically. School programs that emphasize the development of skills to resist social and peer pressure generally produce varying degrees of positive results. Research continues to make more evident the need to focus prevention programs with specific populations in mind.

Treatment: Like prevention programs, drug treatment programs enlist a variety of methods to treat persons dependent upon legal and illegal drugs. There is no single-pronged approach to treatment for drug abuse. Treatment modality may differ radically from one user to the other. The user's background, physical and mental health, personal motivation, and support structure all have serious implications for treatment type. Lumping together the diverse needs of chemically dependent persons for purposes of applying a generic treatment process does not work. In addition, most persons needing and seeking treatment have problems with more than one drug—polydrug use. Current research also correlates drug use with serious mental illness (SMI). Current research by the federal Substance Abuse and Mental Health Services Administration reports that adults with a drug problem are three times more likely to suffer from a SMI. The existing harmful drug use and mental health nexus is exacerbated by the fact that using certain powerful drugs such as methamphetamine push otherwise functioning persons into the dysfunction realm of mental illness. Although treatment programs differ in methods, most provide a combination of key services. These include drug counseling, drug education, pharmacological therapy, psychotherapy, relapse prevention, and assistance with support structures. Treatment programs may be outpatient oriented or residential in nature. Residential programs require patients to live at the facility for a prescribed period of time. These residential programs, often described as therapeutic communities, emphasize the development of social, vocational, and educational skills. The current trend is to increase the availability of treatment programs. One key component of federal drug strategy is to continue to fund and expand the Access to Recovery treatment initiative that began in 2004. This program uses a voucher system to fund drug treatment for individuals otherwise unable to obtain it. This program, now operational in 14 states and one Native American community, allows dependent persons to personally choose care providers, including faith-based care providers. It is hoped that this program will encourage states to provide a wider array of treatment and recovery options. As one example, the state of Missouri has transformed all public drug treatment within the state to an "Access to Recovery-Like" program in which involved persons choose their providers and pay with state vouchers. It is hoped that this and similar programs will allow a more flexible delivery of services that will target large populations of dependent persons who are not reached through other treatment efforts.

Article

Prepared by: Kim Schnurbush, *California State University, Sacramento*
Mark Pullin, *Angelo State University*

Life Skills Training Shields Teens from Prescription Opioid Misuse

Eric Sarlin

Learning Outcomes

After reading this article, you will be able to:

- Discuss how and why life training skills can divert teens from prescription drug abuse.

- Understand cost-effective family-based methods that are effective in reducing teen drug use.

- Discuss the early warning signs of current and potential illicit prescription opioid misuse that can be prevented through early life training skill programs.

The life skills training (LST) prevention intervention, delivered in seventh grade classrooms, helps children avoid misusing prescription opioids throughout their teen years, NIDA-supported researchers report. Coupling LST with the Strengthening Families Program: for Parents and Youth 10–14 (SFP) enhances this protection.

Dr. D. Max Crowley from Duke University, with colleagues from Pennsylvania State University, evaluated the impacts of LST and two other school-based interventions, All Stars (AS) and Project Alert (PA), on teens' prescription opioid misuse. The researchers drew the data for the evaluation from a recent trial of the PROmoting School-community-university Partnerships to Enhance Resilience (PROSPER) prevention program. PROSPER is led jointly by Richard Spoth at Iowa State University and Mark Greenberg at Penn State University, with research funding from NIDA.

The new evaluation also disclosed that communities that implemented LST in the PROSPER trial more than recouped its cost in reduced health, social, and other expenditures related to teen prescription opioid misuse. The researchers recommend that communities consider implementing LST plus SFP to help control the ongoing epidemic of youth prescription opioid misuse. LST was the only intervention of the three tested that was effective by itself, and it was the most effective when the interventions were combined with SFP.

Lessons that Stick

In the PROSPER trial, 14 communities in Iowa and Pennsylvania each selected, from among LST, AS, and PA, the intervention they felt best fit their resources and their youths' risk profile for drug use and other unhealthy and delinquent behaviors. The interventions are all "universal," meaning that they are delivered to all children, not just those who are judged to have elevated risk for problems.

All the interventions involve multiple sessions of classroom instruction addressing the social and psychological factors that lead to experimentation with drugs and other undesirable behaviors. In addition, through games, discussion, role-playing, and other exercises, students practice refusing drugs, communicating with peers and adults, making choices in problem situations, and confronting peer pressure. The programs' curricula focus on helping students to develop practical skills they can apply to resist drug use. Materials, such as worksheets, online content, posters, and videos, augment all three programs.

Each intervention was delivered to all seventh graders in the schools of the PROSPER communities that selected it. Most of the children and their families also received the SFP program during the prior year, when the children were in sixth grade. In SFP, families gather together to watch videos providing advice and instruction toward enhancing family relationships and communication, fostering parenting skills, improving academic performance, and preventing risky behaviors. Group leaders then conduct follow-up lessons and practice exercises.

Dr. Crowley and colleagues previously reported that smaller percentages of children from the 14 PROSPER communities reported illicit drug use and problematic alcohol use in annual follow-up visits conducted through 11th grade, compared to children from 14 matched control communities that did not use any evidence-based prevention program. As well, fewer PROSPER children reported marijuana use in 12th grade.

In their new analysis, the researchers isolated the effects of the three interventions on misuse of prescription opioids. Their analysis showed that LST-only recipients were less likely to report ever having misused these medications than were children in control communities, throughout middle and high school. The prevalence advantage with LST reached 20.2 percent versus 25.9 percent in 12th grade. Pairing LST with SFP increased the advantage to 16.3 percent versus 25.9 percent in 12th grade.

SFP followed by AS helped recipients avoid prescription opioid misuse. However, this combination was less effective than LST plus SFP, resulting in a prevalence advantage, versus control, of 19.6 percent versus 25.9 percent in 12th grade. PA did not significantly reduce misuse of the drugs either alone or in combination with SFP.

Win–Win

Dr. Crowley and colleagues determined that LST's impact on teens' prescription opioid misuse made it a good financial, as well as health, investment for PROSPER communities. They reached this conclusion by:

- Estimating the cost to prevent each case of prescription opioid misuse (by dividing the total cost of LST materials, training, etc., by the number of cases prevented).
- Comparing that number to $7,500, which they estimated, based on previously established figures, is the average expenditure incurred by communities for each single case of teen prescription opioid misuse.

These calculations indicated that PROSPER communities that implemented LST laid out $613 and saved $6,887 for each child that the program prevented from misusing prescription opioids. The corresponding estimates for LST plus SFP indicated expenditures of $3,959 and savings of $3,541 per case averted. Even though communities saved less per benefited child with LST alone, the researchers note, their health benefits were greater and their total savings may have been greater with LST plus SFP, because more cases were prevented.

Numerous studies have shown that LST shields children against other substance use and problem behaviors in addition to LST (see "LST's Broader Impact on Substance Use" section). These benefits presumably would further increase communities' economic advantage in implementing the program.

Dr. Crowley says, "This work illustrates that not only can existing universal prevention programs effectively prevent prescription drug misuse, they can also do so in a cost-effective manner. Our research demonstrates the unique opportunities to combine prevention across school and family settings to augment the larger prevention impact."

LST's Broader Impact on Substance Use

A study by researchers from Iowa State University led by Dr. Richard Spoth yielded results consistent with those of Dr. Crowley's team, providing further support for LST as an effective tool for preventing substance use among youth. Dr. Spoth and colleagues randomized students from 36 Iowa schools into three experimental groups: LST alone, LST plus SFP, and a control group. Dr. Spoth's team periodically collected questionnaire data from the study participants from seventh grade through age 22.

The researchers' findings revealed significant effects of LST on outcomes when the students reached young adulthood, including fewer alcohol-related problems and lower cigarette and substance use. LST's effects were more pronounced for those youth who were at higher risk for substance use. In light of these results, Dr. Spoth and colleagues conclude that LST may delay initiation of substance use and thereby decrease substance use and related problems in early adulthood.

Sources

Crowley, D.M.; Jones, D.E.; Coffman, D.L.; Greenberg, M.T. Can we build an efficient response to the prescription drug misuse epidemic? Assessing the cost effectiveness of universal prevention in the PROSPER trial. *Preventive Medicine* 62: 71–77, 2014.

Spoth, R.; Trudeau, L.; Redmond, C.; Shin, C. Replication RCT of early universal prevention effects on young adult substance misuse. *Journal of Consulting and Clinical Psychology* 82(6):949–963, 2014.

Critical Thinking

1. What are the attractions by teens to prescription opioid drugs?

2. Describe how early warning signs can be observed and enrollment in family-based training methods work to deter drug use.

3. Discuss how the importance of evidence-based preventative interventions (EBPIs) to be utilized in early grades can deter future misuse of licit and illicit drugs by teens and young adults.

Internet References

American Society of Addiction Medicine, Opioid Addiction

http://www.asam.org/docs/default-source/advocacy/opioid-addiction-
disease-facts-figures.pdf

National Institute on Drug Abuse, Advancing Addiction Science

https://www.drugabuse.gov/

Sarlin, Ric, "Life Skills Training Shields Teens from Prescription Opioid Misuse" National Institute on Drug Abuse Research Report, December 3, 2015. National Institutes of Health, U.S. Department of Health and Human Services.

Prepared by: Kim Schnurbush, *California State University, Sacramento*
Mark Pullin, *Angelo State University*

Article

FedEx Indicted on New Criminal Charges in Online Pharmacy Case

Dan Levine

Learning Outcomes

After reading this article, you will be able to:

- Understand the charge of conspiring to launder money as it relates to online pharmacies and delivery companies such as FedEx.

- Become familiar with the online pharmacy ordering process, and that it takes a valid prescription to order medications online.

FedEx Corp faces a new charge of conspiring to launder money in a U.S. criminal case over the company's drug deliveries for rogue online pharmacies despite warnings from law enforcement.

The latest indictment, filed in court on Friday, said FedEx accepted payment from several pharmacies when it knew the revenue was the product of invalid prescriptions.

FedEx was first indicted last month on counts including conspiracy to distribute controlled substances. Senior company managers were repeatedly warned that online pharmacies which had been the subject of criminal prosecutions for supplying drugs without prescriptions were using its services, the indictment said.

Instead of stopping the conduct, FedEx devised policies so it could continue, the filing said.

FedEx pleaded not guilty and in a statement on Friday said it is innocent of the latest charges as well.

"We will continue to defend against this attack on the integrity of FedEx," Senior Vice President Patrick Fitzgerald said.

The company pressed law enforcement for a list of pharmacies so it can stop shipments, he said. "We have asked for a list, and they have sent us indictments," Fitzgerald said.

However in the new indictment, U.S. prosecutors allege FedEx maintained an internal list of hundreds of pharmacies that the company was able to link to a shipping site.

If convicted, FedEx could face fines of up to roughly $1.6 billion.

The case in U.S. District Court, Northern District of California is *United States of America vs. FedEx Corp* et al., 14-cr-380.

Critical Thinking

1. Should a delivery company, such as FedEx, be held responsible for conspiracy to distribute prescription medications if the person(s) they've delivered a package to did not hold a legal prescription for the medications delivered by the company?

2. Should online pharmacies be legal if problems like the one in the article are going to happen?

Internet References

U.S. Department of Justice: Office of Diversion Control
http://www.deadiversion.usdoj.gov/consumer_alert.htm

U.S. Food and Drug Administration, "FDA takes action against thousands of illegal Internet pharmacies"
http://www.fda.gov/NewsEvents/Newsroom/PressAnnouncements/ucm322492.htm

Article

Prepared by: Kim Schnurbush, *California State University, Sacramento*
Mark Pullin, *Angelo State University*

Beating Heroin is More than 12 Steps: It's 18 Years and Going

Tracey Helton Mitchell

Learning Outcomes

After reading this article, you will be able to:

- Discuss the challenges drug addicts, specifically on heroin, face in recovery.

- Explore how being addicted to drugs can drastically change a person's life.

- Understand both the physical and emotional challenges faced by people who are addicted to drugs.

(CNN)—There is a scene in the documentary "Black Tar Heroin: The Dark End of the Street" that continues to resonate with me, despite the 18 years that have passed since 25-year-old me was featured in the film. I was asking the camera, if I wasn't using drugs, "what would I do with my life?" I was pointing to the camera, showing the soft tissue infections on my skin. I was skeletal, living in a filthy hotel room with my boyfriend. I had left my apartment a few years earlier for a spring break trip to San Francisco and had never returned home.

"What would I do with my life?" This continues to be a question. There are two parts to recovery: There is the ceasing of the use and abuse of chemicals. Then, the more difficult process for a person like myself: creating a whole new life. I had fallen so far to the bottom, where would I start? After spending eight years of my life on heroin, what are the steps I need to take to rebuild my life and my sanity?

I was told many things in early recovery: everything from "don't get into a relationships" to "work the 12 steps or die." I have found that the truth is more nuanced.

My recovery process began even before the last time I used drugs. I had made a silent promise to myself that if the opportunity arose, I would take it. I would try to get clean. This attempt

would be a sincere one. I had tried 10 other times but was unable to last beyond a few months, then a few weeks, then a few days. Then, finally, I could go no longer than a day without drugs.

When the police clicked the handcuffs on my wrists, I breathed a sigh of relief. Instead of blaming the world for my situation, I was ready to take an active role in my life. I had deferred these decisions to drugs for so long, the idea of "recovery" was a frightening one. Yet I knew it was one I had to attempt. The alternative was dying as a Jane Doe with a needle hanging out of my arm or getting my throat cut in some sleazy hotel room.

The waves of fear rolled over me in those first few months. The first thing I needed to address was my poor physical condition. I was underweight, covered in soft tissue infections and possibly infected with HIV. After waiting nearly a week for an answer, I had made up my mind that I was going to stay clean. When the test was negative, it merely strengthened my resolve.

The first few months, I found it difficult to sleep at night. This alternated with periods of absolutely no energy, known as PAWS, or postacute withdrawal syndrome. I continued to attend group support meetings, but many days, I felt as if things were completely hopeless. How could a person like me ever stay off drugs? How would I support myself? How could I explain to any "normal" person my former life on the streets of San Francisco? The homelessness, prostitution, and years spent injecting myself with drugs were hard for me to understand.

Slowly, incrementally, I began to see the changes. I began to feel better physically, until one day, I could finally enjoy a warm shower and the food from the commissary. I had the smallest bit of gratitude, enough to push me to the next phase of my recovery.

I was transferred to a residential treatment facility. This was overwhelming to me. It was large, almost a warehouse for users. There were 100 beds and nearly eight men per female resident. I wasn't sure how to navigate social situations. The extent of my conversations for close to a decade had centered around my ability to acquire drugs. I was seated next to people who attempted to engage me in conversations.

I quickly found that many people were not, in fact, there for "recovery." They wanted to get off parole, had no place to live or were forced there by family members.

Many of the male residents gave me validation around my appearance, validation that was inappropriate for the setting. I was completely unaware of this because I had the selective hearing that comes with years of addiction, hearing what I wanted to hear.

After making the mistake of having sex with a male resident, I made another decision to focus on myself. While many people could return home if they didn't complete treatment, my options consisted of jail or living in an alleyway. I wanted more for myself. I began to open up in groups and to counselors. I got my first "chip," celebrating lengths of recovery. I had six months without using drugs.

When it was time to leave the program, my process did not stop there. In reality, it was the beginning. Now, I had to live "life on life's terms. "I had a job, bills and stress. I noticed I was having flashbacks to violence I had endured. I was having nightmares. I felt afraid to be around loud noises and crowded rooms.

I was encouraged to see a therapist. I had rejected the idea outright many times until I got desperate enough to give it a try. "The person is paid to objectively listen to you,"someone told me. I needed that: someone outside my daily life to listen to me.

I was later diagnosed with post-traumatic stress disorder. I had not escaped those years of addiction unscathed. My mind and spirit needed to heal, not just my physical self. I began to open up about my experiences to others. I found that many people had similar experiences. I wasn't crazy or broken; I just needed to heal.

There seems to be no place or person that has not been impacted by the opioid "epidemic" sweeping the United States. On a daily basis, people who are struggling with opioids contact me for insight. I assure them that recovery is possible. There is hope after heroin.

February 27 marked 18 years for me as a recovering person. Recovery is a process. It isn't a place; it is a journey. It isn't a sprint; it is a marathon. It is a lifelong commitment to taking care of yourself.

My entire life has changed. I went from homeless to homeowner. I went from being alone to having a full life with a beautiful family. I went from desperate to fulfilled. It all started with one second, one minute, one hour of knowing I was going to change. By giving up one thing—drugs—I gained everything.

Critical Thinking

1. What types of challenges do drug addicts face as they first step into a recovery program?

2. With regards to the challenges facing drug addicts in recovery, how do physical challenges differ from emotional challenges as they move through the first stages of recovery?

3. Place yourself in the author's shoes and picture yourself looking back 18 years at your drug-addicted self, being filmed in a documentary about heroin addiction. What would you say to your 18-year-old self, knowing what you know about drug addiction?

Internet References

American Addiction Centers, Heroin Withdrawal Timeline
http://americanaddictioncenters.org/withdrawal-timelines-treatments/heroin/

SMART Recovery: Self-Management and Recovery Training
http://www.smartrecovery.org/addiction/heroin.html

TRACEY HELTON MITCHELL is the author of *"The Big Fix: Hope After Heroin"*, which was published in March. She lives in the San Francisco Bay Area with her husband and three children. She works as a manager of peer-based mental health services.

Article

Prepared by: Kim Schnurbush, *California State University, Sacramento*
Mark Pullin, *Angelo State University*

What It's Like to Be on Vivitrol, the Drug that Prevents Heroin Addicts from Getting High

What Comes After Addiction Vivitrol, a Drug Designed to Prevent Heroin Addicts from Getting High, Forces Life into Focus

GENEVIEVE SMITH

Learning Outcomes

After reading this article, you will be able to:

- Understand what Vivitrol is and why it is being used to help heroin addicts.

- Discuss why Vivitrol is being used in prisons prior to inmates being released back into society and why it is so successful.

- Understand the pros and cons of Vivitrol in opioid-addiction treatment programs and why it is not the primary choice for many doctors because of how it needs to be stored.

The first time Gabriel overdosed on heroin, he was technically homeless, crashing on a friend's couch. One morning, the friend went out for groceries and Gabriel shot up. When the friend returned, Gabriel was blue. After coming to in the hospital, Gabriel was stunned that he'd been so close to killing himself, in such a stupid way, and he felt guilty for the pain he'd caused his father, Martin, who had not realized the extent of his son's addiction. Gabriel decided then that he was done with heroin.

The next five times Gabriel overdosed tend to blur together. Sometimes, he wouldn't even go to the emergency room. He'd just sort of wake up someplace and someone would tell him he'd stopped breathing. Sometimes, he'd stay clean for months before slipping up again. But mostly he kept using. He kept using heroin after his son, Jared, was born. He kept using after two friends overdosed at the same time and he had to administer CPR to one, then the other. He kept using after one of his best friends died from an overdose. And he kept using after he went on Suboxone, an opioid relative of methadone. He realized he could take Suboxone in the morning, quiet his heroin hunger pains long enough to go to work, and still shoot up at night. He did this for a couple of years until his doctor refused to continue filling his prescriptions.

The last time Gabriel overdosed was in September 2014. He stopped by his dealer's house after a recovery meeting. On his way home, he went unconscious, and the car swerved into the guardrail on a bridge. The medics had to saw him out.

Martin believed there was an angel looking out for his son. How else to explain his good fortune? That he walked away from the crash with just a couple of broken ribs. That he survived all those overdoses. That when Martin called the local substance-abuse center, the nurses knew to get Gabriel in to see a counselor right away, and that just a few years earlier that counselor, Janet Brannen, had started his town's only group-therapy sessions for opiate addicts, where he went even when he was so sick from withdrawal that he'd have to leave to throw up. That his father stayed with him during the worst of his detox. That he lived in Massachusetts, which subsidized his treatment. That he had Jared, who gave him a reason to stick it out. Not least, that his physician was one of two local doctors willing to prescribe the drug Vivitrol, which made staying off heroin possible when nothing else had, because for the four weeks the drug was in his system, he couldn't, no matter how hard he tried, get high off opiates.

I'd been introduced to Gabriel, which is not his real name, by his half-sister, who is a friend of mine and who had told me about the treatment that seemed to be finally keeping her brother off heroin. Gabriel lives in the Berkshires, and this past spring, on the day of his fourth monthly Vivitrol injection, I went to see him. I brought with me a photographer, Graham MacIndoe, himself a former addict (http://nymag.com/news/features/heroin-graham-macindoe-2014-2/). With a committed girlfriend and a grown son, Graham is very much the best-case scenario of what a life after heroin might look like.

We met Gabriel in the parking lot of the clinic. It was mid-March and sunny but still cold. A third of the houses in the Berkshires are vacation homes, and in the off-season, the landscape felt particularly dormant. Standing by his car in a black fleece jacket and a Dewar's hat, Gabriel, then 24, was built like a high school football player, broad and tall but still soft, with a thin, sculpted goatee, short brown hair, cheeks stained pink. He had diamond studs in his ears and robin's-egg-blue eyes laced with dark lashes, his only blemish a jagged scar down the center of his nose from a fight a few years ago. (He was drunk, not high.) He looked much healthier than I had imagined a recent junkie to look. More surprising, though, was his voice, which was so gentle it seemed to be coming from a smaller person tucked into his great body. Inside the clinic, a nurse ushered us to a small examination room. Gabriel sat on the edge of the beige exam table, legs dangling, as he waited for his doctor, Lara Setti.

The active ingredient in Vivitrol is a drug called naltrexone, which works by blocking heroin's path. It fits the keyhole where heroin would bond to the brain's receptors, but it won't turn the knob. The first forms of naltrexone, released in the '80s, had to be taken every day, which is in part why the drug never caught on as a treatment: You might not be able to fulfill the craving when on naltrexone, but the craving is still there, because for an addict, how to get high is the first thought of the day and the last. The breakthrough with Vivitrol was that four-week window of highlessness, which meant someone in recovery no longer had to keep the faith of sobriety every single day. A once-a-month re-up would suffice. Even then, it is still possible, at least theoretically, to cheat, particularly toward the end of the 28-day cycle when the drug has been partially metabolized. At that point, a committed addict could potentially do enough heroin to get a decent high, albeit a more expensive one, since he'd need enough to overpower the naltrexone lingering in his system.

Still, Vivitrol was a welcome improvement. In the past few years, as it has caught on as a treatment option, drug-court judges have incorporated it into their prison-alternative arsenal, and reentry programs have started giving injections to prisoners before they return home to all the old temptations and triggers. It has been fantastically successful in both keeping prisoners clean and reducing recidivism, though one clinician told me most ex-junkies will try to get high at least once before really understanding what they've signed up for.

Doctors treating the general population have been slower to prescribe the drug, in part because it requires a high level of management. Vivitrol must be kept refrigerated and administered in the office. Getting insurance approval is a nightmare. Without insurance, it's wildly expensive—$1,500 for a single dose. But heroin has increasingly become a white suburban drug—90 percent of new users are white; 75 percent live outside cities. With that shift has come greater political attention and greater pressure to find solutions that don't involve jail time. In October, President Obama made expanding access to medically assisted opioid-addiction treatments like Vivitrol a cornerstone of a new $133 million federal program to combat heroin use (https://www.whitehouse.gov/the-press-office/2015/10/21/fact-sheet-obama-administration-announces-public-and-private-sector).

But it's not just access that has kept Vivitrol unpopular. It has another problem: You have to get heroin out of your system before you can take it. Most addicts Gabriel knew were too terrified of withdrawal to consider going on Vivitrol. You had to want to get clean badly enough that you were willing to wade through 7 to 10 days of pure physical anguish—fevers, vomiting, a hurt that penetrates every ounce of your body. The pain is more bearable if you think you deserve to suffer, if you see suffering as penance for six years of fucking up.

The shot would come at the end of the doctor's visit. It was the easy part, a jab in the hip. Before that, Setti tried to treat everything else. Heroin leaves behind a lingering emptiness, like a stain. The feeling even has a technical name: excessive anhedonia. It's such a pleasing sound for a phrase that means the inability to experience pleasure. The theory goes that opiates flood the brain with so much dopamine that the sober addict becomes numb to the joys of regular life—a beautiful day, a delicious meal, a meaningful conversation. Janet, Gabriel's counselor, had told him to expect it to take two years before he'd be able to fully enjoy himself like a normal person. It was a fact Gabriel repeated often, a way of reminding himself that it wouldn't be like this forever.

Setti was good-naturedly no-nonsense, his coach and cheerleader as much as his doctor. She handed Gabriel a set of dog tags that he was to wear in case he had an accident and lost consciousness. "If you needed a narcotic and they gave you a narcotic, it wouldn't work," she said. "You could be writhing in pain, and they wouldn't understand." She asked Gabriel about his new job, and his son, and whether his antidepressants seemed to be working. She wanted to know how often he was exercising and whom he was hanging out with and whether he was lonely and if he was drinking. It was clear she'd invested in Gabriel, which made sense, since he was her only patient on Vivitrol. None of the others had been willing to go through withdrawal.

She examined Gabriel's depression questionnaire. "So this is interesting," she said. "This is the best you've ever done." It was true. Four months into his treatment, he felt like Jared could tell how much more present his father was. His life had taken on a certain rhythm, one meant to keep him out of trouble: work-gym-home. He had a job at a factory making potter's clay. His new landlord had let him slide on the rent until he got settled, and now he was finally caught up. He was going to the gym six days a week. He was in the best shape of his life. He was even thinking of quitting smoking.

Still, he had trouble answering the question about friends. He had a few close ones and a gym buddy, but most of his old gang he knew he couldn't see, because even if he couldn't do opiates, he could do other things. Alcohol in particular was tricky. Vivitrol blocks the same receptors that make drinking feel euphoric. Gabriel could still get the physical effects of drinking—slow response time, poor motor skills, reduced inhibition—but there was no warm, happy glow, at least not for the first few weeks after his injection. Toward the end of the cycle, he could enjoy a drink, but when he did, he felt his resolve melting a few beers in. He thought he should probably just not drink at all, but he didn't really want to do that either. He asked about upping his dose of antidepressants.

Jared went to preschool in the same building, a community center, as the gym, so father and son would often hang out there in the sun-soaked lounge, where Martin usually joined them. Some days, Jared went home with Gabriel to spend the night. On this day, we ran into Gabriel's ex-girlfriend in the parking lot as she was picking up Jared. We waved to him in the backseat, a smiley 3-year-old with a juice-box mustache. Inside, Martin sat near the window, reading a book on the history of Romanticism.

Martin, who is slight, with a short white beard and a muss of white hair, was dressed head to toe in denim. If you ask Martin where he's lived, he quotes Beckett. In the morning, he wakes up early and feeds the birds in the field behind his apartment, then he writes for three hours. He writes poems. He writes about what he reads. He quotes Emerson to explain this habit. He will tell you this in a voice barely above a whisper. It's that voice that connects father and son, though Gabriel's is loud by comparison.

While Gabriel lifted weights, Martin told me about his guilt at missing all the signs of trouble when his son was a teenager, how he believed Gabriel when he explained away the needle Martin found. He admitted he often doesn't understand his son and wonders if his own interiority is partly to blame for Gabriel's problems. Martin had studied the methods of Rudolf Steiner, the mystic philosopher. He met Gabriel's mother in Wales, where they were both working as caregivers in a Camphill community, a self-sustaining village for the developmentally disabled inspired by Steiner's work. Gabriel was born there. When he was 3, the family moved to another Camphill community in the Hudson Valley. There were no boys his age, so Gabriel often played alone. He hated it, even more so when his mother, who is Dutch, decided to return to the Netherlands. He lived with her for a few years before coming back to live with his father, who had by then moved to the Berkshires.

Martin looked out at the countryside and saw utopia, saw the ability to work with one's hands, saw a way to live well with little. His son looked out and saw guns and ATVs and boredom. He saw Marlboros and trucks. He saw heroin. "Gabriel's thing is four-wheelers, bulking up," Martin said. "I said to him, 'Who the hell is your father? Who was your mother with?' "

Martin was hopeful but cautious about his son's future. "He seems stable now," he said. "You just have to trust that he's committed to the path he's on, but there's always that possibility. So you live with a kind of shadow." He talked about Gabriel's "heartforce," that goodness in him that Martin believed would carry him through. To his addiction, Gabriel had given the years when most of us begin to figure out who we are and what we want. He had talked to his dad about maybe wanting to be a plumber, though so far it was only talk. "He is a young 24," Martin said. "I've told him, What do you really want to do? Who are you? 'What is it you plan to do with your wild and precious life?,' as Mary Oliver said." He grew quiet and looked away. When he started speaking again, there were tears in his eyes.

The clinic where Janet works is housed in an old Victorian. She met us at the door with hugs. "I remember the most striking thing was your eyes," she said to Gabriel. "Fear, sadness, desperation, but also a kind of finality. Sometimes I see folks and I think they're not ready yet. He was ready to get clean."

Janet was full of stories, wisdom handed down from addicts. There was the addict who told her that heroin was the answer to all of life's problems, so why should he quit? And the one who wanted to get high so badly he paid someone to cut out his naltrexone implant—an alternative to the injectable Vivitrol that's released via a microchip embedded in the skin. She talked about how the Vivitrol shot "catapults the person into the possibility of being able to get to who you are really and what you want, because it literally stops you from thinking *I can go do heroin*." One patient told her how he didn't know what to think about with his morning coffee now that he didn't have to think about how to score that day.

Gabriel nodded. Heroin for him, too, had been a revelation. "There's nothing for me like that experience of instantly being wiped free of any pain," he said. "It's unnatural. So once you experience it, what are you supposed to do with that? It's not something that's supposed to be experienced."

Sometimes Gabriel could go a few weeks without thinking about heroin, then it would just pop into his head. Things could be going beautifully, and the thought would cross his mind how much more beautiful they'd be if he were high. Or he'd be driving and he'd see someone he used to get high with or someone who was clearly high at that very moment, and it would hit him—first, a pang of jealousy. Then, slowly, he'd work to remind himself of all the shit that came with the joy.

In those early months, the craving was physical. Now it was contained mostly to his brain, so he could talk his way down more easily. But there were times he'd toyed with the idea of shooting up, especially toward the end of the month, when the drug had partially worn off. "It's weird," he said. "It's sort of like there are two halves of my brain. One is, *This shit's bad, my life is good. I might struggle sometimes but* blah, blah, blah . . . And there's the other half that's like, *I love heroin. This shit is amazing. Don't worry about anything else.*"

Maybe if you had grown up in a town where the main industries seemed to be real estate and antiquing; maybe if you'd never been good at school or at least not very interested; maybe if your dad believed so strongly in the sanctity of childhood and the goodness he saw in you that he pretty much let you roam free and feral; and maybe if your mother was 4,000 miles away and you never stopped missing her; maybe if you'd always felt a little insecure; maybe if as long as you could remember you'd been curious about drugs, you'd wanted to feel big and warm and expansive and confident; maybe if you'd already tried marijuana and cocaine and LSD and mushrooms and oxycodone and MDMA and crack and basically everything you could get your hands on; maybe it wouldn't seem like a big deal to shoot heroin. Maybe you would have done it, too.

And maybe you would have felt like Superman from the moment the needle pricked the skin and that itchy burn like liquid Red Hots spread through your veins; maybe you'd feel invincible; maybe you'd finally feel like you could breathe.

It is much easier to tell the story of addiction than of what happens after. Addiction is the stuff of movies: self-destruction; brushes with death; villains; the chance of rescue, redemption, salvation. But for those who make it out, the rest of the narrative, the long, hard work of putting together a life—it's much less compelling stuff. It's what the rest of us do every day in one way or another. And it is mostly boring and exhausting and not so much fun, or else the fun is at the margins of the tedious, the brief moments between work and bills and child care and

doctors' appointments and grocery shopping and cooking and laundry. The bigger meaning is in there, someplace, but it can be hard to find. Adulthood can sometimes feel like an endless series of administrative tasks, of just getting by, even when we are not grappling with our demons, even when our demons are not particularly menacing.

At dinner, Graham and Gabriel discussed the oldest addicts they'd known, the agony of withdrawal. We talked about more mundane things, too, like child-rearing, but the conversation had a way of snaking back toward heroin. Gabriel had said he loved movies, and when I asked about his favorites, he told me he really likes ones about drugs, which prompted a discussion of which films and shows were the most realistic. (*Requiem for a Dream* got the desperation of wanting to cop right; the dealers in *The Wire* were spot-on.) I asked Gabriel what he thought he might like to do with his life.

"People always ask me that," he said. "'What do you want to do when you grow up?' I've been so caught up in just going through all this stuff that I haven't even had ... I always thought it would be awesome to be in film, to be part of creating something. Something like Graham's doing. You love photo. And that's what you do for a living. I'd love to find something I really love to do." I didn't say then that even if you are lucky enough to do something you love, you will still, from time to time, look at your life and find it lacking. You'll bang around the rooms of your mind, knocking over furniture, grasping for the exit.

As we finished our burgers, Gabriel talked about missing the social part of his old life, the way his friends would run around together on a mission to get fucked up. "A lot of things are boring, and that life is exciting and you're taking risks," he told me. "Getting up and working a normal job, that shit is lame." And yet it was exactly that banality that he aspired to. "You gotta put in your time to earn a living, to pay your bills, to take care of all your responsibilities," he said. "It's almost like I was in a bad accident, and I had to relearn how to talk and walk and stuff."

The first time Gabriel got high while on Vivitrol was two weeks after his seventh injection. In Janet's telling, a friend who was also on the drug discovered that he could get a decent high just a few weeks into the monthly cycle, and he convinced Gabriel to join him. (Percy Menzies, whose addiction-treatment clinic in St. Louis has treated more than 6,000 patients using Vivitrol, told me that it's exceedingly rare to successfully get high before day 21 of the drug's 28-day cycle.) Then his insurance lapsed, and he couldn't afford to pay for the $1,500 injection out of pocket. Soon after, Janet said, his car broke down and the girl he'd been seeing moved to Florida. And just like that, he was using heroin regularly again, even though he hated it and hated himself for doing it. He came to Janet's office in tears, because he'd failed and because he didn't think he could go through the ten days of detox again. Janet helped get him into a methadone program. Even getting him to that first appointment felt to her like a minor miracle. Gabriel had driven to the clinic dope-sick, and his GPS had gotten him lost. He missed his time slot and was told to come back a week later. He called Janet panicked. "There was so much bad heroin going around he was terrified he was either going to overdose and die or get arrested," Janet told me. She managed to get him in to see the doctor, and he texted her later: "I got it. I'm ok. I'm alive." I could hear her voice crack as she recounted the story on the phone. "It was like a car chase, life and death," she said. "I can't even talk about it. I'm too close to it still. These kids are fighting for their lives."

When I asked Gabriel why he relapsed, he was dismissive at first. "I'm no good. I'm an addict. That's why." A little later, he was more circumspect. "It's hard to explain how I hate it so bad and yet why can't I just say no? It's just a wild thing to fathom, you know? It breaks my heart to be going through this." He suggested that maybe he wasn't ready for Vivitrol. "With the methadone, you're still sort of feeding that hunger for the opiates. The Vivitrol is like a full-blast kick to nothing. I think that was good for me, but it also panicked me in a way." But he said he was grateful for those eight drug-free months. "It allowed me to get a taste of what life was like completely sober. It was the happiest I've ever been."

That night back in March, over dinner, Gabriel had told a story he'd heard about euphoric recall. A term from substance-abuse literature, it describes the way addicts will remember their highs, all of the good parts and none of the bad. One guy in Gabriel's group therapy who had been sober a long time now, who had the wife and the career and the stability, said that at the beginning, his memory of the high was an inch from his face, so close he could feel it, but slowly it receded, until it became like the moon. It hangs over him still, but he wouldn't know how to touch it if he tried.

Critical Thinking

1. What is Vivitrol and why is it being used to help heroin addicts? Is Vivitrol an acceptable drug for all heroin users? Why or why not?

2. How is Vivitrol being used in prisons, and how does it assist inmates who are transitioning back into the community?

3. What story in this article caught your attention the most? Do you believe without Vivitrol that this person would have relapsed back into using drugs more easily? Explain your position.

Internet References

Center for Behavioral Health, What is Vivitrol?
http://centerforbehavioralhealth.com/vivitrol/

Food and Drug Administration, Medication Guide for Vivitrol
http://www.fda.gov/downloads/drugs/drugsafety/ucm206669.pdf

Official website for Vivitrol (naltrexone for extended-release injectable suspension)
https://www.vivitrol.com/

Article

Prepared by: Kim Schnurbush, *California State University, Sacramento*
Mark Pullin, *Angelo State University*

Obama Announces New Moves to Fight Opioid and Heroin Abuse Epidemic

Nadia Kounang

Learning Outcomes

After reading this article, you will be able to:

- Discuss Obama's initiative to expand addiction treatment, to include coverage for mental health and substance abuse services across the nation.

- Understand the reasons additional services are needed to combat drug abuse.

- Discuss how opioid addiction has fueled the need for additional drug treatment across the nation.

(CNN) The Obama administration is making it easier for doctors to use anti-addiction drugs in the fight against an exploding epidemic of prescription drug and heroin abuse.

It's part of a package of new initiatives announced Tuesday that includes other efforts to expand addiction treatment and increase coverage for mental health and substance abuse services. These initiatives are in addition to the $1.1 billion he proposed last month.

Overdose deaths from opioids—drugs that include heroin as well as prescription drugs like oxycodone and hydrocodone—continue to be a leading cause of unintentional death for Americans, rising 14 percentfrom 2013 to 2014. Every 19 minutes someone dies from a drug overdose.

Medication-assisted treatment with drugs like methadone and buprenorphine is a key component of the administration's attack on the opioid epidemic. These drugs are used in conjunction with behavioral treatment to help manage an addict's recovery and ease withdrawal from opioid drugs.

In a call to reporters, Michael Botticelli, director of the White House Office of National Drug Control Policy, said, "Expanding access to medication-assisted treatment for opioid-use disorders has been a top priority for this administration. Research clearly shows that this approach, when combined with behavioral therapies, is more effective at sustaining recovery and preventing overdose."

Some critics are concerned that drugs like methadone or buprenorphine could be diverted, or that their use could lead to further addiction.

However, Caleb Banta-Green says we can't ignore their success. "Buprenorphine and methadone cuts mortality rates (of addicts) in half. . . . The fundamental line is that we need to keep people alive," said Banta-Green, a senior research scientist at the Alcohol and Drug Abuse Institute at the University of Washington.

Expanding Treatment

Currently, physicians are limited by law to prescribing buprenorphine to just 100 patients per doctor. The White House is increasing that cap to 200 patients per doctor.

But there's also a limited number of doctors around the country eligible to prescribe the drug, just about 30,000.

Last October, states and private sector groups proposed to double the number of buprenorphine prescribing physicians over the next three years. So far, 2,200 additional physicians have committed to complete training in buprenorphine prescribing, the White House said.

Banta-Green said expanding the number of doctors is key in the fight against an epidemic that is hitting more and more in rural and suburban areas, where access to treatment is limited. "You have to push out care to many more places," he said.

Additional Efforts to Fight Epidemic

In addition to upping the patient limit, the White House also announced an additional $11 million to go toward state efforts to expand medication-assisted treatment programs, as well as another $94 million in new funding for treatment services to 271 community health centers across the country.

On top of expanding access to MAT, the White House announced other initiatives:

- providing an additional $11 million to increase access to naloxone, the opioid overdose reversal drug.
- establishing a Mental Health and Substance Use Disorder Parity Task Force.
- ensuring that mental health and substance use benefits are offered as medical and surgical benefits are for those enrolled in Medicaid and the Children's Health Insurance Program.
- a $7 million initiative by the Department of Justice toward policing and investigating heroin distribution.
- guidance from the Department of Health and Human Services for federally funded needle exchange programs.

Public health experts said they were pleased to see the White House attention to community health centers and needle exchange programs. "We've seen these programs at the front lines of overdose death, bringing people to drug treatment, and addressing the risk of hepatitis C and HIV," said Daniel Raymond, policy director for the Harm Reduction Coalition, an advocacy group working to mitigate the effects of illegal drug use on people and communities.

Banta-Green said the focus on community health centers was key, because they are more likely to be access points for continuous, ongoing addiction care, instead of a hospital or jail.

Obama to Speak about Opioids

What may have the most lasting effort, Raymond said, is the President's address at the National Rx Drug Abuse & Heroin Summit in Atlanta on Tuesday. "That sends a powerful signal," said Raymond.

Obama will be taking part in a panel moderated by CNN's chief medical correspondent, Dr. Sanjay Gupta.

Over the past month, federal agencies have been aggressive in implementing new strategies to help fight the epidemic. The Centers for Disease Control and Prevention issued new opioid prescribing guidelines, stating plainly that opioids were not

first-line therapies. The Food and Drug Administration issued new requirements that immediate-release, or fast-acting, opioids must carry "black box" warning labels. The FDA is also encouraging abuse-resistant formulations of generic opioids. Generics make up 90percent of the market, the FDA said.

Banta-Green says he's been encouraged by the administration's efforts, but he said a key element was missing—guidance and training on how doctors should address these issues with their patients. "This is a lot of attempt to build supply and capacity of services, which is great . . . but it is important that we create tools about these difficult conversations for clinicians."

Many hope that Obama's addressing these issues can help change the stigma attached to addiction and treatment.

"Long Overdue"

"Coming to the summit, he's coming to an audience of over 1,000 people who are not going to be patting him on the back or paying lip service at all. They are anxious for actions and solutions. I think his willingness to come is more than symbolic. We should expect a lot more to see in his final year of his administration, and some of it is long overdue," Raymond said.

Raymond likened the fight against the opioid epidemic to pushing a boulder up a hill. "There are signs that we are getting a handle on the prescription opioid problem, but over the past few years the heroin issue has gotten worse. Now that we're taking more action on heroin, now we're seeing illicit fentanyl get worse. The problem is spiraling," he said.

"We had an over-reliance on prescription painkillers. We're going to be paying for the original sins for many years to come. And the problem (that) could have gotten under control earlier is going to be affecting a whole generation," Raymond said.

Editor's Note: A previous version of this article mistakenly stated opioid overdoses are the leading cause of unintentional death for Americans. It should have stated that drug overdoses overall are the leading cause of unintentional death for Americans.

Critical Thinking

1. Politics aside, what do you think of Obama's initiative to expand addiction treatment, mental health services and substance abuse services across the nation? Explain your answer.
2. Why do you think heroin use has increased in the United States?
3. Do you agree with how restrictive the Food and Drug Administration has made access to opioids in the United States, to include the new "black box" warning labels on opioid prescription drugs?

Internet References

Harm Reduction Coalition
http://harmreduction.org/

The White House, Office of National Drug Control Policy
https://www.whitehouse.gov/ondcp

Article   Prepared by: Kim Schnurbush, *California State University, Sacramento*
                                          Mark Pullin, *Angelo State University*

The Immigrant Doctor Who's Solving West Virginia's Opioid Crisis

A data-driven health commissioner figured out a way to slow overdose deaths. But treating addiction is a much harder problem.

BRIANNA EHLEY

Learning Outcomes

After reading this article, you will be able to:

- Learn about overdose deaths in West Virginia.
- Discuss recommendations made following this study.

CHARLESTON, W.Va.—Last fall, after watching the death toll from opioids climb unchecked for years, Dr. Rahul Gupta, the man in charge of combating one of the worst health crises in America, decided to do something no one had ever tried. He ordered his staff to do an in-depth analysis of every person in his state who had died of a drug overdose over the preceding year—all 887 of them.

Since 2014, West Virginia has held the grim distinction of having the highest overdose death rate in the country, according to Centers for Disease Control figures. In 2016, West Virginia's death rate, according to the most recent federal data, was 52 per 100,000 people—nearly three times the national average. The next highest state, neighboring Ohio, had 39 deaths per 100,000. What West Virginia lacked, though, were the hard numbers that might point officials to a way out of a disaster that showed no signs of abating.

Story Continued Below

"We wanted to know who each person was and what we could have done to help them," Gupta, West Virginia's public health commissioner, told me when I interviewed him in his Charleston office recently. Doctors, he said, know the risk factors for heart disease and use them to screen patients and prescribe treatment. "We didn't have something like that for opioids. We're all sort of trying to address a problem without a lot of data to know how to approach it from a prevention aspect. So we wanted to develop those risk factors."

Over the next 10 weeks, Gupta's staff combed through public databases, Medicaid rolls, medical examiner reports, birth certificates, death certificates and criminal records. They wanted to find out who was at highest risk of an overdose in West Virginia so they could produce a report for the state legislature before its session began in January. The idea was to give policymakers a data-driven road map of how to get the death rate down, who to focus resources on, and what programs and policies might help them achieve it.

The findings ultimately would show a depressing pattern of vulnerability: Men were twice as likely as women to die of an overdose. And those with jobs in blue-collar industries like construction had a higher risk of overdosing than the general population, likely because they take prescription opioids or illicit substances to deal with chronic pain from injuries. "If you're a male between the ages of 35 to 54, with less than a high school education, you're single and you've worked in a blue-collar industry," Gupta said, "you pretty much are at a very, very high risk of overdosing."

The report included recommendations ranging from limiting initial prescriptions for acute pain to seven days to expanding access to medication-assisted therapies by exempting doctors from federal licensing to administer the treatment. Those recommendations were absorbed into legislation that was signed into law by Governor Jim Justice in March.

But there was another finding, one so obvious and urgent Gupta felt his agency had to act on it immediately. In November, Gupta's team realized that about 71 percent of people who had fatally overdosed had received emergency medical treatment sometime before they died. But only about half of that group had been administered naloxone, a medicine that when injected can reverse the effects of opioids within minutes.

"We saw this was clearly a missed opportunity where we could have saved people … so it's critical that whenever these individuals do come into contact with one of the health systems, we take advantage of that opportunity and we do not let that slide."

Over the past three months, the state has also engaged in a full-court press to get naloxone into the hands of as many people as possible. That includes a recent mandate passed by the state legislature (price tag: $1 million) requiring all first responders to carry the overdose antidote and encouraging libraries and public schools—elementary through high school—to stock up on the lifesaving drug. In January, Gupta issued a standing order for naloxone so that individuals don't have to pay out of pocket for the drug, which can cost around $40 per dose. In Cabell County, which surrounds Huntington, the city considered to be the epicenter of the West Virginia epidemic, the number of EMS overdose responses declined 36 percent between the first quarter of 2017 and the first quarter of 2018, according to county figures.

The emergency distribution of naloxone may finally be having an effect on the seemingly unstoppable death toll in West Virginia. Although overdose fatalities in 2017 increased 2 percent to 909 from the year before, deaths slowed by about 25 percent in the second half of the year. Officials caution that number could change as there is often a lag in data. Death reports from 2016 are still trickling in. But federal data also shows a slowdown of overdoses in West Virginia. A CDC snapshot of 2017 hospital data showed that hospitalizations for drug overdoses were slightly down in West Virginia, even at a time when most other states across the country saw a dramatic increase.

"We are expecting improvements in overdose deaths this year with all of these things we're putting into place," Gupta told POLITICO Magazine. "We're thrilled about it, but we still feel that we have a long way to go."

West Virginia's work to get a handle on the drug abuse epidemic comes as Congress and the Trump administration continue to debate the best ways to tackle the crisis nationwide. Congress recently appropriated an additional $4 billion to help address drug abuse, including for programs to help states expand access to treatment and prevention programs as well as law enforcement activities. Surgeon General Jerome Adams recently issued a rare public advisory encouraging more people across the country to carry naloxone.

But as Gupta and most public health experts warn, naloxone isn't going to end the opioid crisis. It's a temporary bandage that saves people but does not treat them. Often many of the same patients who get revived from an overdose end up overdosing again. "We're doing a good job of saving lives," said Jack Luikart, the director of correctional substance abuse control under West Virginia's Military Affairs and Public Safety Department, "but treating addiction, that's where we need to step up our game."

Gupta, the son of an Indian diplomat, was born in India but grew up in a Maryland suburb of Washington. He came to West Virginia in 2009 to lead the Kanawha-Charleston Health Department after doing stints as a local health official in Tennessee and Alabama. He was appointed state public health commissioner by former Democratic Governor Earl Ray Tomblin in December 2014, following his work overseeing the response to the massive chemical spill near Charleston in January 2014.

While leading the local health department, Gupta, 47, watched the opioid crisis develop and then explode. He lobbied the state legislature to require special opioid prescribing training for physicians and pushed measures to crack down on "pill dumping," in which opioid manufacturers send mass quantities of pills to one area, far outpacing demand. Most of the focus then was on limiting prescription opioids, but by the time he took over as state public health commissioner, the opioid crisis had evolved from prescription drug abuse to illicit drug use like heroin and the powerful synthetic opioid fentanyl.

In his first two years as state public health commissioner, the state approved guidelines for opioid prescribers and passed Good Samaritan laws, but, Gupta said, the overdose death data revealed that their work wasn't saving lives. Despite those efforts, the overdose death rate continued to climb. In 2015, 735 West Virginians died of an overdose, according to state figures. The next year that number climbed to 887. "For me, it was the second year in a row that I was seeing the numbers continue to incline," he said. "That's when I said we have to do something different."

The state in 2017 applied for, and received, a number of federal grants that officials used to buy naloxone kits to distribute to communities. The federal government also approved a waiver for West Virginia last fall to allow Medicaid to pay for inpatient substance abuse treatment at certain facilities as part of a push to expand access to care.

But Gupta wanted a more immediate way to get a handle on the deaths, and that's where his overdose analysis project came in. "We were in a rush for time because if there was an opportunity to have legislation passed this year, this was it," he said.

His team turned the report around in three months, partnering with Johns Hopkins University, West Virginia University and Marshall University to come up with a set of 12 policy recommendations. "We didn't want it to sit on the shelf. We wanted to present practical steps that we could put into place immediately," Gupta said.

"We often don't get data-driven policy making in times of an epidemic or a crisis," Gupta said. "We were using this social autopsy of West Virginians who had died to create policy . . . and that's very hard to push back against."

Roughly 91 percent of all overdose victims had a documented history within the state's prescription drug monitoring program, meaning they had previously filled a prescription for an opioid. About half of all female victims had filled an opioid prescription within 30 days of their death. From this finding, lawmakers crafted, and approved, legislation that limited initial opioid prescribing and cracked down on providers found to be inappropriately prescribing opioids to patients.

"The problem is there is so much of it in circulation," Gupta said of prescription opioids.

West Virginia, in the past few years, has taken action to prevent pill dumping, after mass quantities of prescription painkillers flooded into small towns far surpassing necessary amounts. According to a congressional probe by the House Energy and Commerce Committee, over the past 10 years, drug manufacturers have shipped 20 million prescription painkillers to two pharmacies in Williamson, Virginia, a town of about 3,000 people. The Drug Enforcement Administration last month released a proposed rule that would limit how many opioids drug makers can manufacture in an effort to prevent pill dumping.

Gupta said the state is trying to be cautious not to restrict opioids so much that people who actually need them can't access them. "It's very important that we don't forget about those people with legitimate pain. We want minimum disruptors for them," he said, adding that "there's still a role for opioids to play."

Four out of five West Virginians who died from an overdose in 2016 had come into contact with the health system, whether it was during a visit to the emergency room from a prior overdose, or a visit to a clinic for a routine checkup. About 71 percent had or were eligible for Medicaid coverage.

More than half of West Virginians who died of an overdose in 2016 had been incarcerated at some point. That told policy makers that there needed to be more policies built around the incarcerated population.

After that finding, Gupta partnered with the Department of Corrections to develop a number of programs aimed at helping prison and jail inmates who are struggling with addiction. One pilot program, which will be expanded statewide in the summer, gives assisted treatment to inmates with an opioid medication upon their release and then helps connect them to longer term care in the community.

"First, we were like, why do we want to get involved in treatment? That's not our thing … but when we took a look at this, one of the reasons we have contraband in our facilities is because of inmates with addiction," said Luikart, of West Virginia's Military Affairs and Public Safety Department. "So, if we can provide treatment in our prisons and jails, there will be less demand for contraband." He added that by treating addiction, they also hope to cut recidivism, which is high among people with addiction. "That will help with prison overcrowding."

Gupta is data-driven, but he also knows the value of gathering anecdotal evidence. Once a month, Gupta works on the front lines of the epidemic, treating patients with drug addiction at West Virginia Health Right, a charity clinic in Charleston that is also one of the city's two needle exchanges. He treats patients with chronic pain, who became hooked on prescription painkillers and are now self-medicating with illicit drugs that are cheap and easy to find. He tries to direct them into longer-term treatment. "These are mainstream individuals that got entangled into the grips of addiction, and the data shows us that," Gupta said.

He sees patients who have overdosed a half dozen times and who are still not given any kind of follow through or long-term help. On a recent visit to the clinic, he spoke with a woman who had been resuscitated nine times by paramedics.

Michelle Spencer, 37, has been in and out of treatment for several years. After she was rescued from her latest overdose, she was told by paramedics that they wouldn't use the antidote on her again. "They narcanned me so much that they said they aren't willing to do it anymore," Spencer told Gupta during one of his volunteer shifts at West Virginia Health Right. She came to the clinic with her teenage daughter, who is encouraging her to get into, and stick with, treatment. "It's so easy to go and do more," she says.

Spencer's addiction started like many, with prescription drugs, which she stole or bought from friends. Then she switched to methamphetamine, which was easier to find. She says she has bipolar disorder and has been self-medicating for at least a decade. She went to prison for drug possession and was released about three years ago. That's when she started using heroin. Like meth, it was cheap and easy to find. She says she uses several times a day.

The treatment program Gupta has recommended for Spencer, who is on Medicaid, takes several days to get into. Because she was suffering extreme withdrawal symptoms, she begged him to get her into more immediate treatment, fearful that she might use again if she didn't get help immediately.

Spencer was in a common predicament. Out of the more than 2.1 million Americans with opioid use disorder, just 20 percent receive specialty addiction treatment, according to the Substance Abuse and Mental Health Services Administration. It can be particularly challenging to find medication-assisted treatment, which has a proven track record of treating addiction, in rural areas. One of the challenges West Virginia and many other states across the country are facing is how to expand access to that treatment, which is not widely available across the country for a variety of reasons.

Doctors who administer medication-assisted treatment like buprenorphine are required to have federal licensing and waivers that some say are burdensome and deter doctors from getting them. West Virginia recently passed a measure that allows primary care doctors with smaller practices to administer medication-assisted treatment without having to be licensed federally.

West Virginia state Sen. Ron Stollings, who is also a primary care doctor in Madison, West Virginia, said the waiver allows physicians like him, who don't specialize in substance use treatment but come across many patients struggling with addiction.

"You need to realize that if you don't treat them right away, they're more likely to become a statistic—dead from overdose," Stollings said. "The idea is to get someone on medication-assisted treatment early on." He added that he isn't sure how many fellow primary care providers will want to take part in the program, but "it's a tool in the toolbox."

On a recent Tuesday, Chris Rauhecker, a recovering heroin addict who now counsels people with drug addiction, and Lindsey Harmon, a Cabell County paramedic, jumped into an old, unmarked police car and drove into downtown Huntington on a mission to find a homeless man who had overdosed in the public library the day before.

They knew nothing more about him than his name and the county paramedic's report that detailed the overdose incident. He was discovered unconscious on the library's second floor and was revived by paramedics with naloxone. When he woke up, he walked out of the library and back onto the streets.

The scenario is all too common in Huntington, the rural, Appalachian community that's become the epicenter for the opioid abuse epidemic: A person overdoses, paramedics rush to the scene to revive him, and once he's awake, he's free to walk away with an untreated drug addiction and a high chance of overdosing again, with the next time even more likely to be fatal.

Rauhecker and Harmon are part of a small but persistent team that is working to break that cycle. With federal funding and assistance from Gupta's office, Cabell County's Quick Response Team was launched last December to be the link to care for people who suffer from drug overdoses.

The team follows up with drug overdose victims within 72 hours of the incident and helps connect them to long-term treatment. If a patient has a home address, they'll make house visits. If not, they'll check the local shelters and drive around town until they find them. Gupta said Charleston is in the stages of developing its own "QRT" and thinks Huntington's program could serve as a model for other communities nationally that are looking to get a handle on drug overdose deaths.

Rauhecker and Harmon eventually located the man about five blocks from the library near a Sheetz convenience store—known as a local hangout for drug users and dealers. They approached him, introduced themselves as the Cabell County's Quick Response Team and assured him they were there to help, not implicate him. After some convincing, he agreed to go to an inpatient detox facility. They called a local treatment center, secured a bed for him and drove him there.

"By the end of the week, hopefully, if he's still receptive, we'll try to get him into long-term care," Rauhecker says, cautioning that not everyone the team encounters is ready to be helped, and they know there is a process to gaining a patient's trust. Word is catching on about the Quick Response Team. He said more and more often people are expecting them to show up, "sometimes they're even relieved."

Since December 4, the Huntington QRT has connected with 179 patients who had previously suffered a drug overdose. Of that group, 61 people are now in a form of long-term treatment including medication-assisted therapies, residential treatment centers and sober living homes. That's about a 34 percent success rate, which county officials are pleased with since the program is only four months old.

The key to QRT, Larrecsa Cox, a paramedic on the team, explained, is that they treat each patient they meet differently, based on their needs. They spend time talking to the individuals to learn what kind of treatment, if any, they are interested in pursuing. This often means either medication-assisted treatment or an abstinence-based program like a recovery home.

People aren't always receptive. "I wouldn't say they're always glad to see us. Some people don't want us there," Cox said. That doesn't deter the team, which often makes multiple trips a week to a patient's home to follow up and make sure he's sticking to his appointments. QRT members also stay in touch with patients by texting and talking on the phone.

"If they aren't interested, we come back later," Cox said.

Harmon, another paramedic, said she once knocked on the door of a patient's home every day for a month before finally the woman agreed to hear her out. Her persistence paid off: The woman is now in an inpatient facility in another town, and Harmon still texts her to check in.

"Some of these people, you deal with them so much, you kind of get attached to them," Harmon said. She added that many of the people they visit don't have family support systems to help them cope. "In some cases, we become their friends and their family," she said.

"I wish there would have been someone that would have done this for me," said Rauhecker, who has been clean from heroin for 26 months and now works as a recovery coach at Recovery Point, a sober living home in Huntington. He said he is certain he would have gotten help earlier if a team of people had knocked on his door and dedicated their time to getting him treatment.

Rauhecker rides along with the group and uses his own experiences recovering from heroin addiction to relate to patients and help them get connected to longer term care. The QRT also employs someone from a clinic that provides medication-assisted treatment to represent that option.

"What works for one person isn't always going to work for someone else," he said, adding that sometimes patients want to go to a sober living home, while others prefer medication-assisted treatment. Either way, "the biggest thing is that they have to be ready and want to get help; otherwise it's not going to work."

Critical Thinking

1. Dr. Gupta ordered a review of overdose deaths in West Virginia. How was this accomplished and what types of information did his staff review?

2. What were the findings of this in-depth study?

3. Discuss some of the recommendations made as a result of this study.

4. Do you have any other recommendations, as a student taking this course, on what could be done to prevent overdose deaths in the future?

Internet References

Drug Policy Alliance
http://www.drugpolicy.org/

Principles of Drug Addiction Treatment: A Research-Based Guide
www.drugabuse.gov/PODAT/PODATIndex.html

Substance Abuse and Mental Health Services Administration
https://www.samhsa.gov

WebMD
https://www.webmd.com/

Prepared by: Kim Schnurbush, *California State University, Sacramento*
Mark Pullin, *Angelo State University*

Article

Fighting the Opioid Crisis Through Substance Use Disorder Treatment: A Study of a Police Program Model in Illinois

JESSICA REICHERT

Learning Outcomes

After reading this article, you will be able to:

- Discuss the ANGEL program and the program goals.

- Explore some lessons learned by law enforcement agencies while participating in the ANGEL program.

- Discuss how law enforcement can involve the community in programs like ANGEL.

*S**eeking to more effective help individuals suffering from opioid use disorder, police departments across the country are embracing a deflection model that offers treatment access to those in need. Researchers interviewed representatives of seven law enforcement agencies employing treatment program models in Illinois to better understand operations, leverage lessons learned, measure sustainability, and inform other agencies as they implement their own programs.*

The opioid crisis is ravaging U.S. communities and appears to be escalating, as data indicates drug overdose is the leading cause of death among those under age 50.[1] More people are killed by drug overdoses now than car accidents or gun violence.[2] Law enforcement agencies are finding that solely arresting those who misuse opioids has not helped to alleviate the opioid crisis and may, in fact, exacerbate the problem. Seeking to more effectively help individuals suffering from opioid use disorders, police departments across the country are embracing a new program model by offering treatment access to those in need. Individual program names for the deflection, pre-arrest diversion, and front-end diversion model vary by jurisdiction. The effectiveness of drug treatment is well established in literature and the body of research showing effectiveness has been growing.[3]

This police deflection model involves individuals voluntarily walking into police departments and requesting substance use disorder treatment. Police departments pre-arrange services with treatment providers that can be offered to these individuals. Treatment programs often are located an hour away or more and transportation is provided by volunteers, police, or family members. Program administrators develop their own eligibility criteria but typically exclude those with outstanding warrants or violent arrest histories.

The Gloucester Police Department in Massachusetts was the first to implement this model with its ANGEL program in 2015.[4] Since then, more than 138 programs have started in 28 states.[5]

The program model goals include:

- Restoring and save lives.
- Improving access to treatment.
- Reducing substance use.
- Reducing entry or recidivism into the criminal justice system.

- Cutting costs associated with reoffending and repeat calls for service.
- Improving police-community relations.

Although these programs have grown in popularity, little is known about individual program operations, most effective program components, and client outcomes. In summer 2017, Illinois Criminal Justice Information Authority (ICJIA) researchers set out to learn more about the impetus, development, and implementation of police deflection programs in Illinois to better inform communities interested in offering the model. Researchers identified 11 programs operating in the state and one in development. Representatives from seven programs agreed to be interviewed about their programs and included police chiefs, sheriffs, and a state's attorney.

Researchers conducted qualitative phone interviews consisting of 45 open-ended questions that covered interviewee demographics, initiative operations, treatment, data and evaluation, public awareness, funding and resources, training, and lessons learned. In addition, researchers asked interviewees to complete the Program Sustainability Assessment Tool. This tool rates the extent to which components are in place to sustain their program over time.[6] The research was approved by ICJIA's Institutional Review Board and study subjects consented to participation in the survey and interview, as well as to audio-recording of the interview, which researchers transcribed and analyzed.

Program Implementation and Operations

The seven programs examined were relatively new, with the oldest ones in operation since 2015. Four programs were county-wide and three were city-wide. The programs served geographic areas ranging from small towns to counties with larger cities. Most programs involved multi-agency collaboration; 42 police agencies participated in the seven programs examined. The programs had collectively facilitated treatment access for 384 clients. The number of clients linked to treatment ranged from three to 170 clients per program.

All seven programs started in response to the opioid crisis and overdose deaths in their communities. One program was specifically concerned with overdoses among young people and another reported that their community had been experiencing one overdose per week. Four programs were replications of the Gloucester Police Department's ANGEL program and three were based on established programs in Lake and Lee/Whiteside counties.

Program representatives cited helping people gain access to treatment, criminal justice system diversion, and crime and overdose reduction as individual program goals. All programs required clients to walk into the police department for assistance. Several programs transported clients outside of their communities for treatment and two programs sent people out of state. The programs made treatment accessible at all levels of care—detox, outpatient, and residential. While the programs offered no aftercare services for clients post-treatment, one agency reported seeking funding for recovery coaches and a sober living facility.

Three programs had no external funding source. Three had obtained small seed grants ranging from $2,500 to $10,000. Grant funds were used to pay for program advertising and to transport clients to treatment. Treatment was paid for with federal funds (often Medicaid), state funds (through Department of Human Services Division of Alcohol and Substance Abuse), or, in a few cases, private insurance. One program used drug forfeiture funds to offset client treatment costs.

Five programs used social media to raise awareness, five programs were featured in local media outlets, and two programs were promoted using department websites. Some departments developed and disseminated brochures, rented billboards, and purchased screen time at local movie theaters to get the word out. Officers also promoted and marketed their programs on the street to those suffering from substance use disorders.

Programs obtained data from intake forms, treatment providers, and informal follow-up/contact with clients. External evaluations were being conducted of two of the programs.

When asked about lessons learned, those interviewed made several recommendations, including:

- Find champions within the department. A police chief or administrator with an investment in the program can provide support and motivation for staff and raise program awareness.
- Foster solid relationships with select treatment partners to ensure timely placement and a continuum of services available.
- Designate a small team of trained officers to contact treatment providers. These officers should fully understand and support the program, as well as issues around substance use disorders, in order to effectively interact with clients and treatment providers.
- Involve the whole community, including, but not limited to, hospitals, pastors, health department, and 12-step community, which will help to increase awareness and assist more individuals.
- Gain an understanding of the local population as there may be unique needs or obstacles to overcome for some to enter treatment, such as language barriers, immigration status, child care issues, and legal issues.
- Train officers and consult local substance use coalitions or providers to develop training programs. Officers should understand the nature of substance use disorders as a chronic and relapsing condition, as well as the continuum of care for those with substance use disorders.

Program Sustainability

Program representatives completed the Program Sustainability Assessment Tool (PSAT).[7] PSAT uses 40 Likert scale questions to measure sustainability across eight domains—environmental support, funding stability, partnerships, organizational capacity, program evaluation, program adaption, communications, and strategic planning (*Figure 2*).

Figure 3 depicts the average ratings of sustainability by domain based on responses from the seven program representatives. Measured were responses to five statements on each domain measuring the extent to which the program had factors for sustainability (1=Little/no extent, 7=Very great extent).

Although PSAT does not offer cutoff scores, domains with lower average ratings may reflect potential sustainability issues faced by these police program models. The range of scores varied dramatically for some domains. The largest variation from high to low scores was on partnerships, with one program indicating very strong partnerships (7 out of 7) and one indicating very weak partnerships (2.8 out of 7). Partnerships involve community investment, communication, involvement, commitment, and engagement.

The two domains with the lowest average scores were program evaluation (4.5 out of 7) and adaptation (4.9 out of 7) suggesting a need for improvement in those areas. Adaptation focuses on program flexibility and adaptability to changing conditions required to improve quality. Steps to build

Domain	Description
Environmental Support	The political and economic climate within and external to an organization will affect an organization's ability to accomplish needed and desired programs. This component acknowledges the need for internal and external champions of the program to help communicate the program and its benefits to policymakers and stakeholders.
Communications	Increasing program visibility and communicating information about a program's efficacy externally can help garner greater community and stakeholder support for the program. Program efficacy can help build staff buy-in and support from organizational leaders internally.
Funding Stability	The ebbs and flows of funding for a program can make it challenging to maintain the quality and consistency of the program. By planning for stable funding within the strategic process, an organization can better prepare for these ebbs and flows; in particular, through diversification of funding streams.
Partnerships	Stakeholders can help a program with regard to advocacy, connection to resources or expertise, and dissemination of program information. They can help champion a program and provide support in tumultuous political and economic climates.
Organizational Capacity	Organizational capacity refers to the extent of resources, capabilities, knowledge to help maintain a program, the program goals, and program efficacy. Providing sufficient resources (e.g. enough staff, strong leadership, sufficient training) can help increase a programs potential for long-term success.
Program Evaluation	Program evaluation is vital to informing an organization as to the processes and outcomes (efficacy) of a program. Further, this information helps inform planning and program maintenance and can shed light on a program's effectiveness. Collecting information about a program's processes and outcomes can be especially useful in gaining support and funding for the program.
Program Adaptation	Program evaluation is also important when it comes to program adaptation; as a program is implemented, obstacles may come up or specific program components may need adaptation. Program adaptation necessitates flexibility, particularly to a changing environment, and a quality improvement process within the program. Using program evaluation and the current evidence for a program to adapt a program can ensure effective use of resources and positive outcomes.
Strategic Planning	Strategic decision-making, including processes to guide a program's directions, goals, and strategies, helps ensure program alignment within the overall organizational environment. This component is what ties together all previous components into a deliberate, concise, and long-term plan for sustainability rather than making reactionary decisions from day-to-day.

Figure 2 Program Sustainability Assessment Tool Domains

Note: From the Program Sustainability Assessment Tool v2, Washington University

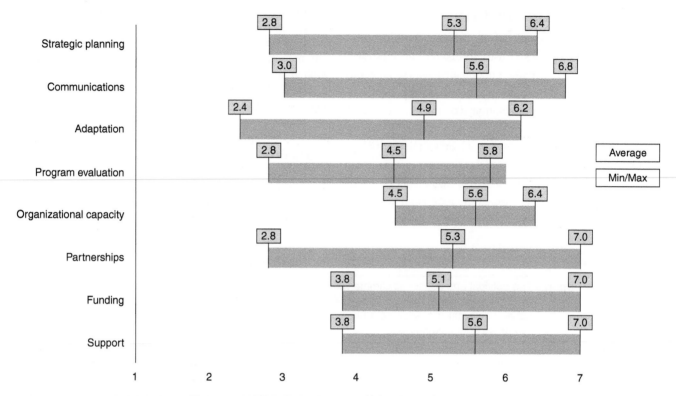

Figure 3 Range and average capacity for program sustainability by domain (n = 6)

Note: From the Program Sustainability Assessment Tool v2, Washington University.

adaptation include prioritizing program components for improvement and communicating frequently with target population to uncover problems and enhance the program. Evaluation and data collection can help programs gain support and funding and identify areas for improvement. In turn, evaluation can help identify areas for adaptation. Programs can review program data and evaluation results while seeking new research and evidence-based practices to guide program changes.

Implications for Policy and Practice

The police interviews highlighted several key issues in deflection model program implementation and operations.

Address Treatment Capacity

Treatment capacity was a common concern, with treatment availability cited as the main obstacle to offering treatment to those in need. Interviewees said waiting lists post-detoxification potentially endangered client safety. One shared that following detox, their clients were on a two- to four-week waiting list,

putting them at risk for relapse and at increased risk for dying from an overdose. However, treatment capacity is an obstacle not easily addressed and capacity is dependent, in part, on the availability of publically-funded healthcare coverage.[8]

Involve the Community

Some programs in this study featured broader community involvement, recognizing the need to foster community support and increase awareness of the program. While all programs involved police departments and treatment providers, just two programs involved the broader community, such as the county health department and mental health board, local recovery-based non-profits, local substance abuse coalition, and faith-based organizations. Research suggests that community engagement in public health issues can have a positive impact.[9]

Although individuals may be hesitant about going to a police department, word-of-mouth can be helpful. One representative noted that police departments are a common-sense point of entry within the community because they are open 24 hours per day, seven days per week, and easily accessible. Those interviewed reported receiving positive responses from the community.

"The police now have an opportunity to work with people struggling with addiction," said one. "People now think of the police as a point of assistance, as opposed to people that they want to avoid and when people begin going through (the program). They realize that it's not a set-up, that there are police officers out there that do care and do want to get people the help they need as opposed to arresting them. I think word will spread in terms of the relationship and how police are viewed and that that will be positive."

One police chief tied the program to a community policing model.

"In my mind, this is the future of law enforcement, that next phase of community policing," he said. "It's a smarter way to do policing and I think that this model really works well with a number of other behavioral health issues. Law enforcement ends up ultimately having to deal with these individuals out at the street level just because that's the nature of our business. We want a better way to help those people and this seems to be a good alternative."

Enhance Officer Training

All departments offered program training for police officers and three provided additional training specifically on substance use addiction. One said the program is beneficial to officers because it puts a "human face" on addiction and officers realize that all kinds of people from all different backgrounds may suffer from addiction.

However, comments from others indicated that officers may need specific training on substance use as a chronic, relapsing mental health condition not governed by willpower in order to understand the need for such programs.[10] One program representative said client motivation and commitment was an obstacle. "They call us just because they want a fix, maybe Methadone," he said. "They're not serious about getting [help for] their addiction. That's been our biggest hurdle."

Secure Sustainable Funding

Although programs are able to operate with little funding and with the use of existing police staff, some representatives indicated a funding need for a program coordinator, possibly a social worker, to oversee operations, as well as recovery coaches. Most reported wanting and seeking long-term sustainable funding. Four applied for federal funding available through the Comprehensive Addiction and Recovery Act and Edward Byrne Memorial Justice Assistance Grant Program.

Conclusion

Police referral to treatment programs represents a new model for policing, designed to help citizens with substance use

disorders at low cost to the municipality.[11] The programs meet a community need, improve community relations, and align with the police charge to help individuals.[12] These programs started in response to the opioid crisis, but will help anyone in need of substance use disorder treatment. Despite established relationships with treatment providers, the main concern of program representatives in Illinois is treatment capacity. To aid in funding of these programs, ICJIA dedicated a portion of Illinois' federal Justice Assistance Grant award toward these programs as a comprehensive law enforcement response to drugs. While it is promising, more research on this model is needed to develop key components, measure outcomes, and gauge sustainability.[13] Programs are encouraged to begin collecting intake and follow-up data to engage in proper evaluation.

Endnotes

1. Katz, J. (2017, June 5). Drug deaths in America are rising faster than ever. *The New York Times*. Retrieved from https://www.nytimes.com/interactive/2017/06/05/upshot/opioid-epidemic-drug-overdose-deaths-are-rising-faster-than-ever.html

2. Centers for Disease Control. (2017). *All injuries*. Atlanta, GA: National Center for Health Statistics. Retrieved from https://www.cdc.gov/nchs/fastats/injury.htm

3. Reichert, J., & Gleicher, L. (2017). *Rethinking law enforcement's role on drugs: Community drug intervention and diversion efforts*. Chicago, IL: Illinois Criminal Justice Information Authority.

4. Gloucester Police Department. (n.d.). For addicts and their friends, families, and caregivers. Retrieved from http://gloucesterpd.com/addicts/

5. Schiff, D. M., Drainoni, M., Bair-Merritt, M., & Rosenbloom, D. (2016). A police-led addiction treatment referral program in Massachusetts. *New England Journal of Medicine*, *375*, 2502-2503.

6. Luke, D. A., Calhoun, A., Robichaux, C., Elliott, M. B., & Moreland-Russell, S. (2014). The Program Sustainability Assessment Tool: A new instrument for public health programs. *Preventing Chronic Disease*, 11, 130184.

7. Schell, S. F., Luke, D. A., Schooley, M. W., Elliott, MB, Herbers, S. H., Mueller, N. B.,& Bunger, A. C. (2013). Public health program capacity for sustainability: A new framework. *Implementation Science*, 8(15). For more information on the Program Sustainability Assessment Tool, Washington University, see https://www.sustaintool.org/

8. Urban, P. (2017, January 16). Cops help addicts get treatment in programs facing uncertain future. *Scientific American*. Retrieved from https://www.scientificamerican.com/article/cops-help-addicts-get-treatment-in-programs-facing-uncertain-future/

9. O'Mara-Eves, A., Brunton, G., Oliver, S., Kavanagh, J., Jamal, F., & Thomas, J. (2015). The effectiveness of community

engagement in public health interventions for disadvantaged groups: a meta-analysis. BMC Public Health, *15*, 129.

10. The National Center on Addiction and Substance Abuse. (2017). *Addiction as a disease*. Retrieved from https://www.centeronaddiction.org/what-addiction/addiction-disease

11. Charlier, J. (2017a) Deflection: A powerful crime-fighting tool that improved community relations. *Police Chief*. Retrieved from http://www.policechiefmagazine.org/deflection-a-powerful-crime-fighting-tool-that-improves-community-relations/

12. Charlier, J. (2017, March 21b). The 'Deflection' survey: Key to reducing re-arrests. *The Crime Report*.

13. Reichert, J., & Gleicher, L. (2017). *Rethinking law enforcement's role on drugs: Community drug intervention and diversion efforts*. Chicago, IL: Illinois Criminal Justice Information Authority.

Critical Thinking

1. Which police department was the first in the nation to implement the ANGEL program, and what are the program goals?

2. Why are some police departments starting to address substance use and abuse differently than simply arresting individuals suffering from use disorders?

3. What were some of the lessons learned by those law enforcement agencies participating in the new programs?

4. How might other law enforcement departments involve the community as a whole in programs as described?

5. Do you see the role of law enforcement as one that solely arrests drug law violators, or do you support the future use of these programs? Explain your answer.

Internet References

Drug and Alcohol Dependence
https://www.drugandalcoholdependence.com/

Drug Policy Alliance
http://www.drugpolicy.org/

National Drug Intelligence Center
https://www.justice.gov/archive/ndic/

U.S. National Institutes of Health's National Library of Medicine (NIH/NLM)
https://www.ncbi.nlm.nih.gov/pmc/

Article

Prepared by: Kim Schnurbush, *California State University, Sacramento*
Mark Pullin, *Angelo State University*

Treatment Approaches for Drug Addiction

NATIONAL INSTITUTE ON DRUG ABUSE

Learning Outcomes

After reading this article, you will be able to:

- Understand the basics of drug addiction and whether or not it can be treated.

- Explore how drug addiction treatment is different for incarcerated individuals compared to the general public.

What is Drug Addiction?

Drug addiction is a chronic disease characterized by compulsive, or uncontrollable, drug seeking and use despite harmful consequences and changes in the brain, which can be long lasting. These changes in the brain can lead to the harmful behaviors seen in people who use drugs. Drug addiction is also a relapsing disease. Relapse is the return to drug use after an attempt to stop.

The path to drug addiction begins with the voluntary act of taking drugs. But over time, a person's ability to choose not to do so becomes compromised. Seeking and taking the drug becomes compulsive. This is mostly due to the effects of long-term drug exposure on brain function. Addiction affects parts of the brain involved in reward and motivation, learning and memory, and control over behavior.

Addiction is a disease that affects both the brain and behavior.

Can Drug Addiction be Treated?

Yes, but it's not simple. Because addiction is a chronic disease, people can't simply stop using drugs for a few days and be cured. Most patients need long-term or repeated care to stop using completely and recover their lives.

Addiction treatment must help the person do the following:
- stop using drugs
- stay drug-free
- be productive in the family, at work, and in society

Principles of Effective Treatment

Based on scientific research since the mid-1970s, the following key principles should form the basis of any effective treatment program:

- Addiction is a complex but treatable disease that affects brain function and behavior.
- No single treatment is right for everyone.
- People need to have quick access to treatment.
- Effective treatment addresses all of the patient's needs, not just his or her drug use.
- Staying in treatment long enough is critical.
- Counseling and other behavioral therapies are the most commonly used forms of treatment.
- Medications are often an important part of treatment, especially when combined with behavioral therapies.
- Treatment plans must be reviewed often and modified to fit the patient's changing needs.
- Treatment should address other possible mental disorders.
- Medically assisted detoxification is only the first stage of treatment.
- Treatment doesn't need to be voluntary to be effective.

- Drug use during treatment must be monitored continuously.
- Treatment programs should test patients for HIV/AIDS, hepatitis B and C, tuberculosis, and other infectious diseases as well as teach them about steps they can take to reduce their risk of these illnesses.

What are Treatments for Drug Addiction?

There are many options that have been successful in treating drug addiction, including:

- behavioral counseling
- medication
- medical devices and applications used to treat withdrawal symptoms or deliver skills training
- evaluation and treatment for co-occurring mental health issues such as depression and anxiety
- long-term follow-up to prevent relapse

A range of care with a tailored treatment program and follow-up options can be crucial to success. Treatment should include both medical and mental health services as needed. Follow-up care may include community- or family-based recovery support systems.

How are Medications and Devices Used in Drug Addiction Treatment?

Medications and devices can be used to manage withdrawal symptoms, prevent relapse, and treat co-occurring conditions.

Withdrawal

Medications and devices can help suppress withdrawal symptoms during detoxification. Detoxification is not in itself "treatment," but only the first step in the process. Patients who do not receive any further treatment after detoxification usually resume their drug use. One study of treatment facilities found that medications were used in almost 80 percent of detoxifications (SAMHSA, 2014). Devices are also being used to reduce withdrawal symptoms. In November 2017, the Food and Drug Administration (FDA) granted a new indication to an electronic stimulation device, NSS-2 Bridge, for use in helping reduce opioid withdrawal symptoms. This device is placed behind the ear and sends electrical pulses to stimulate certain brain nerves.

Relapse Prevention

Patients can use medications to help re-establish normal brain function and decrease cravings. Medications are available for treatment of opioid (heroin, prescription pain relievers), tobacco (nicotine), and alcohol addiction. Scientists are developing other medications to treat stimulant (cocaine, methamphetamine) and cannabis (marijuana) addiction. People who use more than one drug, which is very common, need treatment for all of the substances they use.

- *Opioids:* Methadone (Dolophine®, Methadose®), buprenorphine (Suboxone®, Subutex®, Probuphine®, Sublocade™), and naltrexone (Vivitrol®) are used to treat opioid addiction. Acting on the same targets in the brain as heroin and morphine, methadone and buprenorphine suppress withdrawal symptoms and relieve cravings. Naltrexone blocks the effects of opioids at their receptor sites in the brain and should be used only in patients who have already been detoxified. All medications help patients reduce drug seeking and related criminal behavior and help them become more open to behavioral treatments. A NIDA study found that once treatment is initiated, both a buprenorphine/naloxone combination and an extended release naltrexone formulation are similarly effective in treating opioid addiction. Because full detoxification is necessary for treatment with naloxone, initiating treatment among active users was difficult, but once detoxification was complete, both medications had similar effectiveness.
- *Tobacco:* Nicotine replacement therapies have several forms, including the patch, spray, gum, and lozenges. These products are available over the counter. The U.S. Food and Drug Administration (FDA) has approved two prescription medications for nicotine addiction: bupropion (Zyban®) and varenicline (Chantix®). They work differently in the brain, but both help prevent relapse in people trying to quit. The medications are more effective when combined with behavioral treatments, such as group and individual therapy as well as telephone quitlines.
- *Alcohol:* Three medications have been FDA-approved for treating alcohol addiction and a fourth, topiramate, has shown promise in clinical trials (large-scale studies with people). The three approved medications are as follows:
  - **Naltrexone** blocks opioid receptors that are involved in the rewarding effects of drinking and in the craving for alcohol. It reduces relapse to heavy drinking

and is highly effective in some patients. Genetic differences may affect how well the drug works in certain patients.

- **Acamprosate (Campral®)** may reduce symptoms of long-lasting withdrawal, such as insomnia, anxiety, restlessness, and dysphoria (generally feeling unwell or unhappy). It may be more effective in patients with severe addiction.
- **Disulfiram (Antabuse®)** interferes with the breakdown of alcohol. Acetaldehyde builds up in the body, leading to unpleasant reactions that include flushing (warmth and redness in the face), nausea, and irregular heartbeat if the patient drinks alcohol. Compliance (taking the drug as prescribed) can be a problem, but it may help patients who are highly motivated to quit drinking.
- *Co-occurring conditions:* Other medications are available to treat possible mental health conditions, such as depression or anxiety, that may be contributing to the person's addiction.

How are Behavioral Therapies Used to Treat Drug Addiction?

Behavioral therapies help patients:

- modify their attitudes and behaviors related to drug use
- increase healthy life skills
- persist with other forms of treatment, such as medication

Patients can receive treatment in many different settings with various approaches.

Outpatient behavioral treatment includes a wide variety of programs for patients who visit a behavioral health counselor on a regular schedule. Most of the programs involve individual or group drug counseling, or both. These programs typically offer forms of behavioral therapy such as:

- *cognitive-behavioral therapy,* which helps patients recognize, avoid, and cope with the situations in which they are most likely to use drugs
- *multidimensional family therapy*—developed for adolescents with drug abuse problems as well as their families—which addresses a range of influences on their drug abuse patterns and is designed to improve overall family functioning
- *motivational interviewing,* which makes the most of people's readiness to change their behavior and enter treatment

- *motivational incentives* (contingency management), which uses positive reinforcement to encourage abstinence from drugs

Treatment is sometimes intensive at first, where patients attend multiple outpatient sessions each week. After completing intensive treatment, patients transition to regular outpatient treatment, which meets less often and for fewer hours per week to help sustain their recovery. In September 2017, the FDA permitted marketing of the first mobile application, reSET®, to help treat substance use disorders. This application is intended to be used with outpatient treatment to treat alcohol, cocaine, marijuana, and stimulant substance use disorders.

Inpatient or residential treatment can also be very effective, especially for those with more severe problems (including co-occurring disorders). Licensed residential treatment facilities offer 24-hour structured and intensive care, including safe housing and medical attention. Residential treatment facilities may use a variety of therapeutic approaches, and they are generally aimed at helping the patient live a drug-free, crime-free lifestyle after treatment. Examples of residential treatment settings include:

- *Therapeutic communities*, which are highly structured programs in which patients remain at a residence, typically for 6 to 12 months. The entire community, including treatment staff and those in recovery, act as key agents of change, influencing the patient's attitudes, understanding, and behaviors associated with drug use. Read more about therapeutic communities in the *Therapeutic Communities Research Report* at https://www.drugabuse.gov/publications/research-reports/therapeutic-communities.
- *Shorter-term residential treatment*, which typically focuses on detoxification as well as providing initial intensive counseling and preparation for treatment in a community-based setting.
- *Recovery housing,* which provides supervised, short-term housing for patients, often following other types of inpatient or residential treatment. Recovery housing can help people make the transition to an independent life—for example, helping them learn how to manage finances or seek employment, as well as connecting them to support services in the community.

Challenges of Re-entry

Drug abuse changes the function of the brain, and many things can "trigger" drug cravings within the brain. It's critical for those in treatment, especially those treated at an inpatient facility or prison, to learn how to recognize, avoid, and cope with triggers they are likely to be exposed to after treatment.

Is Treatment Different for Criminal Justice Populations?

Scientific research since the mid-1970s shows that drug abuse treatment can help many drug-using offenders change their attitudes, beliefs, and behaviors towards drug abuse; avoid relapse; and successfully remove themselves from a life of substance abuse and crime. Many of the principles of treating drug addiction are similar for people within the criminal justice system as for those in the general population. However, many offenders don't have access to the types of services they need. Treatment that is of poor quality or is not well suited to the needs of offenders may not be effective at reducing drug use and criminal behavior.

In addition to the general principles of treatment, some considerations specific to offenders include the following:

- Treatment should include development of specific cognitive skills to help the offender adjust attitudes and beliefs that lead to drug abuse and crime, such as feeling entitled to have things one's own way or not understanding the consequences of one's behavior. This includes skills related to thinking, understanding, learning, and remembering.
- Treatment planning should include tailored services within the correctional facility as well as transition to community-based treatment after release.
- Ongoing coordination between treatment providers and courts or parole and probation officers is important in addressing the complex needs of offenders re-entering society.

How Many People Get Treatment for drug addiction?

According to SAMHSA's National Survey on Drug Use and Health, 22.5 million people (8.5 percent of the U.S. population) aged 12 or older needed treatment for an illicit* drug or alcohol use problem in 2014. Only 4.2 million (18.5 percent of those who needed treatment) received any substance use treatment in the same year. Of these, about 2.6 million people received treatment at specialty treatment programs (CBHSQ, 2015).

*The term "illicit" refers to the use of illegal drugs, including marijuana according to federal law, and misuse of prescription medications.

Points to Remember

- Drug addiction can be treated, but it's not simple. Addiction treatment must help the person do the following:
  - stop using drugs
  - stay drug-free
  - be productive in the family, at work, and in society
- Successful treatment has several steps:
  - detoxification
  - behavioral counseling
  - medication (for opioid, tobacco, or alcohol addiction)
  - evaluation and treatment for co-occurring mental health issues such as depression and anxiety
  - long-term follow-up to prevent relapse
- Medications and devices can be used to manage withdrawal symptoms, prevent relapse, and treat co-occurring conditions.
- Behavioral therapies help patients:
  - modify their attitudes and behaviors related to drug use
  - increase healthy life skills
  - persist with other forms of treatment, such as medication
- People within the criminal justice system may need additional treatment services to treat drug use disorders effectively. However, many offenders don't have access to the types of services they need.

Learn More

For more information about drug addiction treatment, visit:
www.drugabuse.gov/publications/principles-drug-addiction-treatment-research-based-guide-third-edition/acknowledgments

For information about drug addiction treatment in the criminal justice system, visit: www.drugabuse.gov/publications/ principles-drug-abuse-treatment-criminal-justice-populations/ principles

For step-by-step guides for people who think they or a loved one may need treatment, visit: www.drugabuse.gov/related-topics/ treatment

This publication is available for your use and may be reproduced **in its entirety** without permission from NIDA. Citation of the source is appreciated, using the following language:

Source: National Institute on Drug Abuse; National Institutes of Health; U.S. Department of Health and Human Services.

References

Center for Behavioral Health Statistics and Quality (CBSHQ). *2014 National Survey on Drug Use and Health: Detailed Tables.* Rockville, MD: Substance Abuse and Mental Health Services Administration; 2015.

Substance Abuse and Mental Health Services Administration (SAMHSA). *National Survey of Substance Abuse Treatment Services (N-SSATS): 2013. Data on Substance Abuse Treatment Facilities.* Rockville, MD: Substance Abuse and Mental Health Services Administration; 2014. HHS Publication No. (SMA) 14-489. BHSIS Series S-73.

National Institute on Drug Abuse, *Treatment Approaches for Drug Addiction.* U.S. Department of Health and Human Services, 2018.

Critical Thinking

1. What is drug addiction?
2. Can drug addiction be treated? If so, how?
3. How is drug addiction treatment different for the incarcerated population?
4. Discuss with a classmate or a small group the "points to remember" at the end of the report. After a brief discussion, decide and argue which point is the most important with regards to drug addiction treatment. If you cannot come to an agreement as to which point is the most important, explain what you feel that way.
5. In your personal opinion, is there any "one" drug treatment for someone addicted to drugs? Explain your answer.

Internet References

Drug and Alcohol Dependence
https://www.drugandalcoholdependence.com/
Drug Policy Alliance
http://www.drugpolicy.org/
National Institute on Drug Abuse
https://www.drugabuse.gov/
Principles of Drug Addiction Treatment: A Research-Based Guide
www.drugabuse.gov/PODAT/PODATIndex.html